Tcl/Tk FOR
REAL PROGRAMMERS

LIMITED WARRANTY AND DISCLAIMER OF LIABILITY

Tcl/Tk FOR REAL PROGRAMMERS

CLIF FLYNT

AP PROFESSIONAL
An imprint of Academic Press

San Diego   London   Boston
New York   Sydney   Tokyo   Toronto

This book is printed on acid-free paper. ∞

ACADEMIC PRESS
A division of Harcourt Brace & Company
525 B Street, Suite 1900, San Diego, CA 92101-4495, USA
http://www.apnet.com

Academic Press
24–28 Oval Road, London NW1 7DX, UK
http://www.hbuk.co.uk/ap/

Library of Congress Cataloging-in-Publication Data

Flynt, Clif.
    Tcl/Tk for real programmers / Clif Flynt.
        p.   cm.
    Includes index.
    ISBN 0-12-261205-1 (acid-free paper). --   ISBN 0-12-261206-X
      1. Tcl (Computer program language)   2. Tk toolkit.   I. Title.
QA76.73.T44F59   1999
005.2'762--dc21
                                                      98-40399
                                                       CIP

Printed in the United States of America
98 99 00 01 02 1P 9 8 7 6 5 4 3 2 1

Contents

v

Contents

Contents

Acknowledgments

You may like to think of the author sitting alone, creating a book in a few weeks. I'm afraid that this idea has as much to do with reality as the Easter Bunny and Santa Claus. Creating this book took the better part of a year and a lot of help from my friends (some of whom I'd never heard of when I started the project).

The first acknowledgment goes to my wife, Carol. For more than a year she has been putting up with "I can't do any work around the house. I've got to finish this chapter," correcting grammar on my rough drafts before I send them out for technical review, editing proofs, making sure that I ate occasionally, and keeping life (almost) sane around here. This book would not have happened without her help.

I also want to thank my editor, Ken Morton, and his editorial assistants Samantha Libby and Jennifer Vilaga. If Ken hadn't been willing to take a chance on my ability to actually finish this book, I'd never have started it, and if Samantha and Jennifer hadn't been there to answer my questions I'd have floundered more than I did.

Julie Champagne, my production editor, did a marvelous job of keeping the final phases of book production on schedule, despite the book being almost twice as long as she expected, the examples all needing to be reformatted, and my missing every deadline.

Alex Safonov provided the final technical review before I declared a chapter done. His comments greatly improved the book, and he earned more thanks than I can give him.

My heartfelt and sincere thanks to the folks who read the early drafts. These folks put duty way above the call of friendship, reading the truly wretched first drafts. Their comments were all invaluable. My thanks to Margaret Bumby, Clark Wierda, Terry Gliedt, Elizabeth Lehmann, Nick DiMasi, Hermann Boeken, Greg Martin, John Driestadt, Daniel Glasser, William Roper, Phillip Johnson, Don Libes, Jeffrey Hobbs, John Stump, Laurent Demailly, Mark Diekhans, David Dougherty, Tod More, Hattie Schroeder, Michael Doyle, Sarah Daniels, Ray Johnson, Mellissa Hirschl, Jan Nijtmans, Forest Rouse, Brion Sarachan, Lindsay F. Marshall, Greg Cronau, and Steve Simmons.

And, finally, my thanks to John Ousterhout and his teams at UC Berkeley, Sun, and now Scriptics. Programming in Tcl has been more productive and given me more pleasure than any tool I've used since I got my first chance to play Lunar Lander on an old IBM 1130.

Preface

Tcl/Tk: GUI Programming for a Gooey World

Alan Watts, the Episcopal priest who popularized Buddhist thought in 1960s California, once wrote that philosophical thinkers can be divided into two basic types: "prickly" and "gooey." The prickly people, by his definition, "are tough-minded, rigorous, and precise, and like to stress differences and divisions between things. They prefer particles to waves, and discontinuity to continuity. The gooey people are tender-minded romanticists who love wide generalizations and grand syntheses. ... Waves suit them much better than particles as the ultimate constituents of matter, and discontinuities jar their teeth like a compressed-air drill." [1]

Watts chose the terms "prickly" and "gooey" carefully, seeking to avoid making one term positive and the other pejorative, and he offered delightful caricatures of the strengths and weaknesses of each type of

---

1. Watts, Alan. "The Book: On the Taboo Against Knowing Who You Are," Vintage Books, 1966.

person. In his view, a constant tension between the two perspectives is healthy in promoting progress toward a more complete understanding of reality.

Western science has long made a similar distinction between two complementary approaches, theoretical and empirical. Prickly theoreticians seek to understand the world through the abstractions of thought, while gooey empiricists return ceaselessly to the real world for the ever-more-refined data that methodical experimentation can yield. The complementarity of the two approaches is widely recognized by scientists themselves. Although most scientists would place themselves squarely in either the theoretical or empirical camp, very few would go so far as to argue that the other approach is without merit. A constant dialectic between empiricism and theory is generally seen to promote the integrity and health of scientific inquiry.

More recently, the advent of computer programming has brought with it a new round in the prickly-gooey dialectic. By temperament, there seem to be two kinds of programmers, whom I will call the planners and the doers. While any good programmer will of course plan his software before building it (and will actually build it after planning it), some programmers (the prickly planners) see planning and designing as the primary activity, after which system-building is relatively automatic. Others (the gooey doers) perceive system design as a necessary and important preparatory stage before the real work of system-building.

Both planners and doers can be excellent programmers, and the best of them excel at both design and execution. However, they may be categorized as planners or doers by their basic world-view, or primary orientation. They show different patterns of strengths and weaknesses, and they can, with skilled management, play complementary roles in large project teams. Still, certain tasks cry out for one type of programmer or the other. The design of software systems to control nuclear weapons, for example, is a task that cries out for exhaustive planning, because the risk of unanticipated errors is too high. The design of a throwaway program that needs to be run just once to calculate the answer to a single question, on the other hand, should probably be built by the fastest methodology possible, robustness be damned. In between these extremes, of course, lie nearly all real-world programming projects, which is why both approaches are useful. They are not, however, always equally well appreciated.

The modern managerial mentality thrives on careful organization, planning, and documentation. It should be no surprise that most managers prefer the planners to the doers; if they were programmers, they would probably be planners themselves. Since they're not programmers, they may easily fail to recognize the value of the skills that the doers bring to the table. Programmers, however, are less likely to make this mistake. In the meager (but growing) literature by and for serious programmers, the role of the doers is more generally recognized. Indeed, planning-oriented programmers often still perceive themselves as the underdogs, and programmer humor shows a deeply rooted skepticism regarding over-planned projects.

Historically, the dialectic between the planners and the doers has been a driving force in the evolution of programming languages. As the planners moved from FORTRAN to Pascal, C, C++, and Java, the doers have moved from COBOL to LISP, BASIC, Perl, and Tcl. Each new generation of language reflected the innovations of both the planners and the doers in the previous generation, but each made most of its own innovations in a single realm, either planning or doing.

Historically, it has been surprisingly hard to make money by inventing even the most wildly successful programming languages. Success is typically highly indirect—being the birthplace of C is certainly a claim that Bell Labs is proud to make, but it's hard to argue that the language was spectacularly meaningful for AT&T's (or Lucent's) bottom line. ParcPlace has perhaps come the closest to a genuine language-invention success story, but it's clearly no Microsoft. Imagine, then, the dilemma in which Sun Microsystems found itself, circa 1994, when its research labs were polishing up two new languages, one prickly and one gooey, each a plausible contender for leadership in the next generation of programming languages. Could any corporation really afford TWO such high-status, low-profit "success" stories?

Sun's decision to promote Java more vigorously than Tcl is hard to argue with. Because most decision-makers are managers, and most managers are planners, Java has always been an easier product to sell. Sun's continued and parallel support for Tcl was correct, even noble, and probably wiser than one could expect from the average large corporation. Still, in the face of the Java juggernaut, the promotion of Tcl has been left, for the most part, to the gooey doers among us. Pragmatic programmers with dirt on their hands, many of us became Tcl advocates for the most practical of reasons: It helped us get our jobs done, and quickly.

One such gooey doer is Clif Flynt, a veteran of countless programming languages who has fallen in love with Tcl for all the neat things it lets him do. Java advocates will often praise that language's abstractions, such as its virtual machine model. Tcl advocates like Clif prefer to grab on to the nuts and bolts and show you how quickly you can get real work done. That's what he does in this book, walking you all the way from the simplest basics to sophisticated and useful examples. If you're in a "doer" state of mind, you've picked up the right language and the right book. It can help you get a lot of jobs done.

Nathaniel Borenstein
Guppy Lake, Michigan

Introduction

Thanks for purchasing this copy of *Tcl/Tk for Real Programmers*. (You did buy this, didn't you?) This book will help you learn Tcl/Tk and show you how to use these tools to increase your programming productivity.

By the time you've finished reading this book, you'll have a good idea of what the strengths and weaknesses of Tcl/Tk are, how you can use the Tcl/Tk libraries and interpreters, and what constitutes an effective strategy for using Tcl/Tk.

This book is aimed at computer professionals from novice to expert level. If you are experienced with computer programming languages, you will be able to skim through the first few chapters getting a feel for how Tcl/Tk works, and then go on to the chapters on techniques and extensions. If you are less experienced, you should read the first chapters fairly carefully to be sure you understand the Tcl/Tk syntax. There are some tricky bits here.

If your primary goal is to learn the Tcl/Tk language quickly, you may want to examine some of the tutorials on the CD-ROM. There are several text and hypertext tutorials under the `tutorials` directory.

The CD-ROM also includes TclTutor, a computer-aided instruction package for learning programming languages. It will introduce the Tcl language in 40 short lessons with interactive examples that you can run, modify, and rerun as you learn more about Tcl.

Every language has some simple tricks and techniques that are specific to that language. Tcl/Tk is no exception. I'll discuss how to best accomplish certain tasks with Tcl/Tk: how to use the list and associative array data structures effectively, how to build modular code using Tcl's software engineering features, and what kinds of programming constructs will help you get your project from prototype to product with the minimal amount of rewriting.

Finally, there are plenty of code snippets, examples, and bits of packages to help you see how Tcl/Tk can be used. These examples are chosen to provide you with some boilerplate procedures that you can add to your programs right now, to help you get from scribbles on paper to a working program.

The CD-ROM includes:

- The longer examples.
- A bonus book of Real World Tcl/Tk applications.
- Tutorials on different aspects of Tcl.
- A printable reference.
- The Tcl style manuals from Scriptics.
- Tcl/Tk tools and extensions discussed in Chapters 13 and 14.
- The Tcl and Tk source code distributions.
- The Tcl and Tk binaries for the Mac, Windows, Linux, and BSDI platforms.

This should give you a good idea of what's coming up. Feel free to skip around the book. It's written to be an overview and reference, not a tutorial.

Where to Get More Information

As much as I would like to cover all the aspects of Tcl/Tk in this book, it isn't possible. Had I but world enough and time, I still wouldn't have enough of either. The Tcl/Tk community and the Tcl/Tk tools are growing too quickly for a book to do more than cover the central core of the language.

You can learn more about Tcl/Tk from these Web references:

`http://www.scriptics.com/`
> Scriptics Home Page: the definitive site for Tcl/Tk information.

`http://www.tclconsortium.org/`
> The Tcl/Tk Consortium: a non-profit organization dedicated to promoting Tcl/Tk.

`http://www.purl.org/NET/Tcl-FAQ`
> comp.lang.tcl FAQ: URLs for several Tcl/Tk FAQs and `comp.lang.tcl`.

`http://www.neosoft.com`
> Tcl/Tk Archives: the official repository for released Tcl/Tk packages.

`http://www.cis.ohio-state.edu/hypertext/faq/usenet/`
`tcl-faq/top.html`
> FAQ repository: the Tcl/Tk FAQ.

`http://www.sco.com/Technology/tcl/Tcl.html`
> Tcl WWW info: URLs for FAQs, conference proceedings, man pages, reference books, and training materials.

`http://www.cs.uoregon.edu/research/tcl/`
> Tcl/Tk FAQs, code, and other resources: URLs for patches, extensions, applications, and other resource sites.

`http://www.wwinfo.com/tcl/usrquery/sea.shtml`
> Database search for Tcl/Tk related items: a search engine for Tcl/Tk related items.

`http://www.net-quest.com/~ivler/cgibook/refs/index.shtml`
> Resources: URLs for mailing lists, newsgroups, books for Tcl/Tk, Perl, HTML, and more.

`http://starbase.neosoft.com/~claird/comp.lang.tcl/`
`tcl-references.html`
> General Tcl/Tk references of interest to Cameron Laird: URLs for tutorials, FAQs, online man pages, books, and more.

`http://cuiwww.unige.ch/eao/www/TclTk.html`
> The World Wide Web virtual library, Tcl and Tk: URLs for tutorials, FAQs, online man pages, books, extensions, applications, and much more.

`http://bmrc.berkeley.edu/people/chaffee/tcltk.html`
> Tcl/Tk for Win32 information: patches and URLs for OLE and ODBC extensions.

`http://home.wxs.nl/~nijtmans/`
> Jan Nijtmans' home page: patches and extensions for Tcl/Tk.

`http://www.cflynt.com`
> Flynt Consulting Services home page: errata and extensions for this book, updated TclTutor.

CHAPTER 1　　　　　*Why Tcl/Tk?*

Your first question is likely to be "What features does Tcl/Tk offer me that other languages don't?" This chapter will give you an overview of the Tcl/Tk features. It will cover the basics of what Tcl/Tk can offer you and what its strengths are compared with several alternatives.

Tcl is a multifaceted language. You can use Tcl as a command scripting language, as a powerful multiplatform interpreted language, or as a library of interpreter calls within another project. The speed with which you can write Tcl scripts makes it useful for single-use scripts to replace repetitive command typing or graphical user interface (GUI) clicking. Tcl has language constructs that make it useful for rapid development prototypes, and Tcl has modularization support to help develop large-scale (100,000+ lines of code) projects.

Tcl is both free software and a commercially supported package. The core Tcl language is supported by Scriptics Corporation (`http://www.scriptics.com`). Scriptics has stated that the interpreter will remain available without charge.

One of the strengths of Tcl is the number of special-purpose extensions that have been added to the language. The most popular extension of Tcl is Tk, which stands for Tool Kit. This extension for graphics programming supports drawing canvases, buttons, menus, etc. The Tk extension is considered part of the Tcl core and is also supported without charge by Scriptics Corporation.

Dr. John Ousterhout received the 1997 Software System Award from the Association for Computing Machinery (ACM) for his work with Tcl/Tk. This award recognizes the development of a software system that has a lasting influence.

The ACM press release says it well:

> The Tcl scripting language and its companion Tk user interface toolkit have proved to be a powerful combination. Tcl is widely used as the glue that allows developers to create complex systems using preexisting systems as their components. As one of the first embeddable scripting languages, Tcl has revolutionized the creation of customizable and extensible applications. Tk provides a much simpler mechanism to construct graphical user interfaces than traditional programming languages. The overall Tcl/Tk system has had substantial impact through its wide use in the developer community and thousands of successful commercial applications.

1.1 Tcl Overview

Tcl stands for Tool Command Language. This name reflects the power that Tcl has as a scripting language for gluing other applications together into a new application.

Tcl was developed by Dr. John Ousterhout while he was at the University of California at Berkeley. He and his group developed simulation packages that needed macro languages to control them. After creating a few on-the-fly languages that were tailored to one application and wouldn't work for another, they decided to create an interpreter library they could merge into the other projects. This provided a common parsing package that could be used with each project and a common base language across the applications.

The original design goal for Tcl was to create a language that could be embedded in other programs and easily extended with new functionality.

Tcl was also designed to execute other programs in the manner of a shell scripting language. By placing a small wrapper around the Tcl library, Dr. Ousterhout and his group created `tclsh`, a program that could be used as an interactive shell and as a script interpreter.

Dr. Ousterhout expected that this solid base for building specialized languages around a common set of core commands and syntax would be useful for building specialized tools. However, as programmers created Tcl extensions with support for graphics, database interaction, distributed processing, etc., they also started writing applications in pure Tcl. In fact, the Tcl language turned out to be powerful enough that many programs can be written using `tclsh` as an interpreter with no extensions.

Today, Tcl is widely used for in-house packages, as a scripting language for commercial products, as a rapid prototyping language, as a framework for regression testing, and for 7×24 mission-critical applications.

1.2 Tcl as a Command Glue Language

A command glue language is used to merge several programs into a single application. Unix programmers are familiar with the concept of using the output from one program as the input of another via pipes. With a glue language, more complex links between programs become possible. For example, several programs that report network behavior can be merged with a glue language to create a network activity monitor.

There are good reasons to use simple glue language scripts in your day-to-day computing work.

1. *A script can glue existing programs into a new entity.* It's frequently faster to glue together several small programs to perform a specific task than it is to write write a program from scratch.

2. *A script can repeat a set of actions faster and more reliably than you can type.* This is not to disparage your typing skills, but if you have to process 50 files in some consistent manner it will be faster to type a five-line script and have that loop through the file names than to type the same line 50 times.

3. *You can automate actions that would otherwise take several sets of window and mouse operations.* If you've spent much time with GUI programs under Microsoft Windows 95, Microsoft Windows NT, or the X Window System, you've probably noticed that there are certain operations you end up doing over and over again but there isn't a hot button you can use to invoke a particular set of button and mouse events. With a scripting language you can automate a set of actions that you do frequently.

4. *The script will remember a set of commands and actions and can act as procedure documentation.*

For example, I create a new release of the TclTutor package (a copy of which is on the CD-ROM accompanying this book) several times a year. This process involves several steps:

- Copy the correct files to a release directory.
- Create a zip file.
- Make the zip file a self-extracting executable.

At each step, there are several mouse selections and button clicks. None of these are particularly difficult or time consuming, but each is a potential error in building the package. I go through this procedure several times while I test that the new distribution works correctly and the new code behaves properly.

I run the process with a small Tcl script. This allows me to work on something else while the files are being copied and zipped. I don't have to worry about missing a file because I released a button too early, and the script ensures a consistent release format. The script is better than I am at remembering all the steps in the release process.

Note that you can use scripts only to control programs that support a non-GUI interface. The GUI-based programs I've worked with have also had a command line interface suitable for my purposes. Others may support script languages of their own or have a dialog-based mode.

1.2.1 Tcl Script Interpreters

Tcl is distributed with two interpreters: `tclsh`, the text-based interpreter, and `wish`, the same basic interpreter with Tk graphics commands added.

You can use the Tcl interpreter (`tclsh`) as you would use Unix shell or MS-DOS `.bat` scripts to control and link other programs and `wish` to create GUI interfaces to these scripts. Tcl provides a more powerful environment than the standard Unix shell or `.bat` file interpreters.

If you've written scripts using the Bourne shell under Unix, or `.bat` files under MS-DOS/MS-Windows, you know how painful it can be to make several programs work together. The constructs that make a good interactive user shell don't necessarily make a good scripting language.

Using Tcl, you can invoke other programs, just as you would with shell or `.bat` scripts, and read any output from those programs into the script for further processing. Tcl provides the string processing and math functionality of `awk`, `sed`, and `expr` without needing to execute other programs. It's easier to write Tcl scripts than Bourne shell scripts with `awk` and `sed`, since you have to remember only a single language syntax. Tcl scripts also run more efficiently, since the processing is done within a single executable instead of constantly executing new copies of `awk` and `sed`.

You can use a `wish` script as a wrapper around a set of programs originally designed for a text-based style user interaction (query/response, or one-at-a-time menu choices) and convert the programs into a modern GUI-based package. This is a very nice way to add a midlife kicker to an older package by hiding the old-style interactions from users more accustomed to graphical environments.

For example, we used a text-based problem-tracking system at one company. The user interface was a series of questions, such as "What product is the problem being reported against?" and "What revision is this product?" It took under an hour to write a wish front end that had buttons to select the products, text entry fields for the revisions and problem descriptions, etc. This GUI invoked the old user interface when the `Submit` button was pressed and relayed the selected values to that program as the prompts were received.

The GUI interface reduced the time and error count for filling out a report by reducing the amount of typing and providing a set of choices for models and revisions.

This technique for updating the user interface is not only quick but also, since the older, well-tested version of the user interface is still used to manipulate the internal data, less likely to introduce new bugs than writing a new interface from scratch.

1.2.2 Tcl Scripts Compared with Unix Shell Scripts

Here are some advantages Tcl provides over Unix shell scripts:

1. *Easier handling of program output.* Parsing the output of the programs a script has spawned is possible but not easy using the Unix shell. With Tcl, it's simple. Instead of saving the original command line variables, changing the field separator, setting the output, and then parsing the line, or invoking awk to process some text, you can read a line from a program's output just as if it had been entered at a keyboard. Then you can use the standard Tcl string and list operators to process the input.

2. *More consistent error handling in Tcl.* It can be difficult to distinguish between an error return and valid output in shell programming. Tcl provides a mechanism that separates the success/failure return of a program from the textual output.

3. *Consistent language.* When you write Unix shell scripts, you end up spawning copies of awk and sed to perform processing the shell can't do. You spend part of your time remembering the arcane awk and sed command syntax, as well as the shell syntax. Using Tcl, you can use a single language to perform all of the tasks—program invocation, string manipulation, computations, etc. You can expend your effort solving the original problem instead of solving language issues.

4. *Speed.* A single self-contained script running within the Tcl interpreter is faster and uses fewer machine resources than a Unix shell script that frequently needs to fork and exec other programs.

   Please note, this is not to say that a program written in Tcl is faster than one written in the C language. A string-searching program written in Tcl is probably slower than a string-finding program written in C. But a script that needs to find strings may run faster with a string-searching subroutine in Tcl than one written for the Unix shell that constantly forks copies of another executable.

When it's appropriate to invoke a special-purpose program, it's easily done in a Tcl script.

5. *GUI support.* You can use Tk to add a graphical interface to your scripts. Under Unix, wish supports the Motif look and feel. According to reports in comp.lang.tcl, a GUI written with wish sometimes runs faster than the same GUI written in C with the Motif library.

1.2.3 Tcl Scripts Compared with MS-DOS .bat Files

Tcl has so much more power than .bat files that there's actually very little comparison. The power of Tcl/Tk more closely resembles that of Visual Basic. Tcl/Tk will be compared with Visual Basic in the next section with the comparison of general-purpose interpreters.

Here are some advantages a Tcl script provides over an MS-DOS .bat file.

1. *Access to the output of programs invoked from script.* The .bat file interpreter simply allows you to run programs, not to access a program's output.

   With Tcl you can start a program, read its output into your script, process that data, send data back to that task, or invoke another task with the modified data.

2. *Control structures.* Tcl has more control structures than .bat files, including while loops, for loops, if/else, and switch.

3. *String manipulation.* .Bat files don't support any string manipulation commands. Tcl provides a very rich set of string searching and manipulation commands.

4. *Math operations.* Tcl provides a full set of arithmetic functions, including arithmetic, trig, and exponential functions and multiple levels of parentheses.

5. *Program control.* An MS-DOS .bat file has very limited control of other programs invoked by the .bat file. Tcl provides a great deal of control.

   In particular, when a GUI program is invoked from a .bat file under Windows 95 or Windows NT, the control may return to the .bat file before the program has ended. This is a problem if you were intending to make use of the results of the first program you invoked in the next program. Tcl can prevent the second program from starting until after the first program has completed its processing, or allow multiple programs to be run simultaneously.

6. *GUI support.* You can use Tk to make your scripts into GUIs. Wish supports a look and feel that match the standard MS Windows look and feel, so scripts you write with wish will look just like programs written in Visual C++, Visual Basic, or other pure MS development environments.

1.3 Tcl as a General-Purpose Interpreter

The Tcl/Tk interpreter provides several advantages over other interpreters:

1. *Multiplatform.* The same script can be run under Microsoft Windows 3.1, Microsoft Windows 95, Microsoft Windows NT, Apple Mac OS, and Unix or Linux. Tcl has also been ported to Digital Equipment VMS and real-time kernels such as VxWorks, from Wind River Systems.

2. *Speed.* As of Tcl version 8.0, the Tcl interpreter does a run-time compilation of a script into a byte code. Running the compiled code allows a Tcl script to run faster than Visual Basic or Perl.

3. *Power.* Tcl supports most of the modern programming constructs.

   - Modularization in the form of subroutines, libraries (including version control), and namespaces.

   - Rich set of variable types: integers, floating point, strings, lists, and associative arrays.

   - Exception handling. The Tcl catch and error commands provide an easy method for handling error conditions.

   - Standard program flow constructs: if, while, for, foreach, and switch.

   - Support for traditional program flow and event-driven programming.

   - Rich I/O implementation. Tcl can perform I/O operations with files, devices, keyboard/screen, other programs, or sockets.

- Powerful string manipulation commands. Tcl includes commands
  for searching and replacing strings or single characters, extracting
  and replacing portions of strings, and converting strings into lists, as
  well as commands that implement regular expressions for searching
  and replacing text.

1.3.1 Tcl/Tk Compared with Visual Basic

Of the currently available languages, Visual Basic is probably the closest
in functionality to Tcl/Tk. Here are a few of the reasons why Tcl/Tk is a
better choice.

1. *Tcl/Tk scripts run on multiple platforms.* Although the primary market for
   software may be the MS-Windows market, you might also want to have
   Apple and Unix markets available to your sales staff.
2. *Tcl/Tk scripts have support for Internet-style distributed processing, including
   security levels.*
3. *Tk provides more and finer control of widgets.* Wish allows you to bind
   actions to graphics objects as small as a single character in a text window or as large as an application window.
4. *Tcl has better support for library modules and version levels.* A Tcl script can
   check for a particular version of its support libraries and not run if they
   aren't available.

The one reason to prefer Visual Basic over Tcl is that you are writing a
package that will interact only with the Microsoft applications that use
Visual Basic as their scripting language. Tcl does not provide good hooks
into the Microsoft applications that are designed to work with Visual Basic.
However, future versions of Tcl may support OLE, etc.

1.3.2 Tcl/Tk Compared with Perl

Tcl/Tk often competes with Perl as an application scripting language. Here
are some of the advantages that Tcl/Tk offers over Perl:

1. *Simpler syntax.* Tcl code can be more easily maintained than Perl code.
   The rich set of constructs available to Perl programmers allows some
   very write-only programming styles. A Perl programmer can write code

that strongly resembles Unix shell language, C code, or awk scripts. Tcl supports fewer syntactic methods of accomplishing the same action, making Tcl code more readable.

2. *Faster.* The Tcl 8.0 interpreter byte compiled code runs faster than Perl 5 interpreter code.

3. *Better GUI support.* Native Perl has no GUI support. A couple of Tk-Perl mergers are available, but Tk is better integrated with Tcl.

1.3.3 Tcl/Tk Compared with Java

The primary language for multiplatform applications today is Java. Tcl and Java have some similarities but are really designed to solve two different problem sets. Java is a system programming language, similar to C and C++, whereas Tcl is an interpreted scripting language. In fact, you can write Tcl extensions in Java, and Tcl can load and execute Java code.

For now, here are some advantages Tcl offers over Java:

1. *Better multiplatform support.* Tcl runs on more platforms than Java. Java requires thread support, which is unavailable on many older Unix platforms. Tcl has also been ported to some real-time kernels such as VxWorks from Wind River Systems.

2. *Faster for prototyping.* The strength of an object-oriented language is that it makes you think about the problem up front and do a careful design before you code. Unfortunately, for many projects, you don't know the requirements up front and can't design a class structure until you understand the solutions better. Tcl/Tk is great for whipping out a quick prototype, seeing what truly answers the user's needs and what wasn't necessary, and then doing a serious design from a solid set of requirements.

3. *Better GUI support.* The Tk widgets are easier to work with and provide higher level support than the Java graphics library.

4. *Configurable security levels.* Tcl supports a different security model than the JavaScript model, making Tcl an ideal language for Internet program development. With Tcl, objects with various origins can be given varying levels of access to your system. For instance, you can give JavaScript-style

restricted system access to an unsigned applet (called a ticklet in Tcl), partial access to a ticklet from a slightly trusted source, or ActiveX-style full access to an applet that is encrypted with a key you truly trust.

5. *Smaller downloadable objects.* Because the Tcl libraries live on the machine where an application runs, there is less to download with a Tcl/Tk application than a similar set of functionality written in Java.

1.4 Tcl as an Extensible Interpreter

Many programming groups these days have a set of legacy code, a set of missions, and a need to perform some sort of rapid development. Tcl can be used to glue these code pieces into new applications.

Using Tcl, you can take the existing project libraries and turn them into commands within a Tcl interpreter. Once this is done, you'll have a language that you can use to develop rapid prototypes or even shippable programs.

Merging the existing libraries into the interpreter gives you a chance to hide sets of calling conventions that may have grown over several years and projects and expose the application programmer to a consistent application programmer interface (API).

This technique gives you a chance to graft a graphics interface over older, non-GUI-based sets of code.

1.5 Tcl as an Embeddable Interpreter

Programs frequently start as a simple proof of concept with hardcoded values. These values quickly evolve into variables that can be set with command line arguments. Shortly after that, the command lines get unwieldy, and someone adds a configuration file and a small interpreter to parse the configuration. The macro language then grows to control program flow as well as variables. Then it starts to get messy.

At the point where you need a configuration file, you can merge in a Tcl interpreter instead of writing new code to parse the configuration file. You can use Tcl calls to interpret the configuration file, and as the requirements expand, you'll be able to use Tcl as a complete language all at once, instead of adding features as people request them.

1.6 Tcl as a Rapid Development Tool

Tcl has a simple and consistent syntax at its core, which makes it an easy language to learn. At the edges, Tcl has many powerful extensions that provide less commonly needed functionality. These extensions range from general-purpose programming extensions such as the [incr Tcl] object-oriented programming extensions, to task-specific extensions, such as the OraTcl and SybTcl extensions for programming the Oracle and Sybase databases.

You can think of Tcl as a simple language with a rich set of libraries.

You can learn enough of the core Tcl commands to start writing programs in under an hour and then extend your knowledge as the need arises. When a task requires some new tools (SQL database interface, for instance), you have to learn only those new commands, not a whole new language. This common core with extensions makes your life as a programmer easier. You can take all the knowledge you gained doing one project and apply most of it to your next project.

This simplicity at the core with complexity in the extensions makes Tcl/Tk very suitable for rapid prototype development projects. During the 1995 Tcl/Tk Workshop, Brion Sarachan described the product that General Electric developed for NBC to control television network distribution (the paper describing this work is printed in the Conference Proceedings of the Tcl/Tk Workshop, July 1995).

The first meeting was held before the contract was awarded and included the engineers, management, and sales staff. After discussing the basic requirements, the sales and management groups continued to discuss schedules, pricing, and such, while the engineers went into another room with a laptop and put together a prototype for what the system could look like. By the time the sales and management staff were done, the engineers had a prototype to show. This turnaround speed had a lot to do with GE being awarded that contract.

In the course of the project, the GE group developed several prototype systems with various levels of functionality for the people at NBC to evaluate. As the project matured, the specifications were changed on the basis of the experience with prototypes.

The ease with which Tcl/Tk code can be extended and modified makes it an ideal platform for this type of a project.

The ability to extend the interpreter is a feature that separates Tcl from the other multiplatform and rapid development languages. Tcl interpreters can be extended in several ways, ranging from adding more Tcl subroutines (called procs in Tcl) to merging C, Java, or even assembly code into the interpreter.

Studies have found that 80% of a program's run time is spent in 20% of the code. The extensible nature of Tcl allows you to win at that game by rewriting the compute-intensive portion in a faster language while leaving the bulk of the code in the more easily maintained and modified script language.

This form of extensibility makes Tcl/Tk useful as the basis for a suite of programs. In a rapid prototype phase, a Tcl/Tk project can evolve from a simple set of back-of-the envelope designs to a quick prototype done entirely in Tcl. As the project matures, the various subroutines can be modified quickly and easily, as they are all written in Tcl. Once the design and the main program flow have stabilized, various Tcl/Tk subroutines can be rewritten in C or Java to get the required performance.

Once one project has evolved to this state, you have an interpreter with a set of specialized commands that can be used to develop other projects in this problem domain. This gives you a platform for better rapid prototyping and for code reuse.

1.7 GUI-Based Programming

The Tcl distribution includes the Tk graphics extensions of Tcl. The Tk extension package provides an extremely rich set of GUI tools, including buttons, menus, drawing surfaces, text windows, and scrollbars.

Any visual object can have procedures and events bound to it so that when a given event happens a particular set of commands is executed. For example, you can instruct a graphics object to change color when the cursor passes over it. You can bind actions to objects as trivial as a single punctuation mark in a text document or as large as an entire display.

1.8 Shipping Products

When it comes time to ship a product, you can either ship the Tcl scripts and Tcl interpreter or merge your Tcl script into an interpreter to create a Tcl-based executable.

The advantage of shipping the Tcl scripts is that competent users (or clever GUIs) can modify and customize the scripts easily. The disadvantages include the need for the user to have the proper revision level of Tcl available for the script to run and the possibility that someone will reverse engineer your program.

A Tcl script can be wrapped into a copy of the interpreter, to create a binary executable that will run only this script. (See the discussion of Jan Nitjmans' plus-patch in Chapter 13.)

With this technique, you can develop your program in a rapid development environment and ship a single program that doesn't require installation of the Tcl interpreter and has no human-readable code.

1.9 Bottom Line

Tcl/Tk is:

1. A shell scripting language
2. A multiplatform language
3. An extensible interpreter
4. An embeddable interpreter
5. A graphics programming language

Tcl/Tk is useful for:

1. Rapid prototyping
2. Shippable product
3. GUI-based projects
4. Multiplatform products
5. Adding GUIs to existing text-oriented programs
6. Adding new functionality to old code libraries

## CHAPTER 2

The Mechanics of Using the Tcl and Tk Interpreters

The first step in learning a new computer language is learning to run the interpreter/compiler and create simple executable programs. This chapter will describe:

- Mechanics of starting the interpreters.
- Starting `tclsh` and `wish` scripts in the interactive mode.
- Exiting the interpreter.
- Running `tclsh` and `wish` scripts from files.

2.1 The `tclsh` and `wish` Interpreters

The Tcl/Tk package is distributed with two script interpreters, `tclsh` and `wish`. `Tclsh` is a text-oriented interpreter that includes the core commands. It's useful for applications that don't require a GUI. `Wish` is the **windowing shell**; it includes the core Tcl interpreter with all the commands that `tclsh` supports and the Tk graphics extensions.

The simplest way to get started playing with Tcl and Tk is to type your commands directly into the interpreter. If you don't already have Tcl installed on your system, please see the instructions in Appendix B for installing Tcl/Tk from the CD-ROM.

2.1.1 Starting the `tclsh` and `wish` Interpreters

The `tclsh` and `wish` interpreters can be invoked from a menu choice or from a command line (with or without additional arguments). Invoking the interpreters from a menu choice or from a command line without arguments executes the interpreter in interactive mode: the interpreter evaluates the commands as you type them. Invoking the interpreter with a file name argument will cause the interpreter to evaluate the script in that file instead of starting an interactive session.

The command line to invoke the `tclsh` or `wish` interpreter (from a shell prompt under Unix or from a DOS command window under Windows 95 or Windows NT) resembles this:

```
C:\tcl\bin\wish.exe ?options? ?scriptName? ?scriptArguments?
```

or

```
/usr/local/bin/tclsh ?options? ?scriptName? ?scriptArguments?
```

The exact path may vary from installation to installation, and the name of the `wish` interpreter may vary slightly depending on how Tcl was installed. The default installation name for the interpreters includes the revision level (e.g., `wish8.0`), but many sites link `wish` to the latest version of the `wish` interpreter. The example paths and interpreter names used throughout this book will reflect some of the variants you can expect.

The command line options can tune the appearance of the `wish` graphics window. You can define the colormap, the name of the window, the size of the initial window, and other parameters on the command line. Some of these options are system dependent, so you should check your online documentation for the options available on your system.

If there are any arguments after the script name, those arguments will be ignored by the `tclsh` or `wish` interpreter and passed directly to the script for evaluation.

2.1.2 Starting `tclsh` or `wish` under Unix

Under Unix, you start `tclsh` as you would start any other program: type `tclsh` at a shell prompt. Be certain the directory containing the `tclsh` you want to invoke is in your **$PATH**.

`/usr/local/bin/tclsh ?scriptName? ?scriptArguments?`

or

`wish ?options? ?scriptName? ?scriptArguments?`

When the `tclsh` or `wish` interpreter starts, it loads several Tcl script files to define certain commands. The location for these files is defined when the interpreters are installed. If the interpreters are moved without being reinstalled, or the support file directories become unreadable, you may get an error message resembling the following when you try to run `tclsh`:

```
application-specific initialization failed:
Can't find a usable init.tcl in the following directories:
    /usr/local/lib/tcl8.0 /usr/local/lib/tcl8.0
/usr/tcl8.0/library /usr/local/library
This probably means that Tcl wasn't installed properly.
```

or this when you try to run `wish`:

```
Application initialization failed:
Can't find a usable tk.tcl in the following directories:
    /usr/local/lib/tk8.0 /usr/local/lib/tk8.0 /usr/local/tk8.0
    /usr/local/lib/tk8.0 /usr/local/library /usr/tk8.0/library
    /usr/library /usr/local/tk8.0/library
This probably means that Tk wasn't installed properly.
```

If this happens, you should reinstall Tcl/Tk, or restore the `init.tcl`, `tk.tcl`, and other files to one of the directories listed in the default search paths. Alternatively, you can find the appropriate `init.tcl` and define the environment variable `TCL_LIBRARY` as that directory. The default location of `init.tcl` can be overridden by setting the environment variable.

You can set the environment variable at your command line.

Using Bourne shell, Korn shell, or bash, this command would resemble:

TCL_LIBRARY=/usr/local/lib/tcl8.0p1 ; export TCL_LIBRARY

Using csh, tcsh, or zsh, the command would resemble:

setenv TCL_LIBRARY /usr/local/lib/tcl8.0p1

When tclsh is run with no command line, it will display a % prompt to let you know the interpreter is ready to accept commands.

When wish starts up, it will open a new window for graphics and will prompt the user with a % prompt in the window where you invoked wish.

2.1.3 Starting tclsh or wish under Microsoft Windows

When you install Tcl under Windows 95 or Windows NT, it will create a **Tcl** menu entry under the **Programs** menu and, within that menu, entries for tclsh and wish. When you select the tclsh menu item, Tcl will create a window for you with the tclsh prompt (%). If you select the wish menu item, it will open two windows: one for graphics and one with the familiar % prompt.

You can also invoke tclsh from a DOS window by typing the complete path and command name. Note that you may need to use the 8.3 version of a directory name under Windows 95.

Windows NT

```
C:> \Program Files\tcl\bin\tclsh80.exe
C:> \Program Files\tcl\bin\wish80.exe
```

Windows 95

```
C:> \Progra~1\tcl\bin\tclsh80.exe
C:> \Progra~1\tcl\bin\wish80.exe
```

Once you have the % prompt, you can type commands directly to the shell. The commands you enter will be interpreted immediately. If your command creates a graphic widget, it will be displayed in the graphics window.

2.1.4 Starting `tclsh` and `wish` on the Mac

When you install Tcl on a Macintosh, it will create an icon that can be double clicked. When you double-click the `tclsh` or `wish` icon, the `tclsh` or `wish` program will be invoked. Invoking `tclsh` will open up one window for commands. Invoking `wish` will open up two windows: one for commands and one to display graphics.

2.1.5 Exiting `tclsh`

You can exit a `tclsh` or `wish` interactive interpreter session by typing the command `exit` at the % prompt.

Under Unix, you can also exit a `wish` program by selecting a **Destroy** icon from the window manager or selecting a **Close** or **Destroy** from a pull-down menu button.

Under Windows 95/NT, you can exit a `wish` task by clicking on the **X** in the border of the windows. This won't work to exit `tclsh`, however; you must use the `exit` command.

2.2 Using `tclsh`/`wish` Interactively

The default `tclsh` prompt is a percent sign (%). When you see this prompt either in the window where you started `tclsh` or in a new window, you can type commands directly into the interpreter. Invoking `tclsh` in this mode is useful when you want to check the exact behavior of a command.

2.2.1 Tclsh as a Command Shell

When `tclsh` and `wish` are used interactively, if you type a command that is not part of the Tcl language, such as `ls` or `dir`, the interpreter will attempt to invoke that program as a subprocess and will display the child's output on your screen. This feature allows you to use the Tcl interpreter as a command shell, as well as an interpreter.

Under Unix the command interpreters also evaluate shell programs. This is the equivalent of having the MS-DOS .bat file interpreter and command.com functionality available at the command line. Experienced users use this feature to write small programs from the command line to accomplish simple tasks.

For instance, suppose you've been busy developing code for a while and you've forgotten which files you changed. If you've got (or can retrieve from an archive) the original code, you can compare all the files in one directory with files with the same name in another directory and put the results in a file with a DIF suffix. The commands at the Bourne, Korn, or Bash shell prompt are:

```
$ for i in *.c
    do
    diff $i ../otherDir/$i >$i.DIF
done
```

You can use tclsh to gain this functionality in the Windows world.

To accomplish the same task under a tclsh shell, type:

```
% foreach i [glob *.c] {
    diff $i ../otherDir/$i >$i.DIF
  }
```

2.2.2 TkConsole—An Alternative Interactive tclsh/wish Shell

Jeffrey Hobbs has written a useful console program, TkConsole, which provides a nicer interface than the simple % prompt.

TkConsole provides:

- A menu-driven history mechanism, to make it easy to find and repeat previous commands.
- An Emacs-like editor interface to the command line, to make it easy to fix typos or modify previous commands slightly.
- Brace and parenthesis matching, to help you keep your code ordered.
- Color coding Tcl command names, to differentiate commands and data.

- The ability to save your commands in a file. This lets you experiment with commands and save your work.
- A menu entry to load and run Tcl command scripts from files.
- Support for opening several new TkConsole displays.

This program is included on the CD-ROM accompanying this book. After you install it, you can invoke it as you would any other script. Under MS-Windows, start it via the **RUN** button, or move it into the **Start** menu. Under Unix, type `tkcons1_1.tcl` at a shell prompt.

Note that although `TkCon` is easier to work with than the interactive `wish` interpreter, it can be used to invoke `wish` scripts, and is more powerful than the Windows command interpreter, it does not deal well with programs that require user interaction after they have been started. It's actually designed to help develop Tcl scripts and to run noninteractive commands.

2.2.3 Evaluating Scripts Interactively

`Tclsh` and `wish` can be used interactively as Tcl program interpreters. This section will discuss typing a short program at the command prompt. The next section will discuss how to run a program saved in a file.

The traditional first program, "Hello, world," is trivial in Tcl:

```
% puts "Hello, world"
Hello, world
```

The `puts` command sends a string to an I/O channel. By default, the standard output is your command window, but the output can be assigned to a file, a TCP/IP socket, or through a pipe to another program. The details of the Tcl commands will be covered in the next chapters.

Printing "Hello, world" is a fairly boring little example, so let's make it a bit more exciting by using the Tk extensions to make it into a graphics program.

In this case, you need to invoke the `wish` interpreter instead of the `tclsh` interpreter.

If you are using the TkConsole program to run these examples, you'll need to load the Tk package by selecting the **Interp** menu, **packages**, and **load Tk**.

Typing this code at the % prompt will display "Hello, world" in a small box in the graphics window:

```
label .1 -text "Hello, world"
pack .1
```

The `label` command tells the `wish` interpreter to construct a graphics widget named `.1` and place the text "Hello, world" within that widget.

The `pack` command causes the label to be displayed. This will be covered in Chapter 8.

When you run this little script you should see a window resembling this on your screen:

2.3 Evaluating Tcl Script Files

Typing a short program at the command line is a good start, but it doesn't create a shippable product. The next step is to evaluate a Tcl script stored in a file on disk.

2.3.1 The Tcl Script File

A Tcl script file is simply an ASCII text file of Tcl commands. The individual commands may be terminated with a newline marker (carriage return or linefeed) or a semicolon. If a command is too long to fit on a single line, making the last character before the newline a backslash will continue the same command line on the next screen line.

For example, here's a simple `tclsh` script that prints several lines of information.

Example 2.3.1-1

Script Code

```
puts "This is a simple command"
puts "this line has two"; puts "commands on it";
puts "this line is continued \
on the next line, but prints one line"
```

Script Output

```
This is a simple command
this line has two
commands on it
this line is continued  on the next line, but prints one line
```

Note that there are *two* spaces between the words continued and on. When the Tcl interpreter evaluates a line with a backslash in it, it replaces the backslash newline combination with a space.

You can write Tcl/Tk programs with any editor that will let you save a flat ASCII file. On the Macintosh, the interactive command window behaves like a standard Macintosh editing window, allowing you to scroll back, copy lines, and save text. Under Unix and Windows, the interactive command window does not support these options, and you'll need to use a separate editor to create and modify your scripts.

In the Unix world, vi and Emacs are common editors. Notepad, Brief, WordPerfect, and MS-Word are suitable editors in the Windows world, and Mac-Write and Alpha are suitable for use on the Macintosh. Note that you must specify an ASCII text file for the output and use hard newlines if you use one of the word processor style editors. Tcl cannot read a word processor's native format.

Mike Doyle and Hattie Schroeder developed a nice editor as an example in their book *Interactive Web Applications with Tcl/Tk* (http://www.eolas.com/tcl). This editor allows you to edit a script, test it within the editor, and save it to disk when you are happy with it. This program is on the CD-ROM included with this book. You may find it useful while you're getting familiar with Tcl. It uses a subset of the Emacs/Brief editor commands and the mouse to position a cursor.

You can also use the TkConsole package to type in Tcl commands and then save them to a file via the **File - Save - History** menu choice. Note that you will probably need to edit this file after you've saved it to delete extra lines.

2.3.2 Evaluating Tcl Script Files

For the time being, let's assume that you've created a file named foo.tcl with this text:

```
label .l -text "The arguments to this script are: $argv"
pack .l
```

There are several ways to evaluate this wish script file. Here are two that will work on Unix or Microsoft systems. Other methods tend to be platform specific and will be covered in the system-specific sections.

You can always evaluate a tclsh or wish script by typing the path to the interpreter, followed by the script, followed by arguments to the script. This works under Windows (from a DOS window, or **Run** menu) or Unix and would look like:

```
C:\tcl8.0\bin\wish80.exe foo.tcl one two three
```

or

```
/usr/local/bin/wish8.0 foo.tcl one two three
```

This will cause a window resembling this to appear on your display:

You can also cause a script to be evaluated by typing source foo.tcl at the % prompt within an interactive wish interpreter session. The source will read and evaluate a script but does not support setting command line arguments.

```
$> wish
% source foo.tcl
```

2.3.3 Evaluating a Tcl Script File under Unix

Under Unix, you can use the technique of placing the name of the interpreter in the first line of the script file. Unfortunately, the shells will only search /bin and /usr/bin for interpreters. If you keep `tclsh` in another directory (for instance, /usr/foo/bin), you'll need to start your script files with the complete path:

```
#!/usr/foo/bin/tclsh
```

This makes a script less portable, since it won't run on a system that has `tclsh` under /usr/bar/bin.

A clever workaround for this is to start your script file with these lines:

```
#!/bin/sh
#\
exec wish "$0" "$@"
```

The trick here is that both Tcl and the shell interpreter use the "#" to start a comment, but the Bourne shell does not treat the \ as a line continuation character, while Tcl does.

The first line (`#!/bin/sh`) invokes the Bourne shell to execute the script. The shell reads the second line (`#\`), sees a comment, and does not process the "\" as a continuation character, so it evaluates the third line (`exec wish "$0" "$@"`). At this point, the shell invokes the `wish` interpreter to evaluate the script, using the full $PATH information as the search path for `wish`.

When the `wish` interpreter reads the script, it interprets the first line as a comment and ignores it and treats the second line (`#\`) as a comment with a continuation to the next line. This causes the Tcl interpreter to ignore `exec wish "$0" "$@"` as part of the comment started on the previous line and the `wish` interpreter starts to evaluate the script.

The last step to making a `tclsh` or `wish` script executable is to `chmod` the file to set the execution bits:

```
chmod 755 foo.tcl
```

or

```
chmod +x foo.tcl
```

2.3.4 Evaluating a Tcl Script File under Microsoft Windows

When Tcl is installed under MS Windows 95 or MS Windows NT, it establishes an association between the .tcl suffix and the wish interpreter. This allows you to run a .tcl script via mouse clicks using the **Run** menu, Internet Explorer, the Find application, etc.

If you desire to use other suffixes for your files, you can define tclsh or wish to process files with a given suffix via the Microsoft Windows configuration menus.

Here's an example of adding a file association between the suffix .tc8 and the tclsh interpreter. This association will invoke the tclsh interpreter to run scripts that are text driven instead of graphics driven.

Select **My Computer - View - Options**, to get the **Options** display.

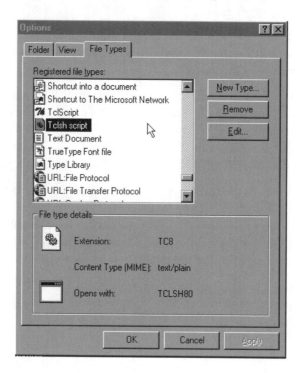

Select the **File Types** card from this display and the New Type button from this card.

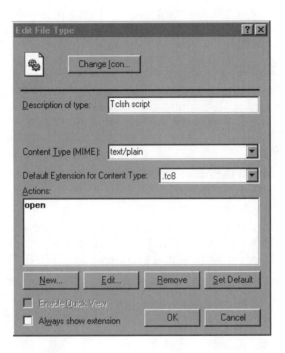

You must provide an open action that points to the interpreter you want to invoke to open files with this suffix. The **Application** to perform the action needs a full path to the interpreter.

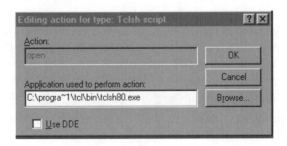

Running scripts via the mouse works well for tclsh- or wish-based programs that don't require any command line arguments. However, when you invoke a script this way, you can't supply command line arguments, and no command window is opened. With no command window opened to receive output, the program loses any output you may have from puts commands, and you can't interact with the program via gets commands.

If you need to invoke a script with command line options, you must invoke the script from a DOS command window.

If you want to avoid typing a long path to invoke your scripts, there are a few options.

1. You can add the path to the Tcl interpreter to your DOS PATH.

   ```
   PATH C:\DOS;C:\PROGRA~1\TCL80\BIN;C:\WINDOWS;\
       C:\WINDOWS\COMMAND
   ```

2. After you've installed tclsh, you can copy the executable (tclsh80.exe) to C:\WINDOWS. C:\WINDOWS is in the MS-Windows default search path. This has the potential to clutter your \WINDOWS directory.

3. You can make a .bat file wrapper for each script. This lets you leave the Tcl executables where they were installed, and you can place the .bat file in your \WINDOWS directory if you want to be able to access the script from any directory.

   C:> TYPE MYSCRIPT.BAT

   **C:\PROGRA~1\TCL80\BIN\TCLSH C:\TCLSCRIPTS\MYSCRIPT.TCL\
       %1 %2 %3 %4 %5**

   This will clutter your **Windows** directory with a .bat file for each script that you use.

4. You can create a .bat file wrapper to invoke tclsh. This is similar to typing out the entire path in some respect, but allows you to put a single small .bat file in C:\WINDOWS, while leaving the Tcl interpreter and libraries in separate directories.

   C:> TYPE TCLSH.BAT

   C:\PROGRA~1\TCL80\BIN\TCLSH %1 %2 %3 %4 %5 %6 %7 %8 %9

   The problem with the .bat file techniques is that .bat files support a limited number of command line arguments. On the other hand, if you need more than nine command line arguments, you might consider using a configuration file.

5. You can write your Tcl programs as .bat files and evaluate them as
   `filename.bat` with this wrapper around the Tcl code:

```
::catch {};#\
@echo off
::catch {};#\
@"C:\tcl\bin\tclsh.exe" %0 %1 %2
::catch {};#\
@goto eof
#your code here
#\
:eof
```

This is similar to the startup described for the Unix Tcl files.

The lines with leading double colons are viewed as labels by the bat file interpreter, while the Tcl interpreter evaluates them as commands in the global namespace.

These lines end with a comment followed by a backslash. The backslash is ignored by the bat file interpreter, which then executes the next line. The Tcl interpreter treats the next line as a continuation of the previous comment and ignores it.

The catch command is discussed in Chapter 5, and namespaces are discussed in Chapter 6.

If you prefer to run your scripts by single word, i.e., `filename` instead of `filename.bat`, you can change the line:

```
@"C:\tcl\bin\tclsh.exe" %0 %1 %2
```

to

```
@"C:\tcl\bin\tclsh.exe" %0.bat %1 %2
```

2.3.5 Evaluating a Tcl Script on the Mac

The concept of the executable script file doesn't really exist on the Mac.

If you wish to evaluate a previously written script on the Mac, you can select the **Source** entry from the **File** menu, and then select the file to execute.

Alternatively, you can type the command to source the script file at the % prompt. In this case, you must use the complete path:

```
source :demos:widget
```

The Tcl 8.0 distribution includes an application Drag & Drop Tclets that converts Tcl script files into small applications that can be launched normally. The first time you invoke this program, it will launch the standard Macintosh file selection mechanism for you to select the **Wish Stub** to use in the future and will prompt you for a name and location for the new program.

You cannot change the **Creator** for a script to make the script evaluated by tclsh (or wish) when you double-click it.

2.4 Bottom Line

1. Tclsh is an interpreter for text-based applications.
2. Wish is the tclsh interpreter with graphics extensions for GUI-based applications.
3. These programs may be used as interactive command shells or as script interpreters.
4. Either interpreter will accept a script to evaluate as a command line argument. A script is an ASCII file with commands terminated by newlines or semicolons. In a script, commands may be continued across multiple lines by making the final character of a line the backslash character.
5. Tclsh scripts may be wrapped in .bat files under Windows 95 and Windows NT, or chmod it to be executable under Unix.
6. Wish scripts that need no arguments may be executed from the RUN menu under Windows 95 and Windows NT.
7. Arguments after the script file name will be passed to the script for evaluation.
8. The command to exit the tclsh or wish interpreters is exit.

CHAPTER 3 — *Introduction to the Tcl Language*

The next four chapters constitute a Tcl language tutorial. This chapter provides an overview of the Tcl syntax, data structures, and some commands. Chapter 4 will discuss in more detail command syntax and how Tcl processes commands and will provide some examples. Chapters 5 and 6 will introduce more commands and techniques and provide examples showing how Tcl data constructs can be used to create complex data constructs such as structures, trees, and classes.

This introduction to the Tcl language is intended to show you how Tcl can be used, rather than be a complete listing of all the commands and all their options. The CD-ROM contains a Tcl/Tk reference guide that contains brief listings of all commands and all options. The online reference pages are the most complete reference for the commands.

If you prefer a more extensive tutorial, please check the CD-ROM under the tutorials directory. You'll find a couple of textual tutorials and a copy of TclTutor, which is a computer-assisted instruction program that covers all of the commands in Tcl and most of the command options.

Chapters 8–11 constitute the Tk tutorial. If you are doing graphics programming, you may be tempted to skip ahead to those chapters and just read about the GUIs. *Don't do it.* Tcl is the glue that holds the graphic widgets together. Tk and the other Tcl extensions build on top of the Tcl foundation. If you glance ahead for the Tk tutorial, plan on coming back to fill in the gaps.

This book will print the command syntax using the font conventions that are used in the Tcl online manual and help pages. This convention is:

`commandname`   The command name appears first in this type font.

`subcommandname`

If the command supports subcommands they will also be in this type font.

`-option`   Options appear in italics. The first character is a dash (–).

`argument`   Arguments to a command appear in italics.

`?-option?`   Options that are not required are bounded by question marks.

`?argument?`   Arguments that are not required are bounded by question marks.

For example:

Syntax: `puts ?-newline? ?channel? outputString`

The command name is `puts`. It may take an option `-nonewline` and it may accept a `channel` as an argument. However, it must have an `output-String` argument.

3.1 Overview of the Basics

The Tcl language has a simple and regular syntax. You can approach Tcl by learning the overall syntax and then learning the individual commands. Because the base interpreter is used for all Tcl extensions, the basic Tcl syntax is used by the extensions.

3.1.1 Syntax

Tcl is a position-based language, not a keyword-based language. There are no reserved strings. The first word of a Tcl command line has a defined meaning: it must be a Tcl command, either a built-in command, a procedure name, or (when `tclsh` is in interactive mode) an external command.

A complete Tcl command is a list of words. The first word must be a Tcl command name or a subroutine name. The following words may be subcommands, options, or arguments to the command. The command is terminated by a newline or a semicolon.

For example, the word `puts` at the beginning of a command is a command name, but `puts` in the second position of a command could be a subcommand or a variable name. The Tcl interpreter keeps separate hash tables for the command names and the variable names, so you can have both a command `puts` and a variable named `puts` in the same function.

Example 3.1.1-1

```
puts "This is a command with one argument";
```
Valid: This is a complete command.

```
x=4
```
Not valid: x is not a command.

```
puts one; puts two;
```
Valid: This line has two commands.

```
puts one puts two
```
Not valid: The first command is not terminated, so Tcl interprets it as a `puts` command with three arguments.

3.1.2 Grouping Words

The spaces between words are important. Since Tcl doesn't have a set of keywords, it scans commands by checking for symbols separated by white space.

The spaces in a Tcl command are used to determine which words are commands, subcommands, options, or data. If a data string has multiple words but needs to be treated as a single set of data, the string needs to be grouped with quotes (`" "`) or curly braces (`{ }`).

Example 3.1.2-1

```
if { $x >2 } {set greater true}
```
> Valid: If the value of x is greater than 2, then the value of greater is set to "true."

```
if{ $x >2 } {set greater true}
```
> Invalid: No space between if and test left brace.

```
if {$x >2}{ set greater true}
```
> Invalid: No space between test and body left brace.

```
set x a b
```
Invalid: Too many arguments to set.

```
set x "a b"
```
Valid: The variable x is assigned the value a b.

```
set x {a b}
```
Valid: The variable x is assigned the value a b.

Quotes and braces are treated differently by the Tcl interpreter. These differences will be discussed in Chapter 4.

3.1.3 Comments

A comment is denoted by putting a pound sign (#) in the position where a command name could be. It is strongly recommended that this be the first character on a line, but it could be the first character after a semicolon.

Example 3.1.3-1

```
# This is a comment
```
> Valid: This is a valid comment.

```
puts "test" ;# Comment after a command.
```
> Valid: But not recommended style.

```
puts "test" # this is a syntax error.
```
> Invalid: The puts command was not terminated.

3.1.4 Data Representation

Tcl does not require that you declare variables before using them. The first time you assign a value to a variable name, it allocates space for the data and adds the variable name to the internal tables.

A variable name is an arbitrarily long sequence of letters, numbers, or punctuation characters. Although any characters (including spaces) *can* be used in variable names, convention is to follow naming rules similar to those in C and Pascal: start a variable name with a letter, followed by a sequence of alphanumeric characters.

The *Tcl Style Guide* recommends that you start local variable names with an uppercase letter and global variable names with a lowercase letter. The rationale for this is that items that are intended for internal use should require more keystrokes than items intended for external use. This document is available on the SunScript Web site (`http://sunscript.sun.com`), the Scriptics Web site (`http://www.scriptics.com/resource/doc/papers/`), and on the CD-ROM (`docco/style.ps`).

A variable is referenced by its name. The value assigned to a variable is accessed by placing a dollar sign (`$`) in front of the variable name. The value of a Tcl variable will always be accessed as a printable string within your script. (Internally, it may be a floating-point value or an integer. That will be discussed in Chapter 12.)

Example 3.1.4-1

`set x four`   Set the value of a variable named `x` to `four`.

`set pi 3.14`   Set the value of a variable named `pi` to `3.14`.

`puts "pi is $pi"`
              Display the string: "pi is 3.14".

`set pi*2 6.28`
              Set the value of a variable named `pi*2` to `6.28`.

`set "bad varname" "Don't Do This"`
              Set the value of a variable named `bad varname` to `Don't Do This`.

Notice that the * symbol in the variable name pi*2 does not mean to multiply in this case. Since the * is embedded in a word, it is simply another character in a variable name. The last example shows how spaces can be embedded in a variable name. This is not recommended style.

3.1.5 Command Results

If a Tcl command fails to execute for a syntactic reason (incorrect arguments, etc.), it will generate an error, display a message about the cause of the error, and stop evaluating the current Tcl script.

If a command can be evaluated successfully, it may return data. That data can be assigned to a variable, used in a conditional statement like an if, or passed to another command.

Enclosing a Tcl command in square brackets causes the command to be evaluated immediately, and the command's return value is available for the script to process. This is the same as putting a command inside backquotes in Unix shell programming.

For example, the set command always returns the value of the variable being set. When x is assigned the value of "apple" in the following example, evaluating the set command returns "apple". When set x "pear" is evaluated within the square brackets, it returns "pear", which is then assigned as the value for y.

Example 3.1.5-1

```
# The set x command returns the contents of the variable.
% set x "apple"
apple
% set y [set x "pear"]
pear
% puts $y
pear
```

In the previous example, the quotes around the word apple are not required by the Tcl interpreter. However, it's good practice to place strings within quotes.

3.2 Data Types

The primitive data type in Tcl is the string, and the composite data types are the list and the associative array. Certain complex objects such as graphic objects, I/O channels, and sockets are accessed via handles. These will be introduced briefly here, with more discussion in the following chapters.

Unlike C, C++, or Java, Tcl is a typeless language. However, certain commands can define what sort of string data they will accept. Thus, the `expr` command, which performs math operations, will generate an error if you try to add 5 to the string "You can't do that".

3.2.1 Strings

All Tcl data are strings. A string can hold alphanumeric or pure numeric data. Numeric data can be represented in Tcl as integers, as floating-point values (with a decimal point), or in scientific notation. The command that receives a string will determine whether the data should be interpreted as numeric or alphabetic.

Example 3.2.1-1

LegitimateStrings

```
set alpha "abcdefg"
```
Assign the string "abcdefg" to the variable `alpha`.

```
set validString "this is a valid string"
```
Assign the string "this is a valid string" to the variable `validString`.

```
set number 1.234
```
Assign the number "1.234" to the variable `number`.

```
set scientificNotation 10e2
```
Assign the number "100" to the variable `scientificNotation`.

```
set msg {Bad input: "Bogus". Try again.}
```
>   Assign the string "Bad input: "Bogus". Try again." to the variable `msg`. Note the internal quotes. Quotes within a braced string are treated as ordinary characters.

```
set msg "Bad input: \"Bogus\". Try again."
```
>   Assign the string "Bad input: "Bogus". Try again." to the variable `msg`. Note that the internal quotes are escaped. This will be explained in detail in the next chapter.

Bad Strings

```
set msg "Bad input: "Bogus". Try again."
```
>   The quotes around `Bogus` aren't escaped and are treated as quotes. The quote before `Bogus` closes the string, and the rest of the line causes a syntax error.

```
set badstring "abcdefg
```
>   Has only one quote.

```
set mismatch {this is not a valid string"
```
>   Quote and brace mismatch.

```
set noquote this is not valid string
```
>   This set of words must be grouped to be assigned to a variable.

3.2.2 Lists

A list is an ordered set of strings, such as "apple pear banana". The first element of this list is "apple", the second element is "pear", etc. The order of the elements can be changed with Tcl commands for inserting and deleting list elements, but the Tcl interpreter will never modify the order of list elements as a side effect of another operation.

A list may be arbitrarily long, and list elements may be arbitrarily long.

Any string can be considered as a list. The first word in a string can be considered to be the first element in a list.

With Tcl 8.0, lists and strings are treated differently within the interpreter. If you are dealing with data as a list, it's more efficient to use the list commands. If you are dealing with data as a string, it's better to use the string commands.

The commands that manipulate lists and strings will be discussed later.

3.2.3 Associative Arrays

The associative array is an array that uses a string to index the array elements, instead of a numeric index the way C, Fortran, and Basic implement arrays. For example, `price(apple)` and `price(pear)` would be associative array variables that could contain the price of an apple or pear.

Example 3.2.3-1

```
set price(apple)  .10
```
> `price` is an associative array. The variable referenced by the index `apple` is set to .10.

```
set price(pear)  .15
```
> `price` is an associative array. The variable referenced by the index `pear` is set to .15.

```
set quantity(apple) 20
```
> `quantity` is an associative array. The variable referenced by the index `apple` is set to 20.

```
set discount(12) 0.95
```
> `discount` is an associative array. The variable referenced by the index `12` is set to 0.95.

3.2.4 Handles

Tcl uses handles to refer to certain special-purpose objects. These handles are returned by the Tcl command that creates the object and can be used to access and manipulate the object. When you open a file, a handle is returned for accessing that file. The graphic objects created by a wish script are also accessed via handles, which will be discussed in the wish tutorial.

Types of handles include:

channel A handle that references an I/O device such as a file, serial port, or TCP socket. A channel is returned by an open or socket call and can be an argument to a puts, read, close, flush or gets call.

graphic A handle that refers to a graphic object created by a wish command. This handle is used to modify or query an object.

http A handle that references data returned by an http::geturl operation. An http handle can be used to access the data that was returned from the http::geturl command or otherwise manipulate the data.

3.3 Tcl Commands

Tcl has a rich set of commands. This section will introduce a subset of those commands. Most of these commands will be used in the examples in the next few chapters. With these few commands you can start writing useful Tcl programs.

3.3.1 Assigning Values to Variables

The command to define the value of a variable is set. It allocates space for a variable and a set of data and assigns the data to that variable.

Syntax: set *varName ?value?*

set Define the value of a variable.

varName The name of the variable to define.

value The data to assign to the variable.

If set is invoked with two arguments, the first argument will be treated as the variable name and the second as a value to assign to that variable.

If set is invoked with a single argument, then that argument must be a variable name and the value of that variable is returned.

Set always returns the value of the variable.

Example 3.3.1-1

```
% set x 1
1
% set x
1
% set y
can't read "y": no such variable
```

3.3.2 Math Operations

Math operations are performed using the incr and expr commands. The incr command provides a fast method of incrementing the value of an integer, and the expr command provides an interface to a general-purpose calculation engine.

The incr command will add an integer value to a variable. The value may be positive or negative, thus allowing the incr command to perform a decrement operation. The incr command is used primarily to adjust loop variables.

Syntax: incr *varName ?incrValue?*

incr   Add a value (default 1) to a variable.

varName   The name of the variable to increment. NOTE: This is a variable name, not a value. Do not start the name with a $. This variable must contain an integer value, not a floating-point value.

?incrValue?   The value to increment the variable by. May be a negative number. This value must be an integer, not a floating-point value.

Example 3.3.2-1

```
%set x 4
4
% incr x
5
% incr x -3
2
```

The expr command is a general-purpose calculation command that will perform arbitrarily complex math operations. Unlike most Tcl commands, expr does not expect a fixed number of arguments. It can be invoked with the arguments grouped as a string or as individual values and operators. Arguments to expr may be grouped with parentheses to control the order of math operations.

The expr command can also evaluate boolean expressions and is used to test conditions by the Tcl branching and looping commands.

Syntax: expr *mathExpression*

Tcl supports these math operations (grouped in decreasing order of precedence):

- + ~ !	Unary minus, unary plus, bitwise NOT, logical NOT
* / %	Multiply, divide, remainder
+ -	Add, subtract
<< >>	Left shift, right shift
< > <= >=	Less than, greater than, less than or equal, greater than or equal
== !=	Equality, inequality
&	Bitwise AND
^	Bitwise exclusive OR
|	Bitwise OR
&&	Logical AND. Produces a 1 result if both operands are nonzero, 0 otherwise.
||	Logical OR. Produces a 0 result if both operands are zero, 1 otherwise.
x?y:z	If-then-else, as in C. If x evaluates to nonzero, then the result is the value of y. Otherwise, the result is the value of z. The x operand must have a numeric value. The y and z operands may be variables or Tcl commands.

Note that the bitwise operations are valid only if the arguments are integers (not floating-point or scientific notation).

The `expr` command also supports these math functions and conversions:

Trigonometric Functions

cosine:	arccosine:	hyperbolic cosine:
cos(*radians*)	acos(*float*)	cosh(*radian*)
sin:	arcsin:	hyperbolic sin:
sin(*radians*)	asin(*float*)	sinh(*radian*)
tangent:	arctangent:	hyperbolic tangent:
tan(*radian*)	atan(*float*)	tanh(*float*)
Euclidean distance:	arctangent of ratio:	
hypot(*float*)	atan2(*float, float*)	

Exponential Functions

natural log:	log base 10:	square root:
log (*float*)	log10 (*float*)	sqrt(*float*)
exponential:	power:	
exp(*float*)	pow(*float, float*)	

Conversion Functions

Largest integer less than a float:	Smallest integer greater than a float:	remainder:
floor(*float*)	ceil(*float*)	fmod(*float, float*)
return closest int:	convert int to float:	convert float to int:
round(*num*)	double(*num*)	int(*num*)
absolute value:		
abs(*num*)		

Random Numbers

seed random number: generate random number:

srand(*num*)   rand()

Example 3.3.2-2

```
% expr rand()*10
3.70896398263
% expr floor(sin(3.14/2)*10)
9.0
% set x [expr int(rand()*10)]
4
% expr atan(((3 + $x) * $x)/100.)
0.273008703087
```

3.3.3 Choices

Tcl supports a simple choice command (if) and a multiple choice command (switch).

The if command tests a condition, and if that condition is true, the script associated with this test is evaluated.

Syntax:

```
if {testExpression1} {
    body1
} ?elseif {testExpression2 } {
    body2
    } ...?
?else {bodyN}?
```

if   Determine whether a code body should be evaluated based on the results of a test. If the test returns true, then the first body is evaluated. If the test is false and a body of code exists after the else, then that code will be evaluated.

testExpression1

If this expression evaluates to true, then the first body of code is evaluated. The expression must be in a form acceptable to the expr command. These forms include

An arithmetic comparison `{$a < 2}`

A string comparison `{ $string != "OK" }`

The results of a command `{ [eof $inputFile] }`

A variable with a numeric `{$AnalysisResult}` value. Zero (0) is considered false, and nonzero values are true.

body1   The body of code to evaluate if the first test evaluates as true.

`elseif`   If *testExpression1* is false, evaluate *testExpression2*.

testExpression2
          A second test to evaluate if the first test evaluates to false.

body2   The body of code to evaluate if the second test evaluates as true.

`?else bodyN?` If all tests evaluate false, this body of code will be evaluated.

In the following example, note the placement of the curly braces (`{}`).

The *Tcl Style Guide* describes the preferred format for `if`, `for`, `proc`, and `while` commands. It recommends that you place the left curly brace of the body of these commands on the line with the command and place the body on the next lines, indented four spaces. The final, right curly brace should go on a line by itself, indented even with the opening command. This makes the code less dense (and more easily read).

Putting the test and action on a single line is syntactically correct Tcl code but can cause maintenance problems later. You will need to make some multiline choice statements, and mixing multiline and single-line commands can make the action statements hard to find. Also, what looks simple when you start writing some code may need to be expanded as you discover more about the problem you are solving. You may as well start with the code laid out to support adding new lines of code.

Because of the way a Tcl command is evaluated, a left curly brace must be at the end of a line of code, not on a line by itself. The reasons for this are discussed in Chapter 4.

Example 3.3.3-1

A Simple Test

```
set x 2
set y 3
if {$x < $y} {
    puts "x is less than y"
}
```

Script Output

x is less than y

The `switch` command allows a Tcl script to choose one of several patterns. The `switch` command is given a variable to test and several patterns. The first pattern that matches the test phrase will be evaluated, and all other sets of code will not be evaluated.

Syntax: `switch ?opt? str pat1 bod1 ?pat2 bod2? ?...? ?default?`

`switch`	Evaluate 1 of N possible code bodies depending on the value of a string.
`?opt?`	One of these possible options:

`-exact`	Match a pattern string exactly to the test string, including a possible "-" character.
`-glob`	Match a pattern string to the test string using the `glob` string match rules. These are the default matching rules.
`-regexp`	Match a pattern string to the test string using the regular expression string match rules.
`--`	Absolutely the last option. The next string will be the *string* argument. This allows strings that start with a dash (–) to be used as arguments without being interpreted as options.

str	The string to match against patterns.
patN	A pattern to compare with the `string`.
bodN	A code body to evaluate if `patN` matches `string`
default	A pattern that will match if no other patterns have matched.

The options -exact, -glob, and -regexp control how the `string` and pattern will be compared.

The rules for glob matching are:

*	Matches 0 or more characters.
?	Matches a single character.
[]	Matches a character in the set defined within the braces.

[abc]	defines abc as the set.
[x-y]	defines all characters alphabetically between x and y (inclusive) as the set

\?	Matches the single character ?.

Notice that the glob rules use [] in a different manner than the Tcl evaluation code. You must protect the braces from tclsh evaluation, or tclsh will try to evaluate the phrase within the braces as a command and will probably fail. Enclosing a glob expression in curly braces will accomplish this. Trust me. I'll explain it in the next chapter.

The regular expression rules are similar in that they allow you to define a pattern of characters in a string but are more complex and more powerful. The regexp command, which is used to evaluate regular expressions, will be discussed in the next chapter.

The switch command can also be written with curly braces around the patterns and body.

Syntax: switch *?option? string {*
        pattern1 body1
        ?pattern2 body2?
        ?default?
    }

When the braces are used, the pattern strings must be hardcoded patterns. When the switch command is used without braces, the pattern strings may be variables, allowing a script to modify the behavior of a switch command at run time.

Example 3.3.3-2

Switch Example

```
set x 7
switch -glob $x {
    "1"     {puts "one"}
    "2"     {puts "two"}
    "3"     {puts "three"}
    {[4-8]}{puts "greater than 3"}
    default{puts "Not 1, 2, or 3"}
}
```

Script Output

greater than 3

3.3.4 Looping

Tcl provides commands that allow a script to loop on a counter, loop on a condition, or loop through the items in a list.

These three commands are:

for: A numeric looping command

while: A conditional loop command

foreach: A list-oriented loop command

The for command is the numeric loop command.

Syntax: for *start test next body*

for   Loop until a condition becomes false.

start   Tcl statements that define the start conditions for the loop.

test   A statement that tests an end condition. This statement must be in a format acceptable to expr.

next
: A Tcl statement that will be evaluated after each pass through the loop. Normally this increments a counter.

body
: The body of code to evaluate on each pass through the loop.

The for command is similar to the looping for in C, Fortran, Basic, etc. The for command requires four arguments; the first (*start*) sets the initial conditions, the next (*test*) tests the condition, and the third (*next*) modifies the state of the test. The last argument (*body*) is the body of code to evaluate while the *test* returns true.

Example 3.3.4-1

For Loop Example

```
for {set i 0} {$i < 2} {incr i} {
    puts "I is: $i"
}
```

Script Output

```
I is: 0
I is: 1
```

The while command is used to loop until a test condition becomes false.

Syntax: while *test body*

while
: Loop until a condition becomes false.

test
: A statement that tests an end condition. This statement must be in a format acceptable to expr.

body
: The body of code to evaluate on each pass through the loop.

Example 3.3.4-2

While Loop Example

```
set x 0;
while {$x < 5} {
    set x [expr $x+$x+1]
    puts "X: $x"
}
```

51

Script Output

```
X: 1
X: 3
X: 7
```

The `foreach` command is used to iterate through a list of items.

Syntax: `foreach listVar list body`

`foreach`	Evaluate the *body* for each of the items in *list*.
`listVar`	This variable will be assigned the value of the list element currently being processed.
`list`	A list of data to step through.
`body`	The body of code to evaluate on each pass through the loop.

Example 3.3.5-3

Foreach Loop Example

```
foreach element [list one two three] {
    puts "this is element: $element"
}
```

Script Output

```
this is element: one
this is element: two
this is element: three
```

3.3.5 String Processing Commands

The `string` and `format` commands provide support for manipulating strings. The `string` subcommands include commands for searching for substrings, identifying string matches, trimming unwanted characters, and converting case. The `format` command generates formatted output from a format descriptor and a set of data.

All Tcl variables are represented as strings. You can use the string manipulation commands with integers and floating-point numbers as easily as with alphabetic strings. When a command refers to a position in a string, the character positions are numbered from 0, and the last position can be referred to as end.

There is more detail on all of the string subcommands in the Tcl reference and the CD-ROM tutorials. The following subcommands will be used in the examples in the next chapters.

The string match command searches a target string for a match to a pattern. It uses the same globbing technique as the switch command uses when invoked with the -glob option.

Syntax: string match *pattern string*

string	Defines this as a string command.
match	Returns 1 if *pattern* matches *string*, else returns 0.
pattern	The pattern to compare to *string*.
string	The string to match against the *pattern*.

The string tolower command converts a string to lowercase letters. Note that this is not done in place. A new string of lowercase letters is returned.

The string toupper command converts strings to uppercase using the same syntax.

Syntax: string tolower *string*

string	Defines this as a string command.
tolower	Returns the string converted to lowercase.
string	The string to convert.

The string first command returns the location of the first instance of a pattern in a test string or -1 if the pattern does not exist in the test string.

Syntax: string first *substr string*

string	Defines this as a command that manipulates strings.
first	Return the location of the first occurrence of *substr* in *string*.

substr   The substring to search for.

string   The string to search in.

The `string length` command returns the number of characters in a string.

Syntax: `string length` *string*

string   Defines this as a string command.

length   Returns the number of characters in *string*.

string   The string.

The `string range` command returns the characters between two points in the string.

Syntax: `string range` *string first last*

string   Defines this as a string command.

range   Returns the characters in *string* between *first* and *last*.

string   The string.

The `format` command emulates the behavior of the C `sprintf` function. It takes as arguments a format description and a set of values that will be used to replace the % fields in the format description. A percent symbol can be generated with a % % field.

The format for the % fields is the same as that used in the C library. The field definition is a string composed of a leading percent sign, two optional fields, and a format definition:

`% ?justification? ?field width? format definition`

- The first character in a replacement field is a `%` symbol.
- The *field justification* may be a plus or minus sign. A minus sign causes the contents of the % field to be left justified. A plus sign causes the contents to be right justified.
- The *field width* is a numeric field. If it is a single integer, it defines the width of the field in characters. If this value is two integers separated by a decimal point, then the first integer represents the total width

of the field in characters, and the second represents the number of digits to the right of the decimal point to display for floating-point formats.

- The format definition is the last character. It must be one of:

c	The argument should be a decimal integer. Replace the field with the ASCII character value of this integer.	`format %c 65` returns A
d or i	The argument should be a decimal integer. Replace the field with the decimal representation of this integer.	`format %d 0xff` returns 255
E or e	The argument should be a numeric value. Replace the field with the scientific notation representation of this integer.	`format %e 0xff` returns 2.550000e+02
f	The argument should be a numeric value. Replace the field with the decimal fraction representation.	`format %f 1.234` returns 1.234
G or g	The argument should be a numeric value. Replace the field with the scientific notation or floating-point representation.	`format %g 1.234e2` returns 123.4
o	The argument should be an integer value. Replace the field with the octal representation of the argument.	`format %o 0xf` returns 17
s	The argument should be a string. Replace the field with the argument.	`format %s 0xf` returns 0xf
u	The argument should be an integer. Replace the field with the decimal representation of this integer treated as an unsigned value.	`format %u -1` returns 4294967295
X or x	The argument should be an integer. Replace the field with the hexadecimal representation of this integer.	`format %x -1` returns ffffffff

The following example shows how you might use the string match, string first, and string tolower commands to check for certain fields in a set of data. In this case, the data is a list of field names and values separated by colons, similar to the export format of a spreadsheet or database program.

Example 3.3.5-1

String and Format Command Examples

```
% set dataString "field4:Value4:Field1:Value1:FIELD2:
VALUE2:field3:value3"
field4:Value4:Field1:Value1:FIELD2:VALUE2:field3:value3

% if {[string match *FIELD2* $dataString]} {
    puts "Matched FIELD2 in dataString"
}
Matched FIELD2 in dataString
% set lowercaseDataString [string tolower $dataString]
field1:value1:field2:value2:field3:value3

% if {[string first field2 $lowercaseDataString] != -1} {
    puts "Found field2 in lowercaseDataString"
}
Found field2 in lowercaseDataString

% for {set i 1} {$i < 5} {incr i} {
    set srch [format "field%d" $i]
    set position($i) [string first $srch $dataString]
    if {$position($i) != -1} {
        puts "$srch is found in dataString"
    } else {
        puts "$srch is NOT found in dataString"
    }
}

field1 is NOT found in dataString
field2 is NOT found in dataString
field3 is found in dataString
field4 is found in dataString

%  if {$position(3) > $position(4)} {
    puts "field3 is after field4"
} else {
    puts "field4 is after field3"
}
```

```
field3 is after field4
%  #
%  # The next code splits field3:value3 from the dataString
%  # And then splits the value3 from the Field/Value pair
%  #
%  set x [string range $dataString $position(3) end]
field3:value3
% set separator [string first ":" $x]
6
% incr separator
7
% set value [string range $x $separator end]
value3
```

3.3.6 List Processing Commands

A list is an ordered set of strings. Lists may be arbitrarily long, and list members can be arbitrarily long. Lists members may be single words or lists. The elements of a list are separated by spaces. If a list element contains a space, then that element is grouped with braces ({}).

A list can be created in several ways:

- By using the set command to assign a list to a variable
- By grouping several arguments into a single list element with the list command
- By appending data to an unused variable with the lappend command
- By splitting a single argument into list elements with the split command

The list command takes several units of data and combines them into a single list. It adds whatever braces may be necessary to keep the list members separate.

Syntax: list *element1 ?element2? ... ?elementN?*

list	Joins the arguments into a list
member	A unit of data to become part of the list

The `lappend` command appends new data to a list, creating and returning a new, longer list. Note that this command will modify the existing list, unlike the `string tolower` command, which returns new data without changing the original.

Syntax: `lappend` *listName* *?element1?* ... *?elementN?*

`lappend`	Joins the arguments into a list
`listName`	The name of the list to append data to
member	A unit of data to add to the list

The `split` command returns the input string as a list. It splits the string wherever certain characters appear. By default, the split location is a whitespace character: a space, tab or newline.

Syntax: `split` *data* *?splitChar?*

`split`	Split data into a list
data	The data to split
?splitChar?	An optional character (or list of characters) to split the data at

The `llength` command returns the number of list elements in a list. Note that this is not the number of characters in a list, it's the number of list elements. List elements may be lists themselves. These lists within a list are each counted as a single list element.

Syntax: `llength` *list*

`llength`	Returns the length of a list
list	The list

The `lindex` command returns a list element referenced by its position in the list.

Syntax: `lindex` *list* *index*

`lindex`	Returns a list entry
list	The list

index   The position of a list entry to return. The first element is element 0. If this value is larger than the list, then an empty string is returned.

Example 3.3.6-1

List Commands Example

```
% set simpleList "This is a six element list"
This is a six element list
% puts "item 3 is [lindex $simpleList 3]"
item 3 is six
%   lappend complex This
This
%   lappend complex "is a three element"
This {is a three element}
%   lappend complex "list with internal lists"
This {is a three element} {list with internal lists}
% puts $complex
This {is a three element} {list with internal lists}
% puts "complex has [llength $complex] members"
complex has 3 members"
% puts "complex is [string length $complex] characters long"
complex is 52 characters long
%   list "this" "creates a" "list"
this {creates a} list
% split "splitting, this string, on commas, creates a list" ","
splitting { this string} { on commas} { creates a list}
```

3.3.7 Associative Array Commands

The associative array uses a string for an array index instead of a number. The associative array is a powerful construct in its own right and can be used to implement composite data types resembling the C struct or even a C++ class object. We'll say more about using associative arrays in Chapter 5.

A variable is denoted as an associative array by placing an index within parentheses after the variable name.

Example 3.3.7-1

Array Example

```
set count(apple) 5
set count(pear) 3
set cost(apple) .10
set cost(pear) .15
set total(apple) [expr $count(apple) * $cost(apple)]
set total(pear)  [expr $count(pear) * $cost(pear)]
puts "Fruit Bill: [expr $total(apple) + $total(pear)]";
```

Script Output

Fruit Bill: 0.95

As with lists, there is a set of commands for manipulating associative arrays. You can get a list of indices for an array, get a list of array indices and values, set array indices and values, or step through an array.

Like the string commands, the array commands are arranged as a set of subcommands of the array command.

The command array names returns a list of the indices that exist for a given array name.

Syntax: array names *arrayName* *?pattern?*

array	Defines this as an array command.
names	Returns a list of the indices used in this array.
arrayName	The name of the array.
pattern	If this option is present, array names will return only indices that match the pattern. Otherwise, array names returns all the array indices.

The array get command returns a list of array indices and the associated values.

Syntax: array get *arrayName*

array	Defines this as an array command.

get   Returns a list of the indices and values used in this associative array.

arrayName   The name of the array.

Example 3.3.7-2

Array Example

```
set fruit(apple.cost) .10
set fruit(apple.count) 5
set fruit(pear.cost) .15
set fruit(pear.count) 3

foreach item [array names fruit *cost] {
    set type [lindex [split $item "."] 0]
    puts "The cost for $type is $fruit($item)"
    puts "There are $fruit($type.count) units in stock"
    puts "The $type inventory is worth: \
            [expr $fruit($item) * $fruit($type.count)]"
}

puts ""
puts "Indices and values of fruit are:\n   [array get fruit]"
```

Script Output

```
The cost for apple is .10
There are 5 units in stock
The apple inventory is worth: 0.5
The cost for pear is .15
There are 3 units in stock
The pear inventory is worth: 0.45

Indices and values of fruit are:
    apple.count 5 apple.cost .10 pear.count 3 pear.cost .15
```

3.4 Input/Output in Tcl

It's difficult to perform any serious computer programming without accepting data and delivering results. Tcl abstracts the input and output commands into two input commands and one output command. Using these three commands, you can read or write to any file, pipe, device, or socket supported by `tclsh` or `wish`. A GUI-based `wish` script can also perform I/O through various graphics widgets but will use these three commands to access files, pipes to other programs, or sockets.

All I/O in Tcl is done through channels. A channel is an I/O device abstraction similar to an I/O stream in C. The Tcl channel device abstraction is extended beyond the stream abstraction to include sockets and pipes in the abstraction layer. The Tcl channel provides a uniform abstract model of the Unix and MS-Windows socket calls, so they can be treated as files.

Channels are accessed by handles, which are returned by the Tcl commands that open channels.

A channel handle can be passed to an I/O command to specify which channel should accept or provide data.

These channels are predefined in Tcl:

stdin   Standard input: keyboard or a redirected file.

stdout   Standard output: usually the screen.

stderr   Error output: usually the screen. Note that MS-Windows does not distinguish between stdout and stderr.

3.4.1 Output

The `puts` command sends output to a channel. It requires a string to output as an argument. By default, this command will append a newline character to the string.

Syntax: puts *?-nonewline? ?channel? outputString*

puts   Send a string to a channel.

?-newline? Do not append a newline to the output.

?channel?   Send output to this channel. Else, send to standard output.

outputString The data to send.

Example 3.4.1-1

```
% puts "Hello, "; puts "World"
Hello,
World
% puts -nonewline "Hello, "; puts "World"
Hello, World
```

3.4.2 Input

The Tcl commands that input data are the gets and read commands. The gets command will read a single line of input from a channel and strip off any newline character. The gets command may return the data that was read or the number of characters that were read. The read command will read a certain number of characters, or until the end of data, and always returns the data read.

The gets command is best for interactive I/O. The read command is best used when there is a large body of text to read in a single read command, such as a file, or a socket connection that will have a large amount of data to deliver to the program.

Syntax: gets *channelID ?varName?*

gets   Read a line of data from a channel.

channelID   Read from this channel.

?varName?   If this variable name is present, the data will be stored in this variable, and the number of characters read will be returned. If this argument is not present, the line of data will be returned.

Example 3.4.2-1

```
% gets stdin               # A user types "Hello, World" at keyboard.
Hello, World
% gets stdin inputString # A user types "Hello, World" at keyboard.
12
% puts $inputString
Hello, World
```

The read command can be invoked to read characters from a channel until the specified number of characters are read, or to read until an End-of-File is returned by the read. If the read command is invoked to read a certain number of characters and an End-of-File is encountered before the requested characters are read, the read will return the available characters and not generate an error. The read command returns the characters read. The read command may strip off the final newline character but by default leaves newlines intact.

Syntax: read *channelID numBytes*

read	Read a certain number of characters from a channel.
channelID	The channel to read data from.
numBytes	The number of bytes to read.

Syntax: read *?-nonewline? channelID*

read	Read data from a channel until an End-of-File (**EOF**) condition.
?-nonewline?	Discard the last character if it is a newline.
channelID	The channel to read data from.

Example 3.4.2-2

```
# Read from stdin until an End-Of-File is encountered
#

% read stdin              # A user types Hello, WorldEOF"
Hello, World
```

```
# Read 5 characters from stdin

% read stdin 5          # A user types Hello, World
Hello
```

3.4.3 Opening Channels

A channel can be created by an open command or by a socket command. The open command can be used to open a channel to a file, a device, or a pipe to another program. The socket command can be used to open a client socket to a server or to open a server socket that will listen for clients.

The open command is used to create a channel to a file, device, or to another program.

Syntax: open *fileName ?access? ?permissions?*

open   Open a file, device, or pipe as a channel and return a handle to be used to access this channel.

fileName   The name of the file or device to open.
If the first character of the name is a pipe (|), then the file-name argument is a request to open a pipe connection to a command. The first word in the filename will be the command name, and subsequent words will be arguments to the command.

?access?   How this file will be accessed by the channel. *Access* may be one of:

     r   Open file for read-only access.

     r+   Open file for read and write access. File must already exist.

     w   Open file for write-only access. Truncate file if it exists.

     w+   Open file for read and write access. Truncate the file if it exists, or create it if it doesn't exist.

a
: Open file for write-only access. File must already exist, and new data will be appended to the file.

a+
: Open file for read and write access. Create the file if it doesn't exist. Append data to an existing file.

?permissions?

If a new file is created, this parameter will be used to set the file permissions. The *permissions* argument will be an integer, with the same bit definitions as the argument to the creat system call on the operating system being used.

Example 3.4.3-1

File Output and Input Example

```
# Open a file for writing
set outputFile [open "testfile" "w"]

# send a line to the output file.
puts $outputFile "This is line 1"
puts $outputFile "This is line 2"
puts $outputFile "This is line 3"

# Close the file
close $outputFile

# Reopen the file for reading
set inputFile [open "testfile" "r"]

# Read a line of text
set numBytes [gets $inputFile string]

# Display the line read
puts "Gets returned $numBytes characters in the string: $string"

# Read the rest of the file
set string2 [read $inputFile]
puts "Read: $string2"

puts "\nOpening a Pipe\n"
# Open a pipe to the ls command
set pipe [open "|ls /" "r"]
```

```
# read the output of the ls command:

while {![eof $pipe]} {
    set length [gets $pipe lsLine]
    puts "$lsLine"
}
```

Script Output

Gets returned 14 characters in the string: This is line 1
Read: This is line 2
This is line 3

Opening a Pipe

bin
boot
bsd
dev
. . .

3.4.4 Client Sockets

The socket command returns a channel for use with socket-based I/O. The socket command can return a client or server socket.

Using the socket command to establish a client socket is as straightforward as opening a file. Server sockets and event-driven code are discussed in the bonus book on the CD-ROM. See the chapter about controlling a National Instruments I/O card.

The first example in Chapter 4 will show how the socket and flush commands can be used.

Syntax: socket *?options? host port*

socket   Open a socket connection.

?options?   Options to specify the behavior of the socket.

–myaddr *addr*   Defines the address (as a name or number) of the client side of the socket. This is not necessary if the client machine has only one network interface.

-myport *port*	Defines the port number for the server side to open. If this is not supplied, then a port is assigned at random from the available ports.
-async	Causes the socket command to return immediately, whether the connection has been completed or not.

host	The host to open a connection to. May be a name or a numeric IP address.
port	The number of the port to open a connection to on the host machine.

3.4.5 Buffered I/O

By default, Tcl I/O is buffered, like the stream-based I/O in the C standard library calls. In many cases, this is the desired behavior. If this isn't what your project needs, you can modify the behavior of the channel or flush the buffer on demand.

The fconfigure command lets you define the behavior of a channel. You can modify several options, including whether the channel should be buffered and the size of the buffer to use. The fconfigure command allows you to configure more options than are discussed in this book. You should read the online documentation for more details.

Syntax: fconfigure *channelId ?name? ?value?*

fconfigure	Configure the behavior of a channel.
channelId	The channel to modify.
name	The name of a configuration field, which includes:

-blocking *boolean*

If set true (the default mode), a Tcl program will block on a gets or read until data is available. If set false, gets, read, puts, flush, and close commands will not block.

-buffering *newValue*

> If *newValue* is set to **full**, the channel will use buffered I/O. If set to **line**, the buffer will be flushed whenever a full line is received. If set to **none**, the channel will flush whenever characters are received.

The fconfigure command was added to Tcl in version 7.5. If you are writing code for an earlier revision of Tcl, or if you want to control when the buffers are flushed, you can use the flush command. The flush command forces buffered data to be written immediately.

Syntax: flush *channelId*

flush   Flush the output buffer of a buffered channel.

channelId   The channel to flush.

3.5 Bottom Line

At this point, you know enough Tcl to write useful programs. There are many Tcl commands that were not covered in this chapter, but you have enough background that you can find the commands you need in the Tcl Command Reference on the CD-ROM.

The next chapter will work through a few examples to show how these commands (and a few new ones) can be used.

- A Tcl command consists of
  1. A command name
  2. Optional subcommand, options, or arguments
  3. A command terminator (either a semicolon (;) or a newline)
- An option will always start with a "-". It may proceed or follow the arguments (depending on the command) and may require an argument itself.
- Tcl is a position-based language rather than a keyword-based language.
- Words and symbols must be separated by at least one whitespace character.

- Multiple words or variables can be grouped into a single argument with braces ({}) or quotes ("").
- Values are assigned to a variable with the set command.

  Syntax: set *varName value*
- Math operations are performed with the expr and incr commands.

  Syntax: expr *mathExpression*

  Syntax: incr *varName ?incrValue?*
- The branch commands are if and switch.

  Syntax: if *{test} {bodyTrue}* else *{bodyFalse}*

  Syntax: switch *?option? string pattern1 body1* \
         ?pattern2 body2? ?default?
- The looping commands are for, while, and foreach.

  Syntax: for *start test next body*

  Syntax: while *test body*

  Syntax: foreach *listVar list body*
- The list operations include list, split, llength, lindex, and lappend.

  Syntax: list *element1 ?element2? ... ?elementN?*

  Syntax: lappend *listName ?element1? ... ?elementN?*

  Syntax: split *data ?splitChar?*

  Syntax: llength *list*

  Syntax: lindex *list index*
- The string processing subcommands include first, match, toupper, tolower, and range.

  Syntax: string first *substr string*

  Syntax: string match *pattern string*

  Syntax: string tolower *string*

  Syntax: string range *string first last*

- The array processing subcommands include names and get.

    Syntax: array names *arrayName ?pattern?*

    Syntax: array get *arrayName*

- I/O is handled by the gets, read, and puts commands.

    Syntax: gets *channelID ?varName?*

    Syntax: read *?-nonewline? channelID*

    Syntax: read *channelID numBytes*

    Syntax: puts *?-nonewline? ?channel? outputString*

- Channels are created with the open and socket commands.

    Syntax: open   *fileName ?access? ?permissions?*

    Syntax: socket *?options? host port*

## CHAPTER 4

Tcl Code
Examples

This chapter will show how Tcl can be used. It will cover command evaluation and substitutions in a series of examples.

The first example in this chapter is a program to open a socket to a remote Post Office Protocol (POP) server and check for mail. This example demonstrates how Tcl I/O and string commands can be used to develop an Internet client.

The second series of examples goes through methods for extracting a particular piece of information from a mass of data. It will demonstrate ways to use the list commands and string commands and will introduce regular expressions and subroutines.

4.1 Pop Client

This example uses several of the commands described in Chapter 3 to make a POP-3 mail client that will contact a remote mail server and report if there are pieces of mail waiting for you.

The POP-3 message protocol is an ASCII conversation between the POP-3 client (your machine) and the POP-3 server (the remote machine). Simply to learn if there is mail waiting, the conversation would resemble this:

```
$> telnet pop.example.com pop3
Trying 123.456.789.012
Connected to 123.456.789.012
Escape character is '^]'.
+OK QPOP (version 2.2-krb-IV) at pop.example.com starting.
<28004.887684070@pop.example.com>
user ImaPopper
+OK Password required for ImaPopper.
pass myPassword
+OK ImaPopper has 1 message (1668 octets).
```

The following example will contact a remote machine and report if any mail is waiting for a hardcoded user. The machine name, user name, and password are all hardcoded in this example. The last example in this chapter will discuss how to get arguments from the command line, how to modularize with subroutines, etc.

The test for +OK is done differently in each test, just to demonstrate some of the different methods of checking for one string in another.

Example 4.1-1

```
#
# Open a socket to a POP server. Report if mail is available
#

set popHost example.com
set popLoginID popclient
set popPasswd SecretPassword

# Open the socket to port 110 (POP3 server)
set popClient [socket $popHost 110]

# Get the first line:
#    +OK QPOP (version ..) at example.com starting...

set line [gets $popClient]

if {[string first "+OK" $line] != 0} {
    puts "ERROR: Did not get expected '+OK' prompt"
```

```
    puts "Received: $line"
    exit;
}

# send the user name
# Note that the socket can be used for both input and output

puts $popClient "user $popLoginID"

# The socket is buffered by default.  Thus we need to
#  either fconfigure the socket to be non-buffered, or
#  force the buffer to be sent with a flush command.

flush $popClient

# Receive the password prompt:
#   +OK Password required for popclient.

set response [gets $popClient]
if {[string match "+OK*" $response] == 0} {
    puts "ERROR: Did not get expected '+OK' prompt"
    puts "Received: $response"
    exit;
}

# Send Password

puts $popClient "pass $popPasswd"
flush $popClient

# Receive the message count:
#    +OK popclient has 0 messages (0 octets).

set message [gets $popClient]
if {![string match "+OK*" $message]} {
    puts "ERROR: Did not get expected '+OK' prompt"
    puts "Received: $message"
    exit;
}

puts [string range $message 3 end]
```

Script Output

popclient has 2 messages (2069 octets).

You can put together a client/server application with just a few lines of Tcl.

Note that the error messages use an apostrophe to quote the +OK string. In Tcl, unlike C and C++, the apostrophe has no special meaning. We'll revisit those lines in Section 4.2.2 and show how they could be written to appear as "ERROR: Did not get expected "+OK" prompt".

4.2 Command Evaluation and Substitutions

Much of the power of the Tcl language is in the mechanism used to evaluate commands. The evaluation process is straightforward and elegant but, like a game of Go, can catch you by surprise if you don't understand how it works.

Tcl processes commands in two steps. First it performs command and variable substitutions, and then it evaluates the resulting string.

Note that *everything* goes through this evaluation procedure. Both internal commands such as set and subroutines that you write are processed by the same evaluation code. A while command, for example, is treated just like any other command. It takes two arguments: a test and a body of code to execute if the test is **true**.

4.2.1 Substitution

The first phase in Tcl command processing is substitution. The command is scanned from left to right, and phrases that should be replaced by their values are substituted. Tcl does two types of substitutions:

- A Tcl command within square brackets ([...]) is replaced by the results of that command. This is referred to as *command substitution*.
- A variable preceded by a dollar sign is replaced by the value of that variable. This is referred to as *variable substitution*.

After these substitutions are done, the resulting command string is evaluated.

4.2.2 Controlling Substitutions with Quotes, Curly Braces, and Backslash

Most Tcl commands expect a certain number of arguments and will generate an error if the wrong number of arguments is presented to them. When you need to pass an argument that consists of multiple words, you must group the words into a single argument with curly braces or quotes.

The difference between grouping with quotes and grouping with braces is that substitutions will be performed on strings grouped with quotes but not on strings grouped with braces.

The backslash may be used to disable the special meaning of the character that follows the backslash. You can escape characters such as the dollar sign, quote, or brace, to disable their special meaning for Tcl.

The error messages in the previous example could be written like this:

```
puts "ERROR: Did not get expected \"+OK\" prompt"
```

to embed quotes in the output string, and create error messages with the string "+OK" instead of '+OK'.

The following examples show how quotes, braces, and backslashes affect the substitutions.

The first example places the argument to puts within curly braces. No substitutions will occur.

Example 4.2.2-1

```
set x 2
set y 3
puts {The sum of  $x and $y is returned by [expr $x+$y]}
```

Script Output

The sum of $x and $y is returned by [expr $x+$y]

In the next example (4.2.2-2), puts has its argument enclosed in quotes, so everything is substituted.

Example 4.2.2-2

```
set x 2
set y 3
puts "The sum of  $x and $y is returned by [expr $x+$y]"
```

Script Output

The sum of 2 and 3 is returned by 5

In Example 4.2.2-3, the argument is enclosed in quotes, so substitution occurs, but the square brackets are escaped with backslashes to prevent Tcl from performing a command substitution.

Example 4.2.2-3

```
set x 2
set y 3
puts "The sum of  $x and $y is returned by \[expr $x+$y\]"
```

Script Output

The sum of 2 and 3 is returned by [expr 2+3]

Example 4.2.2-4 escapes the dollar sign on the variables to prevent them from being substituted and also escapes a set of quotes around the expr string. If not for the backslashes before the quotes, the quoted string would end with the second quote. Sets of brackets nest, whereas quotes do not.

Example 4.2.2-4

```
set x 2
set y 3
puts "The sum of \$x + \$y is returned by \"\[expr \$x+\$y\]\""
```

Script Output

The sum of $x + $y is returned by "[expr $x+$y]"

4.2.3 Steps in Command Evaluation

When a Tcl interpreter evaluates a command, it makes only one pass over that command to do substitutions. It does not loop until a variable is fully resolved. However, if a command includes another Tcl command within brackets, the command processor will be called recursively until there are no further bracketed commands. When there are no more phrases to be substituted, the command is evaluated, and the result is passed to the previous level of recursion to substitute for the bracketed string.

The next example shows how a command is evaluated. The recursion level is shown by the indentation level.

Let's examine this command:

```
set x [expr [set a 3] + 4 + $a]
```

The command is scanned left to right for the first phrase to be substituted. The scanner encounters the left square bracket, and the command evaluator is reentered with that subset of the command.

```
expr [set a 3] + 4 + $a
```

This command is again scanned, and again there is a bracket, so the command evaluator is called again with that subset:

```
set a 3
```

There are no more levels of brackets and no substitutions to perform, so this command is evaluated, the variable a is set to the value 3, and 3 is returned.

The recursive call returned 3, so the bracketed command is replaced by 3, and the command now resembles this:

```
expr 3 + 4 + $a
```

The variables are now substituted, and $a is replaced by 3, making the new command:

```
expr 3 + 4 + 3
```

This is evaluated, and the result (10) is returned.

The substitution is performed, and the command is now:

```
set x 10
```

This is evaluated, the variable x is set to 10, and tclsh returns 10.

In particular, notice that the variable a was not defined when this command started but was defined within the first bracketed portion of the command. If this command had been written in another order:

```
set x [expr $a + [set a 3] + 4 ]
```

- if a had not been previously defined, it would generate an error. If a had been previously defined, the command would return an unexpected result.

4.3 Looking for a Needle in a Haystack

A common programming task is extracting one piece of information from a large mass of data. This section will discuss several methods for doing that and introduce several more Tcl concepts and commands along the way.

For the application, we'll find the Scriptics home page in a a list of uniform resource locators (URLs) for some Tcl information and archive sites.

This is the starting data, extracted and modified from a browser's bookmark file.

```
% set urls {
"http://zazu.maxwell.syr.edu/nt-tcl/" "NT Extentions for TCL"
"http://sunscript.sun.com/" "SunScript Home Page"
"http://www.scriptics.com/" "Scriptics Corporation"
"http://www.wwinfo.com/tcl/usrquery/sea.shtml"\
    "Database Search"
"http://www.teamwave.com/tcl.html" "Tcl/Tk in TeamWave"
"http://www.msen.com/~clif" "Clif Flynt's Home Page"
"http://www.worldaccess.nl/~nijtmans/" "Tcl/Tk Plus patches"
"http://www.neosoft.com/tcl/default.html"\
    "Tcl/Tk Code Archives"
"http://www.sco.com/Technology/tcl/Tcl.html" "SCO Tcl/Tk info"
"http://expect.nist.gov/" "Expect Home Page"
}
```

4.3.1 Converting a String into a List

Since the data has multiple lines, one solution is to convert the lines into a list and then iterate through the list to check each line.

Example 4.3.1-1

Splitting Data into a List

```
#
# Split data into a list at the newline markers
#
set urlList [split $urls "\n"]

#
# display the list
#
puts $urlList
```

Script Output

```
{}
 {"http://zazu.maxwell.syr.edu/nt-tcl/" "NT Extentions for
TCL"}
 {"http://www.scriptics.com/" "Scriptics Corporation"}
 {"http://www.wwinfo.com/tcl/usrquery/sea.shtml" "Database
Search" }
 {"http://www.teamwave.com/tcl.html" "Tcl/Tk in TeamWave"}
 {"http://www.msen.com/~clif "Clif Flynt's Home Page"}
 {"http://www.worldaccess.nl/~nijtmans/" "Tcl/Tk Plus
patches"}
 {"http://www.neosoft.com/tcl/default.html" "Tcl/Tk Code
Archives"}
 {"http://www.sco.com/Technology/tcl/Tcl.html" "SCO Tcl/Tk
info"}
 {"http://expect.nist.gov/" "Expect Home Page"}
 {}
```

Note that the empty lines after the left bracket and before the right bracket were converted to empty list entries. This is an artifact of the way the starting data was defined. If it had been defined as:

```
% set urls {"http://zazu.maxwell.syr.edu/nt-tcl/"\
    "NT Extentions for TCL"
"http://sunscript.sun.com/" "SunScript Home Page"
"http://www.scriptics.com/" "Scriptics Corporation"
"http://www.wwinfo.com/tcl/usrquery/sea.shtml"\
    "Database Search"
"http://www.teamwave.com/tcl.html" "Tcl/Tk in TeamWave"
"http://www.msen.com/~clif" "Clif Flynt's Home Page"
"http://www.worldaccess.nl/~nijtmans/" "Tcl/Tk Plus patches"
"http://www.neosoft.com/tcl/default.html"\
    "Tcl/Tk Code Archives"
"http://www.sco.com/Technology/tcl/Tcl.html" "SCO Tcl/Tk info"
"http://expect.nist.gov/" "Expect Home Page"}
```

the empty list elements wouldn't be created, but the example would be a bit less readable. This example code won't be bothered by the empty lists, but you may need to check for that condition in other code you write.

4.3.2 Examining the List with a `for` Loop

Now that the data is a list, we can iterate through it using the numeric `for` loop introduced in Chapter 3.

Syntax: for *start test next body*

Example 4.3.2-1

Search using a For Loop

```
for {set pos 0} {$pos < [llength $urlList]} {incr pos} {
    if {[string first "Scrip" [lindex $urlList $pos]] >= 0} {
        puts "SCRIPTICS PAGE:\n    [lindex $urlList $pos]"
    }
}
```

Script Output

```
SCRIPTICS PAGE:
    "http://www.scriptics.com/" "Scriptics Corporation"
```

Let's do a line-by-line examination of this script.

- ```
  for {set pos 0} {$pos < [llength $urlList]} {incr pos} {
  ```

  This line calls the `for` command. The `for` command takes four arguments, *start, test, next,* and a *body* to evaluate. You'll notice that this line has only three arguments on it, *start, test,* and *next,* but no *body.* There is only a left curly bracket for the body of this command.

  Tcl treats an end-of-line condition as the end of a command unless the end-of-line is escaped with a backslash or the end-of-line comes within a grouped string. The curly brackets around a command make that a grouped string. So, placing the curly bracket at the end of the `for` line tells the Tcl interpreter to continue reading until it reaches the matching close bracket, and treat that entire mass of code as the *body* for this `for` command.

  The following code would generate an error:

  ```
  % for {set i 1} {$i < 10} {incr i}
    {
    set x [expr $x + $i]
    }
  ```

  A Tcl interpreter reading the line `for {set i 1} {$i < 10} {incr i}` would find a `for` command, *start, test,* and *next* arguments, and would then see the end-of-line and nothing to tell the interpreter that the next line might be part of this command. The interpreter would return this error to inform the programmer that the command could not be parsed correctly:

  wrong # args: should be "for start test next command"

  The *Tcl Style Guide* from the Tcl development group at Sun recommends that you place the body of an `if`, `for`, `proc`, or `while` command on a separate line from the rest of the command, with just the left bracket on the line with the command to inform the compiler that the body of the command is continued on the following lines.

  This code is correct:

  ```
  for {set i 0} {$i < 100} {incr i} {
      puts "I will write my code to conform to the standard"
  }
  ```
  ```

Notice that the arguments to the `for` command in both sets of example code are grouped with curly braces, not quotes. If the arguments were grouped with quotes, a substitution pass would be done on the arguments before passing them to the `for` command. The variable `pos` has not been defined, so attempting a substitution would result in an error. If `pos` had already been defined (perhaps in a previous `for` loop), then variable substitutions would be performed and the first line would be passed to the `for` command resembling this:

```
for {set pos 0} "10 < 10" {incr pos} {
```

With the variables in the *test* already substituted, the *test* will always either fail or succeed (depending on the value of the variable), and the loop won't do what you expect.

For the same reason, the `body` of a `for` command should be grouped with braces instead of quotes. You don't want any variables to be substituted until the loop body is evaluated.

Given that no substitution happens to the variables enclosed in curly braces, you may be wondering how the code in one scope (within the `for` command) can access the variables in another scope (the code that invoked the `for` command).

The Tcl interpreter allows commands to declare which scope they should be evaluated in. This means that the code implementing commands such as `for`, `if`, and `while` can be invoked as procedures, which can be evaluated in the scope of the code that called them. This gives these commands access to the variables that were enclosed in curly braces and allows the substitution to be done as the command is being evaluated, instead of before the evaluation.

For internal commands such as `for`, `if`, and `while` the change of scope is done within the Tcl interpreter. Tcl script procedures can also use this facility with the `uplevel` and `upvar` commands, which will be described in Chapter 6. There are examples using the `uplevel` and `upvar` commands in Chapters 7, 9, 10, 11, and 13.

The `start` and `next` arguments to the `for` command are also evaluated in the scope of the calling command. Thus, `pos` will have the last value that was assigned by the `next` phrase when the `for` loop is complete and the line of code after the body is evaluated.

- `if {[string first "Scrip" [lindex $urlList $pos]] >= 0} {`

Like the `for` command, the `if` command accepts an expression and a body of code. If the expression is true, the body of code will be evaluated. As with the `for` command, the test expression goes on the same line as the `if` command, but only the left brace of the body is placed on that line.

The test for the `if` is grouped with brackets, just as is done for the `for` command.

Within the `test` expression, there are two nested Tcl commands. These will be evaluated, innermost command first, before the expression is evaluated. The string `[lindex $urlList $pos]` will be replaced by the item at position `$pos` in the list. Then the string `[string first "Scrip" listEntry]` will be replaced by either the position of the string `Scrip` in the target string or -1 if `Scrip` is not in the `listEntry` being examined.

- `puts "SCRIPTICS PAGE:\n [lindex $urlList $pos]"`

If the `test` evaluates to true, then the `puts` command will be evaluated; otherwise, the loop will continue until `$pos` is greater than the number of entries in the list.

4.3.3 Using the `foreach` Command

Using a `for` command to iterate through a list is familiar to people who have coded in C or Fortran, which are number-oriented languages. Tcl is a string- and list-oriented language, and there are better ways to iterate through a list.

For instance, we could use the `foreach` command instead of the `for` command to loop through the list.

Syntax: `foreach varname list body`

Example 4.3.3-1

Search Using a Foreach Loop

```
foreach item $urlList  {
    if {[string first "Scriptics" $item] >= 0} {
        puts "SCRIPTICS PAGE:\n    $item"
    }
}
```

Script Output

SCRIPTICS PAGE:
    "http://www.scriptics.com/" "Scriptics Corporation"

Using the `foreach` command the code is somewhat simpler, because the `foreach` command returns each list element instead of requiring the `lindex` commands to extract the list elements.

4.3.4 Using the `string match` instead of `string first`

There are other options that can be used for the `test` in the `if` statement.

Example 4.3.4-1

Search Using a `string match` Test

```
%   foreach item $urlList   {
        if {[string match {*[Ss]criptics*} $item]} {
            puts "SCRIPTICS PAGE:\n      $item"
        }
    }
```

Script Output

SCRIPTICS PAGE:
    "http://www.scriptics.com/" "Scriptics Corporation"

Notice that the pattern argument to the `string match` command is enclosed in braces to prevent Tcl from performing command substitutions on it. The pattern includes the asterisks because `string match` will try to match a complete string, not a substring. The asterisk will match to any set of characters. The pattern `{*[Ss]criptics*}` causes `string match` to accept as a match a string that has the string **scriptics** or **Scriptics** with any sets of characters before or after.

4.3.5 Using `lsearch`

We could also extract the Scriptics site from the list of URLs using the `lsearch` command. The `lsearch` command will search a list for an element that matches a pattern.

Syntax: lsearch *?mode? list pattern*

lsearch	Returns the index of the first list element that matches *pattern* or -1 if no element matches the pattern.
?mode?	The type of match to use in this search. *?mode?* may be one of:

	-exact	The list element must exactly match the pattern.
	-glob	The list element must match pattern using the glob rules.
	-regexp	The list element must match pattern using the regular expression rules.

list	The list to search.
pattern	The pattern to search for.

Example 4.3.5-1

Search Using a lsearch

```
set index [lsearch -glob $urlList "*Scriptics*"]
if {$index >= 0} {
    puts "SCRIPTICS PAGE:\n    [lindex $urlList $index]"
}
```

Script Output

```
SCRIPTICS PAGE:
     "http://www.scriptics.com/" "Scriptics Corporation"
```

4.3.6 The regexp Command

The regular expression commands in Tcl provide finer control of string matching than the glob method, more options, and much more power.

4.3.6.1 Regular Expression Matching Rules

Starting with the smallest units, and building up...

- The smallest part of a regular expression is an *atom*.

An atom may be:

Definition	Example	Description
A single character	x	Will match the character x
A range of characters enclosed in brackets	[a-q]	Will match any lowercase letter between a and q (inclusive)
A period	.	Will match any character
A caret	^	Matches the beginning of a string
A dollar sign	$	Matches the end of a string
A backslash sequence	\^	Inhibits treating *, &, $, +, ^, etc. as special characters and matches the exact character
A regular expression enclosed in parentheses	([Tt]cl)	Will match that regular expression

- *Atoms* can be combined into *pieces*.

A piece is an atom followed by:

Definition	Example	Description
Another atom	ab	Matches if each atom matches in sequence
An asterisk	a*	Matches 0 or more occurrences of the preceding atom (a)
A plus	a+	Matches 1 or more occurrences of the preceding atom
A question mark	[a-z]?	Matches 0 or 1 occurrence of the preceding atom
Another piece	[a-z]?[0-9]	Matches a letter followed by 0 or 1 more letters, followed by a number

- *Pieces* can be combined into a *regular expression*.

A regular expression may be:

Definition	Example	Description
An atom	T	If the atom is matched, the regular expression is true.
A piece	[TtCcLl]*	If the piece is matched, the regular expression is true.
Multiple pieces separated by "	"	([Tt]cl)|([Tt]k)	If any piece is matched, the regular expression is true.

The range atom ([a-z]) needs a little more explanation, since there are actually several rules to define a range of characters.

A *range* consists of square brackets enclosing:

Definition	Example	Description
A set of characters	[tcl]	Any of the letters within the brackets may match the target.
Two characters separated by a dash	[a-z]	The letters define a range of characters that may match the target.
A character preceded by a caret, if the caret is the first letter in the range	[^,]	Any character *except* the character after the caret may match the target.
Two characters separated by a dash and preceded by a caret, if the caret is the first letter in the range	[^a-z]	Any character *except* characters between the two characters after the caret may match the target.

A piece or atom can be enclosed within parentheses and will then be considered as a single atom. For instance,

([a-z][0-9])+

would look for repeating patterns of a single letter followed by a single digit and would match to one or more of these letter-number patterns.

The regular expression commands will return the largest block of text that matches the regular expression. Thus a regular expression such as:

A.+B

would match any set of characters bounded by A and B.

If the text were AbcdAefgBhijB, several combinations of letters would match the pattern. The regular expression code would select the longest (the entire string) as the match instead of the shortest (AefgB).

The Tcl commands that implement the regular expression matching are regexp and regsub.

Syntax: regexp *?opt? expr string ?fullmatch? ?submatch?*

regexp   Returns 1 if *expr* has a match in *string*. If *matchVar* or *subMatchVar* arguments are present, they will be assigned the matched substrings.

opt   Options to fine-tune the behavior of regexp. May be one of:

        -nocase   Ignores the case of letters when searching for a match.

        -indices   Stores the location of a match, instead of the matched characters, in the *submatch* variable.

        --   Marks the end of options. Arguments that follow this will be treated as a regular expressions even if they start with a dash.

expr   The regular expression to match with *string*.

string   The string to search for the regular expression.

?fullmatch?   If there is a match, and this variable is supplied to regexp, the entire match will be placed in this variable.

?submatch?

        If there is a match, and this variable is supplied to regexp, the Nth parenthesized regular expression match will be placed in this variable. The parenthesized regular expressions are counted from left to right and outer to inner.

Example 4.3.6.1-1

Example Script

```
# Match a string of uppercase letters,
#   followed by a string lowercase letters
#   followed by a string uppercase letters

regexp {([A-Z]*)(([a-z]*)[A-Z]*)} "ABCdefgHIJ" a b c d e

puts "The full match is: $a"
puts "The first parenthesized expression matches: $b"
puts "The second parenthesized expression matches: $c"
puts "The third parenthesized expression matches: $d"
puts "There is no fourth parenthesized expression: $e"
```

Script Output

```
The full match is: ABCdefgHIJ
The first parenthesized expression matches: ABC
The second parenthesized expression matches: defgHIJ
The third parenthesized expression matches: defg
There is no fourth parenthesized expression:
```

Syntax: `regsub ?options? expression string subSpec varName`

regsub	Copies *string* to the variable *varName*. If *expression* matches a portion of *string*, then that portion is replaced by *subSpec*.
options	Options to fine-tune the behavior of regsub. May be one of:

	-all	Replace all occurrences of the regular expression with the replacement string. By default, only the first occurrence is replaced.
	-nocase	Ignores the case of letters when searching for match.
	--	Marks the end of options. Arguments that follow this will be treated as regular expressions, even if they start with a dash.

expression	A regular expression that will be compared with the target string.
string	A target string with which the regular expression will be compared.
subSpec	A string that will replace the regular expression in the target string.
varName	A variable in which the modified target string will be placed.

Example 4.3.6.1-2

regsub Example

```
set bad "This word is spelled wrung"
regsub "wrung" $bad "correctly" good
puts $good
```

Script Output

```
This word is spelled correctly
```

4.3.6.2 Back to the Example

We could use the regexp command in place of the string command to search for Scriptics. This code would resemble:

Example 4.3.6.2-1

Search Using a regexp Test

```
foreach item $urlList  {
  if {[regexp {[Ss]criptics} $item]} {
     puts "SCRIPTICS PAGE:\n    $item"
  }
}
```

Script Output

```
SCRIPTICS PAGE:
    "http://www.scriptics.com/" "Scriptics Corporation"
```

Or, we could just use the regexp command to search the original text for a match rather than the text converted to a list. This saves us a processing step.

Example 4.3.6.2-2

Search All Data Using `regexp`

```
set found [regexp "(\[^\n]*\[Ss\]criptics\[^\n]*)" $urls\
    fullmatch submatch]
if {$found} {
    puts "SCRIPTICS PAGE:\n    $submatch"
}
```

Script Output

SCRIPTICS PAGE:
    "http://www.scriptics.com/" "Scriptics Corporation"

Let's take a careful look at the regular expression in Example 4.3.6.2-2.

First, the expression is grouped with quotes instead of braces. This is done so that the Tcl interpreter can substitute the \n with a newline character. If the expression were grouped with braces, then the characters "\n" would be passed to the regular expression code, which would interpret the backslash as a `regexp` escape character and would look for an ASCII "n" instead of the newline character.

However, since we've enclosed the regular expression in quotes, we need to escape the braces from the Tcl interpreter with backslashes. Otherwise, the Tcl interpreter would try to evaluate [^\n] as a Tcl command in the substitution phase.

Breaking the regular expression into pieces, we have:

[^\n]*   Match zero or more characters that are *not* newline characters

[Ss]criptics
                Followed by the word scriptics or Scriptics

[^\n]*   Followed by zero or more characters that are *not* newline characters

This will match a string that includes the word scriptics and is bounded by either newlines or the start or end of the string.

If `regexp` succeeds in finding a match, it will place the entire matching string in the `fullmatch` variable. The portion of the string that matches the portion of the expression between the parentheses is placed in `submatch`. If the regular expression has multiple sets of expressions within parentheses, then these portions of the match will be placed in submatch variables in the order in which they appear.

4.3.7 Creating a Procedure

Identifying one datum in a stream of data is the kind of application that should be generalized and placed in a procedure. This procedure is a good place to reduce the line of data to the information we actually want.

4.3.7.1 The `proc` Command

The Tcl subroutines are known as `procs`, because they are defined with the `proc` command. Note that `proc` is a Tcl command, not a declaration. Remember, Tcl is a typeless language and has no declarations.

The `proc` command takes three arguments that define a procedure: the procedure name, the argument list, and the body of code to evaluate when the procedure is invoked. When the `proc` command is evaluated it adds the procedure name, arguments, and body to the list of known procedures.

The command looks very much like declaring a subroutine in C or Fortran, but you should remember that `proc` is a command, not a declaration.

Syntax: `proc name args body`

Example 4.3.7.1-1

```
#
# Define a proc
#
proc demoProc {arg1 arg2} {
    puts "demoProc called with $arg1 and $arg2"
}

# Now, call the proc
demoProc 1 2
demoProc alpha beta
```

Script Output

```
demoProc called with 1 and 2
demoProc called with alpha and beta
```

4.3.7.2 Variable Scope

Most computer languages support the concept that variables can be accessed only within certain scopes. For instance, in C, a subroutine can access only variables that are either declared in that function (local scope) or have been declared outside all functions (the extern, or global scope).

Tcl supports the concept of local and global scopes. A variable declared and used within a proc can be accessed only within that proc, unless it is made global with the global command. The Tcl scoping rules will be covered in painful detail in Chapters 6 and 7.

Tcl also supports the concept of namespaces, similar in some ways to the FORTRAN named common or a C++ static class member. The namespace command will be discussed in Chapter 6.

4.3.7.3 A findUrl proc

This proc will find a line that has a given substring, extract the URL from that string, and return just the URL. It can accept a single line of data or multiple lines separated by newlines.

Example 4.3.7.3-1

findUrl

```
# findUrl -
#       Finds a particular line of data in a set of lines
# Arguments:
#       match       A string to match in the data
#       text        Textual data to search for the pattern.
#                   Multiple lines separated by newline
#                   characters.
# Results:
#       Returns the line which matched the match string, or ""
#
proc findUrl {match text} {
    set url ""
    set found [regexp -nocase "\[^\n]*$match\[^\n]*"\
        $text match]
```

```
    if {$found} {
        regexp {"(http:[^"]+)"} $match m url
    }
    return $url
}

# Invoke the procedure to
# search for a couple of well known sites
#
puts "SCRIPTICS SITE: [findUrl Scriptics $urls]"
puts "SCO SITE: [findUrl sco $urls]"
```

Script Output

```
SCRIPTICS SITE: http://www.scriptics.com/
SCO SITE: http://www.sco.com/Technology/tcl/Tcl.html
```

In this example, we've used the -nocase switch in the regexp call, instead of using the range atom. This lets us call the proc with a simple string and not worry about case. When regexp finds a match, it places that line in the match variable.

The url variable is set with another regexp command that extracts a string within quotes that starts with the characters "http: from the match variable.

4.3.8 Making a Script

As a final step in this set of examples, we'll create a script that can read the bookmark file of a well-known browser, extract a URL that matches a command line argument string, and report that URL.

4.3.8.1 Global Information Variables

This script will need to read the bookmark file, process the input, find the appropriate entry or entries, and report the result. Because the bookmark files are stored differently under Unix, Mac OS and MS Windows, the script will have to to figure out where to look for the file.

Tcl has several global variables that describe the version of the interpreter, the current state of the interpreter, the environment in which the interpreter is running, etc. These variables include:

argv   A list of command line arguments.

argc   The number of list elements in argv.

env   An associative array of environment variables.

tcl_version   The version number of a Tcl interpreter.

tk_version   The version number of a Tk interpreter.

tcl_pkgPath   A list of directories to search for packages to load.

errorInfo   After an error occurs, this variable contains information about where the error occurred within the script being evaluated.

errorCode   After an error occurs, this variable contains the error code of the error.

tcl_platform   An associative array describing the hardware and operating system that the script is running under.

The tcl_platform associative array has several indices that describe the environment that the script is running on. These indices include:

byteOrder   The order of bytes on this hardware. Will be LittleEndian or BigEndian.

osVersion   The version of the OS on this system.

machine   The CPU architecture (i386, sparc, etc.).

platform   The type of operating system. Will be macintosh, unix, or windows.

os   The name of the operating system. On a Unix system this will be the value returned by uname -s. For MS-Windows systems it will be Win32s (DOS/Windows 3.1 with 32-bit DLL), Windows NT, or Windows 95.

We'll use the tcl_platform global variable to determine the system on which the script is running. Once we know the system on which the script is running, we can set the default name for the bookmark file, open the file, and read the contents.

4.3.8.2 The Executable Script

Aside from those additions, this script uses the code we've already developed.

Example 4.3.8.2-1

```
#!/bin/sh
#\
exec tclsh "$0" "$@"
################################################################
# geturl.tcl
# Clif Flynt -- clif@cflynt.com
#
# Extracts a URL from a netscape bookmark file
#
################################################################
# findUrl --
#
#       Finds a line in the text string that matches the
#       pattern string.  Extracts the URL from that line.
#
# Arguments:
#       match    The pattern to try and match
#       text     The string to search for a match in.
#
# Results:
#       Returns the matched URL, or ""

proc findUrl {match text} {
    set found [regexp -nocase "\n(\[^\n]+$match\[^\n]+)\n" \
            $text fullmatch submatch]
    if {$found} {
        regexp {"(http:[^"]+)"} $submatch match url
    } else {
        set url ""
    }
    return $url
}

################################################################
```

```tcl
#
# Check for a command line argument
#
if {$argc != 1} {
    puts "geturl.tcl string"
    exit -1;
}

#
# Set the bookmark file name depending on the current system.
#
switch $tcl_platform(platform) {
    unix        {
        set bookmarkName "$env(HOME)/.netscape/bookmarks.html"
    }
    windows     {
        set bookmarkName\
            "C:/program files/netscape/navigator/bookmark.htm"
    }
    mac         {
        # Find the exact path, with possible unprintable
        # characters.
        set path [glob\
            "Macintosh HD:System *:Preferences:\
            Netsc*:Bookmarks.html"]

        # Strip the { and } from the name returned by glob.
        set bookmarkName [string trim $path "{}"]
    }
    default     {
        puts "I don't recognize the platform:\
            $tcl_platform(platform)"
        exit -1;
    }
}
#
```

```
# Open the bookmark file, and read in the data
#
set bookmarkFile [open "$bookmarkName" "r"]
set bookmarks [read $bookmarkFile]
close $bookmarkFile

#
# print out the result.
#
puts "[findUrl $argv $bookmarks]"
```

4.4 Speed

The question that always arises is "How fast does it run?" This is usually followed by "Can you make it run faster?" The time command times the speed of other commands.

Syntax: time *cmd ?iterations?*

time	Returns the number of microseconds per iteration of the command.
cmd	The command to be timed. Put within curly braces if you don't want substitutions done twice.
?iterations?	The number of times to evaluate the command. When this argument is defined, the time command returns the average time for these iterations of the command.

The time command evaluates a Tcl command passed as the first argument. The cmd argument will go through the normal substitutions when time evaluates it, so you probably want to put the cmd variable within curly braces.

We've tried several methods for extracting a single datum from a mass of data. Now, let's look at the relative speeds:

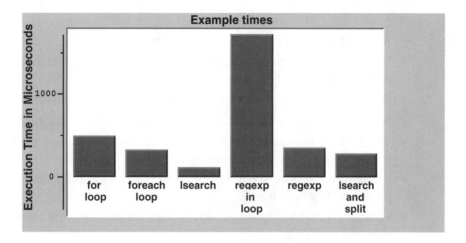

Comparison of Execution Speeds (Tcl8.0p2/BSDI Unix/P166)

The last column in this graph is the combined time that it takes to perform the lsearch and split. Given a set of data that must be split into a list before it can be searched with the lsearch command, an accurate comparison between searching with a regular expression and searching with lsearch should include the time for converting the data to a list.

Regular expressions are very powerful, but slow. Most of the time in a regular expression search is used by the regular expression compilation, the setup time. When you can do a single search over an entire string, regular expressions are almost as fast as iterating through a list or converting a string to a list and using lsearch.

The graph was created with the Blt extension. Blt will be discussed in Chapter 13.

4.5 Bottom Line

There are some tricks in Tcl that may not be apparent until you understand how Tcl commands are evaluated.

- A Tcl command is evaluated in a single pass.
- The Tcl evaluation routine is called recursively to evaluate commands enclosed within braces.
- Substitution will be performed on strings grouped with quotes.
- Substitutions will not be performed on strings grouped with braces ({}).
- Variables exist in either a local or global scope or can be placed in private namespaces. Namespaces are discussed in Chapter 6.
- A Tcl procedure may execute in its default scope or in the scope of a procedure in its call tree.
- Searching a list with lsearch is faster than iterating through a list checking each item.
- The time command can be used to tune your code.

    Syntax: time *cmd ?iterations?*

- Regular expression string searches are performed with the regexp command.

    Syntax: regexp *?opt? expr str ?fullmatch? ?submatch?*

- Regular expression string substitutions are performed with the regsub command.

    Syntax: regsub *?opt? expr str subSpec varName*

- Subroutines are defined with the proc command.

    Syntax: proc *name args body*

CHAPTER 5 — *Using Lists and Arrays*

This chapter will demonstrate how lists and arrays can be used to group data into constructs similar to structures, linked lists, and trees. The first examples will show how lists can be used to group data in ordered and unordered formats. The next section will discuss using associative arrays instead of structures, and the final set of examples will show how associative arrays and naming conventions can be used to create a tree-structured container object.

Tcl has been accused of being unsuited for serious programming tasks because of the simplicity of its data types. Whereas C++ has integers, floats, pointers, structs, and classes, Tcl has just strings, lists, and associative arrays. These simple constructs are usually sufficient. This chapter will demonstrate some techniques for using Tcl data constructs in place of the more traditional structs, linked lists, etc.

For some applications, such as dealing with an interface to a relational database management system (RDBMS), the Tcl data constructs are more suited to the interface than a C structure. Tcl handles an empty return from a database query more intuitively than some other languages.

If you are familiar with compiled languages such as C or Pascal, you may want to consider why you use particular constructs in your programs instead of others. In some cases, you may do so because of the machine and language architecture, rather than because the problem and the data structure match. In some cases you'll find that the Tcl data types are better suited than the more familiar constructs.

When programming in compiled languages such as C or Pascal, there are several reasons for using linked lists:

- Linked lists provide an open-ended data structure; you don't need to declare the number of entries at compile time.
- Data can be added to or deleted from linked lists quickly.
- Entries in a linked list can be easily rearranged.
- Linked lists can be used as container classes for other data.

All of these features are supported by the Tcl list. In fact, the internal implementation of the Tcl list allows data items to be swapped with fewer pointer changes than exchanging entries in a linked list. This allows commands such as lsort to run very efficiently.

The important reason for using linked lists is that you have data that can be conceptualized as a list of items. The Tcl list is ideal for this purpose, and as a programmer you can spend your time developing the algorithm for handling your data, instead of developing a linked list subroutine package.

A binary tree is frequently used in C or Pascal in order to search for data efficiently. In Tcl, the indices of an associative array are stored in a very efficient hash table. Rather than implementing a binary tree for data access purposes, you can use an associative array and get the speed of a good hash algorithm for free. Depending on the depth of your tree, the hash search is very likely to be faster than a binary search, without the overhead of balancing the tree.

Tcl is most commonly used for applications that are not speed critical, and the speed of the list or array is generally adequate. If your application grows and becomes speed bound by Tcl data constructs, you can extend the interpreter with other faster data representations. Extending the interpreter will be covered in Chapter 12.

5.1 Using the Tcl List

A Tcl list can be used whenever the data can be conceptualized as a sequence of data items. These items could be numeric, such as a set of graph coordinates, or textual, such as a list of fields from a database or even another list.

5.1.1 Manipulating Ordered Data with Lists

Lists can be used to manipulate data in an ordered format. Data exported from spreadsheets and database programs are frequently arranged as strings of fields delimited by a field separator. The Tcl list is an excellent construct for organizing such data.

You can treat a list as an ordered set of data and use the `lindex` command to retrieve data from fixed locations within a list.

Code maintenance becomes simpler if you use a set of variables to define the locations of the fields in a list, rather than hardcoding the positions in the `lindex` commands. The mnemonic content of the variable names makes the code more readable. This technique also allows you to add new fields without having to go through all your code to change hardcoded index numbers.

Chapter 3 showed how a comma-delimited line could be split into a Tcl list with each field becoming a separate list element. The next example manipulates three records with fields separated by colons. Each record has four fields in a fixed order: key value, last name, first name, and e-mail address. The example converts the records to lists with the `split` command and then merges the lists into a single list with the `lappend` command. After the data has been converted to a list, the `lsearch` command is used to find individual records in this list, the `lreplace` command is used to modify a record, and then the list is converted back to the original format.

With this example, there are also two new list manipulation commands, the `join` command and `lreplace`.

The `join` command is the flip side of the `split` command. It will join the members of a list into a single string.

Syntax: join *?joinString?*

join   Join the elements of a list into a single string.

?joinString? Use this string to separate list elements. Defaults to a space.

The lreplace command will replace one or more list elements with new elements or can be used to delete list elements.

Syntax: lreplace *list first last ?element element ...?*

lreplace   Return a new list with one or more elements replaced by zero or more new elements.

list   The original list.

first   The position of the first element in the list to be replaced.

last   The position of the last element in the list to be replaced.

element   A list of elements to replace the orginal elements. If this list is shorter than the number of fields defined by *first* and *last*, elements will be deleted from the original list.

Example 5.1.1-1

Position-Oriented Data Example

```
# Set up a list

lappend data [split "KEY1:Flynt:Clif:clif@cflynt.com" : ];
lappend data [split "KEY2:Doe:John:jxd@example.com" : ];
lappend data [split "KEY3:Doe:Jane:janed@example.com" : ];

# data new data is a list of lists.
# { {KEY1 Flynt Clif clif@cflynt.com}
#    {KEY2 Doe John jxd@example.com} ...}

# Find the record with KEY2

set position [lsearch $data "KEY2 *"]
```

```
# Extract a copy of that record

set record [lindex $data $position]

# Assign the record positions to mnenomically named variables

set keyIndex 0;
set lastNameIndex 1;
set firstNameIndex 2;
set eMailIndex 3;

# Display fields from that record

puts "The Email address for Record [lindex $record $keyIndex] \
    ([lindex $record $firstNameIndex]) was \
     [lindex $record $eMailIndex]"

# Modify the eMail Address

set newRecord [lreplace $record $eMailIndex $eMailIndex \
    "joed@example.com"]

# Confirm change

puts "The Email address for Record [lindex $newRecord $keyIndex] \
    ([lindex $newRecord $firstNameIndex]) is \
     [lindex $newRecord $eMailIndex]"

# Update the main list

set data [lreplace $data $position $position $newRecord]

# Convert the list to colon delimited form, and display it.

foreach record $data {
    puts "[join $record :]"
}
```

Script Output

```
The Email address for Record KEY2   (John) was jxd@example.com
The Email address for Record KEY2   (John) is joed@example.com
```

```
KEY1:Flynt:Clif:clif@cflynt.com
KEY2:Doe:John:joed@example.com
KEY3:Doe:Jane:janed@example.com
```

5.1.2 Manipulating Unordered Data with Lists

In some applications information may become available at irregular intervals and in an indeterminate order. It may not be feasible to build a fixed-position data record in this case.

One solution to this problem is to declare a string to identify each piece of expected data, create a list of identifiers and data, and append this list to a primary list as the data becomes available.

Since a Tcl list can contain sublists, you can use the list to implement an unordered collection of Key/Value pairs. The records in the next example consist of two element lists. The first element is a field identifier, and the second element is the field value. The order of these Key/Value pairs within a record is irrelevant. There is no position-related information, because each field contains an identifier as well as data.

The next example uses the procedure getDatum to simulate a system that provides data in an irregular order. The getDatum procedure returns data as a list of three elements: a record identifier, the field identifier, and the field data. The example merges the items with the same record identifier into a single list and then manipulates the data.

Note the use of the global variable position. This variable is initialized in the global scope to maintain its data between invocations of getDatum. If it existed only in the scope of the proc, the variable would be created and destroyed whenever getDatum was called, losing the previous value.

Example 5.1.2-1

Keyed Pair List Example

```
#------------------------------------------------------------
#
# This returns successive entries in the list, simulating a
# system that provides information as it becomes available
```

```tcl
set position 0;

proc getDatum {} {
    global position;

     # Define simulated random order data

    set rawDataList [list \
        [list KEY1 {First Name} Clif] \
        [list KEY2 Email jxd@example.com] \
        [list KEY2 {First Name} John] \
        [list KEY3 {Last Name} Doe] \
        [list KEY3 {First Name} Jane] \
        [list KEY1 {Last Name} Flynt] \
        [list KEY3 Email janed@example.com] \
        [list KEY1 Email clif@cflynt.com] \
        [list KEY2 {Last Name} Doe] ]

    #
    # Select the next item in the list, if not at end.

    if {$position < [llength $rawDataList]} {
        set data [lindex $rawDataList $position]
        incr position
    } else {
        set data ""
    }

    # Ship it.
    return $data;
}
#-------------------------------------------------------------

# Create an empty data list

set dataList "";

# The data returned by getDatum are fixed position lists.
# These are the definitions of the positions.
```

```
set keyIndex 0
set fieldIDIndex 1
set fieldDatumIndex 2

# Populate the dataList

while {[set data [getDatum]] != ""} {
    set key [lindex $data $keyIndex]
    set fieldID [lindex $data $fieldIDIndex]
    set fieldDatum [lindex $data $fieldDatumIndex]

    #
    # If new key, create a new sublist

    if {[lsearch $dataList "*{KEY $key}*" ] == -1} {
        lappend dataList [list [list KEY $key]]
    }

    #
    # Extract the sublist with this key, merge in the new data,
    # and restore the list

    set recordLocation [lsearch $dataList "*{KEY $key}*"]
    set record [lindex $dataList $recordLocation]
    lappend record [list $fieldID $fieldDatum]
    set dataList [lreplace $dataList $recordLocation \
        $recordLocation $record]
}

#
# Display the raw data

for {set i 0} {$i < [llength $dataList]} {incr i} {
    puts "$i: [lindex $dataList $i]"
}

# Get the record with Key KEY1

set record [lindex $dataList [lsearch $dataList "*KEY KEY1*"]]
```

```
# Display fields from the record with KEY1

set namePos [lsearch $record {{FirstName}*}]
puts "\nFirst Name for record KEY1: \
     [lindex [lindex $record $namePos] 1]"
puts "Email Address for record KEY1: \
     [lindex [lindex $record [lsearch $record {Email *}]] 1]"
```

Script Output

```
0: {KEY KEY1} {{First Name} Clif} {{Last Name} Flynt}
{Email clif@cflynt.com}
1: {KEY KEY2} {Email jxd@example.com} {{First Name} John}
{{Last Name} Doe}
2: {KEY KEY3} {{Last Name} Doe} {{First Name} Jane} {Email
janed@example.com}

First Name for record KEY1:  Clif
Email Address for record KEY1:  clif@cflynt.com
```

For most lists this technique works well. However, the time for the lsearch command to find an entry increases linearly with the position of the item in the list. Lists longer than 5000 entries become noticeably sluggish.

The pairing of data to a key value can also be done with associative arrays. The arrays use hash tables instead of a linear search to find a key, so the speed does not degrade as more records are added.

5.2 Using the Associative Array

The Tcl associative array can be used just like a C or Fortran array by setting the indices to numeric values. If you are familiar with Fortran or Basic programming, you might be familiar with coding constructs like this:

C Arrays

```
int values[5];

char desc[5][80];
```

Tcl Array

```
set values(0) 1;

set desc(0) "First"
```

Continued

C Arrays	Tcl Array

```
values[0] = 1;
strcpy(desc[0], "First");
```

When programming in Tcl, you can link the value and description together more efficiently by using a nonnumeric index into the associative array.

```
set value("First") 1;
```

Data that consist of multiple items that need to be grouped together are frequently collected in composite data constructs like a C struct or a Pascal record. These constructs allow the programmer to deal with a single data entity, instead of several entities, when the data must be manipulated as a unit and still allow single items to be manipulated individually.

Grouping information in a struct or record is conceptually a naming convention that the compiler enforces for you. When you define the structure, you name the members and define what amount of storage space they will require. Once this is done, the algorithm developer generally doesn't need to worry about the internal memory arrangements. The data could be stored anywhere in memory, so long as it can be accessed by name when necessary.

You can group data in an associative array variable by using different indices to indicate the different items being stored in that associative array, which is conceptually the same as a structure.

C Structure	Tcl Array

```
struct {
   int  value;
   char desc[80];
} var;


var.value = 1;
strcpy(var.desc,"First");
```

```
set var(value) 1
set var(desc) "First"
```

It may not be immediately obvious, but the Tcl variable var groups the description and value together just as a struct would do.

Another common C data construct is the array of structs. Again, so far as your algorithm is concerned, this is primarily a naming convention. By treating the associative array index as a list of fields, separated by some obvious character (in the following example, a period is used), this functionality is available in Tcl.

Array of C Structures	Tcl Array
```struct {```	```set var(0.value) 1```
``` int value;```	```set var(0.desc) "First"```
``` char desc[80];```	```set var(1.value) 2```
```} var[5];```	```set var(1.desc) "Second"```

```
var[0].value = 1;
strcpy(var[0].desc, "First");
var[1].value = 2;
strcpy(var[1].desc, "Second");
```

You can create naming conventions to group data in Tcl. The Tcl interpreter does not require that you adhere to any naming convention, but you can enforce a convention by writing procedures to hide the conventions from people using a package.

The next sections will describe a more complex set of naming conventions that are hidden from the package user behind a set of procedures.

5.3 New Commands

Before we get into the next set of examples, there are some new commands to discuss. The next examples use the Tcl exception handling calls error and catch, the file system interaction commands file and glob, the introspection command info, and the file load command source.

5.3.1 Exception Handling in Tcl

The default action for a Tcl interpreter when it hits an exception condition is to halt the execution of the script and print out the data in the `errorInfo` global variable.

The simplest method of modifying this behavior is to use the `catch` command to intercept the exception condition before the default error handler is invoked.

Syntax: `catch` *script ?varName?*

catch	Catch an error condition and return the results rather than aborting the script.
script	The Tcl script to evaluate.
varName	Variable to receive the results of the script.

The `catch` command catches an error in a script and returns a success or failure code rather than aborting the program and displaying the error conditions. If the script runs without errors, `catch` returns 0. If there is an error, `catch` returns 1, and the `errorCode` and `errorInfo` variables are set to describe the error.

There are circumstances in a program in which you want to generate an exception. For instance, while checking the validity of user-provided data, you may want to abort processing if the data is obviously invalid. The Tcl command for generating an exception is `error`.

Syntax: `error` *informationalString ?errorInfo? ?errorCode?*

error	Generate an error condition. If not caught, display the `informationalString` and stack trace and abort the script evaluation.
informationalString	Information about the error condition.
errorInfo	A string to initialize the `errorInfo` string. Note that more information about the error may be appended to this string.
errorCode	An identifying error number to be placed in the global variable `errorCode`.

The next example shows some ways of using the catch and error commands.

Example 5.3.1-1

```
#
# Will generate an error if first or second arguments are
#  not numeric.
# Will invoke the error command to
#  generate an error if the arguments are valid.

proc errorProc {first second} {

    # This will fail if $first is non-numeric or 0
    set dummy [expr 1/$first]

    # This will not generate an error.
    #  $fail will be non-zero if $second is non-numeric.
    set fail [catch {expr 5 * $second} result]
    # if $fail is set, generate an error
    if {$fail} {
        error "Bad second argument"
    }

    error "errorProc always fails" "evaluating error" 123
}
```

Example Script

```
puts "call errorProc with a 0 argument"
if {[catch {errorProc 0 a} returnString]} {
    puts "errorProc failed because of: $returnString\n"
}

puts "call errorProc with a bad second argument"
set fail [catch {errorProc 1 X} returnString]

if {$fail} {
    puts "Failed in errorProc"
    puts "Return string: $returnString"
    puts "Error Info: $errorInfo\n"
}

puts "call errorProc with valid arguments"
```

```
set fail [catch {errorProc 1 1} returnString]

if {$fail} {
    if {$errorCode == 123} {
        puts "errorProc failed as expected"
        puts "returnString is: $returnString"
        puts "errorInfo: $errorInfo"
    } else {
        puts "errorProc failed for an unknown reason"
    }
}
```

Script Output

```
call errorProc with a 0 argument
errorProc failed because of: divide by zero

call errorProc with a bad second argument
Failed in errorProc
Return string: Bad second argument
Error Info: Bad second argument
    while executing
"error "Bad second argument""
    (procedure "errorProc" line 11)
    invoked from within
"errorProc 1 X"

call errorProc with valid arguments
errorProc failed as expected
returnString is: errorProc always fails
errorInfo: evaluating error
    (procedure "errorProc" line 1)
    invoked from within
"errorProc 1 1"
```

5.3.2 Interacting with the File System

The glob and file commands provide support for interacting with the file system. These commands allow a script to examine the contents of directories, move files, create new directories, examine file creation dates, etc.

The `glob` command returns a list of the directory entries that match a path expression. The expression is evaluated using the same globbing rules that are used by the `switch` and `string match` commands. In the `glob` command the pattern is compared with the contents of the file system.

For instance, this code returns a list of all files in C:\windows that end in the .COM suffix:

```
% glob C:/windows/*.com
C:/windows/COMMAND.COM  C:/windows/WIN.COM
```

Note that I used the forward slash of a Unix-style path, rather than the Microsoft backward slash. Tcl uses the backward slash (\) as an escape character. The Tcl commands that access a file system will translate Unix-style file names into machine-specific formats.

Syntax: `glob ?-nocomplain? ?--? pattern ?pattern?`

`glob`	Return a list of directory entries that match a pattern.
`-nocomplain`	If a directory is empty, return an empty string instead of generating an error.
`--`	Identifies the end of options, all following arguments are patterns even if they start with a dash.
`pattern`	The pattern (or patterns) to match on the file system.

The `file` command provides more tools for interacting with a file system. It has several subcommands that provide support for transforming file paths from system-dependent format into a neutral (Unix-style) format, obtaining the attributes of files, determining the types of files, copying files, deleting files, etc. Check the online documentation for your version of Tcl for the complete list of subcommands.

Syntax: `file subCommand pathName ?arg ...?`

`file`	Interact with the file system.
`subCommand`	The `subCommand` defines the interaction. Interactions include:

`type`	Returns the type of a file. Types include:		
		file	*pathName* is a normal file.
		directory	*pathName* is a directory.
		link	*pathName* is a link to another file.
		characterSpecial	*pathName* is a character-oriented device.
`nativename`	Returns *pathName* in the proper format for the current platform.		
`delete`	Deletes the file referenced by *pathName*.		
`exists`	Returns 1 if *pathName* exists, or 0 if not.		
`isdirectory`	Returns 1 if *pathName* is a directory, 0 if not.		
`isfile`	Returns 1 if *pathName* is a regular file, 0 if not.		
pathName	The path to the directory entry with which to interact.		
`?arg...?`	Arguments that `subCommands` require.		

5.3.3 Examining the State of the Tcl Interpreter

The Tcl interpreter can be queried about its current state. It can report whether a procedure or variable has been defined, what a procedure body or argument list is, the current level in the procedure stack, etc.

The next examples will use only one of the `info` subcommands. See the online documentation for details of the other subcommands.

The `info exists` command can be used to query whether or not a variable has been used. This can be used to initialize a variable on the first pass through a section of code.

Syntax: `info exists    varName`

`info exists`   Returns 1 if a variable exists in the local or global scope, else returns 0.

`varName`   The name of the variable being tested.

5.3.4 Loading Code from a Script File

The `source` command loads a file into an existing Tcl script. It is similar to the `#include` in C, the `source` in shell programming, and the `require` in Perl.

This command lets you build packages that you can load into your scripts when you need particular functionality, which allows you to modularize your programs. This is the simplest of the Tcl commands that implement libraries and modularization. We'll discuss `package` and `namespace` in Chapter 7.

Syntax: `source fileName`

`source`   Load a file into the current Tcl application and evaluate it.

`fileName`   The file to load.

Macintosh users have two options to the `source` command that aren't available on other platforms:

Syntax: `source -rsrc resourceName ?fileName?`
Syntax: `source -rsrcid resourceId ?fileName?`

These options allow one script to source another script from a TEXT resource. The resource may be specified by resourceName or resourceID.

5.4 Trees in Tcl

You don't need to use a binary tree in Tcl for speed, because the associative array gives you fast access to array indices. However, sometimes the underlying data is best represented as a tree.

A set of data in which a single large entity is composed of several smaller entities that are again subdivided can be best represented as a tree. For example, a file system is a single large disk divided into directories, which are further divided into subdirectories and files. A set of data that has inherent order (with possible branches), such as the steps in an algorithm, can be represented as a tree.

Unfortunately, Tcl doesn't provide a tree construct as a built-in data type. However, it's not difficult to create one using the associative array and a naming convention. This section will build a package of subroutines and data to construct and manipulate trees. It would be difficult to use this package if a programmer were required to learn the naming convention and write code that conforms to this convention. Therefore, the names are all generated by the procedures in this package, and the programmer is given a handle to use to access the trees and nodes.

5.4.1 Tree Package Description

In this section I discuss how to use and implement a tree data object in Tcl. A few procedures will be shown and discussed in this chapter to demonstrate how the package works. The complete code for the package is on the CD-ROM under examples/chapter5.

The tree is implemented using a naming convention for the indices of an associative array. This naming convention lets us create multiple separate trees, each of which has parent and child references. A parent node can reference multiple child nodes, and a child node references a single parent. Trees can be as deep as the data requires.

When a node is created, a handle is returned. This handle is passed to the procedures that manipulate the tree, so the programmer never needs to see the naming conventions.

5.4.2 Tree Package Naming Conventions

Since this package is built around a naming convention, we'll examine that first.

This package defines a single associative array to hold the trees and their nodes. This array is a global variable (so that all the procedures can access it) named `Tree_InternalArray`.

`Tree_InternalArray` has indices that are used for

- Internal housekeeping.
- Defining a node.
- Defining a node's parent.
- Defining a node's children.
- Attaching Key/Value sets of data to a node.
- Attaching Key/Value sets of data to the entire tree.

The naming convention used in this package is to treat each associative array index as multiple fields separated by periods. These fields identify the tree and node, as well as the type of data associated with this index.

The structure of the indices is shown next. The fields that are generated by the tree procedures are shown in italic type. The fields that have fixed values are shown in normal type.

- Tree Housekeeping Indices

  Index: base
  Example: `Tree_InternalArray(base)`

  - This index contains a counter that is incremented each time a new tree is created. It is used to create unique identifiers for each tree.

    base   Identifies this index as containing the base value for trees.

  Index: *treeID*.base
  Example: `Tree_InternalArray(tree0.base)`

  - This index contains a counter that is incremented each time a new node is created. It is used to create unique identifiers for each node within a given tree.

treeID   The word `tree` followed by a unique number. This field identifies the members of a tree. All nodes in a tree will have the same unique number.

base   Identifies this index as containing the base value for nodes in a tree.

- Tree Structure Indices

Index: *treeID.nodeID*
Example: `Tree_InternalArray(tree0.1)`

- This node is set when a node is created and is used by the internal procedures to confirm that a handle references a valid node. It does not contain any useful data.

treeID   The tree identifier

nodeID   The node identifier

Index: *treeID.nodeID*`.children`
Example: `Tree_InternalArray(tree0.1.children)`

- This index contains a list of the handles of the children for the node identified by *treeID.nodeID*

treeID   The tree identifier

nodeID   The node identifier

children
          Denotes this index as the child list.

Index: *treeID.nodeID*`.parent`
Example: `Tree_InternalArray(tree0.1.parent)`

- This index contains the handle of the parent of the node identified by *treeID.nodeID*

treeID   The tree identifier

nodeID   The node identifier

parent   Denotes this index as the parent handle.

- Key/Value Data Indices

Index: *treeID.nodeID*`.node.Key`
Example: `Tree_InternalArray(tree0.1.node.nodeKey1)`

- These indices allow nodes to be used as container objects. A script can store arbitrary data in an index identified by the tree/node identifier and a Key and later retrieve that data with the node and Key identifiers.

  treeID   The tree identifier

  nodeID   The node identifier

  node   A marker to denote that this Key/Data pair is associated with a particular node rather than the entire tree.

  Key   The Key for a Key/Value data pair. The data is stored in the associative array variable referenced by this index.

Index: *treeID*.tree.Key
Example: Tree_InternalArray(tree0.tree.treeKey1)

- These indices attach data to the tree, instead of a single node. The data can be retrieved with any node handle and Key.

  treeID   The tree identifier

  nodeID   The node identifier

  tree   A marker to denote that this Key/Data pair is associated with the entire tree, not just one node.

  Key   The Key for a Key/Value data pair. The data is stored in the associative array variable referenced by this index.

The package consists of several procs that can be accessed from a user script and a few internal procs that are used only by the tree package procs.

The *Tcl Style Guide* from Scriptics and Sun Microsystems recommends that you start procedure names intended for use within a package with an uppercase letter and use lowercase letters to start the procedures intended for external use. It also recommends that all entry points in a package start with a recognizable string, to avoid name conflict when someone needs to load several packages.

The procs that provide the program interface to this package all start with tree. The internal variables and procedures start with the word Tree.

The commands this package implements are:

Syntax: `treeCreate`

`treeCreate`   Create a new, empty tree and return a handle for the root node.

Syntax: `treeCreateChild` *parent*

`treeCreateChild`

>Create a new node, attached to a given parent. Return the handle for the new node.

parent   The handle for the parent to be attached to the new child.

Syntax: `treeGetChildList` *parent*

`treeGetChildList`

>Return a list of all the children attached to a parent node or an empty list if the parent has no children.

parent   The handle for the parent.

Syntax: `treeGetParent` *node*

`treeGetParent`

>Return the parent of a node if the node has a parent.

node   The handle for the node.

Syntax: `treeSetNodeValue` *node* *Key* *Value*

`treeSetNodeValue`

>Set a `Key` and `Value` pair in a node.

node   The handle for the node.

Key   The identifier for this datum.

Value   The value for this datum.

Syntax: `treeGetNodeValue` *node* *Key*

`treeGetNodeValue`

>Returns the value associated with a `Key` in this node.

node   The handle for the node.

Key   The identifier for this datum.

Syntax: `treeSetTreeValue` *anyNode Key Value*

`treeSetTreeValue`
Set a `Key` and `Value` pair in an entire tree.

`anyNode`   The handle for any node in the tree.

`Key`   The identifier for this datum.

`Value`   The value for this datum.

Syntax: `treeGetTreeValue` *anyNode Key*

`treeGetNodeValue`
Returns the value associated with a `Key` in this tree.

`anyNode`   The handle for any node in this tree.

`Key`   The identifier for this datum.

Here's an example to show the tree being used:

Example 5.4.2-1

Example Script

```
# Load the script file that defines the procedures and
# Tree_InternalArray
source tree.tcl

# Create a Tree. The root node is returned.
set root [treeCreate]

# attach some data to the Key "displayText" of the root node
treeSetNodeValue $root displayText "We can see"

# Create a child attached to the root
# and attach some data to the "displayText" key in the child

set child1 [treeCreateChild $root]
treeSetNodeValue $child1 displayText "the forest for"

# Create another child attached to the root
# and attach some data to "displayText" Key in the new child
```

```
set child2 [treeCreateChild $root]
treeSetNodeValue $child2 displayText "the trees."

puts "[treeGetNodeValue $root displayText]"

foreach child [treeGetChildList $root] {
    puts "[treeGetNodeValue $child displayText]"
}
```

Script Output

```
We can see
the forest for
the trees.
```

This example produces a tree that resembles this:

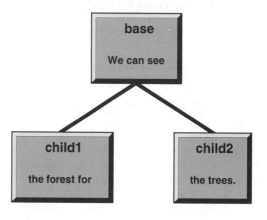

5.5 Tree Package Implementation

Now that we've introduced a simple application of the tree package, let's look at the implementation.

5.5.1 Getting the Parts of a Name

Most of the procedures in this package will need to separate a node name into parts. Therefore, this is a good function to put into a proc. This proc is named TreeGetNameParts. It will split a node name at the periods and return the *treeID* and the *nodeID*.

Usually, a Tcl proc will return a single value, or a list of values, which the calling script will parse appropriately. In this case, the program flow is simpler if TreeGetNameParts returns the *treeID* and *nodeID* in two separate variables.

To do this, we'll use the Tcl upvar command. Chapter 4 discussed briefly that the for, while, and if commands evaluate their scripts in the variable scope of the calling script and mentioned that the uplevel command would allow a script to execute within a different variable scope. The upvar command allows a Tcl script to declare that a particular variable will be evaluated in a different variable scope than the script that's being evaluated.

This is conceptually the same as passing a variable by reference in C and C++. The scope at which a variable can be evaluated, however, is not limited to just the scope immediately above the current script. It could be any level up to the global scope.

Syntax: upvar *?level? var1 localVar1 ?var2? ?localVar2?*

upvar	Causes a variable to be evaluated in a higher variable scope than the code currently being evaluated.
?level?	An optional level to describe the level at which the variable should be evaluated. This value may be a number or the # symbol followed by a number.
	If this is a number, it represents the number of levels higher in the procedure stack at which this variable should be evaluated. If 1, the variable will be evaluated in the scope of the calling process; if 2, it will be evaluated in the scope of the process above that.
	If the number is preceded by a # sign, then it represents the procedure call level down from the global scope (#0). In this form #0 is the global scope, #1 is a proc called from the global scope, #2 is a proc called from that proc, etc.
	The level defaults to 1, the level of the script that invoked the current proc.

var1   The name of a variable in the higher scope to link to a local variable.

localVar1

The name of a variable in the local scope. This variable can be used in this script as a local variable. Setting a new value to this variable will change the value of the variable in the other scope.

Note that an individual array index may be passed by value to a procedure, but Tcl does not pass entire arrays by value. Whenever you need to pass an entire array to a procedure, you must use the upvar command to link to the array in the calling script's scope.

Example 5.5.1-1

TreeGetNameParts

```
############################################################
# proc TreeGetNameParts {name Base IdNum} --
#   Internal proc for splitting a name into parts
# Arguments:
#   name:     The name to split
#   Base:     The name of the Tcl variable to receive the base name
#   IdNum:    The name of the Tcl variable to receive the ID number
#
#   No valid Return, sets two variables in the calling proc.

proc TreeGetNameParts {name Base IdNum} {
    global Tree_InternalArray

    upvar $Base base
    upvar $IdNum idNum

    set namelst [split $name "."]
    set base [lindex $namelst 0]
    set idNum [lindex $namelst 1]
}
```

Example

```
TreeGetNameParts tree1.2 treeName nodeID
puts "Tree Name is: $treeName.  Node ID is: $nodeID"
```

Script Output

Tree Name is: tree1.   Node ID is: 2

5.5.2 Creating a New Tree

The command for creating a new tree in this package is treeCreate. It increments the counter in Tree_InternalArray(base), creates the new tree name, and sets the Tree_InternalArray(*treeName*.base) counter to 0, the start value for the node ID numbers. After this is done, a new node is created to be the top node in this tree, and the handle for the new node is returned.

Example 5.5.2-1

TreeGetNameParts

```
proc treeCreate {} {
    global Tree_InternalArray

    #
    # Create the unique name for this tree.

    set primaryName "tree$Tree_InternalArray(base)"
    incr Tree_InternalArray(base)

    #
    # Can't have two trees with the same name.
    # This should never happen, but just in case...

    if {[array name Tree_InternalArray $primaryName.base] != ""} {
        error "$primaryName already exists"
    }

    #
    # Set the initial unique ID for nodes in this tree.
    #
```

```
    set Tree_InternalArray($primaryName.base) 0
    #
    # Create the root node
    #
    set rootNode [TreeCreateNode $primaryName.base]

    #
    # Looks good, ship it!
    #
    return $rootNode
}
```

Example

```
set tree [treeCreate ]
puts "The root node for this tree is: $tree"
```

Script Output

The root node for this tree is: tree0.1

5.5.3 Creating a New Child Node

The proc to create a new node is treeCreateChild. This proc creates a node, adds its handle to the parent node's list of children, and puts the parent's handle in the parent index of the new node. The treeCreateChild proc calls two other internal procs: one to create a node (TreeCreateNode) and another to link the node to the parent (TreeAddChild).

TreeCreateNode creates an orphan node, with no parent and no children.

Syntax: TreeCreateNode *treeID*

TreeCreateNode

> Create a new node. Confirm that the tree exists, and increment the unique ID.

treeName   The name of the tree, either *treename*.base or a node name.

Syntax: TreeAddChild *parent child*

TreeAddChild   Confirms that the child exists. Adds the child's handle to the parent's child list and sets the child's parent index.

130

parent   The parent to receive this child node.

child   The new child node to be added to the parent.

The following example shows the three procedures that are used to create a new child: the public entry point and the two internal procs. In this example, the internal procs are called to show the steps in creating a child node.

Since all of the interaction between the programmer and the Tree package is done with handles returned by the Tree package, the application programmer will never need to know the internal naming conventions of the Tree package. In this example the array indices are displayed to show how the package works.

Example 5.5.3-1

```
##############################################################
# proc treeCreateChild {parent}   --
#   Creates a child of a given parent
#
# Arguments:
#       parent: The parent node to contain this new node
# Results:
#       Creates a new node.
#       Adds the child to the parent node.
#       Returns the handle for the new node
#
proc treeCreateChild {parent} {
    global Tree_InternalArray

    TreeGetNameParts $parent primary idNum

    set child [TreeCreateNode $primary.base]

    TreeAddChild $parent $child
    return $child
}

##############################################################
# proc TreeCreateNode {rootname} --
#  Create a new node (unattached) in this tree
# Arguments:
```

```
#     rootname:  The name of a node in the tree
#
# Results:
#    Creates a new node.
#    Returns a handle to use to identify this node.
#
proc TreeCreateNode {rootname} {
    global Tree_InternalArray

    TreeGetNameParts $rootname primary idNum

    set val [incr Tree_InternalArray($primary.base)]
    set childname "$primary.$val"
    set Tree_InternalArray($childname) OK
    return $childname
}


##################################################################
#  proc TreeAddChild {parent child} --
#   Adds a node to the child list of the parent node, and sets
#   child's parent pointer to reflect the parent node.
#
# Arguments:
#       parent: The parent node
#       child:  New child node being added to the parent.
#
# Results:
#       Adds the child and updates lists & pointers
#       No valid return.
#
proc TreeAddChild {parent child} {
    global Tree_InternalArray

    if {[array name Tree_InternalArray $parent] == ""} {
        error "TreeAddChild: Parent $parent does not exist "
    }

    if {[array name Tree_InternalArray $child] == ""} {
        error "TreeAddChild: Child $child does not exist "
    }
```

```
    TreeGetNameParts $parent primary parentID

    TreeGetNameParts $child primary childID

    if {[info exists \
       Tree_InternalArray($primary.$childID).parent]} {
         error "$child already has parent: \
           $Tree_InternalArray($primary.$childID.parent)"
    }

    # Add this handle to the parent's list of children.
    lappend Tree_InternalArray($primary.$parentID.children \
         $child

    # Set this node's parent index to reference the parent's
    # handle
    set Tree_InternalArray($primary.$childID.parent) $parent
}
```

Example Script

```
#
# Create a tree
#

set root [treeCreate]

#
# Create two detached nodes
#

set node2 [TreeCreateNode $root]
set node3 [TreeCreateNode $root]

#
# Declare root to be the parent node to node2 and node3
#

TreeAddChild $root $node2
TreeAddChild $root $node3
puts "root is: $root -- node2 is: $node2 -- node3 is: $node3"
puts "the parent of node2 is: [treeGetParent $node2]"
```

```
puts "root has these children: [treeGetChildList $root]\n"

#
# Create a node4 as a child of node3
#

set node4 [treeCreateChild $node3]

puts "the parent of node4 is: [treeGetParent $node4]"
puts "node3 has these children: [treeGetChildList $node3]\n"

puts "Tree_InternalArray has these indices:"

foreach index [lsort [array names Tree_InternalArray]] {
    puts "$index"
}
```

Script Output

```
root is: tree0.1 -- node2 is: tree0.2 -- node3 is: tree0.3
the parent of node2 is: tree0.1
root has these children: tree0.2 tree0.3

the parent of node4 is: tree0.3
node3 has these children: tree0.4

Tree_InternalArray has these indices:
root
tree0.1
tree0.1.children
tree0.2
tree0.2.parent
tree0.3
tree0.3.children
tree0.3.parent
tree0.4
tree0.4.parent
tree0.base
```

The Tcl tree example demonstrates what can be done with naming conventions. Because the naming convention is so important to this package, we'll examine it in detail.

base
: This index references the value that will be used to create unique tree names. The value associated with this index is initialized to 0 when the `tree.tcl` file is sourced and incremented each time a new tree is created.

tree0.base
: This index references the value that will be used for the unique ID (the second field) in each index. The value associated with this index is initialized to 0 when a tree is created and incremented each time a new node is created.

tree0.1
: This is the node root that was returned from treeCreate. There will never be a `tree0.parent.1` index, since the root node cannot have a parent. The array variable referenced by this index contains the value `""`.

tree0.1.children
: This is the list of children for the base node, `tree0.1`. The array variable referenced by this index contains `tree0.2 tree0.3`.

tree0.2
: This node was created and then declared as a child node to `tree0.1`. The array variable referenced by this index contains the value `OK`.

tree0.2.parent
: This index references the name of the parent node for `tree0.2`: `tree0.1`.

tree0.3
: This node was created and then declared as a child node to `tree0.1`. Later in the script, `tree0.4` was created as a child node to this node. The array variable referenced by this index contains the value `OK`.

tree0.3.children
: This index references a list of the child nodes for `tree0.3`. The value associated with this array index is `tree0.4`.

tree0.4   This node was created as a child node to tree0.3. The array
                 variable referenced by this index contains the value OK.

tree0.4.parent
                 This index references the name of the parent to tree0.4:
                 tree0.3.

5.5.4 Tree Package as a Container Class

The Tree package also allows the programmer to attach data to a node and
access it via a Key. This lets you use the Tree package similarly to the way
you would use a container class in C++ or Java.

The procs that implement this are treeSetNodeValue and treeGetNode-
Value, to set and retrieve values from a node based on the Key provided.
Similar code implements the procedures treeSetTreeValue and tree-
GetTreeValue, which set and retrieve values that are attached to the entire
tree and available to all nodes.

Example 5.5.4-1

```
##############################################################
#   proc treeSetNodeValue {node key value} --
#         Sets the value of a Key/Value pair in a node.
#
# Arguments:
#         node:    The node to set the Key/Value pair in
#         key:     An identifier to reference this value
#         value:   The value for this identifier
#
# Results:
#         Sets a Key/Value pair in this node.
#         Returns the value
#
proc treeSetNodeValue {node key value} {
    global Tree_InternalArray

    if {[array name Tree_InternalArray $node] == ""} {
        error "treeSetNodeValue: Node $node does not exist "
    }

    set Tree_InternalArray($node.node.$key) $value
```

```
        return $value
}


###############################################################
#   proc treeGetNodeValue {node key} --
#          Returns a value from a Key/Value pair, if it has
#          previously been set.
#
# Arguments:
#          node:   The node to get the Key/Value pair from
#          key:    The identifier to get a value for
#
# Results:
#          Returns the value from a previously set Key/Value pair
#
proc treeGetNodeValue {node key} {
    global Tree_InternalArray

    if {[array name Tree_InternalArray $node] == ""} {
        error "treeGetNodeValue: Node $node does not exist "
    }

    if {[array name Tree_InternalArray $node.node.$key] == ""} {
        error "treeGetNodeValue: Key $key does not exist "
    }

    return $Tree_InternalArray($node.node.$key)
}
```

Example Script

```
#
# Create a tree
#
set tree [treeCreate]

#
# Create two nodes attached to the root node.
#
set node1 [treeCreateChild $tree]
set node2 [treeCreateChild $tree]

#
```

```
# Set values in node1 and node2
#
treeSetNodeValue $node1 keyA "Value for node1:KeyA"
treeSetNodeValue $node2 keyA "Value for node2:KeyA"

treeSetNodeValue $node1 keyB "Value for node1:KeyB"
treeSetNodeValue $node2 keyB "Value for node2:KeyB"

#
# Retrieve the values.
#
puts "node1 has values:"
puts "  keyA: [treeGetNodeValue $node1 keyA]"
puts "  keyB: [treeGetNodeValue $node1 keyB]"

puts "node2 has values:"
puts "  keyA: [treeGetNodeValue $node2 keyA]"
puts "  keyB: [treeGetNodeValue $node2 keyB]"

#
# Set a value for the entire tree, via node 1

treeSetTreeValue $node1 TreeKeyA "Value A for tree"

#
# Retrieve it via node 2

puts "\nTreeKeyA: [treeGetTreeValue $node2 TreeKeyA]"
```

Script Output

```
node1 has values:
  keyA: Value for node1:KeyA
  keyB: Value for node1:KeyB
node2 has values:
  keyA: Value for node2:KeyA
  keyB: Value for node2:KeyB

TreeKeyA: Value A for tree
```

The tree created in this example resembles this:

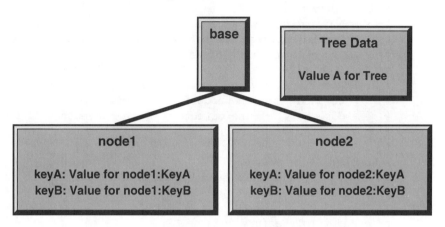

5.6 Using the Tree Package

Now that we've gone over the internals of the tree package, let's see a simple example of how it can be used.

This example builds a tree structure from the first two levels of a file directory and then prints out that directory tree.

The tree package is contained in a file named `tree.tcl`. The `source tree.tcl` command loads `tree.tcl` into the script and makes the `treeCreate`, `treeSetNodeValue`, etc. procs available for use.

In this example we use the `catch` command to examine directories without aborting the program if the directory is empty or our script does not have read permission.

Example 5.6-1

```
#!/usr/local/bin/tclsh

source tree.tcl
```

```
##################################################################
# proc addDirToTree
#       Add a directory to a node.
#       Create children for each directory entry, and set the
#           name and type of each child.
#
# Arguments:
#       treeNode        The node for this directory.
#       directory       The directory whose contents will be added
#                       to the tree.
#
# Results:
#       The Tree is increased by the number of items in this
#       directory.

proc addDirToTree {treeNode newDir} {

    # If this isn't a directory, it has no subordinates.

    if {[file type $newDir] != "directory"} {
        error "$newDir is not a directory. Can't add to tree."
    }

    # If the treeNode node hasn't been updated with name and
    # type, do so now.

    if {[catch {treeGetNodeValue $treeNode name}]} {
        treeSetNodeValue $treeNode name $newDir
        treeSetNodeValue $treeNode type directory
    }

    # An empty or unreadable directory will return a fail
    #       for the glob command
    # If the directory can be read, the list of names will be
    #       in fileList.

    set fail [catch {glob $newDir/*} fileList]

    if {$fail} {
        return;
    }
```

```
        # Loop through the names in fileList

        foreach name $fileList {
            set node [treeCreateChild $treeNode]
            treeSetNodeValue $node name $name
            treeSetNodeValue $node type [file type $name]
        }
}

# Create a tree structure

set root [treeCreate]

# Add the initial directory and its directory entries
#     to the tree structure

addDirToTree $root [file nativename /]

# If any children are directories, add their entries to the
#     tree as new nodes

foreach entry [treeGetChildList $root] {
    if {[treeGetNodeValue $entry type] == "directory"} {
        addDirToTree $entry [treeGetNodeValue $entry name]
    }
}

# Print out the tree in the form:
# Dir1
#     Dir1/Entry1
#     Dir1/Entry2
# Dir2
#     Dir2/Entry3
#     Dir2/Entry4

foreach entry [treeGetChildList $root] {
    puts "[treeGetNodeValue $entry name]"
    if {[treeGetNodeValue $entry type] == "directory"} {
        foreach sub [treeGetChildList $entry] {
```

```
                puts "     [treeGetNodeValue $sub name]"
            }
        }
    }
```

Script Output

```
...
/usr
    /usr/var
    /usr/contrib
    /usr/X11
    /usr/bin
    /usr/lib
    ...
/bsd
/bin
    /bin/chmod
    /bin/cp
    /bin/csh
    /bin/date
    ...
/dev
    /dev/apm
    /dev/audio
    ...
...
```

5.7 Speed Considerations

So, how do lists and associative arrays compare when it comes to accessing a particular piece of data? The following example shows the results of plotting the list and array access times with Tcl 8.0 and Tcl 7.6. In each case the last added element of a list or array was accessed.

The time to access the last element in a list increases linearly with the length of the list. In Tcl 8.0 the list handling code was rewritten to improve the performance, but even with that performance improvement, the access speed for array elements is much faster and does not degrade as the number of elements increases.

Also note that the performance between lsearch and an array access is not significantly different with Tcl 8.0 until you exceed 500 elements in the list. If your lists are shorter than 500 elements, you can use whichever data construct fits your data best.

This timing test was done on a P166 platform running BSDI Unix. Your mileage will vary.

Example 5.7-1

List Element Access Time

```
for {set i 0} {$i < 5000} {incr i } {
  set x "abcd.$i.efg"
  lappend lst $x
  puts "$i [lindex [time {lsearch $lst $x} 50] 0]"
}
```

Array Element Access Time

```
for {set i 0} {$i < 4000} {incr i } {
  set x "abcd.$i.efg"
  set arr($i) $x
  puts "$i [lindex [time {set y $arr($i)} 50] 0]"
}
```

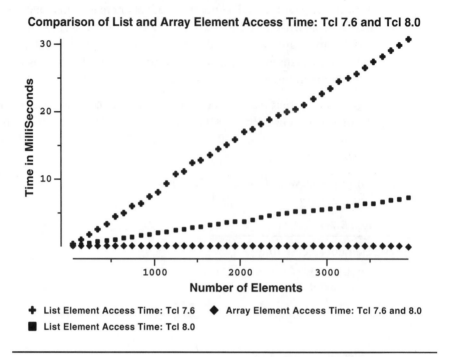

Comparison of List and Array Element Access Time: Tcl 7.6 and Tcl 8.0

5.8 Bottom Line

This chapter has demonstrated several ways to use Tcl lists and associative arrays.

1. Lists can be used to organize information as position-oriented data or as Key/Value pairs.

2. Naming conventions can be used with associative array indices to provide the same functionality as structures, arrays of structures, and container classes.

3. A variable can contain the name of another variable, providing the functionality of a pointer.

4. The `catch` command is used to catch an error condition without causing a script to abort processing.

   Syntax: catch *script ?varName?*

5. The `file` command provides access to the filesystem.

   Syntax: file type *pathName*
   Syntax: file nativename *pathName*
   Syntax: file delete *pathName*
   Syntax: file exists *pathName*
   Syntax: file isdirectory *pathName*
   Syntax: file isfile *pathName*

6. The `glob` command returns directory entries that match a particular pattern.

   Syntax: glob *?-nocomplain? ?--? pattern ?pattern?*

7. The `source` command loads and evaluates a script.

   Syntax: source *fileName*

8. The `upvar` command causes a variable to be evaluated in a different variable scope than the current script.

   Syntax: upvar *?level? var1 localVar1 ?var2? ?localVar2?*

9. The `error` command generates an error condition.

   Syntax: error *infoString ?newErrInfo? ?newErrCode?*

10. The `lreplace` command replaces one or more list elements with 0 or more new celements.

    Syntax: lreplace *list first last ?element element ...?*

11. The `join` command will convert a list into a string, using an optional character as the element separator.

    Syntax: join *?joinString?*

12. Accessing an array element is much faster than using `lsearch` to find a list element.

Procedure Techniques

One key to writing modular code is dividing large programs into smaller subroutines. Tcl supports the common programming concept of subroutines—procedures that accept a given number of arguments and return one or more values. Tcl also supports procedures with variable numbers of arguments and procedures with arguments that have default values. The Tcl interpreter also allows scripts to rename procedures or create new procedures while the script is running.

This chapter will discuss:

- Defining the arguments to procedures.
- Renaming and deleting procedures.
- Examining a procedure's body and arguments.
- Performing Tcl variable and command substitutions upon a string.
- Constructing and evaluating command lines within a script.
- Turning a set of procedures and data into an object.

The last example in this chapter will show how to extend the Tree example from Chapter 5 into a tree object.

6.1 Arguments to Procedures

When the `proc` command is invoked to create a new procedure, the new procedure is declared with a name, a list of arguments, and a body to evaluate when the procedure is invoked.

When a procedure is called, the Tcl interpreter counts the arguments to confirm that there are as many arguments in the procedure call as there were in the procedure definition.

If a procedure is called with too few arguments, the Tcl interpreter will generate an error message resembling this:

```
no value given for parameter "arg1" to "myProcedure"
```

If a procedure is called with too many arguments, the Tcl interpreter will generate an error message resembling this:

```
called "myProc" with too many arguments
```

This run-time checking helps you avoid the silent errors that occur when you modify a procedure to take a new argument and miss changing one of the procedure calls. However, there are times when you don't know the number of arguments (as with the `expr` command) or you want an argument to be optional, with a default value when the argument is not present (as 1 is the default increment value for the `incr` command).

You can easily define a procedure to handle a variable number of arguments or define a default value for an argument in Tcl.

6.1.1 Variable Number of Arguments to a Procedure

You can define a procedure that takes a variable number of arguments by making the final argument in the argument list the word `args`. When a procedure with `args` as the last argument is called with more arguments than expected, the Tcl interpreter will concatenate the arguments that weren't assigned to declared variables into a list and assign that list to the variable `args`, instead of generating a `too many arguments` error.

Note that args must be the last argument in the argument list to get the excess arguments assigned to it. If there are other arguments after the args argument, then args is treated as a normal argument.

In the following example, the procedure showArgs requires at least one argument. If there are more arguments, they will be placed in the variable args.

Example 6.1.1-1

```
#
# A proc that accepts a variable number of args
#
proc showArgs {first args} {
puts "first: $first"
puts "args: $args"
}
```

Example Script

```
puts "Called showArgs with one arg"
showArgs oneArgument

puts "\nCalled showArgs with two args"
showArgs oneArgument twoArgument

puts "\nCalled showArgs with three args"
showArgs oneArgument twoArgument threeArgument
```

Script Output

```
Called showArgs with one arg
first: oneArgument
args:

Called showArgs with two args
first: oneArgument
args: twoArgument

Called showArgs with three args
first: oneArgument
args: twoArgument threeArgument
```

6.1.2 Default Values for Procedure Arguments

The technique for setting a default value for an argument is to define the argument as a list; the first element is the argument name, and the second is the default value. When the arguments are defined as a list and a procedure is called with too few arguments, the Tcl interpreter will substitute the default value for the missing arguments, instead of generating a no value given for parameter... error.

Example 6.1.2-1

```
#
# A proc that expects at least one arg, and has defaults for 2
#
proc showDefaults {arg1 {numberArg 0} \
        {stringArg {default string}}} {
    puts "arg1: $arg1"
    puts "numberArg: $numberArg"
    puts "stringArg: $stringArg"
}
```

Example Script

```
puts "\nCalled showDefaults with one argument"
showDefaults firstArgument

puts "\nCalled showDefaults with two arguments"
showDefaults firstArgument 3

puts "\nCalled showDefaults with three arguments"
showDefaults firstArgument 3 "testing"
```

Script Output

```
Called showDefaults with one argument
arg1: firstArgument
numberArg: 0
stringArg: default string

Called showDefaults with two arguments
arg1: firstArgument
numberArg: 3
stringArg: default string

Called showDefaults with three arguments
arg1: firstArgument
```

```
numberArg: 3
stringArg: testing
```

The procedure showDefaults must be called with at least one argument. If only one argument is supplied, then numberArg will be defined as 0, and stringArg will be defined as default string.

Note that the order of the arguments when a procedure is invoked must be the same as the order when the procedure was defined. The values are assigned in the order in which they appear in the procedure definition. For example, you cannot call procedure showDefaults with arguments for arg1 and stringArg but use the default for numberArg. The second value in the procedure call will be assigned to the second variable in the procedure definition.

You cannot create a procedure that has an argument with a default before an argument without a default.

If you created a procedure like this:

```
proc badProc {{argWithDefault dflt} argWithOutDefault} {...}
```

and called it with a single argument, it would be impossible for the Tcl interpreter to guess which variable that argument was intended for.

6.2 Renaming or Deleting Commands

Procedures are created with the proc command. Sometimes you may also need to rename or delete a procedure. For example, if you need to use two sets of Tcl code that both have a processData procedure, you can source one package, rename the processData procedure to package1processData, and then source the second package. You can also do this with the Tcl packages that will be discussed in Chapter 7.

If you've had to deal with name collisions in libraries and DLLs before, you'll appreciate this ability. When you use the technique shown later in this chapter to extend a data item into an object, you'll want to delete the object method procedure when the data object is destroyed.

The `rename` command lets you change the name of a command or procedure. If you rename a procedure to an empty string, the procedure is deleted.

Syntax: `rename` *oldName* *?newName?*

`rename`	Rename a procedure.
oldName	The current name of the procedure.
?newName?	The new name for the procedure. If this is an empty string, the procedure is deleted.

The following example shows the procedure `alpha` renamed to beta and then deleted.

Example 6.2-1

```
proc alpha {} {
    return "This is the alpha proc"
}
```

Example Script

```
puts "Invocation of procedure alpha: [alpha]"
rename alpha beta
puts "Invocation of procedure beta: [beta]"
rename beta ""
beta
```

Script Output

```
Invocation of procedure alpha: This is the alpha proc
Invocation of procedure beta: This is the alpha proc
invalid command name "beta"
```

6.3 Getting Information about Procedures

The Tcl interpreter is a very introspective interpreter. A script can get information about most aspects of the interpreter while the script is running. The `info` command that was introduced in Chapter 5 provides information about the interpreter.

These four `info` subcommands will return information about the procedures that have been defined:

info commands *pattern*

> Return a list of commands with names that match a pattern.

info procs *pattern*

> Return a list of procedures with names that match a pattern.

info body *procName*

> Return the body of a procedure.

info args *procName*

> Return the arguments of a procedure.

The `commands` subcommand will list the available commands that match a `glob` pattern. This command is useful when you are debugging code that runs in several namespaces (discussed in Chapter 7) and you need to know what commands are defined where.

Syntax: info commands *pattern*

info commands

> Returns a list of commands in the local and global scope that match the pattern.

pattern

> A glob pattern to attempt to match.

The `info body` command will return the body of a procedure. This can be used to generate and modify procedures at run time and when debugging scripts that generate new procedures while they are running.

Syntax: info body *procName*

info body

> Returns the body of a procedure.

procName

> The procedure from which the body will be returned.

The `info args` command returns the argument list of a procedure. Again, this is useful when debugging code that has generated its own procedures.

Syntax: info args *procName*

info args

> Returns a procedure's argument list.

procName

> The procedure from which the arguments will be returned.

The next example shows how you can check that a procedure exists and create a slightly different procedure from it.

Example 6.3-1

Example Script

```
#
# Define a simple procedure.

proc alpha {args} {
    puts "proc alpha is called with these arguments: $args"
}

#
# Confirm that the procedure exists

if {[info commands alpha] != ""} {
    puts "There is a procedure named alpha"
}

#
# Get the argument list and body from the alpha procedure
set alphaArgs [info args alpha]
set alphaBody [info body alpha]

#
# Change the word "alpha" in the procedure body to "beta"

regsub "alpha" $alphaBody "beta" betaBody

#
# Create a new procedure "beta" that will display its arguments.

proc beta $alphaArgs $betaBody

#
# Run the two procedures to show their behavior

alpha How 'bout
beta them Cubs.
```

Script Output

```
There is a procedure named alpha
proc alpha is called with these arguments: How 'bout
proc beta is called with these arguments: them Cubs.
```

6.4 Substitution and Evaluation of Strings

Section 4.2 discussed how the Tcl interpreter evaluates a script: the interpreter examines a line, performs a pass of command and variable substitutions, and then evaluates the resulting line. A Tcl script can access these interpreter functions to perform substitutions on a string or even evaluate a string as a command. This is one of the unusual strengths in Tcl programming. Most interpreters don't allow access to their parsing and evaluation sections to the program that is being interpreted.

The two commands that provide access to the interpreter are subst and eval.

6.4.1 Performing Substitution on a String

The subst command performs a single pass of variable and command substitutions on a string and returns the modified string. This is the first phase of a command being evaluated, but the actual evaluation of the command does not happen. If the string includes a square-bracketed command, the command within the brackets will be evaluated as part of this substitution.

The subst command can be used when you need to replace a variable with its contents but do not want to evaluate it as a command. The following example shows how subst can be used to combine the contents of two variables into a variable name.

Syntax: subst *string*

subst   Perform a substitution pass upon a string. Do not evaluate the results.

string   The string upon which to perform substitutions.

Example 6.4.1-1

Example Script

```
% set x var
var
% set y name
name
% set varname "this is a test"
```

```
this is a test
% puts $${x}${y}
$varname
% subst $${x}${y}
this is a test
```

6.4.2 Evaluating a String as a Tcl Command

The eval command concatenates its arguments into a string and then evaluates that string as if it were text in a script file. The eval command allows a script to create its own command lines and evaluate them.

You can use eval to write data-driven programs that effectively write themselves based on the available data. You can also use the eval command to write agent-style programs, where a task on one machine sends a program to a task on another machine to execute. These techniques (and the security considerations) will be described as they come up in the next chapters.

Syntax: eval *arg ?args?*

eval   Evaluate the arguments as a Tcl script.

arg ?args?   These arguments will be concatenated into a command line and evaluated.

The next example evaluates several lines of text to increment a variable.

Example 6.4.2-1

Example Script

```
set cmd(0) {set a 1}
set cmd(1) {puts "start value of A is: $a"}
set cmd(2) {incr a 3}
set cmd(3) {puts "end value of A is: $a"}

for {set i 0} {$i < 4} {incr i} {
    eval $cmd($i)
}
```

Script Output

```
start value of A is: 1
end value of A is: 4
```

6.5 Working with Global and Local Scopes

The Tcl scope rules and their relation to the upvar and uplevel commands can be confusing. This section will discuss scopes and the upvar and uplevel in a bit more detail than they've been discussed previously and show how uplevel and upvar commands behave.

This discussion will be expanded again in Chapter 7, when we discuss the namespace command. For now, a namespace is a technique for encapsulating procedure and variable names.

6.5.1 Global and Local Scope

The global scope is the primary scope in a Tcl script. All Tcl commands and any procedures that are not defined within a namespace are maintained in this scope. All namespaces and procedures can access commands and variables maintained in the global scope.

Any variable declared global or defined outside a procedure is maintained in the global scope. Variables maintained in the global scope are kept until either the script exits or they are explicitly destroyed with the unset command. These variables can be accessed from any other scope by declaring the variable to exist in the global scope with the global command. Note that the global command must be evaluated before that variable name is used in the local scope. The Tcl interpreter will generate an error if you try to declare a variable to be global after using it in a local scope.

```
set globalVar "I'm global"

proc goodProc {} {
    global globalVar
```

```
    # The next line prints out
    #"The globalVar contains: I'm  global"
    puts "The globalVar contains: $globalVar"
}

proc badProc {} {
set globalVar "This defines 'globalVar' in the local scope"

    # The next line causes an error
    global globalVar
}
```

When a procedure is evaluated, it creates a local scope. Variables are created in this scope as necessary and are destroyed when the procedure returns. The variables used within a procedure are visible to other procedures called from that procedure but not to procedures outside the current call stack.

When a new procedure is defined within a procedure, the new procedure is defined in the global scope and is not deleted when the procedure that defined the new procedure returns.

Each time a procedure invokes another procedure, another local scope is created. These nested procedure calls can be viewed as a stack, with the global scope at the top and each successive procedure call stacked below the previous ones.

A procedure can access variables within the global scope or within the scope of the procedures that invoked it via the upvar and uplevel commands. The upvar command will link a local variable to one in a previous (higher) stack scope.

Example 6.5.1-1

Example Script

```
proc top {topArg} {
    set localArg [expr $topArg+1]
    puts "Before calling bottom localArg is: $localArg"
    bottom localArg
    puts "After calling bottom, localArg is: $localArg"
}

proc bottom {bottomArg} {
```

```
    upvar $bottomArg arg
    puts "bottom is passed $bottomArg with a value of $arg"
    incr arg
}

top 2
```

Script Output

```
Before calling bottom localArg is: 3
bottom is passed localArg with a value of 3
After calling bottom, localArg is: 4
```

The uplevel command will concatenate its arguments and evaluate the resulting command line in a previous scope. The uplevel is like eval, except that it evaluates the command in a different scope instead of the current scope.

The following example shows a set of procedures (stack1, stack2, and stack3) that call each other and then access and modify variables in the scope of the procedures that called them. All of these stack procedures have a local variable named x. Each is a separate variable. Note that procedure stack1 cannot access the variables in the scope of procedure stack2, although stack2 can access variables in the scope of stack1.

Note that the procedure b1 is not part of the call stack. It cannot access the variable x within the local procedure scopes, but it can access the global variable x.

Example 6.5.1-2

```
# Create procedure stack1 with a local variable x.
#    display the value of x, call stack2, and redisplay the
#    value of x

proc stack1 {} {
  set x 1;
  puts "X in stack1 starts as $x"
  stack2
  puts "X in stack1 ends as $x"
  puts ""
}
```

```
# Create procedure stack2 with a local variable x.
#   display the value of x, call stack3, and redisplay the
#   value of x

proc stack2 {} {
  set x 2;
  puts "X in stack2 starts as $x"
  stack3
  puts "X in stack2 ends as $x"
}

# Create procedure stack3 with a local variable x.
#   display the value of x,
#   display the value of x in the scope of procedures that
#   invoked stack3 using relative call stack level.
#   Add 10 to the value of x in the proc that called stack3
#        (stack2)
#   Add 100 to the value of x in the proc that called stack2
#        (stack1)
#   Add 200 to the value of x in the global scope.
#   display the value of x using absolute call stack level.

proc stack3 {} {
  set x 3;

  puts "X in stack3 starts as $x"

  puts ""

  # display the value of x at stack levels relative to the
  # current level.

  for {set i 1} {$i <= 3} {incr i} {
      upvar $i x localX
      puts "X at upvar $i is $localX"
  }

  puts "\nx is being modified from procedure stack3\n"

  # Evaluate a command in the scope of procedures above the
  # current call level.

  uplevel 1 {incr x 10}
  uplevel 2 {incr x 100}
  uplevel #0 {incr x 200}
  puts ""
```

```
  # display the value of x at absolute stack levels

  for {set i 0} {$i < 3} {incr i} {
      upvar #$i x localX
      puts "X at upvar #$i is $localX"
  }
  puts ""
}

proc b1 {} {
    # Declare that X exists in the global scope -
    # do not create an x in the local scope.
    global x;

    puts "X in global scope is: $x"
}
```

Example Script

```
set x 0;
puts "X at global scope is $x"
stack1
b1
```

Script Output

```
X at global scope is 0

X in stack1 starts as 1
X in stack2 starts as 2
X in stack3 starts as 3

X at upvar 1 is 2
X at upvar 2 is 1
X at upvar 3 is 0

x is being modified from procedure stack3

X at upvar #0 is 200
X at upvar #1 is 101
X at upvar #2 is 12

X in stack2 ends as 12
X in stack1 ends as 101

X in global scope is 200
```

The scopes in the preceding example resemble the left side of the following diagram when the procedure stack3 is being evaluated. Each local procedure scope is nested within the scope of the procedures that called it.

When the uplevel 1 {incr x 10} command is evaluated it causes the string incr x 10 to be evaluated one scope higher than the current stack3 scope, which is the stack2 scope. The uplevel #0 {incr x 200} command is evaluated at absolute scope level 0, or the global scope. The evaluation level for a command uplevel #1 would be the first level down the call stack, stack1 in this example.

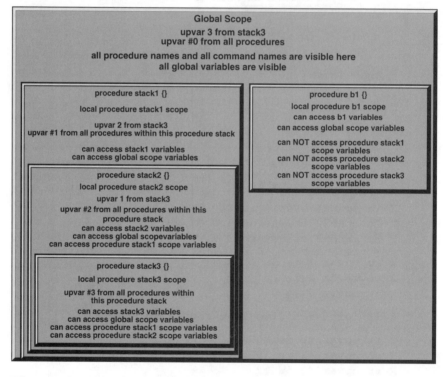

The preceding example demonstrates how procedures can access all levels above them in the call stack but not levels below.

The procedure b1 that is called from the global level is unable to access any variable in the local scope of the procedure stack1. The local variable scope for procedure stack1 exists only while stack1 is being evaluated.

6.6 Making a Tcl Object

Chapter 3 mentioned that Tcl keeps separate hash tables for commands, associative array indices, and variables and that the first word in a Tcl command string must be a command name. These features mean that any name can be defined as both a variable name and a procedure name. The interpreter will know which is meant by the position of the name in the command line.

This section will discuss techniques for using the same label as a variable name or array index and a procedure name. For example, the `newTreeObject` procedure will define an array index and also create a procedure with the same name. It will return the name of the procedure.

This lets us implement the object-oriented programming concept of having methods attached to a data object. The implementation of a Tcl object is much different from the implementation of a C++ or Java object, but the programming semantics are very similar.

Table 6.6-1

C++	Tcl
`object = new Object(arg);`	`set myTree [newTreeObject]`
`object->method(arg1, arg2);`	`$mytree method arg1 arg2`

6.6.1 An Object Example

For a simple example, here's some code that creates variables with the name of a common fruit and then creates a procedure with the same name that tests whether or not its argument is a valid color for this fruit.

Example 6.6.1-1

Example Script

```
set fruitList [list {apples {red yellow green}} {bananas yellow} \
        {grapes {green purple}}]

foreach fruit $fruitList {
    # 1) Extract the info we'll use from the list
```

```
        set fruitName [lindex $fruit 0]
        set fruitColors [lindex $fruit 1]

        # 2) Create a variable with the name of the fruit.
        #     The contents will be the fruit's possible colors.
        eval set $fruitName [list $fruitColors]

        # 3) Create a body for a procedure that compares the
        #     argument to a list of colors.
        set body [format \
            {if {[lsearch "%s" $clr] != -1} {
                return 1
            } else {
                return 0
            } } \
            $fruitColors]

        # 4) Define the procedure.
        proc $fruitName {clr} $body
}
# Loop through the fruits, and ask the user for a color
#   Read the input from the keyboard.
#   Compare it to valid colors.
foreach fruit [list apples bananas grapes ] {
    puts "What color are $fruit?"
    gets stdin answer
    if {[eval $fruit [list $answer]]} {
        puts "Correct, $fruit can be $answer"
    } else {
        puts "No, $fruit are [subst $$fruit]"
    }
}
```

Script Output

```
What color are apples?            # User types red
Correct, apples can be red
What color are bananas?           # User types red
No, bananas are yellow
What color are grapes?            # User types red
No, grapes are green purple
```

There are a few things to notice in that example.

Note that in section #2 the `fruitColors` argument to the `eval` command is placed within a `list` command. When the `eval` command collects its arguments, it concatenates them into a string. It does not maintain the arguments as separate units. If the line were written as:

```
eval set $fruit $color
```

then the first line to be evaluated (after variable substitutions) would be:

```
set apples red yellow green
```

This is an error, since a set command can only accept two arguments.

By putting the second argument within the `list` command, the colors are grouped, and the line being evaluated resembles:

```
set apples {red yellow green}
```

Whenever you don't know the number of words that will be in an argument to the `eval` command but you need the argument to be treated as a single entity, it's best to group the argument with the `list` command.

In section #3, the body of the fruit procedures is created with the `format` command. The body for this procedure needs to be able to access the procedure argument `$clr` and also have the values for `$fruitColors` substituted into the `lsearch` command.

The `format` command returns this body for the `apples` procedure:

```
if {[lsearch "red yellow green" $clr ] != -1} {
    return 1
} else {
    return 0
}
```

Using the `format` command is one method of creating a string with some `$variable` values substituted, while others are included as `$variable`. The next section, building the tree object, will demonstrate another technique.

The $answer value is passed to the $fruit procedure inside a `list` command for the same reason that the `color` argument is passed to eval in a list. User input can be almost anything, and the code has to be defensive. For example, without the list enclosing the $answer a user could type in [proc apples {a} {return 1}] to force the program to generate a correct response.

6.6.2 Creating a Tree Object

The tree subroutines discussed in Chapter 5 returned an index into the global associative array Tree_InternalArray. This index is used as a handle to identify the node being referenced.

This handle name can also be defined as a procedure name, just as the variable names were used in the previous example.

Rather than adding code to convert the handle into a procedure each time we create a new tree or add a node, we can write a new procedure (newTreeObject) that will:

1. Call the treeCreate procedure to create a new tree.
2. Define a procedure with the same name as the handle treeCreate returned.
3. Return that name for the program to use as a procedure for manipulating the tree.

In the previous example, we created a procedure that had a single purpose. We can also make a procedure that will perform any of several actions based on a subcommand name. In the next examples, that procedure will be named TreeObjProc, which will be discussed after describing the newTreeObject procedure.

The following code shows the newTreeObject procedure.

Example 6.6.2-1

```
##############################################################
# proc newTreeObject {} --
#   Creates a new Tree object, and returns an object for
#       accessing the base node.
# Arguments:
#   None

proc newTreeObject {} {
```

```
    set treeId [treeCreate]
    proc $treeId {args} "return \[TreeObjProc $treeId \$args]"

    return $treeId
}
```

The first line in this procedure is a call to the `treeCreate` proc that we created in Chapter 5, which returns a handle for the base node of this tree.

The second line is a `proc` command that defines the new procedure to evaluate for this node. This line adds a new procedure to the interpreter with the same name as the handle. The new procedure will take an undefined number of arguments (the `args` argument), and the body of this procedure will return the results of evaluating the procedure `TreeObjProc`.

Instead of using the `format` command, as was done in the last example, this example uses the backslash to inhibit substitutions from occurring on certain strings. Note what is escaped in the body of the new procedure.

The entire body is enclosed with quotes, not braces. This allows substitutions to occur within the body before the `proc` command is evaluated. The variable substitution on the variable `$treeId` places the handle for this node in the body of the procedure.

Because the body is enclosed in quotes, not braces, the opening square bracket before `TreeObjProc` must be escaped to prevent `TreeObjProc` from being evaluated during the substitution phase of evaluating the `proc` command. The backslash will leave the square brackets as part of the procedure body, causing `TreeObjProc` to be evaluated when the new procedure is evaluated.

The same is true of the dollar sign preceding the `args` argument to `TreeObjProc`. If not for the backslash, the interpreter would try to replace `$args` with the contents of that variable while evaluating the `proc` command. This would generate an error, because `args` will be defined in the new procedure but is not defined in `newTreeObject`.

After the substitutions, the body that is passed to the `proc` command resembles this:

```
{return [TreeObjProc tree1.node.1 $args]}
```

6.6.3 Defining the Object's Method

The `TreeObjProc` is the largest part of the tree object package. This procedure takes two arguments: the name of the node to manipulate (which is set when the node's procedure is defined) and a list of arguments. The first entry in the list will be a subcommand that defines which `tree.tcl` procedure to evaluate, and the rest of the list will be arguments that will be passed to that procedure.

All of the procedures that were defined in the tree example in Chapter 5 are supported in TreeObjProc.

```
##############################################################
# proc TreeObjProc {node methodArgs} --
#     Primary method for tree objects.
#     Parses the subcommand and calls the appropriate
#     tree.tcl proc.
#
# Arguments:
#     node:           The internal name for this node.
#     methodArgs:     A list, the first member is the subcommand
#                     name, subsequent (optional) members are
#                     arguments to be passed to the tree.tcl
#                     command.
#
# Results:
#     Calls other procedures which may produce output,
#         create new objects, delete objects, etc.

proc TreeObjProc {node methodArgs} {

    set subCommand [lindex $methodArgs 0]
    set cmdArgs [lrange $methodArgs 1 end]

    switch $subCommand {
    {set} {
            # Set the Key/Value pair associated with this node.
            # could be set -node key value
            #           set -tree key value
            #           set key value    -- Default to node.
            if {[llength $cmdArgs] == 3} {
                set option [lindex $cmdArgs 0]
```

```
                set key [lindex $cmdArgs 1]
                set val [lindex $cmdArgs 2]
        }\
        elseif {[llength $cmdArgs] == 2} {
                set option "-node"
                set key [lindex $cmdArgs 0]
                set val [lindex $cmdArgs 1]
        } else {
                error "$node set ?-node? ?-tree? key value"
        }
        if {[string match $option "-node"]} {
                return [treeSetNodeValue $node $key $val]
        }\
        elseif {[string match $option "-tree"]} {
                return [treeSetTreeValue $node $key $val]
        } else {
                error "$node set ?-node? ?-tree? key value"
        }
        }
{get} {
        # return the Key/Value pair associated with this node.
        #  May be:
        #  get -node key
        #  get -tree key
        #  get -best key  -- return node, value
        #  or tree value if no node value exists
        #  get key  -- treat as best.
        if {[llength $cmdArgs] == 2} {
                set option [lindex $cmdArgs 0]
                set key [lindex $cmdArgs 1]
                set val [lindex $cmdArgs 2]
        }\
        elseif {[llength $cmdArgs] == 1} {
                set option "-best"
                set key [lindex $cmdArgs 0]
                set val [lindex $cmdArgs 1]
        } else {
                error "$node set ?-node? ?-tree? key value"
        }
```

```
switch -exact -- $option {
{-node} {
return [treeGetNodeValue $node $key]
      }
{-tree} {
return [treeGetTreeValue $node $key]
      }
{-best} {
set fail [catch \
    {treeGetNodeValue $node $key} returnVal]
if {!$fail} {
      return $returnVal
}
return [treeGetTreeValue $node $key]
      }
default {
error "$node set ?-node? ?-tree? key value"
      }
   }
}
{add} {
   # Add a child node to this node.
   set newNode [treeCreateChild $node]
   proc $newNode {args} " \
         return \[TreeObjProc $newNode \$args]"
   return $newNode
}

   {delete} {
   # remove this node
   # and remove the proc from the proc hash table
   # If cmdArgs == "-r", delete recursively.
   if {[string match $cmdArgs "-r"]} {
         foreach child [$node childList] {
         $child delete -r
         catch {rename $child ""}
         }
         }
         # delete this node.
         treeDeleteNode $node
         rename $node ""
}
```

```
{destroyTree} {
     # destroy this tree completely
     # Find the base of the tree, and delete all nodes
     #  and their associated procs
     set base [$node base]
     $base delete -r

     # then destroy the base.
     treeDestroyTree $node
}
{childList} {
     # return a list of children
     return [treeGetChildList $node]
}
{search} {
     # return a list of keys defined in this tree
     #   that match a pattern
     return [treeSearchKey $node $cmdArgs]
}
{siblingList} {
     # return a list of children
     return [treeGetSiblingList $node]
}
{parent} {
     # returns the parent of a node
     return [treeGetParent $node]
}
{valueList} {
     # returns a list of ids and values
     return [treeGetNodeValueList $node]
}
{base} {
     # returns the ultimate ancestor of a node.
     return [treeGetRoot $node]
}
{dump} {
     # dump the contents of this node
     return [treeDump $node $cmdArgs]
}
default {
     # Should not be here, this is an error
```

```
        set methods {set, get, add, delete \
            destroyTree childList, parent, valueList, \
            base, dump, \
            siblingList search}
        error "Bad method: $subCommand\n use $methods"
    }
  }
  return ""
}
```

There are a few points to note about this code.

The `TreeObjProc` procedure uses `rename` to delete the procedure associated with a node when the node is deleted. Once a node is deleted, there is no longer a procedure call with that name.

The subcommand strings are shorter and simpler than the procedures defined in `tree.tcl`. The `tree.tcl` tree package needs to use long names starting with a unique string to avoid conflicts with other packages that may be loaded. (Imagine how many packages might have a procedure named "process-Data".) Within the `TreeObjProc`, however, there are no conflicts with other Tcl commands or procedures, so simple subcommand names can be used.

The `set` and `get` commands use an option (`-tree` or `-node`) to declare whether the Key being set should be attached to a single node or to the complete tree. In the `tree.tcl` script, setting a value in the tree and setting one in a node are two separate procedures. By default, the `set` and `get` commands set the a Key/Value pair for a node. The following example uses the default action for these commands.

Here's the example from Chapter 5 rewritten to use the treeObj class instead of the tree functions.

Example 6.6.3-1

Example Script

```
#!/bin/sh
#\
exec tclsh "$0" "$@"

source ../Tree/treeObj.tcl
```

```
############################################################
# proc addDirToTree
#       Add a directory to a node.
#       Create children for each directory entry, and set the
#       name and type of each child.
#
# Arguments:
#       parent          The parent node for this directory.
#       directory       The directory to add to the tree.
#
# Results:
#       The Tree is made longer by the number of entries in this
#       directory.

proc addDirToTree {parent newDir} {

    #
    # If this isn't a directory, it has no subordinates.
    #

    if {[file type $newDir] != "directory"} {
        error "$newDir is not a directory. Can't add to tree."
    }

    #
    # If the parent directory hasn't been updated with name and
    # type, do so now.
    #
    if {[catch {$parent get name}]} {
        $parent set name $newDir
        $parent set type directory
    }

    #
    # An empty or unreadable directory will return a fail for
    # the glob command
    # If the directory can be read, the list of names will be in
    # fileList.
    #

    set fail [catch {glob $newDir/*} fileList]

    if {$fail} {
        return;
```

```
    }
    #
    # Loop through the names in fileList
    #
    foreach name $fileList {
        set node [$parent add]
        $node set name $name
        $node set type [file type $name]
    }
}
```

Example Script

```
#
# Create a tree structure
#
set base [newTreeObject]

#
# Add the initial directory and its directory entries to the
# tree structure
#
addDirToTree $base [file nativename C:/]

#
# If any children are directories, add their entries to the
# tree as sub-children.
#
foreach entry [$base childList] {
    if {[$entry get type] == "directory"} {
        addDirToTree $entry [$entry get name]
    }
}

#
# Print out the tree in the form:
# Dir1
#     Dir1/Entry1
#     Dir1/Entry2
# Dir2
#     Dir2/Entry3
#     Dir2/Entry4
#
```

```
foreach entry [$base childList] {
    puts "[$entry get name]"
    if {[$entry get type] == "directory"} {
        foreach sub [$entry childList] {
            puts "    [$sub get name]"
        }
    }
}
```

Script Output

C:/IO.DOS
C:/MSDOS.DOS
C:/COMMAND.DOS
C:/COMMAND.COM
C:/BOOTLOG.PRV
C:/CONFIG.SYS
C:/NETLOG.TXT
C:/DRVSPACE.BIN
C:/AUTOEXEC.BAT
C:/CONFIG.WIN
C:/Program Files
    C:/Program Files/Common Files
    C:/Program Files/PLUS!
    C:/Program Files/The Microsoft Network
    C:/Program Files/Microsoft Exchange
    C:/Program Files/Accessories
    C:/Program Files/Tcl
    C:/Program Files/Seagate
    C:/Program Files/WinZip
C:/tcltutor
    C:/tcltutor/nopty.tcl
    C:/tcltutor/icon
    C:/tcltutor/TclTutor.bat
    ...
C:/WINDOWS
    C:/WINDOWS/INF
    C:/WINDOWS/COMMAND
    C:/WINDOWS/SYSTEM
    ...

The preceding example is very similar to the example in Chapter 5, since most of the code deals with the file system, not with the tree. However, it's a bit easier to follow with the shorter subcommand names used instead of the long tree procedures.

There are two problems with this tree object.

1. The associative array `Tree_InternalArray` sits at the global scope, where any code can access it easily.

2. The script that wishes to use the treeObject needs to know the directory where `treeObj.tcl` is stored, and `treeObj.tcl` needs to be able to find `tree.tcl`.

Chapter 7 will discuss the `namespace` and `package` commands. The examples will show how to use the `namespace` command to hide the `Tree_InternalArray` in a private namespace and how to use the `package` command to create a package that can used without the script needing to know the location of the files it loads.

6.7 Bottom Line

- A procedure can be defined as taking an undefined number of arguments by placing the `args` argument last in the argument list.

- A procedure argument with a default value is defined by declaring the argument as a list. The second list element is the default value.

- When a Tcl procedure is evaluated, it creates a local scope for variables. This local scope stacks below the scope of the code that invoked the procedure.

- A Tcl script can access all of the scopes above it in the procedure call stack.

- Tcl procedures can be constructed and evaluated in a running program.

- Data items can be treated as objects by creating a procedure with the same name as the data item and using that procedure to manipulate the data item.

- The `rename` command renames or removes a command or proc.
  Syntax: `rename` *oldName ?newName?*

- The `subst` command performs a pass of command and variable substitutions upon a string.
  Syntax: `subst` *string*

- The `eval` command will evaluate a set of arguments as a Tcl command.
  Syntax: `eval` *arg ?args?*

- The `info commands` command will return a list of commands that are visible in the current scope and match a pattern.
  Syntax: `info commands` *pattern*

- The `info args` command will return the arguments of a procedure.
  Syntax: `info args` *procName*

- The `info body` command will return the body of a procedure.
  Syntax: `info body` *procName*

- The `global` command declares that a variable exists in the global scope.
  Syntax: `global`*varName1 ?varName2...varNameN?*

CHAPTER 7   *Namespaces and Packages*

The `namespace` and `package` commands help you write modular and reusable code in Tcl. These commands implement two different concepts that work together to make it possible to write more modular code. The `namespace` command lets you organize the code and data within a package safely, while the `package` command provides tools for organizing code modules into libraries.

The `namespace` command lets you collect data and procedure names in a private scope where they won't interact with other data and procedure names. This lets you load new procedures without cluttering the global space (avoiding name collisions) and protects data from unintentional corruption.

The `package` command groups a set of procedures that may be in separate files into a single entity. Other scripts can then declare which packages they will need and what versions of those packages are acceptable. The Tcl interpreter will find the directories where the packages are located, determine what other packages are required, and load them when they are needed. The `package` command can load both Tcl script files and binary shared libraries or DLLs.

This chapter will discuss:

- The namespace scope.
- Encapsulating Tcl procedures and data in namespaces.
- Nesting one namespace within another.
- Modularizing Tcl scripts into packages.
- Nesting packages within namespaces.

And, of course, in the final example, we'll revisit the Tree script and extend it into a package that uses nested namespaces for the data and procedures.

7.1 Namespaces and Scoping Rules

In Chapter 6 we discussed the Tcl global and procedure variable scopes. This section will expand on that discussion and introduce the `namespace` and `variable` commands. These commands allow the Tcl programmer to create private areas within the program in which procedure and variables names will not conflict with other names.

7.1.1 Namespace Scope

Namespaces provide encapsulation similar to that provided by C++ and other object-oriented languages. Namespace scopes have some of the characteristics of the global scope and some characteristics of a procedure local scope. A namespace can be viewed as a global scope within a scope.

Namespaces are similar to the global scope in that:

- Procedures created at any scope within a namespace are visible at the top level of the namespace.
- Variables created in a namespace scope (outside a local procedure scope) are maintained between execution of code within the namespace.

- Variables created in a namespace scope (outside a local procedure scope) can be accessed by any procedure that is being evaluated within that namespace.
- While a procedure defined within a namespace is being evaluated, it creates a local scope within that namespace, not within the global namespace.

Namespaces are similar to local procedure scopes in that:

- Code being evaluated within a namespace can access variables and procedures defined in the global space.
- All namespaces are contained within the global scope.
- Namespaces can nest within each other.

Namespaces also have some unique features:

- A namespace can declare certain items (procedures or variables) to be exportable. Exportable items can be made visible in the global scope.
- A nested namespace can keep procedures and variables hidden from higher level namespaces.

The following diagram shows the scopes in a script that contains two namespaces (example and demo), each of which contains procedures named proc1 and proc2. Because the procedures are in separate namespaces, they are different procedures. If a script tried to define two proc1 procedures at the global level, the second definition would overwrite the first.

In this example, ::example::proc1 and ::example::proc2 are procedures that are both called independently, while ::demo::proc2 is called from ::demo::proc1. The demo::proc2 is displayed within demo::proc1 to show that the procedure local scopes nest within a namespace just as they nested within the stack example in the previous chapter.

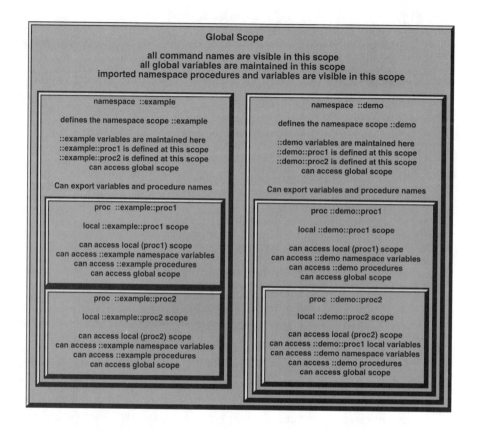

7.1.2 Namespace Naming Rules

A namespace can contain other namespaces, creating a tree structure similar to a filesystem. The naming convention for namespaces is similar to the filesystem naming convention.

- Instead of separating entities with slashes (/ or \), namespace entities are separated with double colons (::)
- The global scope is the equivalent to a filesystem "/" directory. It is identified as "::".

- Namespace identifiers that start with a double colon (::) are absolute identifiers and are resolved from the global namespace. Namespace identifiers that do not start with a double colon are relative identifiers and are resolved from the current namespace.

  An entity identified as `::foo::bar::baz` represents an entity named `baz`, in the `bar` namespace, which was created within the `foo` namespace, which was created in the global scope.

  An entity identified as `foo::bar` represents an entity named `bar` that exists in the namespace `foo`. The namespace `foo` is a child namespace in the current namespace.

- Namespace identifiers are relative if they do not start with a double colon.

  An entity identified as `bar::baz` represents an entity named `baz` that is a member of the namespace `bar`, which was created in the current scope. The current scope may be global, a procedure's local scope, or another namespace.

7.1.3 Accessing Namespace Entities

In C++, Java, or other strongly object-oriented languages, private data is completely private and other objects can't access it. In Tcl, the namespaces are advisory private areas. An entity (procedure or data) in a namespace can always be accessed if your script knows the full path to that entity.

A script can publish the entities within a namespace that it considers public with the `namespace export` command, and other scripts can import entities from the namespace into their local scope with the `namespace import` command. (Both of these will be discussed later in this section.)

In many cases you'll want to access namespace procedures by their full identifier, rather than import the procedures into your script's global scope.

- Using the namespace identifier for an entity makes it easier to figure out what package a procedure or data originated from.
- Using the namespace identifier removes the possibility of name collisions when you load a new package with the same procedure and data names.

7.1.4 Why Use Namespaces?

So, if you always access namespace members by their full path, and namespaces don't provide truly private data, why should you use a namespace instead of having your own naming convention?

- The namespace naming conventions are enforced by the interpreter. This provides a consistent naming convention across packages, making it easier to merge multiple packages to get the functionality you need.

- Namespaces nest. Scripts in one namespace can invoke another namespace and access that namespace by a relative name.

- Namespaces conceal their internal structure from accidental collisions with other scripts and packages. Data and procedures named with a naming convention exist in the global scope.

- A package can be loaded multiple times in different namespaces without interfering with other instantiations of the package.

7.1.5 The `namespace` and `variable` Commands

The `namespace` command has many subcommands, but most Tcl applications will need to use only the `eval`, `export`, and `import` commands. The `children` command is not required for using namespaces but provides some information that is useful in determining what namespaces exist within which scopes.

The `variable` command declares that a variable exists within a namespace. It is similar to the `global` command.

The `namespace eval` command concatenates the arguments into a string and evaluates them within a defined namespace. If the defined namespace does not already exist, it is created.

Procedures and variables can be defined in the argument to the `namespace eval` command. When the `namespace eval` command is evaluated, these procedures and variables are created within that namespace scope.

Syntax: namespace eval *namespaceID arg ?args?*

namespace eval

> Create a namespace, and evaluate the script *arg* in that scope. If more than one *arg* is present, the arguments are concatenated together into a single command to be evaluated.

namespaceID   The identifying name for this namespace.

arg ?args?   The script or scripts to evaluate within namespace *namespaceID*.

It's often necessary to permit certain portions of a namespace to be imported into other scopes. For example, you will probably want to allow the procedures that provide the application programmer interface (API) to your package to be imported into other namespaces but not allow the importation of private data and internal procedures.

The namespace export command lists the entities within a namespace scope that can be imported by other scopes.

Syntax: namespace export *pattern ?patterns?*

namespace export

> Export members of the current namespace that match the patterns. Exported names can then be imported into other scopes. The patterns are in glob format.

pattern ?patterns?

> Patterns that represent procedure names and data names to be exported.

The namespace import command imports an entity in a namespace into the current scope. When a procedure that was defined within a namespace is imported into the global scope, it becomes visible to all scopes and namespaces.

Syntax: namespace import *?-force? ?pattern?*

namespace import

> Imports variable and procedure names that match a *pattern*.

-force   If this option is set, an import command will overwrite existing commands with new ones from the *pattern* namespace. Otherwise, namespace import will return an error if a new command has the same name as an existing command.

pattern   The patterns to import. The pattern must include the *namespaceID* of the namespace from which items are being imported. There will be more details on naming rules in the next section.

The `namespace children` returns a list of the namespaces that are visible from a scope.

Syntax: `namespace children  ?scope? ?pattern?`

`namespace children`

> Returns a list of the namespaces that exist within *scope*. (If *scope* is not defined, the current scope is used.)

`?scope?`
> The namespace scope from which the list of namespaces will be returned. If this argument is not present, the list of namespaces visible from the current scope will be returned.

`?pattern?`
> Return only namespaces that match a glob pattern. If this argument is not present, all namespaces are returned.

The `variable` command declares that a variable is to be maintained within a namespace. These variables will not be destroyed when the namespace scope is exited. A variable defined with the `variable` command is equivalent to a variable defined in the `global` scope, except that the variable name is visible only within the scope of the namespace. This feature allows you to define persistent data that will be local to a namespace, easily accessed by all procedures in the namespace, and not pollute the global namespace.

Syntax: `variable varName ?value? ?varName2? ?value2?`

`variable`
> Declare a variable to exist within the current namespace. The arguments are pairs of name and value combinations.

`varName`
> The name of a variable.

`?value?`
> An optional value for the variable.

7.1.6 Creating and Populating a Namespace

A namespace is created with the `namespace eval` command. Because all the arguments with a `namespace eval` command are evaluated as a Tcl script, any command that can be evaluated can be used as an argument to the `namespace eval` command. This includes procedure definitions, setting variables, creating graphics widgets, etc.

A namespace can be populated with procedures and data either in a single namespace eval command or in multiple invocations of the namespace eval command.

The following example shows a namespace procedure that provides a unique number by incrementing a counter. The counter variable, staticVar, is maintained within the uniqueNumber namespace. The getUnique procedure, which is also defined within the uniqueNumber namespace, can access this variable easily, but code outside the uniqueNumber namespace cannot.

Example 7.1.6-1

Example Script

```
#
# Create a namespace.
namespace eval uniqueNumber {
    #
    # staticVar is a variable that will be retained between
    # evaluations
    # This declaration defines the variable and its initial
    # value.

    variable staticVar 0;

    #
    # allow getUnique to be imported into other scopes

    namespace export getUnique

    #
    # return a unique number by incrementing staticVar

    proc getUnique {} {
        #  This declaration of staticVar is the equivalent of a
        #     global - if it were not here, then a staticVar
        #     in the local procedure scope would be created.

        variable staticVar;
        return [incr staticVar];
    }
}

# Display the currently visible namespaces:
```

```
puts "Visible namespaces from the global scope are: \n \
    [namespace children]\n"

# Display "get*" commands that are visible in the global
#   scope before import

puts "Before import, global scope contains these \"get*\" \
    commands: \n  [info commands get*]"

# Import all exported members of the namespace uniqueNumber

namespace import ::uniqueNumber::*

# Display "get*" commands that are visible in the global
#   scope after importing
puts "After import, global scope contains these \"get*\" \
    commands: \n [info commands get*] \ n"

# Run getUnique a couple times to prove it works

puts "first Unique val: [getUnique]"
puts "second Unique val: [getUnique]"

# Display the current value of the staticVar variable

puts "staticVar: \
    [namespace eval uniqueNumber {set staticVar}]"

# The next line generates an error condition because
#     staticVar does not exist in the global scope.

puts "staticVar is: $staticVar"
```

Script Output

```
Visible namespaces from the global scope are:
   ::uniqueNumber

Before import, global scope has these "get*" commands:
   gets
After import, global scope contains these "get*" commands:
   gets getUnique

first Unique val: 1
second Unique val: 2
staticVar: 2
can't read "staticVar": no such variable
```

There are a few points to note in this example:

- The procedure `getUnique` can be declared as an exported name before the procedure is defined.

- After the `uniqueNumber` namespace is defined, there are two namespaces visible from the global scope—the `::uniqueNumber` namespace and the `::tcl` namespace. The `::tcl` namespace is always present when the Tcl interpreter is running.

- The `namespace import ::uniqueNumber::*` command imports all exported entities from `::uniqueNumber` into the global scope.

- The value of the `staticVar` variable can be accessed via the `namespace eval`. It can also be accessed as `::uniqueNumber::staticVar`.

- The `staticVar` variable is initialized by the line `variable staticVar 0` when the namespace is created. This code is equivalent to placing

  ```
  set staticVar 0
  ```

  within the arguments to `namespace eval`, which would cause the variable to be defined at the top scope of the `uniqueNumber` namespace.

7.1.7 Namespace Nesting

If procedures in two namespaces need functionality that exists in a third namespace, there are a couple of options. They can create a shared copy of the third namespace in the scope of the first two namespaces, or each can create a copy of the third namespace nested within its own namespace scope.

One advantage of nesting the third namespace is that it creates a unique copy of the persistent data defined within the third namespace. If a namespace is shared, then that data is also shared.

The next example shows the `unqiueNumber` namespace being nested within two separate namespaces (`Package1` and `Package2`). This allows each procedure in `Package1` and `Package2` to get unique numbers with no gaps between numbers.

If the `uniqueNumber` namespace were created at the global level and shared by `Package1` and `Package2`, then whenever either package called `getUnique` the unique number would be incremented.

Example 7.1.7-1

```
#
# This procedure creates a uniqueNumber namespace in the scope of
# the script that invokes it.

proc createUnique {} {
  uplevel 1 {
      namespace eval uniqueNumber {
          variable staticVal 0
          namespace export getUnique;
          proc getUnique {} {
              variable staticVal
              return [incr staticVal]
          }
      }
  }
}

# Create the Package1 namespace,
#  Create a uniqueNumber namespace within the Package1 namespace
# The Package1 namespace includes a procedure to report unique
# numbers

namespace eval Package1 {
  createUnique
  namespace import uniqueNumber::*

  proc pack1demo {} {
      return "pack1demoUnique.[getUnique]"
  }
}

# Create the Package2 namespace,
#  Create a uniqueNumber namespace within the Package2 namespace
# The Package2 namespace includes a procedure to report unique
# numbers

namespace eval Package2 {
  createUnique
  namespace import uniqueNumber::getUnique

  proc pack2demo {} {
      return "pack2demoUnique.[getUnique]"
  }
}
```

Example Script

```
puts "Package1 example returns: [::Package1::pack1demo]"
puts "invoking Package1::getUnique directly returns: \
    [Package1::getUnique]"
puts "Package1 example returns: [::Package1::pack1demo]"
puts ""
puts "Package2 example returns: [::Package2::pack2demo]"
puts "Package2 example returns: [::Package2::pack2demo]"
puts "Package2 example returns: [::Package2::pack2demo]"
```

Script Output

```
Package1 example returns: pack1demoUnique.1
invoking Package1::getUnique directly returns: 2
Package1 example returns: pack1demoUnique.3

Package2 example returns: pack2demoUnique.1
Package2 example returns: pack2demoUnique.2
Package2 example returns: pack2demoUnique.3
```

Note that the createUnique process uses the uplevel to force the namespace eval to happen at the same scope as the code that invoked createUnique. By default, a procedure will be evaluated in the scope in which it was defined. Since the createUnique procedure is created in the global scope, it will, by default, create the getUnique namespace as a child namespace of the global space. By using the uplevel command, we force the evaluation to take place in the scope of the calling script: within the package namespace.

Here's what the namespaces look like after the previous example has been evaluated.

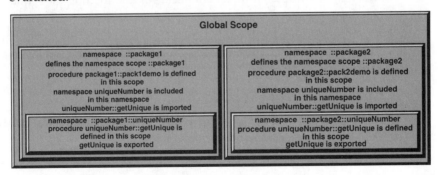

7.2 Packages

The `namespace` command allows you to encapsulate information and procedures within a script. The `package` commands allow you to group a set of procedures that may be in multiple files and identify them with a single name. The `package` command provides library functionality, while the `namespace` command provides encapsulation functionality.

This section will discuss how to turn a set of procedures into a package that can be automatically loaded by other scripts.

I've been calling a script with a collection of procedures and variables that work together to perform related functions a package. What's been developed so far in the examples isn't *really* a package in the Tcl sense, although it's close.

What's missing is the `package provide` command, which declares that this collection of procedures and variables is identified by a single identifier (the package name) and that this collection constitutes a particular revision of that package.

When a set of procedures have been identified this way, they can be indexed and loaded automatically when they are needed by a script.

The Tcl `package` command provides a framework for:

- Automatically loading files when a procedure defined within those files is required.
- Tracking the version numbers of packages and loading the requested version.
- Defining whether the file to be loaded is a script file (discussed here) or shared library/DLL (discussed in Chapter 12, Building Extensions).

7.2.1 How Packages Work

When a set of code is defined as a package, an index file is created that lists the procedures that are included in that package.

When the Tcl interpreter encounters an unrecognized command, it invokes a script that checks to see if that command is available in a known package.

If the procedure is not defined in any known package, then the Tcl interpreter reports an error. If the command can be acquired by loading a package, the interpreter does so and then evaluates the command line that caused the error again (presumably successfully).

The Tcl interpreter will search the index files in the directories listed in the global variable auto_path. The auto_path variable is defined in the init.tcl script, which is loaded when a Tcl or Tk interpreter is started.

This section will discuss how to generate the index files and how to add your package directories to the list of index files to be searched.

Note that when you create an index for a package that has procedures defined within a namespace, only the procedure names listed in a namespace export command will be indexed.

7.2.2 Internal Details: The Files and Variables Used with Packages

These files and global variables are used to find and load a package.

auto_path   global variable   The auto_path variable contains a list of the directories that should be searched for package index files.

The auto_path variable is defined in the init.tcl script, which is loaded when a tclsh interpreter is started.

On Unix systems, init.tcl will probably be found in /usr/local/lib/tcl8.0 or some variant, depending on your installation and the revision number of your tclsh. On Windows systems, init.tcl is stored in \Program Files\Tcl\lib\tcl8.0, or some variant depending again on your version of Tcl and the base directory in which you installed the Tcl interpreter.

auto_index	global array	The auto_index array is indexed with the names of procedures defined in pkgIndex.tcl files. The data associated with each index is the command to evaluate which will load the package that defines the procedure.

This command will resemble:

```
source /usr/myLibs/package.tcl
```

pkgIndex.tcl	file	These files contain a list of procedures defined by the packages in that directory. The pkgIndex.tcl files are created with the pkg_mkIndex command.

7.2.3 Package Commands

The package command has several subcommands. These are the ones you'll use to turn your scripts into a package.

The pkg_mkIndex command creates a package index file. It is not evaluated when a script is being evaluated, but it is evaluated when a package is being installed or tested.

The pkg_mkIndex command scans the files identified by the *patterns* for package provide commands and uses information in that command and the procedure definitions to create a file named pkgIndex.tcl in the current directory.

Syntax: pkg_mkIndex *dir pattern ?pattern?*

pkg_mkIndex	Creates an index of available packages. This index is searched by package require when it is determining where to find the packages.
dir	The directory in which the packages being indexed reside.
pattern ?patterns?	Glob-style patterns that define the files that will be indexed.

When the `pkg_mkIndex` command has finished evaluating the files that match the `pattern` arguments, it creates a file named `pkgIndex.tcl` in the `dir` directory. The `pkgIndex.tcl` file contains:

- The names of the packages defined in the files that matched the patterns.
- The version level of these packages.
- The names of the procedures defined in those packages.
- The name of the command to use to load the package.

The `pkg_mkIndex` will overwrite an existing `pkgIndex.tcl` file. If you are developing more than one package in a single directory, you will need to enter the name of each file every time you update the index. In this case, it may become simpler to create a two-line script that lists all the files:

```
#!/usr/local/bin/tclsh
pkg_mkIndex [pwd] file1.tcl file2.tcl file3.tcl
```

The `package provide` command defines the name and version of the package the procedures in this file are part of. This command is used in the scripts that provide procedures for other scripts to use.

Syntax: `package provide` *packageName ?version?*

`package provide`

> Declares that procedures in this script module are part of the package *packageName*. Optionally declares which *packageName* version this file represents.

`packageName`   The name of the package that will be defined in this script.

`?version?`   The version number of this package.

The `pkg_mkIndex` command looks for a `package provide` command in a file. It uses the package name and version information to generate an entry in the `pkgIndex.tcl` file with the name and version of the package and a list of all the procedures defined in this file.

When you place a `package provide` command in a Tcl script file, it tells the Tcl interpreter that all of the procedures in the file are members of a package.

You can use multiple files to construct your package, provided that there is a `package provide` command in each file.

Note that if you have multiple package provide commands with different *packageName* arguments in a source file, all the procedures in that source file will be members of all the packages described in the package provide commands. In this case, if any package listed in the package provide commands is required, then all the procedures will be loaded. You cannot define two separate, nonoverlapping packages in a single source file.

If you put multiple package provide commands with identical *packageName* but different *version* arguments, the pkg_mkIndex will generate an error.

The package require command declares that a procedure defined in a particular package will be used in this script. This command is used by scripts that use procedures defined in other files.

Syntax: package require ?-exact? *packageName* ?*versionNum*?

package require

> Informs the Tcl interpreter that this package may be needed during the execution of this script. The Tcl interpreter will attempt to find the package and be prepared to load it when required.

-exact

> If this flag is present, then *versionNum* must also be present. The Tcl interpreter will load only that version of the package.

packageName   The name of the package to load.

?versionNum?   The version number to load. If this parameter is provided, but -exact is not present, then the interpreter will allow newer versions of the package to be loaded, provided they have the same major version number (see Section 7.2.4 for details of version numbering). If this parameter is not present, any version of packageName may be loaded.

The package require command checks the pkgIndex.tcl files in the search path (defined in auto_path) and selects the best match to the version number requested. If the -exact flag is used, it will select an exact match to that version number. If versionNum is defined and the -exact is not set, the largest minor revision number greater than versionNum will be selected. If versionNum is not defined, then the highest available version will be selected. If an acceptable revision cannot be found, package require will generate an error.

Once the appropriate file has been identified, the global array auto_index is updated. The indices of this array are the names of procedures, and the data associated with each index is a Tcl command that will load the file that contains the procedure.

By delaying the loading of files until a procedure is required, Tcl avoids lengthy initialization times. By scanning the indices first and building the arrays, the interpreter can run until it needs a command that is not currently defined. At that point, the interpreter loads the script that defines the command and continues running. If a package is marked by the package require command, but no commands from that package are actually used, the Tcl interpreter never loads the file.

Note that when a package is loaded automatically it is loaded into the global scope, where the code that loads unknown procedures is evaluated. If you want to nest a namespace within another namespace and use the package require command to find the correct version of the package, you will need to force the package to load immediately. You can use the Tcl eval command to evaluate the command that the package require placed in auto_index. This will be discussed in more detail in the next set of tree examples.

7.2.4 Version Numbers

The package command has some notions about how version numbers are defined. The rules for version numbers are:

- Version numbers are one or two positive integers separated by periods, i.e., 1.2 or 75.19.

- The first integer in the string is the major revision number. As a general rule, this is changed only when the package undergoes a major modification. It is expected that there will be no application interface modifications within a major revision, but there may be changes such that code that worked with one major revision will not work with another.

- The second integer is the minor revision number. This corresponds to an intermediate release. You can expect that bugs will be fixed, performance enhanced, and new features added, but code that worked with a previous minor revision should work with later minor revisions.

- The revision numbers are compared integer by integer. Revision 2.0 is more recent than revision 1.99.

7.2.5 Package Cookbook

7.2.5.1 Creating a Package

1. Create the Tcl source file or files. You can split your package procedures across several files if you wish.

2. Add the command

   ```
   package provide packageName versionNumber
   ```

   to the beginning of these Tcl source files.

3. Invoke tclsh. If you have several revisions of Tcl installed on your system, be certain to invoke the correct tclsh. The package command was introduced with revision 7.6 and was modified slightly in Tcl 8.0 and Tcl 8.1.

4. At the % prompt, type

   ```
   pkg_mkIndex directory fileNamePattern ?Pattern2...?
   ```

   You may include multiple file names in this command. The pkg_mkIndex command will create a new file named pkgIndex.tcl with information about the files that were listed in the pkg_mkIndex command.

7.2.5.2 Using a Tcl Package

1. If the package is not located in one of the Tcl search directories listed by default in the auto_path variable, you must add the directory that contains the package's pkgIndex.tcl file to your search list. This can be done as follows:

   - Add a line resembling

     ```
     lappend auto_path /usr/project/packageDir
     ```

     in the beginning of your Tcl script.

   - Set the environment variable TCLLIBPATH to include your package directory. The environment variable need not include the path to the default Tcl library.

- Add your package directory to the `auto_path` definition in the `init.tcl file`. This file will be located in the Tcl library directory. The location of that directory is an installation option.

2. Add the line

   ```
   package require packageName ?versionNumber?
   ```

   in the beginning of your script.

3. If you need the package to load immediately, follow the `package require` command with

   ```
   global auto_index      # if this is within a procedure
   eval $auto_index(packageProcedureName)
   ```

There is more discussion about why this `eval` command is needed in the next section.

7.3 A Tree Object Package with Namespaces

This section will describe how to turn the `tree.tcl` and `treeObject.tcl` scripts we've developed into a pair of scripts that implement a tree object package with most of the commands protected within namespaces.

7.3.1 Adding Namespace and Package to `tree.tcl`

The first step in this process is to make the procedures defined within the `tree.tcl` file into a package with the procedures and variables enclosed within a namespace.

The beginning code for `tree.tcl` (which had been a set of Tcl procedure definitions) now looks like this:

Example 7.3.1-1

```
package provide tree 1.0

namespace eval tree {

# Export the public entry points

namespace export treeCreate treeCreateChild treeDestroyTree \
    treeDeleteNode
```

```
namespace export treeGetChildList treeGetParent treeSetNodeValue
namespace export treeGetNodeValue treeGetNodeValueList \
    treeGetRoot treeDump
namespace export treeSetTreeValue treeGetTreeValue \
    treeGetTreeValueList
namespace export treeGetSiblingList

# Tree_InternalArray is the array in which all nodes and trees
# reside.
# It is a persistent data object, shared among all procedures
# within this namespace.

variable Tree_InternalArray

# Initialize the base counter.

set Tree_InternalArray(base) 0;

#
proc treeCreate {} {
    variable Tree_InternalArray;
    #
    # Create the unique name for this tree.

    set primaryName "tree$Tree_InternalArray(base)"
    incr Tree_InternalArray(base)

    #
    # Set the initial unique ID for nodes in this tree.
    #
    set Tree_InternalArray($primaryName.base) 0;

    #
    # Create the root node
    #
    set rootNode [TreeCreateNode $primaryName.base]

    #
    # Looks good, ship it!
    #
    return $rootNode
}
....
}
```

The package provide tree 1.0 line informs Tcl that this file defines the tree package, revision level 1.0.

The namespace eval tree { evaluates all the following code as being within the tree namespace. This includes all of the procedure definitions and the Tree_InternalArray variable that had previously been maintained in the global namespace.

The namespace export commands allow the entry points to be accessed (and namespace imported) by other programs. The pkg_mkIndex command will put only exported names into the pkgIndex.tcl file; thus, any procedure that can be called from code outside the package should be listed here. Note that the internal tree procedure TreeGetNameParts is not listed here.

The Tree_InternalArray is declared to be a namespace variable with the variable Tree_InternalArray command. This line is not required. Simply defining a value for Tree_InternalArray would be sufficient. I prefer to make an explicit declaration.

Next, the base unique value for defining trees is set, and the treeCreate procedure is defined.

The procedure definition for treeCreate is identical to the original, except that the line global Tree_InternalArray has been changed to variable Tree_InternalArray. The other procedure definitions follow this pattern: the only change between the original procedure and the procedure within a namespace is that the word global is changed to variable.

If the Tree_InternalArray definition were left global, instead of being changed to variable, then the variable Tree_InternalArray would be created in the global scope instead of the namespace scope. The code would still work correctly, but we would not gain the encapsulation that the namespace command provides.

7.3.2 The Tree Object in a Namespace

Putting a namespace around the tree object described in Section 6.3 is a bit trickier. The treeObject package will nest the tree namespace within the treeObject namespace, rather than placing both namespaces at the global level. There will be one entry point (`newTreeObject`) in the global scope, where all scripts can access it, and the other procedure (`TreeObjProc`) inside the `treeObject` namespace, where it is hidden from most scripts.

By nesting the `tree` namespace within the `treeObject` namespace the `treeObject` acquires a private copy of the tree data and functions. This insulates the `treeObject` from possible collisions with other packages that might also be using the `tree` package.

The set of namespaces will resemble this after the `treeObject` package is loaded:

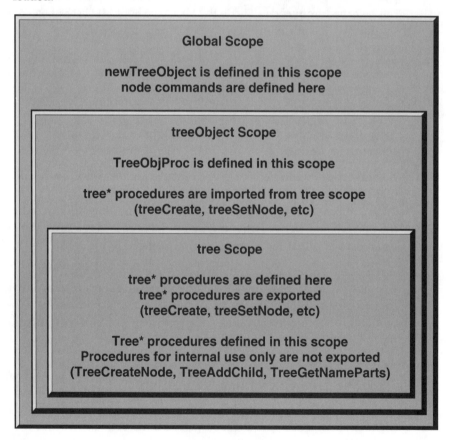

The code that implements this is:

Example 7.3.2-1

```
package provide treeObject 1.0

##############################################################
# proc newTreeObject {} --
#  Creates a new Tree object, and returns an object for
#    accessing the base node.
# Arguments:
#   NONE
#
# NOTE: This procedure is in global scope.
#
proc newTreeObject {} {
    set treeId [treeObject::tree::treeCreate]

    proc $treeId {args} "
        return \[treeObject::TreeObjProc $treeId \$args]
    "

    return $treeId
}

#
# These procedures are defined within the treeObject namespace
#

namespace eval treeObject {

#
# The tree package is required.  This causes the Tcl
#     interpreter to search the pkgIndex.tcl files and
#     set the fields in auto_index
#
package require tree 1.0

#
# In order to import the tree procedures, we need to force
#     the package to load.
```

```
#
# The package is identified with an absolute namespace
#  path in auto_index(), so that's how we identify it here.
# However, since we are loading the package within the
#  treeObject namespace, the package will be nested within
#  treeObject.

if {[info exists auto_index(::tree::treeCreate)]} {
    eval $auto_index(::tree::treeCreate)
    namespace import tree::*
}
################################################################
# proc TreeObjProc {node methodArgs} --
#   ...
# Results:
#    Calls other procedures which may produce output,
#       create new objects, delete objects, etc.
proc TreeObjProc {node methodArgs} {
    set subCommand [lindex $methodArgs 0]
...
```

Again, the package provide command defines this package as being the treeObject package.

The newTreeObject procedure has been changed from the original version to reflect the fact that this procedure is defined in a different scope than other procedures in the treeObject package, and the procedures in the tree package are defined in a namespace nested within that.

The treeCreate procedure is invoked by its relative namespace path. The relative path from the current scope is used here because the current scope could be the global scope, or the treeObject namespace could be nested within another namespace.

The procedure definition for the new tree node that is defined within newTreeObject invokes treeObject::TreeObjProc by a relative path for the same reason.

The next line, namespace eval treeObject {, starts the definition of the treeObject namespace.

The next set of lines nests the `tree` namespace within the `treeObject` namespace.

The `package require tree` line causes the Tcl interpreter to search the `pkgIndex.tcl` files for information on how to load the `tree` package. When the source for the `tree` namespace is identified, those methods are stored in the `auto_index` variable.

As mentioned previously in this chapter, if we wait for the unknown procedure to be invoked to load the `tree` package automatically, it will be loaded at the global level, not nested within the `treeObject` package.

The next line, `if {[info exists auto_index(::tree::treeCreate)]}`, tests to confirm that one of the expected indices into `auto_index` has been set. This index should be set. The only way for it not to be set is for another `tree` package to be defined in your search path that doesn't have a `treeCreate` procedure defined.

If this index into `auto_index` exists, it will contain a command script that will load the `tree` package (and resolve the undefined procedure `treeCreate`). It will resemble

```
source /usr/TclPackages/treeName.tcl
```

with a directory path that reflects where `treeName.tcl` is installed on your system.

The next line:

```
eval $auto_index(::tree::treeCreate)
```

evaluates the script and loads the `tree` package.

The last line in setting up the namespace is to import the procedures from the `tree` namespace into the `treeObject` namespace. This is done with the command `namespace import tree::*`, which will import all the entities exported from `tree`. Note that these procedure names are being imported into the `treeObject` namespace, not into the global namespace. Importing into this space simplifies writing the `treeObject` code without polluting the global space.

7.3.3 Procedures and Namespace Scopes

What happens if you evaluate a command in a namespace that is not defined in that namespace? When Tcl evaluates a command, it tries first to evaluate a version of the command that is local to the current namespace. If that fails, it attempts to evaluate the command in the global namespace. Tcl does not promote a command through a series of nested namespaces.

The following example creates a tree object, adds a child, and then displays what tree procedures are available at which scopes. The procedures created for the new tree nodes, tree0.1 and tree0.2, are available at the global scope, along with the procedure for creating new trees, newTreeObject All the other procedures in this package are hidden in the namespaces. Notice that TreeAddChild and TreeCreateNode are not exported from the tree namespace. They are visible within the tree namespace but not the treeObject namespace.

Note that when the info commands is evaluated in the ::treeObject::tree namespace, the output includes the tree commands in the ::treeObject::tree and global scopes, but not in the ::treeObject scope.

The info commands command reports only the procedures that are visible in the scope where the command is evaluated. Tcl will not search the parent namespace to find a procedure; thus, commands in the parent namespace are not visible from a child namespace.

Example 7.3.3-1

Example Script

```
# Include the Tree directory in the auto search path
lappend auto_path "../Tree"

package require treeObject 1.0

# Create a new tree and a child node - two nodes total.

set base [newTreeObject]
set child1 [$base add]

# Display the commands defined in the global scope
```

```
puts "Tree Commands defined at global scope: \
    \n    [lsort [info commands *ree*]]"

# Display the commands defined in the
#    treeObject namespace scope

set treeObjectCmds [lsort [info commands ::treeObject::* ]]

# The regsub command replaces the string "::treeObject::"
# with "" in each of the commands listed in treeObjectCmds
# to make the names more readable.

regsub -all {::treeObject::} $treeObjectCmds "" treeObjectCmds

puts "\nTree Commands defined at treeObject scope: \
    \n $treeObjectCmds"

# Display the commands defined in the
#    treeObject::tree namespace scope

set treeCmds [lsort [info commands ::treeObject::tree::*]]
regsub -all {::treeObject::tree::} $treeCmds "" treeCmds

puts "\nTree Commands defined at treeObject::tree scope: \
    \n    $treeCmds"

set treeCmds [lsort [namespace eval ::treeObject::tree \
    {info commands *ree*}]]
puts "Tree Commands visible from treeObject::tree scope:\
    \n    $treeCmds"

puts "tree0.1 body: [info body tree0.1]"
```

Script Output

Tree Commands defined at global scope:
**   newTreeObject tree0.1 tree0.2**

Tree Commands defined at treeObject scope:
**   TreeObjProc treeCreate treeCreateChild**
treeDeleteNode treeDestroyTree treeDump treeGetRoot
treeGetChildList treeGetNodeValue treeGetNodeValueList
treeGetParent treeGetSiblingList treeGetTreeValue
treeGetTreeValueList treeSearchKey treeSetNodeValue
treeSetTreeValue

```
Tree Commands defined at treeObject::tree scope:
    TreeAddChild TreeCreateNode TreeGetNameParts
treeCreate treeCreateChild treeDeleteNode
treeDestroyTree treeDump treeGetRoot treeGetChildList
treeGetNodeValue treeGetNodeValueList treeGetParent
treeGetSiblingList treeGetTreeValue treeGetTreeValueList
    treeSearchKey treeSetNodeValue treeSetTreeValue

Tree Commands visible from treeObject::tree scope:
    TreeAddChild TreeCreateNode TreeGetNameParts
newTreeObject tree0.1 tree0.2 treeCreate treeCreateChild
treeDeleteNode treeDestroyTree treeDump treeGetRoot
treeGetChildList treeGetNodeValue treeGetNodeValueList
treeGetParent treeGetSiblingList treeGetTreeValue
treeGetTreeValueList treeSearchKey treeSetNodeValue
treeSetTreeValue

tree0.1 body:
        return [treeObject::TreeObjProc tree0.1 $args]
```

7.4 Bottom Line

Tcl libraries (packages) can be built from one or more files of Tcl scripts.

The package commands provide support for declaring what revision level of a package is provided and what revision level is required.

Tcl namespaces can be used to hide procedures and data from the global scope.

- The namespace commands manipulate the namespaces.
  - The namespace eval command evaluates its arguments within a particular namespace.

    Syntax: namespace eval *namespaceID arg ?args?*

  - The namespace export command makes its arguments visible outside the current scope.

    Syntax: namespace export *pattern ?patterns?*

- The `namespace import` will make the entities within a namespace local to the current scope.

  Syntax: `namespace import` *?-force? ?pattern?*

- The `variable` command declares a variable to be static within a namespace. The variable is not destroyed when procedures in the namespace scope complete processing.

  Syntax: `variable` *varName ?value? ?varName2? ?value2?*

- The `package` commands provide methods for manipulating packages.

  - The `package provide` command declares the name of a package being defined in a source file.

    Syntax: `package provide` *packageName ?version?*

  - The `package requires` command declares what packages a script may require.

    Syntax: `package require ?-exact?` *packageName ?versionNum?*

- The `pkg_mkIndex` command creates the `pkgIndex.tcl` file that lists the procedures defined in appropriate files.

  Syntax: `pkg_mkIndex` *dir pattern ?pattern?*

CHAPTER 8   *Introduction to Tk Graphics*

Everyone knows the fun part about computer programming is the graphics. The Tk graphics package lets a Tcl programmer enjoy this fun too. Tk is a package of graphics widgets that provide the tools to build complete graphic applications. Tk supports the usual GUI widgets like buttons and menus, complex widgets like color and file selectors, and data display widgets like an editable text window and an interactive drawing canvas.

The user interaction widgets include buttons, menus, scrollbars, sliders, pop-up messages, and text entry widgets. A script can display either text or graphics with the text and canvas widgets.

Tk provides three algorithms to control the layout of a display and a widget to group widgets.

Finally, if none of the standard widgets do what you want, the Tk package supports low-level tools at both the script and C API levels to build your own graphical widgets.

The Tk widgets are very configurable. For most widgets, you can set the background colors, foreground colors, and border widths. Some classes of widgets have special-purpose options such as font, line color, and behavior when selected. This chapter will discuss some of the more frequently used options but won't try to be complete. Consult the online manual pages with your installation for a complete list of options supported with your version of Tcl/Tk.

Like most GUI packages, the Tk package is geared toward event-driven programming. If you are already familiar with event-driven programming, skip to Section 8.1. If not, the next paragraphs will give you a quick overview of event-driven programming.

Using traditional programming, your program watches for something to happen and then reacts to it. For instance, user interface code resembles this:

```
while {![eof stdin]} {
    gets command
    switch $command {
        "cmd1" {doCmd1}
        "cmd2" {doCmd2}
        default {unrecognized command}
    }
}
```

The user interface code will wait until a user types in a command and then evaluate that command. In between commands, the program does nothing. While a command is being evaluated, the user interface is inactive.

With event-driven programming there is an event loop that watches for events, and when an event occurs it invokes the procedure that was defined to handle that event. This event may be a button press, a clock event, or data becoming available on a channel. Whenever the program is not processing a user request, it is watching for events.

In this case, the user interface pseudocode resembles:

```
WHEN {user types a carriage return} {parseUserInput}
  WHEN {clock registers 00 seconds} {updateClockDisplay}
  WHEN {user presses button A} {buttonA_Command}
  processEventLoop
```

With Tk, the details of registering procedures for events and running an event loop are handled largely behind the scenes. At the time you create a widget you can register a procedure to be evaluated whenever the widget is selected, and the event loop simply runs whenever there is no other processing going on.

8.1 Creating a Widget

The standard form for the command to create a Tk widget is:

Syntax: WidgetClass *widgetName* *requiredArguments* *?options?*

WidgetClass   A primitive widget type, such as `button`, `label`, or `scrollbar`.

widgetName   The name for this widget. Must conform to the naming Tk conventions that are described in the next section.

required Arguments
     Some Tk widgets have required arguments.

?options?   Tk widgets support a large number of options that define the fonts, colors, actions to be taken when the widget is selected, etc.

For example, this line:

```
label .hello -text "Hello, World."
```

will create a label widget named `.hello`, with the text `Hello, World`.

As part of creating a widget, Tcl creates a command named `widgetName`. After the widget is created, your script can interact with the widget via this command. This is similar to the way the tree object was created and manipulated in Chapter 6. Tk widgets support commands for setting and retrieving configuration options, querying the widget for its current state, and other widget-specific commands such as scrolling the view, selecting items, and reporting selections.

The `label` in the preceding example will appear in the default window. When the `wish` interpreter starts, it creates a default window for graphics named ".".

8.2 Conventions

There are a few conventions for widgets supported by Tk. These conventions include naming conventions for the widgets and colors and the conventions for describing screen locations, sizes and distances.

8.2.1 Widget Naming Conventions

A widget or window name must start with a period and may be followed by a label. The label may start with a lowercase letter, digit, or punctuation mark. After the first character, other characters may be upper- or lowercase letters, numbers, or punctuation marks (except periods). It's recommended that you use a lowercase letter to start the label.

The Tk graphics widgets are named in a tree fashion, similar to a filesystem or the naming convention for namespaces. Instead of the slash used to separate filenames, widget and window names are separated by periods. Thus, the root window is named ".", and a widget created in the root window could be named .widget1.

Some widgets can contain other widgets. In that case, the widget is identified by the complete name from the top dot to the referenced widget. Tk widgets must be named by absolute window path, not relative. Thus, if widget one contains widget two, which contains widget three, you would access the last widget as .one.two.three.

A widget path name must be unique. You can have multiple widgets named .widget1 if they are contained in different widgets, e.g., .main.widget1 and .subwin.widget1.

8.2.2 Color Naming Conventions

Colors may be declared with a color name (red, green, lavender, etc.) or with a hexadecimal representation of the red/green/blue intensities.

The hexadecimal representation starts with the # character, followed by 3, 6, 9, or 12 hexadecimal digits. The number of digits used to define a color must be a multiple of three. The number will be split into three hexadecimal values, with an equal number of digits in each value, and assigned to the red, green, and blue color intensities in that order. The intensities range from 0 (black) to 0xF, 0xFF, 0xFFF, or 0xFFFF (full brightness), depending on the number of digits used to define the colors.

Thus, #f00 (bright red, no green, no blue) creates deep red, #aa02dd (medium red, dim green, medium blue) creates purple, and #ffffeeee0000 (bright red, bright green, no blue) creates a golden yellow.

8.2.3 Dimension Conventions

The size or location of a Tk object is given as a number followed by an optional unit identifier. The numeric value is maintained as a floating-point value. Even pixels can be described as fractions. If there is no unit identifier, then the numeric value defaults to pixels. You can describe a size or location in inches, millimeters, centimeters, or points (1/72 of an inch) by using the unit identifiers shown in the following examples.

15.3	15.3 pixels
1.5i	1 1/2 inches
10m	10 millimeters (1 cm)
1.3c	1.3 centimeters (13 mm)
90p	90 points (1 1/4 inches)

8.3 Common Options

The Tk widgets support many display and action options. Fortunately, these options have reasonable default values associated with them; thus you don't need to define every option for every widget you use.

These are some common options supported by many Tk widgets. They will be described once here, rather than with each widget that supports these options. Widget-specific options will be defined with the individual widget discussions.

The complete list of options and descriptions is in the Tcl/Tk online documentation under options.

-background *color*

> The background color for a widget.

-borderwidth *width*

> The width of the border to be drawn around widgets with three-dimensional effects.

-font *fontDescriptor*

> The font to use for widgets that display text. Fonts will be discussed more in Chapter 10, with the text widget.

-foreground *color*

> The foreground color for a widget. This is the color that text will be drawn in a text widget or on a label. It accepts the same color names and descriptions as -background.

-height *number*

> The requested height of the widget in pixels.

-highlightbackground *color*

> The color rectangle to draw around a widget when the widget does not have input focus.

-highlightcolor *color*

> The color rectangle to draw around a widget when the widget has input focus.

-padx *number* -pady *number*

> The -padx and -pady options request extra space (in pixels) to be placed around the widgets when they are arranged in another widget or the main window.

-relief *condition*

> The three-dimensional relief for this widget: condition may be raised, sunken, flat, ridge, solid, or groove.

-text *text*   The text to display in this widget.

-textvariable *varName*
> The name of a variable to associate with this widget. The contents of the variable will reflect the contents of the widget. e.g., the textvariable associated with an entry widget will contain the characters typed into the entry widget.

-width *number*
> The requested width of the widget in pixels.

8.4 Determining and Setting Options

The value of an option can be set when a widget is created or can be queried and modified after the widget is created using the cget and configure commands.

The cget subcommand will return the value of a widget option.

Syntax: *widgetName* cget *option*

widgetName   The name of this widget.

cget   Return the value of a single configuration option.

option   The name of the option to return the value of.

The configure subcommand will either return a single configuration option value, return all the configuration options available for a widget, or allow you to set one or more configuration options.

Syntax: *widgetName* configure *?opt1? ?val1? ?opt2? ?val2?*

widgetName   The widget being set/queried.

configure   Return or set configuration values.

opt1   The first option to set/query.

?val1?   The value to set for *option1*.

If configure is evaluated with no options, then a list of all the available options and values is returned.

If configure is evaluated with a single option, it returns a list consisting of the option name, the name and class that can be used to define this option in the windowing system resource file, the default value for the option, and the current value for the option.

If configure is evaluated with option value pairs, it will set the options to the defined values.

The following example creates a button that uses the configure command to change its label when it is clicked. We'll go over the -command option and the pack command later in this chapter.

Example 8.4-1

Example Script

```
set clickButton [button .b1 -text "Please Click Me" \
        -command {.b1 configure -text "I've been Clicked!"}]
pack .b1
```

Script Results

Before Click

After Click

8.5 The Basic Widgets

These primitive widgets are supported in the Tk 8.0 distribution:

button   A clickable button that may evaluate a command when it is selected.

radiobutton   A set of on/off buttons and labels, one of which may be selected.

checkbutton   A set of on/off buttons and labels, many of which may be selected.

entry	A widget that can be used to accept a single line of textual input.
message	Creates a new window with a text message.
label	A widget with read-only text in it.
scale	A slider widget that can call a procedure when the selected value changes.
menubutton	A button that displays a scrolldown menu when clicked.
menu	A holder for menu items. This is attached to a menubutton.
listbox	Creates a widget that displays a list of options, one or more of which may be selected. The listbox may be scrolled.
scrollbar	Attaches a scrollbar to widgets that support a scrollbar. Will call a procedure when the scrollbar is modified.
frame	A container widget to hold other widgets.
toplevel	A window with all the borders and decorations supplied by the window manager.
text	A widget for displaying and optionally editing large bodies of text.
canvas	A drawing widget for displaying graphics and images.

8.6 Introducing Widgets: `label`, `button`, and `entry`

The `label`, `button`, and `entry` widgets are the easiest widgets to use. The `label` widget simply displays a line of text, the `button` widget evaluates a Tcl script when it is selected, and the `entry` widget accepts user input.

All Tcl widget creation commands return the name of the widget they created. A good coding technique is to save that name in a variable and access the widget through that variable rather than hardcoding the widget names in your code.

Syntax: `label` *labelName* `?option1? ?option2?` ...

`label`	Create a `label` widget.
`labelName`	The name for this widget.
option	Valid options for `label` include:

`-font` *fontDescriptor*

> Defines the font to use for this display. Font descriptors will be discussed in Chapter 10.

`-textvariable` *varName*

> A variable that contains the display text.

`-text` *displayText*

> Text to display. If `-textvariable` is also used, the variable will be set to this value when the widget is created.

Note that the options can be defined in any order in the following example.

Example 8.6-1

Example Script

```
set txt [label .l1 -relief raised -text \
    "Labels can be configured with text"]
pack $txt
set var [label .l2 -textvariable label2Var -relief sunken]
set label2Var "Or by using a variable"
pack $var
```

Script Output

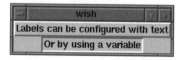

The `button` widget will evaluate a script when a user clicks it with the mouse. The script may be any set of Tcl commands, including procedure calls. By default, a script attached to a widget will be evaluated in the global scope. The scope in which a widget's `-command` script will be evaluated can be modified with the `namespace current` command, which will be discussed in Section 9.6.

Syntax: button *buttonName* *?option1?* *?option2?* ...

button   Create a button widget.

buttonName   The name to be assigned to the widget.

?options?   Valid options for button include:

-font *fontDescriptor*

> Defines the font to use for this button. Font descriptors will be discussed in Chapter 10.

-command *script*

> A script to evaluate when the button is clicked.

-text *displayText*

> The text that will appear in this button. A newline character (\n) can be embedded in this text to create multiline buttons.

Example 8.6-2

Example Script

```
set theLabel [label .l1 -text "This is the beginning text"]
set myButton [button .b1 -text "click to modify label" \
    -command "$theLabel configure -text \
        {The Button was Clicked}"]
pack $theLabel
pack $myButton
```

Script Results

Before Click

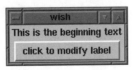

After Click

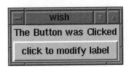

The `entry` widget allows a user to enter a string of data. This data can be longer than will fit in the widget's displayed area. The widget will automatically scroll to display the last character typed and can be scrolled back and forth with the arrow keys or by attaching the widget to a scrollbar (we'll get to scrollbars later in this chapter).

The `entry` widget can be configured to reflect its contents in a variable, or your script can query the widget for its contents.

Syntax: *entry entryName ?options?*

entry	Create an `entry` widget.
entryName	The name for this widget
?options?	Valid options for `label` include:

-font *fontDescriptor*

Defines the font to use for this display. Font descriptors will be discussed in Chapter 10.

-textvariable *VarName*

The variable named here will be set to the value in the entry widget.

-justify *side*

Justify the input data to the left margin of the widget (for entering textual data) or the right margin (for entering numeric data). Values for this option are `right` or `left`.

Example 8.6-3

Example Script

```
set input [entry .e1 -textvariable inputval]
set action [button .b1 -text "Convert to UPPERCASE" \
    -command {set inputval [string toupper $inputval]} ]
pack $input
pack $action
```

Script Results

| *Before Click* | *After Click* |

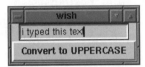

Note that the button command in Example 8.6.2 was enclosed within quotes, while the command in Example 8.6.3 was enclosed within curly brackets. In Example 8.6.2 we want the variable `theLabel` to be replaced by the actual name of the variable while the `button` command is being evaluated. The command being bound to the button is:

```
.l1 configure -text {The Button was Clicked}
```

Thus, if we change the contents of the variable `theLabel`, the command will still configure the original widget that it was linked to, .l1, not the window now associated with $thelabel.

In Example 8.6.3, we do not want the substitution to occur when the button is created, we want the substitution to occur when the button is clicked. When the command is placed within brackets, the command bound to the button is:

```
set inputval [string toupper $inputval]
```

and $inputval will be replaced by the contents of the `inputval` variable when the button is selected.

If the command for Example 8.6.3 were enclosed in quotes, the command bound to the button would have been:

```
set inputval [string toupper ""]
```

since the variable `inputval` is empty. In this case, clicking the button would cause the entry field to be cleared.

8.7 *Widget Layout:* `frame`, `place`, `pack`, *and* `grid`

Stacking one widget atop another is useful for extremely simple examples, but real-world applications need a bit more structure. Tk includes three layout managers, `place`, `pack`, and `grid`, and a widget to group other widgets, the `frame`.

The layout managers allow you to describe how the widgets in your application should be arranged. The layout managers use different algorithms for describing how a set of widgets should be arranged. Thus, the options supported by the managers have little overlap.

All of the window managers support the `-in` option, which defines the window in which a widget should be displayed. By default, a widget will be displayed in its immediate parent widget. For example, a button named `.mainButton` would be packed in the root (.) window, while a button named `.buttonFrame.controls.offButton` would default to being displayed in the `.controls` widget, which is displayed in the `.buttonFrame` widget.

Using the tree-style naming conventions and default display parent for widgets makes code easier to read. This technique documents the widget hierarchy in the widget name. However, the default display parent can be overridden with the `-in` option if your program requires this control.

8.7.1 The `frame` Widget

You frequently need to group a set of widgets when you are designing a display. For instance, you'll probably want all the buttons placed near each other and all the results displayed as a group. The Tk widget for grouping other widgets is the `frame`.

The `frame` is a rectangular container widget that groups other widgets. You can define the height and width of a `frame` or let it automatically size itself to fit the contents.

Syntax: `frame` *frameName* `?options?`

`frame`	Create a `frame` widget.
frameName	The name for the `frame`.

?options?   The options for a `frame` include:

-height *numPixels*
                 Height in pixels.

-width numPixels
                 Width in pixels.

-background *color*
                 The color of the background.

-relief ?sunken?raised?
                 Defines how to draw the border edges—
                 can make the `frame` look raised or sunken.
                 The default is not to display relief borders.

-borderwidth *width*
                 Sets the width of the decorative borders.
                 The `width` value may be any valid size
                 value (as described in Section 8.2.3).

A display can be divided into frames by functionality; for example, an application that interfaces with a database would have an area for the user to enter query fields, an area with the database displays, an area of buttons to generate searches, etc. This could be broken down into three primary frames: `.entry-Frame`, `.displayFrame`, and `.buttonFrame`. Within each of these frames would be the other widgets, with names such as `.entryFrame.userName`, `.display-Frame.securityRating`, and `.buttonFrame.search`.

8.7.2 The `place` Command

The `place` command lets you declare precisely where a widget should appear in the display window. This location can be declared as an absolute location or a relative location based on the size of the window. Applications that use few widgets or need precise control are easily programmed with the `place` layout manager. For most applications, however, the `place` layout manager has too much programmer overhead.

Syntax: place *widgetName option ?options?*

place   Declare the location of a widget in the display.

widgetName   The name of the widget being placed.

option   The `place` command requires at least one of these placement options:

- An absolute location in pixels

  `-x` *xLocation*

  `-y` *yLocation*

- A relative location given as a fraction of the distance across the window

  `-relx` *xRelativeLocation*

  `-rely` *yRelativeLocation*

- The parent window for this widget. The parent may be a frame or a top-level window, such as ".".

  `-in` *windowName.*

The following example uses the `place` command to build a simple application that calculates a 15% sales tax on purchases. As you can see, there is a lot of overhead in placing the widgets. You need a good idea of how large widgets will be, how large your window is, etc. in order to make a pretty screen.

Example 8.7.2-1

Example Script

```
# Create the "quit" and "calculate" buttons
set quitbutton [button .quitbutton -text "Quit" -command "exit" ]

set gobutton [button .gobutton -text "Calculate Sales Tax" \
        -command {set salesTax [expr $userInput * 0.15]}]

# Create the label prompt, and entry widgets
set input [entry .input -textvariable userInput]
set prompt [label .prompt -text "Base Price:"]

# Create the label and result widgets
set tax [label .tax -text "Tax :"]
set result [label .result -textvariable salesTax -relief raised]
```

```
# Set the size of the window
. configure -width 250 -height 100

# Place the buttons near the bottom
place $quitbutton -relx .75 -rely .7
place $gobutton -relx .01 -rely .7

# Place the input widgets near the top.
place $prompt -x 0 -y 0
place $input -x 70 -y 0

# Place the results widgets in the middle

place $tax -x 0 -y 30
place $result -x 40 -y 30
```

Script Result

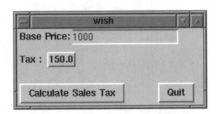

8.7.3 The **pack** Command

The pack command is quite a bit easier to use than place. With the pack command, you declare the positions of widgets relative to each other and let the pack command worry about the details.

Syntax: pack *widgetName ?options?*

pack   Place and display the widget in the display window.

widgetName   The widget to be displayed.

?options?   The pack has many options. These options are the most used:

                  -side *side*   Declares that this widget should be packed
                                  closest to a given side of the parent window.
                                  The side argument may be one of top, bot-
                                  tom, left, or right. The default is top.

-expand *boolean*

> If set to 1 or yes, the widget will be expanded to fill available space in the parent window. The default is 0: do not expand to fill the space. The boolean argument may be one of 1,yes,0, or no.

-fill *direction*

> Defines whether a widget may expand to fill extra space in its parcel. The direction argument may be

none	Do not fill
x	Fill horizontally
y	Fill vertically
both	Fill both horizontally and vertically

> The default is none.

-padx *number*

> Declares how many pixels to leave as a gap between widgets.

-pady *number*

> Declares how many pixels to leave as a gap between widgets.

-after *widgetName*

> Pack this widget after (on top of) *widgetName*.

The pack algorithm works by allocating a rectangular parcel of display space and filling it in a given direction. If a widget does not require all the available space in a given dimension, the parent widget will "show through" unless the -expand or -fill option is used.

The following example shows how a label widget will be packed with a frame with various combinations of the -fill and -expand options being used.

Example 8.7.3-1

Example Script

```
# Create a root frame with a black background, and pack it.

frame .root -background black
pack .root

# Create a frame with two labels to allocate 2 labels worth of
# vertical space.
# Note that the twoLabels frame shows through where the top
# label doesn't fill.

frame .root.twoLabels -background gray50
label .root.twoLabels.upperLabel -text "twoLabels no fill top"
label .root.twoLabels.lowerLabel -text "twoLabels no fill lower"

pack .root.twoLabels -side left
pack .root.twoLabels.upperLabel -side top
pack .root.twoLabels.lowerLabel -side bottom

# Create a frame and label with no fill or expand options used.
# Note that the .nofill frame is completely covered by the
# label, and the root frame shows at the top and bottom

frame .root.nofill -background gray50
label .root.nofill.label -text "nofill, noexpand"

pack .root.nofill -side left
pack .root.nofill.label

# Create a frame and label pair with the -fill option used when
# the frame is packed.
# In this case, the frame fills in the Y dimension to use all
# available space, and the label is packed at the top of
# the frame. The .fill frame shows through below the label.

frame .root.fill_frame -background gray50
label .root.fill_frame.label -text "fill frame"

pack .root.fill_frame -side left -fill y
pack .root.fill_frame.label

# Create a label that can fill, while the frame holding it will
# not.
```

```
# In this case, the frame is set to the size required to hold
# the widget, and the widget uses all that space.

frame .root.fill_label -background gray50
label .root.fill_label.label -text "fill label"

pack .root.fill_label -side left
pack .root.fill_label.label -fill y

# Allow both the frame and widget to fill.
# The frame will fill the available space,
#   but the label will not expand to fill the frame.

frame .root.fillBoth -background gray50
label .root.fillBoth.label -text "fill label and frame"

pack .root.fillBoth -side left -fill y
pack .root.fillBoth.label -fill y

# Allow both the frame and widget to expand and fill.
# The -expand option allows the widget to expand into extra
# space.
# The -fill option allows the widget to fill the available
# space.

frame .root.expandFill -background gray50
label .root.expandFill.label -text "expand and fill label and
frame"

pack .root.expandFill -side left -fill y -expand y
pack .root.expandFill.label -fill y -expand y
```

Script Results

The pack command is good at arranging widgets that will go in a line or need to fill a space efficiently. It's somewhat less intuitive when you are trying to create a complex display.

The solution to this problem is to construct your display out of frames and use the pack command to arrange widgets within the frame, and again to arrange the frames within your display.

For many applications, grouping widgets within a frame and then using the pack command is the easiest way to create the application.

The following example will show a fairly common technique of making a frame to hold a label prompt and an entry widget.

Example 8.7.3-2

Example Script

```
# Create the frames for the widgets

set buttonFrame [frame .buttons]
set inputFrame [frame .input]
set resultFrame [frame .results]

# Create the widgets
set quitbutton [button .buttons.quitbutton -text "Quit" \
    -command "exit"]
set gobutton [button .buttons.gobutton -text \
    "Calculate Sales Tax" \
        -command {set salesTax [expr $userInput * 0.15]}]

set input [entry .input.input -textvariable userInput]
set prompt [label .input.prompt -text "Base Price:"]

set tax [label .results.tax -text "Tax :"]
set result [label .results.result -textvariable salesTax \
    -relief raised]

# Pack the widgets into their frames.

pack .buttons.quitbutton -side right
pack .buttons.gobutton -side right

pack $input -side right
pack $prompt -side left

pack $tax -side left
pack $result -side left

# Pack the frames into the display window.
```

```
pack .buttons -side bottom
pack $inputFrame -side top

# The left example image is created by setting
#     withFill to 0 outside this code snippet.
# The right example image is created by setting
#     withFill to 1 outside this code snippet.

if {$withFill} {
    pack $resultFrame -after $inputFrame -fill x
} else {
    pack $resultFrame -after $inputFrame
}
```

Script Results

With `-fill`	*Without* `-fill`
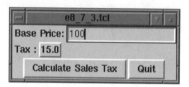	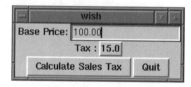

Note the way the `-side` option is used in the previous example. The buttons are packed with `-side` set to `right`. The `pack` command will place the first widget with a `-side` option set against the requested edge of the parent frame. Subsequent widgets will be placed as close to the requested side as possible without displacing a widget that previously requested that side of the frame.

The `-fill x` option to the `pack $resultFrame` allows the frame that holds the `$tax` and `$result` widgets to expand to the entire width of the window, as shown in the **With -fill** result.

By default, a frame is only as big as it needs to be to contain its child widgets. Without the `-fill` option, the `resultFrame` would be the narrowest of the frames and would be packed in the center of the middle row, as shown in the **Without -fill** result. With the `-fill` option set to fill in the X dimension, the frame can expand to be as wide as the window that contains it, and the widgets packed on the left side of the frame will line up with the left edge of the window instead of lining up on the left edge of a small frame.

If you want a set of widgets .a, .b, and .c to be lined up from left to right, you can pack them as

```
pack .a -side left
pack .b -side left
pack .c -side left
```

8.7.4 The **grid** Command

Many graphic layouts are conceptually grids. The grid layout manager is ideal for these sorts of applications, since it lets you declare that a widget should appear in a cell at a particular column and row. The grid manager then determines how large columns and rows need to be to fit the various components.

Syntax: grid *widgetName ?widgetNames? option*

grid	Place and display the widget in the display window.
widgetName	The widget to be displayed.
?options?	The grid has many options. This is a minimal set:

    -column *columnNumber*
            The column position for this widget.

    -row *rowNumber*
            The row for this widget.

    -columnspan *columnsToUse*
            How many columns to use for this widget. Defaults to 1.

    -sticky *side*
            Which edge of the cell this widget should "stick" to. Values may be n, s, e, w, ns, or ew.

The -sticky option lets your script declare that a widget should "stick" to the north (top), south (bottom), east (right), or west (left) edge of the grid that it's placed within. By default, a widget is centered within its cell.

Any of the options for the grid command can be reset after a widget is packed with the grid configure command.

Syntax: grid configure *widgetName* -option *optionValue*

grid configure

        Change one or more of the configuration options for a widget previously positioned with the grid command.

widgetName   The name of the widget to have a configuration option changed.

-option -optionValue

        The option and value to modify (or set).

Example 8.7.4-1

Example Script

```
set quitbutton [button .quitbutton -text "Quit" -command "exit" ]

set gobutton [button .gobutton -text "Calculate Sales Tax" \
        -command {set salesTax [expr $userInput * 0.15]}]

set input [entry .input -textvariable userInput]
set prompt [label .prompt -text "Base Price:"]

set tax [label .tax -text "Tax :"]
set result [label .result -textvariable salesTax -relief raised]

grid $quitbutton $gobutton -row 3

grid $prompt $input -row 1

grid $tax $result -row 2 -sticky w
```

Script Output

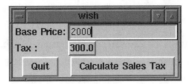

8.7.5 Working Together

The different layout managers can be used together to get the screen layout you desire. In the rules defined in the following, .f1 and .f2 are frames that contain other widgets.

Within a single frame, any single layout manager can be used.	This is valid:

```
pack .f1.b1 -side left
grid .f2.b1 -column 1 -row 3
```

Within a single frame, the grid and pack cannot be mixed.

This is not valid:

```
pack .f1.b1 -side left
grid .f1.b2 -column 1 -row 3
```

The place can be used with either the grid or pack command.

This is valid:

```
pack .f1.b1 -side left
place .f1.label -x 25 -y 10

grid .f2.b1 -column 1 -row 3
place .f2.label -xrel .1 -yrel .5
```

Frames can be arranged with either grid or pack regardless of which layout manager is used within the frame.

This is valid:

```
pack .f1.b1 -side left
grid .f2.b1 -column 1 -row 3

grid .f1 -column 0 -row 0
grid .f2 -column 1 -row 0
```

8.8 *Selection Widgets:* radiobutton, checkbutton, menu, *and* listbox

Allowing the user to select one (or more) items from a list is a common program requirement. The Tk graphics extension provides these selection widgets: radiobutton, checkbutton, menu, and listbox.

8.8.1 **radiobutton** and **checkbutton**

The radiobutton and checkbutton widgets are very similar. The primary difference is that the radiobutton will allow the user to select only one of the entries, whereas the checkbutton will allow the user to select multiple items from the entries.

8.8.1.1 **radiobutton**

The radiobutton widget displays a label with a diamond-shaped status indicator next to it. When a radiobutton is selected, the indicator changes color to show which item has been selected, and any previously selected radiobutton is deselected.

Syntax: radiobutton *radioName ?options?*

radiobutton   Create a radiobutton widget.

radioName   The name for this radiobutton widget.

?options?   Options for the radiobutton include:

-command *script*

A script to evaluate when this button is clicked.

-variable *varName*

The variable defined here will contain the value of this button when the button is selected. If this option is used, the -value must also be used.

-value *value*

The value to assign to the variable.

The -variable and -value options allow the radiobutton widget to be attached to a variable that will be set a particular value when the button is selected. By using the -command, a script can be assigned to be evaluated when the button is selected. If the -variable and -value options are used, the script will be evaluated after the new value has been assigned to the widget variable.

The next example shows how the magic shop in a computerized Fantasy Role Playing game can be modernized.

Note the foreach {item cost} $itemList command. This style of the foreach command (using a list of variables instead of a single variable) was introduced in Tcl version 7.4. It is useful when stepping through a list that consists of repeating fields, like the name price name price data in itemList.

Example 8.8.1.1-1

Example Script

```
#
# Update the displayed text in a label
proc updateLabel {myLabel item} {
    global price;

    $myLabel configure -text \
    "The cost for a potion of $item is $price gold pieces"
}

# Create and display a label
set l [label .l -text "Select a Potion"]
grid $l -column 0 -row 0 -columnspan 3

# A list of potions and prices

set itemList [list "Cure Light Wounds" 16 "Boldness" 20 \
    "See Invisible" 60]

set position 0
foreach {item cost} $itemList {
    radiobutton .b_$position -text $item -variable price \
    -value $cost -command [list updateLabel $l $item]
    grid .b_$position -column $position -row 1
    incr position
}
```

Script Result

All of the `radiobutton` widgets in this example share the global variable `price`. The variable assigned to the `-variable` option is used to group `radiobutton` widgets. For example, if you had two sets of `radiobuttons`, one for magic potions and one for magic scrolls, you would need to use two different variable names, such as `potionPrice` and `scrollPrice`.

If you assign each `radiobutton` a different variable, the `radiobuttons` will be considered as separate groups. In this case, all the buttons can be selected at once and cannot be deselected, since there would be no other button in their group to select.

Note that the variable `price` is declared as a global in the procedure `updateLabel`. The variables attached to Tcl widgets default to being in the global scope.

The `updateLabel` procedure is called with an item name and uses the variable `price` to get the price. The `$price` value could be passed to the procedure by defining the `-command` argument as:

```
-command [list updateLabel $1 $item $cost]
```

This example used the variable for demonstration purposes. Either technique for getting the data to the procedure can be used.

8.8.1.2 `checkbutton`

The `checkbutton` widget allows multiple items to be selected. The `checkbutton` widget displays a label with a square status indicator next to it. When a `checkbutton` is selected, the indicator changes color to show which item has been selected. Any other checkbuttons are not affected.

The checkbutton widget supports a -variable option, but unlike the case of radiobutton, you must use a separate variable for each widget, instead of sharing a single variable among the widgets. Using a single variable will cause all of the buttons to select or deselect at once, instead of allowing you to select one or more buttons.

Syntax: *checkbuttoncheckName ?options?*

checkbutton   Create a checkbutton widget.

checkName   The name for this checkbuttonwidget.

?options?   Valid options for the checkbutton widget include:

-variable *varName*

> The variable defined here will contain the value of this button when the button is selected.

-onvalue *valueWhenSelected*

> The value to assign to the variable when this button is selected. Defaults to 1.

-offvalue *valueWhenDeSelected*

> The value to assign to the variable when this button is not selected. Defaults to 0.

Example 8.8.1.2-1

Example Script

```
#
# Update the displayed text in a label
proc updateLabel {myLabel item} {
    global price;

    set total 0
    foreach potion [array names price] {
        incr total $price($potion)
    }

    $myLabel configure -text "Total cost is $total Gold Pieces"
}
```

```
# Create and display a label
set l [label .l -text "Select a Potion"]
grid $l -column 0 -row 0 -columnspan 3

# A list of potions and prices

set itemList [list "Cure Light Wounds" 16 "Boldness" 20 \
        "See Invisible" 60 "Love Potion Number 9" 45]

set position 1
foreach {item cost} $itemList {
    checkbutton .b_$position -text $item \
        -variable price($item) -onvalue $cost -offvalue 0 \
        -command "[list updateLabel $l $item]"
    grid .b_$position -row $position -column 0 -sticky w
    incr position
}
```

Script Output

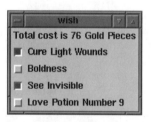

8.8.2 Pull-down Menus: `menubutton` and `menu`

The Tk `menubutton` widget is the ubiquitous pull-down menu that we've all become so fond of.

Creating a pull-down menu with Tk requires two widgets: the `menubutton` that appears on the screen and a nondisplayable `menu` that is attached to the `menubutton` and contains the menu entries.

Syntax: menubutton *buttonName* *?options?*

menubutton   Create a `menubutton` widget.

buttonName   The name for this `menubutton`.

?options? The menubutton supports many options. Some of the more useful are:

-text *displayText*

The text to display on this button.

-textvariable *variableName*

The variable that contains the text to be displayed.

-underline *underlinePosition*

Selects a position for a hotkey.

-menu *menuName*

The name of the *menu* widget associated with this menubutton.

The -text and -textvariable options can be used to control the text displayed on a button. If a -textvariable option is declared, then the button will display the contents of that variable. If both a -text and -textvariable are defined, then the -textvariable variable will be initialized to the argument of the -text option.

The -underline option lets you define a hotkey to select a menu item. The argument to the -underline option is the position of a character in the displayed text. The character at that position will be underlined. If that character and the ALT key are pressed simultaneously, the menubutton will be selected.

A menu widget is a nondisplayable container widget that holds the menu entries to be displayed.

Syntax: menu *menuName ?options?*

menu Create a menu widget.

menuName The name for this menu widget. Note that this name must be a child name to the parent menubutton. For example, if the menubutton is .foo.bar, the menu name must resemble .foo.bar.baz .

?options?   The *menu* widget supports several options. A couple that are unique to this widget are:

-postcommand *script*

>   A script to evaluate just before a menu is posted.

-tearoff boolean

>   Allows (or disallows) a menu to be removed from the menubutton and displayed in a permanent window. This is enabled by default.

Once a menu widget has been created, it can be manipulated via several widget subcommands. The ones that will be used in these examples are:

Syntax: *menuName add   type ?options?*

menuName add

>   Add a new menu entry to a menu.

type   The type for this entry. May be one of:

separator   A line that separates one set of menu entries from another.

cascade   Defines this entry as one that has another menu associated with it, to provide cascading menus.

checkbutton Same as the stand-alone checkbutton widget.

radiobutton Same as the stand-alone radiobutton widget.

command   Same as the stand-alone button widget.

?options?   A few of the options that will be used in the examples are:

-command *script*

>   A script to evaluate when this entry is selected.

-accelerator *string*

>Displays the string to the right of the menu entry as an accelerator. This action must be bound to an event. Binding will be covered in Chapter 9.

-label *string*

>The text to display in this menu entry.

-menu *menuName*

>The menu associated with a cascade menu item. Valid only for cascading menus.

-variable *varName*

>A variable to be set when this entry is selected.

-value *string*

>The value to set in the associated variable.

-underline *position*

>The position of the character in the text for this menu item to underline and bind for action with this menu entry. This is equivalent to the -underline option that the menubutton supports.

Alternatively, the command *menuName insert* can be used to insert items into a menu. This command supports the same options as the add command. The *insert* command allows your script to define the position to insert this entry before.

The insert and delete commands require an *index* option. An index may be specified in one of these forms:

number   The position of the item in the menu. Zero is the topmost entry in the menu.

active   The entry that is currently active (selected). If no entry is selected, this is the same as none.

end or last   The bottom entry in the menu. If the menu has no entry, this is the same as none.

@number   The entry that contains (or is closest to) the Y-coordinate defined by number.

pattern   The first entry with a label that matches the glob style pattern.

Syntax: menuName insert index type ?options?

menuName insert

Insert a new entry before position index.

index   The position to insert this entry before.

Syntax: menuName delete index1 index2

menuName delete

Delete menu entries.

index1 index2

Delete the entries between the numeric indices index1 and index2, inclusive.

Syntax: menuName index string

menuName index

Return the numeric index of the menu entry with the label string.

string   The string displayed in a -label option for a menu entry.

The following example shows how the various menus are created and how they look. In actual fact, you cannot pull down all the menus at once. You can, however, use the tear-off strip (select the dotted line at the top of the menus) to create a new window and have multiple windows displayed.

Example 8.8.2-1

Example Script

```
#-------------------------------------------------------------
# Create a checkbutton menu - Place it on the left
#
```

```
set checkButtonMenu [menubutton .mcheck \
    -text "checkbuttons" -menu .mcheck.mnu]
set checkMenu [menu $checkButtonMenu.mnu]

grid $checkButtonMenu -row 0 -column 0

$checkMenu add checkbutton -label "check 1" \
    -variable checkButton(1) -onvalue 1
$checkMenu add checkbutton -label "check 2" \
    -variable checkButton(2) -onvalue 2

#------------------------------------------------------------
# Create a radiobutton menu - Place it in the middle
#
set radioButtonMenu [menubutton .mradio \
    -text "radiobuttons" -menu .mradio.mnu]
set radioMenu [menu $radioButtonMenu.mnu]

grid $radioButtonMenu -row 0 -column 1

$radioMenu add radiobutton -label "radio 1" \
    -variable radioButton -value 1
$radioMenu add radiobutton -label "radio 2" \
    -variable radioButton -value 2

#------------------------------------------------------------
# Create a menu of mixed check, radio, command, cascading and
# menu separators

set mixButtonMenu [menubutton .mmix -text "mixedbuttons"  \
        -menu .mmix.mnu -relief raised -borderwidth 3]
set mixMenu [menu $mixButtonMenu.mnu]

grid $mixButtonMenu -row 0 -column 2

#-----------------------------------
# Two command menu entries
#
$mixMenu add command -label "command 1" -command "doStuff 1"
$mixMenu add command -label "command 2" -command "doStuff 2"

#-----------------------------------
# A separator, and two radiobutton menu entries
#
$mixMenu add separator
$mixMenu add radiobutton -label "radio 3" \
```

```
        -variable radioButton -value 3
$mixMenu add radiobutton -label "radio 4" \
    -variable radioButton -value 4

#-----------------------------------
# A separator, and two checkbutton menu entries
#
$mixMenu add separator
$mixMenu add checkbutton -label "check 3" \
    -variable checkButton(3) -onvalue 3
$mixMenu add checkbutton -label "check 4" \
    -variable checkButton(4) -onvalue 4

#-----------------------------------
# A separator, a cascading menu, and two sub menus
#    within the cascading menu
#
$mixMenu add separator
$mixMenu add cascade -label "cascader" \
    -menu $mixMenu.cascade
menu $mixMenu.cascade
$mixMenu.cascade add command -label "Cascaded 1"\
    -command "doStuff 3"
$mixMenu.cascade add command -label "Cascaded 2"\
    -command "doStuff 3"

#
# Define a dummy proc for the command buttons to invoke.
proc doStuff {args} {
    puts "doStuff called with: $args"
}
```

Script Results

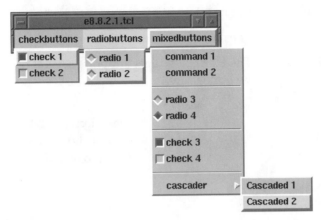

Note that the radio buttons in Example 8.8.2-1 all share the variable radioButton even though they are in separate menus. Selecting a radio item from the mixedbuttons window deselects an item selected in the radiobuttons menu.

You may notice that some of the menu entries are highlighted differently than others (the **radiobuttons** menubutton and **check 1** checkbutton, for instance). The cursor was over these windows when I made the screen dumps. When the cursor passes over a button or menu item, it changes color to announce that it is active.

8.8.3 listbox

The listbox widget allows the user to select items from a list of items. The listbox widget can be configured to select one entry, similar to a radiobutton, or multiple entries, similar to a checkbutton.

The listbox can be queried to return the positions of the selected items. This can be used to index into a list or array of information, or the listbox can be queried about the text displayed at that position.

Syntax: `listbox` *`listboxName ?options?`*

`listbox`   Create a `listbox` widget.

`listboxName`   The name for this *`listbox`*.

`?options?`   The `listbox` widget supports several options. Three useful options are:

`-selectmode` *`style`*

Sets the selection style for this `listbox`. The default mode is `browse`. This option may be set to one of:

`single`   Allows only a single entry to be selected. Whenever an entry is clicked, it is selected, and other selected entries are deselected.

`browse`   Allows only a single entry to be selected. Whenever an entry is clicked, it is selected, and other selected entries are deselected. When the cursor is dragged across entries with the left mouse button depressed, each entry will be selected when the cursor crosses onto it and deselected when the cursor passes off.

`multiple`   Allows multiple entries to be selected. An entry is selected by clicking upon it (if not already selected).

| | A selected entry can be deselected by clicking it. |
| extended | Allows a single entry to be selected, or multiple contiguous entries to be selected by dragging the cursor over the entries. |

-exportselection *boolean*

If this is set true, then the contents of the listbox will be exported for other X11 tasks, and only a single listbox selection may made. If you wish to use multiple listbox widgets with different selections, set this option to FALSE. This defaults to TRUE.

-height *numLines*

The height of this listbox in lines.

When a listbox is created, it is empty. The listbox widget supports several commands for manipulating the listbox contents. These are a few that will be used in the next chapters:

Syntax: *listboxName insert index element ?elements?*

insert	Inserts a new element into a listbox.
index	The position to insert this entry before. The word end causes this entry to be added after the last entry in the list.
element	A text string to be displayed in that position. This must be a single line. Embedded newlines are printed as backslash-N, instead of generating a new line.

Syntax: *listboxName delete first ?last?*

delete	Delete entries from a listbox.
first	The first entry to delete. If there is no *last* entry, only this entry will be deleted.
last	The last entry to delete. Ranges are deleted inclusively.

Syntax: *listboxName curselection*

curselection

> Returns a list of the indices of the currently selected items in the `listbox`.

Syntax: *listboxName get   first ?last?*

get
: Returns a list of the text displayed in the range of entries identified by the indices.

first
: The first entry to return.

last
: The last entry to return. If this is not included, only the first entry is returned. The range returned is inclusive.

In the next example, some selections were made before the graphic and report were created.

Example 8.8.3-1

Example Script

```
# Create the left listbox, defined to allow only a single
# selection
#
listbox .lSingle -selectmode single -exportselection no
grid .lSingle -row 1 -column 0
.lSingle insert end "top" "middle" "bottom"

# Create the right listbox, defined to allow multiple items to
# be selected.
#
listbox .lMulti -selectmode multiple -exportselection no
grid .lMulti -row 1 -column 1
.lMulti insert end "MultiTop" "MultiMiddle" "MultiEnd"

# Create a button to report what's been selected
#
button .report -text "Report" -command "report"
grid .report -row 0 -column 0 -sticky e

# And a procedure to loop through the listboxes,
#   and display the selected values.
#
```

```
proc report {} {
  foreach widget [list .lSingle .lMulti] {
      set selected [$widget curselection]
      foreach index $selected {
         set str [$widget get $index]
         puts "$widget has index $index selected - $str"
      }
  }
}
```

Script Results

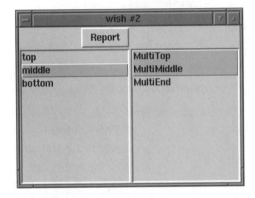

Script Output

```
.lSingle has index 1 selected - middle
.lMulti has index 0 selected - MultiTop
.lMulti has index 1 selected - MultiMiddle
```

8.9 Scrollbar

Since the listbox doesn't allow variables or commands to be associated with its selections, it seems less useful than the button or menu widgets. The listbox becomes important when you need to display a large number of selection values and you connect the listbox with a scrollbar widget.

8.9.1 The Basic `scrollbar`

The `scrollbar` widget allows you to show a portion of a widget's information by using a bar with arrows at each end and a slider in the middle. To change the information displayed, a user clicks the arrows or bar or drags the slider. At this point, the `scrollbar` informs the associated widget of the change. The associated widget is responsible for displaying the appropriate portion of its data to reflect that change.

Syntax: `scrollbar scrollbarName ?options?`

`scrollbar`   Create a `scrollbar` widget.

`scrollbarName`

    The name for this `scrollbar`.

`options`   This widget supports several options. The `-command` option is required.

    `-command "procName ?args?"`

        This defines the command to invoke when the state of the `scrollbar` changes. Arguments that define the changed state will be appended to the arguments defined in this option.

    `-orient direction`

        Defines the orientation for the scrollbar. The `direction` may be `horizontal` or `vertical`. Defaults to `vertical`.

    `troughcolor color`

        Defines the color for the trough below the slider. Defaults to the default background color of the frames.

A `scrollbar` interacts with another widget by invoking the defined command whenever the state of the `scrollbar` changes. The widgets that support scrolling (`listbox`, `text`, and `canvas`) have procedures defined to allow them to be scrolled.

The `listbox`, `text`, and `canvas` widgets support several commands for interacting with the scrollbar. These will be discussed in more detail later in this chapter. An overview of them is as follows:

Syntax: *widgetName xview   options*

Syntax: *widgetName yview   options*

xview   Change the displayed area of a widget in the X dimension.

yview   Change the displayed area of a widget in the Y dimension.

Syntax: *widgetName yscrollcommand   options*

Syntax: *widgetName xscrollcommand   options*

yscrollcommand

> The command to send back to the scrollbar if the widget view shifts in the Y dimension, so that the scrollbar may reflect the state of the display widget.

xscrollcommand

> The command to send back to the scrollbar if the widget view shifts in the X dimension, so that the scrollbar may reflect the state of the display widget.

The `listbox` also needs to know that it is associated with a scrollbar. When the listbox changes its display, it will invoke the `set` subcommand to inform the scrollbar of the change. The `set` subcommand is supported by the `scrollbar` to modify the location of the slider.

Also note the `-fill y` option to the `pack` command. This informs the `pack` layout manager that this widget should expand to fill the available space and that it should expand in the y direction. Without this option, the `scrollbar` would consist of two arrows with a 1-pixel-tall bar to use the minimal space.

The equivalent `grid` option is `-sticky ns` to tell the `grid` layout manager that the ends of the widget should stick to top and bottom of the frame.

The following example shows a scrollbar connected with a listbox.

Example 8.9.1-1

Example Script

```
# Create the scrollbar and listbox.
#
scrollbar .scroll -command ".box yview"
listbox .box -height 4 -yscrollcommand ".scroll set"

# Pack them onto the screen - note expand and fill options
#
pack .box -side left
pack .scroll -side right -fill y

# Fill the listbox.
#
.box insert end 0 1 2 3 4 5 6 7 8 9 10
```

Script Result

8.9.2 scrollbar Details

In normal use, the programmer can just set the -command option in the scrollbar and the -yscrollcommand or -xscrollcommand in the widget the scrollbar is controlling, and everything will work as expected. For some applications, though, you need to understand the details of how the scrollbar works.

This is the sequence of events that occurs when a scrollbar is clicked:

1. The user clicks an arrow or bar or drags a slider.
2. The scrollbar invokes the defined procedure. (.box yview)
3. The widget changes the displayed information to reflect the change.
4. The widget invokes a scrollbar command to modify the scrollbar appearance. (.scroll set)

These `scrollbar` subcommands support the interaction between the `scrollbar` and the associated widget.

Syntax: `scrollbarName set first last`

set   Sets the size and location of the slider.

first   A fraction representing the beginning of the displayed data in the associated widget (e.g., 0.25) informs the scrollbar that the associated widget starts displaying data at that point (e.g., the 25% point). The scrollbar will place the starting edge of the slider one fourth of the way down the bar.

end   A fraction representing the end of the displayed data in the associated widget (e.g., 0.75) informs the scrollbar that the associated widget stops displaying data at that point (e.g., the 75% point). The scrollbar will place the ending edge of the slider three fourths of the way down the bar.

Syntax: `scrollbarName get`

get   Returns the current state of the widget. This will be the result of the most recent set command.

When the user modifies the state of the `scrollbar`, the `scrollbar` will append a set of arguments to the string defined with the `-command` option and will evaluate that string. The arguments that the `scrollbar` appends to that string will be one of the following:

User Action	Arguments
click an arrow	`scroll ?-?1 unit`
click the bar	`scroll ?-?1 page`
drag the slider	`moveto fraction`

In the preceding example, when the scrollbar is manipulated, a command of the form

`.box yview scroll 1 unit`

or

`.box yview moveto .25`

would be created by the scrollbar and then evaluated by the Tcl interpreter. The listbox would change the display to show the requested area and generate the following command:

```
.scroll set .25 .60
```

When this command is evaluated, the scrollbar will change its display to put the slider in the proper location.

8.9.3 Intercepting `scrollbar` Commands

The next example shows how you can use this knowledge about how the scrollbar works to use a single scrollbar to control two listbox widgets.

This example uses a couple of previously unmentioned subcommands of the listbox widget. These are:

Syntax: *listboxName size*

size   Returns the number of entries in a listbox.

Syntax: *listboxName yview moveto fraction*

yview moveto

This is one of the subcommands designed for interaction with the scrollbar. It moves the listbox display window such that the top entry is the entry described by the *fraction* argument.

fraction   A fraction representing the percentage of the list that should be skipped before displaying the first list entry (e.g., .25 means that 25% of the list should be skipped, and the entry that is one fourth of the way down the list should be the first entry displayed).

Example 8.9.3-1

Example Script

```
# Create the two listboxes

listbox .leftbox -height 5 -exportselection 0
listbox .rightbox -height 5 -exportselection 0
```

```
# And fill them.  The right box has twice as many entries as
#     the left.

for {set i 0} {$i < 10} {incr i} {
    .leftbox insert end "Left Line $i"
    .rightbox insert end "Right Line $i"
    .rightbox insert end "Next Right $i"
}

# Display the listboxes.

grid .leftbox -column 0 -row 0
grid .rightbox -column 2 -row 0

# Create the scrollbar, set the initial slider size, and
# display
#
scrollbar .scroll -command \
    "moveLists .scroll .leftbox .rightbox"
.scroll set 0 .20
grid .scroll -column 1 -row 0 -sticky ns

##############################################################
# proc moveLists {scrollbar listbox1 listbox2 args}--
#     Controls two listboxes from a single scrollbar
#     Shifts the top displayed entry and slider such that both
#     listboxes start and end together.  The list with the most
#     entries will scroll faster.
#
# Arguments
#   scrollbar  The name of the scrollbar
#   listbox1   The name of one listbox
#   listbox2   The name of the other listbox
#   args       The arguments appended by the scrollbar widget
#
# Results
#   No valid return.
#   Resets displayed positions of listboxes.
#   Resets size and location of scrollbar slider.

proc moveLists {scrollbar listbox1 listbox2 args} {

    # Get the height for the listboxes - assume both are the same.
    #
    set height [$listbox2 cget -height]
```

```
# Get the count of entries in each box.
#
set size1 [$listbox1 size]
set size2 [$listbox2 size]

if {$size1 > $size2} {
    set size ${size1}.0
} else {
    set size ${size2}.0
}

# Get the current scrollbar location
#
set scrollPosition [$scrollbar get]

# And figure out what the top displayed entry is.
#
set top1 [expr int($size1 * [lindex $scrollPosition 0])]
set top2 [expr int($size2 * [lindex $scrollPosition 0])]

# Parse the arguments added by the scrollbar widget
#
set cmdlst [split $args]

switch [lindex $cmdlst 0] {
    "scroll" {
        set count [lindex $cmdlst 1]
        set unit [lindex $cmdlst 2]

        # Determine whether the arrow or the bar was
        #  clicked (is the command "scroll 1 unit"
        #  or "scroll 1 page")

        if {[string first units $unit] >= 0} {
          set increment [expr 1 * $count];
        } else {
         set increment [expr $height * $count];
        }

        # Set the new fraction for the top of the list
        #
        set topfract1 [expr ($top1 + $increment)/$size]
        set topfract2 [expr ($top2 + $increment)/$size]
    }
```

```
    "moveto" {
      # Get the fraction of the list to display as top
      #
      set topfract [lindex $cmdlst 1]

      # And shift it for the appropriate
      #     size of the listboxes.
      set topfract1 [expr $topfract * ($size1/$size)]
      set topfract2 [expr $topfract * ($size2/$size)]
    }
  }

  # Move the listboxes to their new location
  #
  $listbox1 yview moveto $topfract1
  $listbox2 yview moveto $topfract2

  # Reposition the scrollbar slider
  set topfract [expr ($topfract1 > $topfract2)? \
      $topfract1:$topfract2]
  $scrollbar set $topfract \
      [expr $topfract + (($height-1)/$size)]
}
```

Script Result

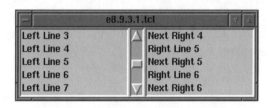

Note the calls to yview in the previous example. The yview and xview subcommands set the start location for the data in a listbox. The first argument (scroll or moveto) is used to determine how to interpret the other arguments.

When a `scrollbar` and a `listbox` are connected in the usual manner, with a line resembling

```
scrollbar .scroll -command ".box yview"
```

the `scrollbar` widget will append arguments describing how to modify the data to the arguments supplied in the -command argument and the new string will be evaluated. The arguments appended will start with either the word `scroll` or the word `moveto`.

For example, if an arrow were clicked in scrollbar .scroll, the command evaluated would be:

```
.box yview scroll 1 unit
```

The .box procedure would parse the first argument (`yview`) and evaluate the `yview` procedure. The `yview` code would parse the argument `scroll 1 unit` to determine how the listbox should be modified to reflect scrolling 1 unit down.

In the previous example, the slider doesn't behave exactly as described for the default `scrollbar` procedures. Because we are scrolling lists of two different sizes, the slider size is set to reflect the fraction of data displayed from the larger listbox. The position of the slider reflects the center of the displayed data, rather than the start point. By changing the parameters to `$control set` you can modify that behavior. For instance, you could position the slider to reflect the condition of one `listbox` and treat the other listbox as a slave.

8.10 The `scale` Widget

The `scale` widget will allow a user to select a numeric value from within a given range. It creates a bar with a slider, similar to the `scrollbar` widget, but without arrows at the ends.

When the user moves the slider, the `scale` widget can either evaluate a procedure with the new slider location as an argument, or set a defined variable to the new value, or perform both actions.

Syntax: scale *scaleName* *?options?*

scale	Create a scale widget.
scaleName	The name for this scale widget.
?options?	There are many options for this widget. The minimal set is:

-orient *orientation*

> Whether the scale should be drawn horizontally or vertically: *orientation* may be *horizontal* or *vertical*. The default orientation is vertical.

-length *numPixels*

> The size of this scale. The height for vertical widgets and the width for horizontal widgets. The *height* may be in any valid distance value (as described in Section 8.2.3).

-from *number* One end of the range to display. This value will be displayed on the left side (for horizontal scale widgets) or top (for vertical scale widgets).

-to *number* The other end for the range.

-label *text* The label to display with this scale.

-command *script*

> The command to evaluate when the state changes. The new value of the slider will be appended to this string, and the resulting string will be evaluated.

-variable *varName*

> A variable that will contain the current value of the slider.

-resolution *number*

> The resolution to use for the scale and slider. Defaults to 1.

-tickinterval *number*

> The resolution to use for the scale. This does not affect the values returned when the slider is moved.

The next example shows two `scale` widgets being used to display temperatures in Celsius and Fahrenheit scales. You can move either slider and the other slider will change to display the equivalent temperature in the other scale.

Example 8.10-1

Example Script

```
#................................................
# Convert the Celsius temperature to Fahrenheit
#
proc celsiusTofahren {ctemp} {
    global fahrenheit

    set fahrenheit [expr ($ctemp*1.8) + 32]
}
#................................................
# Convert the Fahrenheit temperature to Celsius
#
proc fahrenToCelsius {ftemp} {
    global celsius

    set celsius [expr ($ftemp-32)/1.8]
}
#................................................
# Create a scale for fahrenheit temperatures
#
set fahrenscale [scale .fht -orient horizontal \
        -from 0 -to 100 -length 250 \
        -resolution .1 -tickinterval 20 -label "Fahrenheit" \
        -variable fahrenheit -command fahrenToCelsius]
#................................................
# Create a scale for celsius temperatures.
#
set celscale [scale .cel -orient horizontal \
        -from -20 -to 40 -length 250 \
```

```
        -resolution .1 -tickinterval 20 -label "Celsius"   \
        -variable celsius -command celsiusTofahren]

# Pack the widgets.
pack $fahrenscale -side top
pack $celscale -side top
```

Script Results

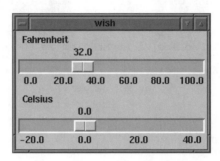

8.11 New Windows

When the wish interpreter is initialized, it creates a top-level graphics window. This window will be drawn with whatever decorations your display system provides and will expand to fit whatever other widgets are placed within it.

If you find you need another, separate window, one can be created with the toplevel command.

Syntax: toplevel   *windowName ?options?*

toplevel   Creates a new top-level window.

windowName   The name for the window to create. The name must start with a period and conform to the widget naming conventions.

?options?   Valid options for the *toplevel* widget include: -borderwidth, -highlightbackground, highlightcolor, -relief, -background, -height, -width.

Example 8.11-1

Example Script

```
# Create a label in the original window
#
label .l -text "I'm in the original window"

# Create a new window, and a label for it
#
toplevel .otherTopLevel
label .otherTopLevel.l -text "I'm in the other window"

# Display the labels.
#
pack .l
pack .otherTopLevel.l
```

Script Output

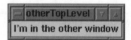

By default, the window name is shown in the top window decoration. This can be modified with the wm title command. The wm command gives the Tk programmer access to the services provided by the window manager. These services vary slightly between window managers and operating systems. You should read the online documentation for the subcommands supported by the wm command.

8.12 Interacting with the Event Loop

The Tk event loop is processed whenever the interpreter is not evaluating a command or procedure. It's best to write your code to spend as little time as possible within procedures. However, some tasks just plain take a while, and you may need to schedule passes through the event loop while your procedure is running.

You can force the Tcl interpreter to evaluate the event loop with the update command.

Syntax: update *?idletasks?*

update Process the event loop until all pending events have been processed.

idletasks Do not process user events or errors. Process only pending internal requests such as updating the display.

A classic error in event-driven GUI programming is to perform some task in a loop, with a command to modify the display, and not force the display to update. In this case, only the last screen modification is displayed.

The next example shows a simple loop to put characters into a label. Without the update in the loop, the task would pause for several seconds and then display the complete string. The update command causes the characters to be displayed one at a time.

Example 8.12-1

Example Script

```
#
# Create the label.
label .l -text "" -width 40
pack .l

# Assign some text.
set str "Tcl makes programming Fun"

# And add new text to the label one character at a time.

for {set i 1} {$i < [string length $str]} {incr i} {
    .l configure -text [string range $str 0 $i]
    update
    #
    # Mark time for a second or so.
    #
    for {set j 0} {$j < 1000} {incr j} {
        set x [expr $j.0*2]
    }
}
```

8.13 Scheduling the Future: `after`

The previous example uses a busy loop to cause the script to pause between inserting characters into the `label`. This is a pretty silly waste of CPU time, and Tcl provides a better way to handle this.

The `after` command will perform one of two tasks:

- If called with a single numeric argument, it will pause for that many milliseconds.
- If called with a numeric argument and a script, it will schedule that script to be run the requested number of milliseconds in the future and continue processing the current script.

Syntax: after *milliseconds ?script?*

after   Pause processing of the current script, or schedule a script to be processed in the future.

milliseconds

The number of milliseconds to pause the current processing, or the number of seconds in the future to evaluate another script.

script   If this argument is defined, this script will be evaluated after *milliseconds* time has elapsed.

The next example shows the `after` command being used instead of the busy loop. Then it shows events being scheduled in the future to remove the characters from the label.

Example 8.13-1

Example Script

```
#
# Create the label.
label .l -text "" -width 40
pack .l

# Assign some text.
set str "Tcl makes programming Fun"

# And add new text to the label one character at a time.
```

```
for {set i 1} {$i < [string length $str]} {incr i} {
    .l configure -text [string range $str 0 $i]
    update

    after 1000
}

##############################################################
# proc shortenText {widget}--
#    Remove the first character from the displayed string of a
#    widget
# Arguments
#    widget    The name of a widget with a -text option
#
# Results
#    Removes the first character from the text string of the
#    provided widget  if one exists.
#
#    Schedules itself to run again if the -text string wasn't
#    empty.
proc shortenText {widget} {
    # Get the current text string from the widget
    #
    set txt [$widget cget -text]

    # If it's empty, we're done.
    #
    if {$txt == ""} {
        return;
    }

    # shorten the string
    #
    set txt [string range $txt 1 end]

    # Update the widget
    #
    $widget configure -text $txt

    # And schedule this procedure to be run again in 1 second.
    #
    after 1000 shortenText $widget
}
shortenText .l
```

The first loop (filling the widget) is the type of process that occurs immediately to programmers who are used to working in non-event-driven paradigms.

The style of programming demonstrated by the `shortenText` procedure use of the `after` command is less intuitive but more versatile.

In the first style, the event loop is checked only once per second. If there were an ABORT button, there would be a noticeable lag between a button click and the task being aborted. Using the second style, the GUI will respond immediately.

8.13.1 Canceling the Future

Sometimes, after you've carefully scheduled things, plans change and schedules need to change.

When the `after` command is evaluated, it returns a handle for the event that was scheduled in the future. This handle can be used to manipulate the list of scripts scheduled for evaluation. In particular, you can use this handle to cancel an event:

Syntax: `after cancel` *handle*

`after cancel`

> Cancel a script that was scheduled to be evaluated in the future.

handle   The handle for this event that was returned by a previous `after` *time script* command.

We'll use the `after cancel` command in the next chapter.

8.14 Bottom Line

This chapter has introduced most of the Tk primitive widgets. The mega-widgets (fileboxes, color selectors, etc.), the `text` widget, and the `canvas` widget will be covered in the next three chapters.

The Tk primitive widgets provide the tools necessary to write GUI-oriented programs with support for buttons, entry widgets, graphics display widgets, scrolling listboxes, menus, and numeric input.

Tk widgets can be arranged on the display using the `place`, `grid`, or `pack` layout manager.

The `update` command can be used to force a pass through the event loop during long computations.

The `after` command can be used to pause an application or to schedule a script for evaluation in the future.

The `after cancel` command can be used to cancel a script that was scheduled to be evaluated in the future.

CHAPTER 9

The canvas *Widget, Images, and Events*

Chapter 8 described many of the Tk widgets that support GUI programming. This chapter will discuss the canvas widget, Tcl events, and the Tcl image object. It will show how events can be connected to a drawable item on a canvas or an entire widget and how to use a canvas to build your own GUI widgets.

The canvas is the Tk widget drawing surface. You can draw lines, arrows, rectangles, ovals, text, or random polygons in various colors with various fill styles. You can also insert images in X-Bitmap, PPM (Portable PixMap), PGM (Portable GrayMap), or GIF (Graphical Interface Format) format (other formats are supported in various Tk extensions, which will be discussed in Chapter 13). If that's not enough, you can write C code to add new drawing types to the canvas command.

As mentioned in Chapter 8, Tk is event oriented. Whenever a cursor moves or a key is pressed, an event is generated by the windowing system. If the focus for your window manager is on a Tk window, that event is passed to the Tk interpreter, which can then trigger actions connected with graphic items in that window.

The `bind` command links scripts to the events that occur on graphic items such as widgets or displayed items in a canvas or text widget. Events include mouse motion, button clicks, key presses, and window manager events such as refresh, iconify, or resize.

After we've discussed the `canvas` and `bind` command, I'll show you how to use them to create a toolbar widget similar to the ones in MS-Windows and Netscape.

9.1 Overview of the canvas Widget

Your application may create one or more canvas widgets and map them to the display with any of the layout managers `pack`, `grid`, or `place`. The canvas owns all items that are drawn on it. These items are maintained in a display list and their position in that list determines which items will be drawn on top of others. The order in which items are displayed can be modified.

9.1.1 Identifiers and Tags

When an item is created on a canvas, a unique numeric identifier is returned for that item. The item can always be identified and manipulated by referencing that unique number.

You can also attach a `tag` to an item. A tag is an alphanumeric string that can be used to group canvas items. A single tag can be attached to multiple items, and multiple tags can be attached to a single item.

A set of items that share a tag can be identified as a group by that tag. For example, if you composed a blueprint of a house, you could tag all of the plumbing with `plumbing` and then tag the hot water pipes with `hot`, the cold water pipes with `cold`, and the drains with `drain`. You could highlight all of the plumbing with a command like:

```
$blueprint configure plumbing -outline red
```

Two tags are defined by default in a canvas widget:

all   Identifies all of the drawable items in a canvas.

current   Identifies the topmost item selected by the cursor.

9.1.2 Coordinates

The canvas coordinate origin is the upper left-hand corner. Larger Y coordinates move down the screen, and larger X coordinates move to the right. The coordinates can be declared in pixels, inches, millimeters, centimeters, or points (1/72 of an inch), as described for dimensions in Section 8.2.3.

The coordinates are stored internally using floating-point format, which allows a great deal of flexibility for scaling and positioning items. Note that even pixel locations can be fractional.

9.1.3 Binding

You can cause a particular script to be evaluated when an event associated with a displayed item occurs. For instance, when the cursor passes over a button, an ENTER event is generated by the window manager. The default action for the enter event is to change the button color to denote the button as active. Some widgets, such as the button widget, allow you to set the action for a button click event during widget creation with the -command option. All widgets can have actions linked to events with the bind command, which we'll discuss in detail later in this chapter.

The canvas widget takes the concept of binding further and allows you to bind an action to events that occur on each drawable item within the canvas display list. For instance, you can make lines change color when the cursor passes over them or bind a procedure to a button click on an item.

You can bind actions to displayed items either by tag (to cause an action to occur whenever an item tagged as plumbing is clicked, for instance) or by ID (to cause an action when a particular graphic item is accessed).

For instance, you could bind a double mouse click event to bringing up a message box that would describe an item. A plumber could then double click on a joint and see a description of the style of fitting to use, where to buy it, and an expected cost.

9.2 *Creating a* canvas

Creating a canvas is just as easy as creating other Tk widgets. You simply invoke the canvas command to create a canvas and then tell one of the layout managers where to display it.

As with the other Tk commands, a command will be created with the same name as the canvas widget. You will use this command to interact with the canvas, creating items, modifying the configuration, etc.

Syntax: canvas *canvasName* *?options?*

canvas   Create a canvas widget.

canvasName   The name for this canvas.

?options?   Some of the options supported by the canvas widget are:

-background *color*
> The color to use for the background of this image. The default color is light gray.

-closeenough *distance*
> Defines how close a mouse cursor must be to a displayable item to be considered *on* that item. The default is 1.0 pixel. This value may be a fraction and must be positive.

-scrollregion *boundingBox*
> Defines the size of a canvas widget. The bounding box is a list, left top right bottom, that defines the total area of this canvas, which may be larger than the displayed area.

These coordinates define the area of a canvas widget that can scrolled into view when the canvas is attached to a scrollbar widget.

This defaults to `0 0 width height`, the size of the displayed canvas widget.

-height *size* The height of the displayed portion of the canvas. If `-scrollregion` is declared larger than this and scrollbars are attached to this canvas, this defines the height of the window into a larger canvas.

The `size` parameter may be in pixels, inches, millimeters, etc.

-width *size* The width of this canvas widget. Again, this may define the size of a window into a larger canvas.

-xscrollincrement *size*

The amount to scroll when scrolling is requested. This can be used when the image you are displaying has a grid nature, and you always want to display an integral number of grid sections and not display half-grid sections.

-yscrollincrement *size*

The amount to scroll when scrolling is requested. This can be used when the image you are displaying has a grid nature, and you always want to display an integral number of grid sections and not display half-grid sections.

9.3 Creating Displayable Canvas Items

There are several widget subcommands associated with the procedure created when you create a canvas widget. The subcommand for drawing items on a canvas is the create subcommand. This subcommand creates a graphic item in a described location. Various options allow you to specify the color, tags, etc. for this item. The create subcommand returns the unique number that can be used to identify this drawable item.

The create subcommand includes a number of options that are specific to the class of item. Most drawable items support the following options (except when the option is not applicable to that class of drawable; for instance, line width is not applicable to a text item).

-width *width*

> The width of line to use to draw the outline of this item.

-outline *color*

> The color to draw the outline of this item. If this is an empty string, the outline will not be drawn. The default color is black.

-fill *color*   The color with which to fill the item if the item encloses an area. If this is an empty string (the default), the item will not be filled.

-stipple *bitmap*

> The stipple pattern to use if the -fill option is being used.

-tag *tagList*   A list of tags to associate with this item.

The items that can be created with the create subcommand are:

LINE *canvasName* **create line** *x1 y1 x2 y2 ?xn yn? options*

Create a polyline item. The x and y parameters define the ends of the line segments. Options for the line item include:

-arrow *end*   Specifies which end of a line should have an arrow drawn on it. The end argument may be one of:

> * first   The first line coordinate.
> * last   The end coordinate.

- both   Both ends.
- none   No arrow (default).

-fill *color*   The color to draw this line.

-smooth *boolean*

If set to true, this will cause the described line segments to be rendered with a set of Bezier splines.

-splinesteps *number*

The number of line segments to use for the Bezier splines if -smooth is defined true.

ARC   *canvasName* **create arc** *x1 y1 x2 y2 options*

Create an arc. The parameters *x1 y1 x2 y2* describe a rectangle that would enclose the oval of which this arc is a part. Options to define the arc include:

-start *angle*   The start location in degrees for this arc. The *angle* parameter is given in degrees. The 0-degree position is at 3:00 (the rightmost edge of the oval) and increases in the counterclockwise direction. The default is 0.

-extent *angle*

The number of degrees counterclockwise to extend the arc from the start position. The default is 90 degrees.

-style *styleType*

The style of arc to draw. This defines the area that will be filled by the -fill option. May be one of:

- pieslice   The ends of the arc are connected to the center of the oval by two line segments (default).
- chord   The ends of the arc are connected to each other by a line segment.
- arc   Draw only the arc itself. Ignore -fill options.

-fill *color*   The color to fill the arc, if -style is not arc.

RECTANGLE

> ***canvasName* create rectangle *x1 y1 x2 y2 options***

Create a rectangle. The parameters *x1 y1 x2 y2* define opposite corners of the rectangle.

OVAL ***canvasName* create oval *x1 y1 x2 y2 options***

Create an oval. The parameters *x1 y1 x2 y2* define opposite corners of the rectangle that would enclose this oval.

POLYGON

> ***canvasName* create polygon *x1 y1 x2 y2 ... xn yn options***

Create a polygon. The *x* and *y* parameters define the vertices of the polygon. A final line segment connecting xn, yn to x1, y1 will be added automatically.

The polygon item supports the same -smooth and -splinesteps options as the line item.

TEXT ***canvasName* create text *x y options***

Create a text item.

The text item has these unique options:

-anchor *position*

> Describes where the text will be positioned relative to the x and y locations.
>
> The position argument may be one of:
>
> - center—Center the text on the position (default).
> - n s e w ne se sw nw—one or more sides of the text to place on the position. If a single side is specified, then that side will be centered on the x/y location. If two adjacent sides are specified, then that corner will be placed on the x/y location. For example, if position is defined as w, the text will be drawn with the center of the left edge on the specified x/y location. If position is defined as se, the bottom rightmost corner of the text will be on the x/y location.

-justify *style*

> If the text item is multiline (has embedded newline characters), this option describes whether the lines should be right justified, left justified, or center justified. The default is left.

-text *text*   The text to display.

-font *fontDescriptor*

> The font to use for this text.

-fill *color*   The color to use for this text item.

BITMAP *canvasName create bitmap x y options*

Create a two-color bitmap image. Options for this item include:

-anchor *position*

> This option behaves as described for the text item.

-bitmap *name*

> Defines the bitmap to display. May be one of:
>
> @file.xbm   The name of a file with bitmap data.
>
> bitmapName   The name of one of the predefined bitmaps.

The Tcl 8.0 distribution includes these bitmaps for the PC, Mac, and Unix platforms:

info	questhead	question	hourglass	warning

error	gray12	gray25	gray50	gray75

The Mac platform supports these additional bitmaps:

accessory   A desk accessory

application   A generic application

caution	An exclamation point inside a triangle
cdrom	A CD-ROM icon
document	A generic document
edition	The edition symbol
floppy	A floppy disk
folder	A generic folder
note	A face with a speech balloon
pfolder	A locked folder
preferences	The folder icon with a preferences symbol
querydoc	A database document icon
ramdisk	A ramdisk icon (floppy disk with chip)
stationery	Document stationery
stop	A stop sign
trash	The trash can

IMAGE *canvasName* **create image** *x1 y1 options*

Create a displayed image item. An image can be created from a GIF, PPM, PGM, or X-Bitmap image. The image command will be discussed later in this chapter.

The create image command was introduced several revisions after the create bitmap command. The create image is similar to the create bitmap command but can be used with more image formats and is more easily extended.

The create image command uses the same -anchor option as the create bitmap.

The image to be displayed is described with the -image option:

-image *imageName*

> The name of the image to display. This is the identifier handle returned by the image command.

9.3.1 An Example

The following example creates some simple graphic items to display a happy face.

Example 9.3.1-1

Example Script

```
# Create the canvas and display it.

canvas .c -height 140 -width 140 -background white
pack .c

# Create a nice big circle, colored gray
.c create oval 7 7 133 133 -outline black -fill gray80 -width 2

# And Two little circles for eyes
.c create oval 39 49 53 63 -outline black -fill black
.c create oval 102 63 88 49 -outline black -fill black

# A Starfleet insignia nose
.c create polygon 70 67 74 81 69 77 67 81 -fill black

# A big Happy Smile!
.c create arc 21 21 119 119 -start 225 -extent 95 -style arc \
        -outline black -width 3
```

Script Results

9.4 More Canvas Widget Subcommands

The create subcommand is only one of the subcommands supported by a canvas widget. This section will introduce some of them with examples of how they can be used.

9.4.1 Modifying an Item

You can modify a displayed item after creating it with the `itemconfigure` command. This command behaves like the `configure` command for Tk widgets, except that it takes an extra argument to define the item.

Syntax:

`canvasName itemconfigure tagOrId ?opt1? ?val1? ?opt2 val2?`

`itemconfigure`

        Return or set configuration values.

`tagOrId`   Either the tag or the id number of the item to configure.

`opt1`   The first option to set/query.

`?val1?`   The value to set for *option1*.

Example 9.4.1-1

Example Script

```
# Create a canvas with a white background

set canv [canvas .c -height 50 -width 250 -background white]

# Create some text colored the default black.

set top [ $canv create text 125 20 \
    -text "This text can seen before clicking the button"]

# Create some text colored white.
# It won't show against the background.

set bottom [ $canv create text 125 30 -fill white \
    -text "This text can seen after clicking the button"]
# Create a button which will use itemconfigure to change the
#  colors of the two lines of text.

set colorswap [button .b1 -text "Swap colors" \
    -command "$canv itemconfigure $top -fill white;\
            $canv itemconfigure $bottom -fill black;"]

# Pack them
```

```
pack $canv -side top
pack $colorswap -side bottom
```

Script Results

Before Click

After Click

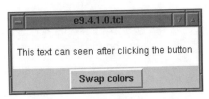

9.4.2 Changing the Display Coordinates of an Item

The previous happy face example simply displayed some graphic items but didn't save the identifiers. The next example creates the happy face and saves the item for one eye to use with the canvas widget subcommand coords. The coords subcommand lets you change the coordinates of a drawable item after the item has been displayed. You can use this to move an item or change an item's shape.

Syntax: *canvasName* coords *tagOrId ?x1 y1? ... ?xn yn?*

coords   Return or modify the coordinates of the item.

tagOrId   A Tag or unique ID that identifies the item.

?x1 y1?...   Optional x and y parameters. If these arguments are absent, the current coordinates are returned. If these are present, they will be assigned as the new coordinates for this item.

Example 9.4.2-1

```
###############################################################
# proc wink {canv item }--
#     Close and re-open an 'eye' item.
# Arguments
#   canv        The canvas that includes this item.
#   item        An identifier for the 'eye' to wink
#
# Results
```

```
#     Converts Y coords for the specified item to center, then
#     restores them.
#     The item is in its original state when this proc returns.
proc wink {canv item } {
    #
    # Get the coordinates for this item, and split them into
    #    left, bottom, right and top variables.
    set bounding [$canv coords $item]

    set left [lindex $bounding 0]
    set bottom [lindex $bounding 1]
    set right [lindex $bounding 2]
    set top [lindex $bounding 3]

    set halfeye [expr int($top-$bottom)/2]

    # Loop to close the eye

    for {set i 1} {$i < $halfeye} {incr i } {
        $canv coords $item $left [expr $top - $i] $right \
            [expr $bottom + $i];
        update
        after 100
    }

    # Loop to re-open the eye

    for {set i $halfeye} {$i >= 0} {incr i -1} {
        $canv coords $item $left [expr $top - $i] \
            $right [expr $bottom + $i];
        update
        after 100
    }
}
```

Example Script

```
# Create the canvas and display it.

canvas .c -height 140 -width 140 -background white
pack .c

# Create a nice big circle, colored gray
.c create oval 7 7 133 133 -outline black -fill gray80 -width 2
```

```
# And Two little circles for eyes
.c create oval 39 49 53 63 -outline black -fill black
set righteye [.c create oval 102 63 88 49 -outline black \
    -fill black]

# A Starfleet insignia nose
.c create polygon 70 67 74 81 69 77 67 81 -fill black

# A big Happy Smile!
.c create arc 21 21 119 119 -start 225 -extent 95 -style arc \
        -outline black -width 3

# Now, wink at the folks

wink .c $righteye
```

Script Output

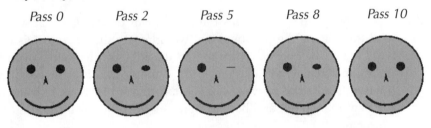

Pass 0   Pass 2   Pass 5   Pass 8   Pass 10

Note that the coords subcommand, like most of the canvas widget subcommands, will accept either an ID or a tag to identify the item. The righteye item could also have been created with this line:

```
.c create oval 102 63 88 49 -outline black \
    -fill black -tag righteye
```

and the wink procedure evaluated as:

```
wink .c righteye
```

Also notice the update command in the wink loops. If this were left out, the display wouldn't update between changes. There would be a pause while the new images were calculated, but the display would never change.

9.4.3 Moving an Item

An item can be moved with the move subcommand as well as with the coords subcommand. The move subcommand supports relative movement, while the coords command supports absolute positions.

Syntax: *canvasName* move *tagOrId xoffset yoffset*

move   Move an item by a defined distance.

tagOrId   A Tag or unique ID that identifies the item.

xoffset yoffset

                The values to add to the item's current coordinates to define the new location. Note that positive values will move the item to the right and lower on the canvas.

For rectangle and oval items the coordinates define the opposite corners and thus define the rectangle that would cover the item. In this case, it's easy to use the coords return to find the edges of the item. If you have a multipointed polygon like a star, for example, finding the edges is a bit more difficult. The canvas widget subcommand bbox returns the coordinates of the top left and bottom right corners of a box that would enclose the item.

Syntax: *canvasName* bbox *tagOrId*

bbox   Return the coordinates of a box sized to enclose a single item or multiple items with the same tag.

tagOrId   A Tag or unique ID that identifies the item. If a tag is used and multiple items share that tag, then the return is the bounding box that would cover all the items with that tag.

The next example creates a star and bounces it around within a rectangle. Whenever the bounding box around the star hits an edge of the rectangle, the speed of the star is decreased and the direction is reversed.

Example 9.4.3-1

Example Script
```
#
# Create the canvas and display it
```

```
canvas .c -height 150 -width 150
pack .c

# Create an outline box for the boundaries.

.c create rectangle 3 3 147 147 -width 3 -outline black \
    -fill white

# Create a star item

.c create polygon 1 15  3 10  0 5  5 5  8 0  10 5  16 5  12 10 \
    14 15  8 12 -fill black -outline black -tag star
# Set the initial velocity of the star

set xoff 2
set yoff 3

#
# Move the item

while {1} {
    set box [.c bbox star]

    set left [lindex $box 0]
    set top [lindex $box 1]
    set right [lindex $box 2]
    set bottom [lindex $box 3]

    # If the star has reached the left margin, heading left,
    #  or the right margin, heading right, make it bounce.
    # Reduce the velocity to 90% in the bounce direction to
    # account for elasticity losses, and reverse the X
    #  component
    # of the velocity.

    if {(($xoff < 0) &&  ($left <= 3)) ||
        (($xoff > 0) && ($right >= 147))} {
       set xoff [expr -.9 * $xoff]
    }

    # The same for the Y component of the velocity.

    if {(($yoff < 0) && ($top <= 3)) ||
        (($yoff > 0) && ($bottom >= 147))} {
       set yoff [expr -.9 * $yoff]
    }
```

```
        .c move star $xoff $yoff
        update;
}
```

Script Output

Pass 1	Pass 3	Pass 5	Pass 7	Pass 9

Tk stores the location of items in floating-point coordinates; thus the bouncing star doesn't completely stop until the x and y velocities fall below the precision of the floating-point library on your computer. The star will just move more and more slowly until you get bored and abort the program.

9.4.4 Finding Items, Raising and Lowering Items

The canvas can be searched for items that meet certain criteria, such as their position in the display list, their location on the canvas, or their tags. The canvas widget subcommand that searches a canvas is the find subcommand. It will return a list of unique IDs for the items that match its search criteria. The list is always returned in the order in which the items appear in the display list, the first item displayed (the bottom if there are overlapping items) first, etc.

The items in a canvas widget are stored in a display list. The items are rendered in the order in which they appear in the list, thus items that appear later in the list will cover items that appear earlier in the list.

An item's position in the display list can be changed with the raise and lower subcommands.

Syntax: *canvasName* raise *tagOrId ?abovetagOrId?*

raise   Move the identified item to a later position in the display list, making it display above other items.

tagOrId   A Tag or unique ID that identifies the item.

?abovetagOrId?

The Id or Tag of an item that this item should be above. By default, items are moved to the end position in the display list (top of the displayed items). With this option, an item can be moved to locations other than the top. In fact, you can raise an item to just above the lowest item, effectively lowering the item.

Syntax: *canvasName* lower *tagOrId ?belowtagOrId?*

lower   Move the identified item to an earlier position in the display list, making it display below other items.

tagOrId   A Tag or unique ID that identifies the item.

?belowtagOrId?

The Id or Tag of an item that this item should be directly below. By default, items are moved to the first position in the display list (bottom of the displayed items). With this option, an item can be moved to locations other than the bottom. You can lower an item to just below the top item, effectively raising the item.

Syntax: *canvasName* find *searchSpec*

find   Find displayable items that match the search criteria and return that list.

searchSpec   The search criteria. May be one of:

all   Return all the items in a canvas in the order in which they appear in the display list.

withtag *Tag*   Returns a list of all items with this tag.

above *tagOrId*

Returns the single item just above the one defined by tagOrId. If a Tag refers to multiple items, then the last (topmost) item is used as the reference.

below *tagOrId*

> Returns the single item just below the one defined by tagOrId. If a Tag refers to multiple items, then the first (lowest) item is used as the reference.

enclosed *x1 y1 x2 y2*

> Returns the items that are totally enclosed by the rectangle defined by *x1, y1* and *x2, y2*. The x and y coordinates define opposing corners of a rectangle.

overlapping *x1 y1 x2 y2*

> Returns the items that are partially enclosed by the rectangle defined by *x1, y1* and *x2, y2*. The x and y coordinates define opposing corners of a rectangle.

closest *x y ?halo? ?start?*

> Returns the item closest to the X/Y location described with the *x* and *y* parameters.
>
> If more than one item overlies the X/Y location, the one that is later in the display list is returned.
>
> The *halo* parameter is a positive integer that is added to the actual bounding box of items to determine whether they cover the X/Y location.
>
> The *start* parameter can be used to step through a list of items that overlie the X/Y position. If this is present, the item returned will be the highest item that is before the item defined by the *start* parameter.
>
> For example, if the display list contained the item IDs (in this order): 1 2 3 4 9 8 7 6 5 and all items overlapped position 100,50, Then the command

```
$canvasName find -closest 100 50 0 8
```

would return item 9, the item immediately below 8.

The next example shows some overlapping items and how their position in the display list changes the appearance of the display. This example redefines the default font for the text items. This will be explained in the next section.

Note how the upvar command is used with the array argument. In Tcl, arrays are always passed by reference, not by value. Thus, if you need to pass an array to a procedure, you will call the procedure with the name of the array and use upvar to reference the array values.

Example 9.4.4-1

```
################################################################
# proc showDisplayList {canv array}--
#     Prints the Display List for a canvas.
#     Converts item ID's to item names via an array.
# Arguments
#     canv                 Canvas to display from
#     array         The name of an array with textual names for the
#                   display items
# Results
#     Prints output on the stdout.

proc showDisplayList {canv array} {
    upvar $array id

    set order [$canv find all]

    puts "display list (numeric): $order"

    puts -nonewline "display list (text):      "

    foreach i $order {
        puts -nonewline "$id($i) "
    }
    puts ""
}
```

Example Script

```
canvas .c -height 150 -width 170
pack .c
```

```tcl
# create a light gray rectangle with dark text.

set tclSquare \
        [.c create rectangle 10 20 110 140 \
        -fill gray70 -outline gray70 ]
set tclText [.c create text 60 50 -text "Tcl\nIs\nTops" \
        -fill black -anchor n -font [list times 22 bold ] \
        -justify center ]

# create a dark gray rectangle with white text.

set tkSquare \
        [.c create rectangle 60 20 160 140 -fill gray30 \
        -outline gray30 ]
set tkText [.c create text 110 50 -text "Tk\nTops\nTcl" \
        -fill white -anchor n -font [list times 22 bold ] \
        -justify center ]

# Initialize the array with the names of the display items
#       linked to the unique number returned from the
#       canvas create.

foreach nm [list tclSquare tclText tkSquare tkText] {
    set id([subst $$nm]) "$nm"
}

# Update the display and canvas
update;

# Show the display list

puts "\nAt beginning"
showDisplayList .c id

# Pause to admire the view
after 1000

# Raise the tclSquare and tclText items to the end \
#       (top) of the display list

.c raise $tclSquare
.c raise $tclText

# Update, display the new list, and pause again
update;
puts "\nAfter raising tclSquare and tclText"
```

```
showDisplayList .c id
after 1000

# Raise the tkText to above the tclSquare (but below tclText)
.c lower $tkText $tclText

# Update and confirm.
update;
puts "\nAfter 'lowering' tkText"
showDisplayList .c id

puts ""
puts "Find reports that $id([.c find above $tclSquare]) \
        is above tclSquare"
puts "Find reports that $id([.c find below $tclSquare]) \
        is below tclSquare"
puts "and items: [.c find enclosed 0 0 120 150] are \
        enclosed within 0,0 and 120,150"
```

Script Output

```
At beginning
display list (numeric): 1 2 3 4
display list (text):     tclSquare tclText tkSquare tkText

After raising tclSquare and tclText
display list (numeric): 3 4 1 2
display list (text):     tkSquare tkText tclSquare tclText

After 'lowering' tkText
display list (numeric): 3 1 4 2
display list (text):     tkSquare tclSquare tkText tclText

Find reports that tkText is above tclSquare
Find reports that tkSquare is below tclSquare
and items: 1 2 are enclosed within 0,0 and 120,150
```

Script Results

Beginning *After* raise *After* lower

9.4.5 Fonts and Text items

Fonts can be just as complex a problem as some 6000 years of human endeavor with written language can make them. They can also be quite simple. I'm just going to discuss the platform-independent, simple method of dealing with fonts. Other methods are described in the online documentation under `font`.

The pre-8.0 releases of Tk name fonts use the X Window System naming convention of

```
-foundry-family-weight-slant-setwidth-addstyle-pixel-point-
resx-resy-spacing-width-charset-encoding.
```

If you need to work with a version of Tk earlier than 8.0, you are probably on a Unix system and can determine a proper name of an available font with the X11 command `xlsfonts` or `xfontsel`.

With the 8.0 release of Tcl and Tk, life became much simpler: a font is named with a list of attributes: `family ?size? ?style? ?style?`

If the Tcl interpreter can't find a font that will match the font you requested, it will find the closest match. It is guaranteed that a font will be found for any syntactically correct set of attributes.

`family`	The family name for a font. On all systems `times`, `helvetica`, and `courier` are defined. A list of the defined fonts can be obtained with the `font families` command.
`size`	The size for this font. If this is a positive value, it is the size in points (1/72 of an inch). The scaling for the monitor is defined when Tk is initialized. If this value is a negative number, it will be converted to positive and will define the size of the font in pixels. Defining a font by point size is preferred and should cause applications to look the same on different systems.
`style`	The style for this font. May be one or more of `normal` (or `roman`), `bold`, `italic`, `underline` or `overstrike`.

Information about fonts can be obtained with the `font` command. As usual, I'll discuss only some of the more commonly used subcommands.

Syntax: `font families ?-displayof windowName?`

`font families`

> Returns a list of valid font families for this system.

`-displayof windowName`

> If this option is present, it defines the window (`frame`, `canvas`, `topwindow`) to return this data for. By default, this is the primary graphics window ".".

The `font measure` command is useful when you are trying to arrange text on a display in an aesthetic manner.

Syntax: `font measure font ?-displayof windowName? text`

`font measure` The `font measure` command returns the number of horizontal pixels that the string `text` will require if rendered in the defined font.

`font` The name of the font, as described above.

`-displayof windowName`

> If this option is present, it defines the window (`frame`, `canvas`, `topwindow`) to return this data for. By default, this is the primary graphics window ".".

`text` The text to measure.

If Tk can't get an exact match to the requested font on your system, it will find the best match. You can determine what font is actually being used with the `font actual` command.

Syntax: `font actual font ?-displayof windowName?`

`font actual` Return the actual font that will be used when `font` is requested.

`font` The name of the requested font.

`-displayof windowName`

> If this option is present, it defines the window (`frame`, `canvas`, `topwindow`, etc.) to return this data for. By default, this is the primary graphics window ".".

With Tk 8.1, Tcl and Tk begin to support the Unicode character fonts. These are encoded by preceding the four-digit Unicode value with "\u". You can get information on the Unicode character sets at http://Unicode.org.

Unicode provides a standard method for handling letters other than the US ASCII alphabet. The Unicode alphabet uses 16 bits to describe 65,536 letters. Each alphabet is assigned a range of numbers to represent its characters. With Unicode, you can represent Japanese katakana, Korean hangul, French, Russian, or any other major alphabet.

The following example steps through the fonts available on a generic Unix system and displays some sample text in ASCII and Unicode. Note that if the Unicode fonts are not supported in a given font, the Unicode numbers are displayed instead. This example was run using Tcl/Tk version 8.1a2. Unicode support is just being added in this revision. By the time you read this book, more Unicode support will be available.

Example 9.4.5-1

Example Script

```
canvas .c -height 950 -width 800
pack .c

set ypos 15

set families [font families]

foreach family $families {
    .c create text 4 $ypos -font [list times 18 bold] \
        -text "$family" -anchor nw
    .c create text 240 $ypos -font [list $family 18] \
        -text "test line -- UNICODE: \u30Ab \u042f \u3072" \
        -anchor nw
    .c create text 4 [expr $ypos+25] -font [list roman 14] \
        -text "[font actual [list $family 18]]" -anchor nw
    .c create line 4 [expr $ypos+45] 800 [expr $ypos+45]
    incr ypos 50
}
```

Script Results

```
e9.4.5.tcl

fixed                          test line -- UNICODE: 力 Я ひ
-family fixed -size 15 -weight normal -slant roman -underline 0 -overstrike 0

fangsong ti                    test line -- UNICODE: 力 Я ひ
-family {fangsong ti} -size 15 -weight normal -slant roman -underline 0 -overstrike 0

charter                        test line -- UNICODE: 力 Я ひ
-family charter -size 16 -weight normal -slant roman -underline 0 -overstrike 0

lucidatypewriter               test line -- UNICODE: 力 Я ひ
-family lucidatypewriter -size 16 -weight normal -slant roman -underline 0 -overstrike 0

lucidabright                   test line — UNICODE: 力 Я ひ
-family lucidabright -size 16 -weight normal -slant roman -underline 0 -overstrike 0

times                          test line -- UNICODE: 力 Я ひ
-family times -size 16 -weight normal -slant roman -underline 0 -overstrike 0

song ti                        test line -- UNICODE: 力 Я ひ
-family {song ti} -size 15 -weight normal -slant roman -underline 0 -overstrike 0

helvetica                      test line -- UNICODE: 力 Я ひ
-family helvetica -size 16 -weight normal -slant roman -underline 0 -overstrike 0

mincho                         τεστ λινε -- ΥΝΙΧΟΔΕ: 力 Я ひ
-family mincho -size 15 -weight normal -slant roman -underline 0 -overstrike 0

courier                        test line -- UNICODE: 力 Я ひ
-family courier -size 16 -weight normal -slant roman -underline 0 -overstrike 0

lucida                         test line -- UNICODE: 力 Я ひ
-family lucida -size 16 -weight normal -slant roman -underline 0 -overstrike 0

utopia                         test line -- UNICODE: \u30ab \u042f \u3072
-family fixed -size 12 -weight normal -slant roman -underline 0 -overstrike 0

nil                            test line -- UNICODE: \u30ab \u042f \u3072
-family fixed -size 12 -weight normal -slant roman -underline 0 -overstrike 0

clean                          test line -- UNICODE: \u30ab \u042f \u3072
-family clean -size 15 -weight normal -slant roman -underline 0 -overstrike 0

terminal                       test line -- UNICODE: \u30ab \u042f \u3072
-family terminal -size 13 -weight normal -slant roman -underline 0 -overstrike 0

symbol                         τεστ λινε — ΥΝΙΧΟΔΕ: ∴ υ30αβ ∴ υ042φ ∴ υ3072
-family symbol -size 16 -weight normal -slant roman -underline 0 -overstrike 0

gothic                         τεστ λινε -- ΥΝΙΧΟΔΕ: ∴υ30αβ ∴υ042φ ∴υ3072
-family gothic -size 15 -weight normal -slant roman -underline 0 -overstrike 0

new century schoolbook         test line -- UNICODE: \u30ab \u042f \u3072
-family {new century schoolbook} -size 16 -weight normal -slant roman -underline 0 -overstrike 0
```

9.4.6 Using a Canvas Larger than the View

When you create a canvas with the `canvas` *name* command, you can provide `-width` *xsize* and `-height` *ysize* arguments to define the size of the canvas to display on the screen.

If you don't also use a -scrollregion argument, then the canvas will be *xsize* by *ysize* in size, and the entire canvas will be visible.

The -scrollregion command will let you declare that the actual canvas is larger than its visible portion.

For example,

```
canvas .c -width 200 -height 150 -scrollregion {0 0 4500 2000}
```

creates a window 150 pixels high and 200 pixels wide into a canvas that is actually 4500×2000 pixels.

If you attach scrollbars to this canvas, you can scroll this 200×150 pixel window around the larger space.

The -xscrollincrement and -yscrollincrement arguments will let you set how much of the canvas should scroll at a time. For instance, if you are displaying a lot of text in a canvas, you would want to set the -yscroll- increment to the height of a line. This will cause the canvas to display full lines of text, instead of displaying partial lines at the top and bottom of the canvas as you scroll through the text.

The next example shows a checkerboard pattern with each square labeled to show its position in the grid. Because the -xscrollincrement is set to the size of a square, the full width of each square is displayed. Because the -yscrollincrement is half the size of a square, half the height of a square can be displayed.

Notice that the -scrollregion can include negative coordinates as well as positive. You can draw any location in a canvas, but you won't be able to scroll to it unless you've set the -scrollregion to include the area you've drawn to.

For example, if you've got a complex image to create and you don't know what the size will be until it's drawn, you can draw the image to a canvas and then determine the bounding box for the image with the command

```
set coords[canvasName bbox all]
```

.

The bounding box for all the items in the display can be used to define the scroll region.

Example 9.4.6-1

Example Script

```
canvas .c -width 200 -height 150 -scrollregion \
        {-100 -200 4500 2000} -yscrollcommand \
        ".scrollY set" -xscrollcommand ".scrollX set" \
        -xscrollincrement 50 -yscrollincrement 25

scrollbar .scrollY -orient vertical -command ".c yview"
scrollbar .scrollX -orient horizontal -command ".c xview"

grid .c -row 0 -column 0
grid .scrollY -row 0 -column 1 -sticky ns
grid .scrollX -row 1 -column 0 -sticky ew

for {set y -200} {$y < 2000} {incr y 50} {
    set bottom [expr $y + 50]
    for {set x -100} {$x < 4500} {incr x 50} {

        set right [expr $x+50]

        if {(($y + $x) % 100) == 50} {
            set textColor white
            set fillColor black
        } else {
            set textColor black
            set fillColor white
        }
        .c create rectangle $x $y $right $bottom \
                -fill $fillColor -outline gray30
        .c create text [expr $x+25] [expr $y+25] \
                -text "$x\n$y" -font \
                [list helvetica 18 bold] -fill $textColor

    }
}
```

Script Results

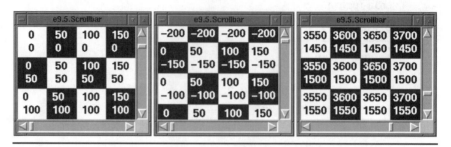

9.5 *The* bind *and* focus *Commands*

Section 9.1.3 mentioned that an event can be linked to a canvas item, and when that event occurs it can trigger an action. You can also bind actions to events on other widgets. This section will discuss how this is done.

Most of the Tcl widgets have some event bindings defined by default. For example, when you click on a button widget, the default action for the ButtonPress event is to evaluate the script defined in the -command option.

9.5.1 The **bind** Command

The bind command links an event to a widget and a script. If the event occurs while the focus is on that widget, the script associated with that event will be evaluated.

Syntax: bind *widgetName eventType script*

bind	Define an action to be executed when an event associated with this widget occurs.
widgetName	The widget to have an action bound to it.
eventType	The event to trigger this action. Events can be defined in one of three formats:
	alphanumeric A single printable (alphanumeric or punctuation) character defines a KeyPress event for that character.

<<virtualEvent>>

> A virtual event defined by your script with the event command.

<modifier-type-detail>

> This format precisely defines any event that can occur. The fields of an event descriptor are described below. Where two names are together, they are synonyms for each other. For example, either Button1 or B1 can be used to the left mouse button click.

modifier

There may be one or more occurrences of the modifier field, which describes conditions that must exist when an event defined by the type field occurs. For example, Alt and Shift may be pressed at the same time as a letter KeyPress.

Not all computers support all the available modifiers. For instance, few computers have more than three buttons on the mouse, and most general-purpose computers don't support a Mod key.

The modifiers Double and Triple define double or triple mouse clicks.

Valid values for modifier are:

Button1	Button2	Button3	Button4	Button5
B1	B2	B3	B4	B5
Mod1	Mod2	Mod3	Mod4	Mod5
M1	M2	M3	M4	M5
Meta	Alt	Control	Double	Triple
M				
Shift	Lock			

type

This field describes the type of event. Only one type entry is allowed in an event descriptor.

Valid values for type are:

KeyPress	ButtonPress	KeyRelease	ButtonRelease
Key	Button		
Enter	Leave	FocusIn	FocusOut
Colormap	Configure	Deactivate	Destroy
Activate	Circulate	Gravity	Map
Motion	Property	Reparent	Unmap
Visibility	Expose		

detail
The detail provides the final piece of data to identify an event precisely. The value that the detail field can take depends on the contents of the type field.

type	detail
ButtonPress ButtonRelease	detail will be the number of a mouse button (1–5). If the button number is specified, only events with that button will be bound to this action.
	If no detail is defined for a Button-Press or ButtonRelease event, then any mouse-button event will be bound to this action.
KeyPress KeyRelease	detail will specify a particular key such as a or 3.
	Nonalphanumeric keys are defined by names such as Space or Caps_Lock. An X11 Manual will list all of these, or you can run xkeycaps on a Unix/Linux system to get a list of the available key types.
	If no detail is defined for a KeyPress or KeyRelease event, then any keyboard event will be bound to this action.

Bind Examples

Event Definition	Description
`<B1-Motion>`	This event is generated if the left mouse button is pressed and the mouse moves, i.e., when you drag an item on a screen.
`a`	Generates an event when the `a` key is pressed.
`Shift_L`	This does not generate an event. `Shift_L` is not an alphanumeric.
`<Shift_L>`	This event is generated when the left shift key is pressed. No event is generated when the key is released.
`<KeyRelease-Shift_L>`	Generates an event when the left shift key is released.
`<Control-Alt-Delete>`	Generates an event if all three are pressed simultaneously. Not a recommended event for PC-based hardware platforms. :-)

The `bind` command can pass information about the event that occurred to the script that is to be evaluated. This is done by including references to the events in the `script` argument to the `bind` command. The complete list of the information available about the event is defined in the `bind` online documentation. The information that can be passed to a script includes:

`%x`   The X component of the cursor's location in the current window when the event occurs.

`%y`   The Y component of the cursor's location in the current window when the event occurs.

`%b`   The button that was pressed or released if the event is a `ButtonPress` or `ButtonRelease`.

`%k`   The key that was pressed or released if the event is a `KeyPress` or `KeyRelease`.

`%A`   They ASCII value of the key pressed or released if the event is a `KeyPress` or `KeyRelease`.

%T	The type of event that occurred.
%W	The pathname of the window in which the event occurred.

Bind Examples

...`<KeyPress>` `{keystroke %k}`	Will invoke the procedure `keystroke` with the value of the key when a `KeyPress` event occurs.
...`<Motion>` `{moveitem %x %y}`	Will invoke the procedure `moveitem` with the x and y location of the cursor when a `Motion` event occurs.

9.5.2 The Canvas Widget **bind** Subcommand

Events can be bound to a drawable item in a `canvas` just as they are bound to widgets. The command to do this uses the same values for *eventType* and *script* as the `bind` command uses:

Syntax: *canvasName* bind *tagOrId eventType script*

The following example is a blueprint drawing with information attached to the items in the drawing, as was suggested in Section 9.1.1. Notice that both the `canvasName` `bind` command and the Tk widget `bind` command are used to bind actions to the events.

In the `setInfo` proc below, when a canvas item is double-clicked, it creates a label to display the information about that item. When the cursor enters one of the labels on the right, the displayable items with that tag are highlighted.

Example 9.5.2-1

```
##############################################################
# proc setInfo {canv obj txt}--
#    sets the 'information' associated with an item.
#    binds displaying the information to a double-click event
#    binds highlighting to <enter> and <leave> events.
# Arguments
#    canv    The canvas that contains this item
#    obj     The item identifier
#    text    Text to display when the item is double clicked.
```

```
#
# Results
#    Creates 3 bindings for the item - Enter, Leave, and
#    double-click
#
proc setInfo {canv item txt} {
    global highlight background normal

    # display the info text when the item is double-clicked

    $canv bind $item  <Double-ButtonPress-1> \
        "label .info -text \"$txt\" ; grid .info -column 0 -row 1"

    # delete any old info text when the cursor enters this item
    # outline this item in highlight color

    $canv bind $item  <Enter> "catch {destroy .info}; \
        .c itemconfigure $item  -outline $highlight"

    # return the outline color to normal when the cursor is not
    # over this item.

    $canv bind $item  <Leave> ".c itemconfigure $item \
        -outline $normal"
}
```

Example Script

```
set background white
set highlight black
set normal gray75

#
# Create a canvas, and display it
#
canvas .c -height 250 -width 400 -background $background
grid .c -row 0 -column 0 -columnspan 2

#
# Draw the outline of the outside of a rectangular house, and
#    define the info for the outside wall.

set house(exterior) [.c create rectangle 8 8 389 248 -width 2 \
        -outline $normal -tag [list exterior wall siding]]
```

```
setInfo .c $house(exterior) \
    "Exterior Wall - white aluminum siding"

#
# Draw the outline of the inside of a rectangular house,
#  and define the info for the interior walls.

set house(interior) [.c create  rectangle 11 11 385 244 \
    -width 1 -outline $normal -tag {interior wall paint}]

setInfo .c $house(interior) "Interior wall, paint pale green"

#
# Create a door for this house.
#

set house(frontdoor) [.c create rectangle 220 8 250 11 \
    -fill $normal -outline $normal -tag \
    [list exterior door paint]]

setInfo .c $house(frontdoor) "Outside door, paint blue"

#
# And a wall to separate the kitchen from the rest of the house.
#

set house(kitchen) \
    [.c create polygon \
    160 150   165 150   165 244   160 244 \
    160 155   50 155   50 150 \
    -outline $normal -tag [list interior paint] -fill ""]

setInfo .c $house(kitchen) "Kitchen wall, paint white"

#
# And finally bedroom/bathroom walls
#

set house(bed.bath) \
    [.c create polygon \
    250 254   250 155   200 155   200 150   350 150   350 155 \
    255 155 255 254 \
    -outline $normal -tag [list interior paint] -fill ""]

setInfo .c $house(bed.bath) "Bedroom & Bathroom walls \
    \n paint white"
```

```
#
# Make a list of the info tags for this drawing, and bind these
# items to highlight the associated tagged items when the list
# items are entered or left.
#
set ypos 1
foreach l [list exterior interior siding paint ] {
    label .$l -text $l
    bind .$l <Enter> ".c itemconfigure $l -outline $highlight "
    bind .$l <Leave> ".c itemconfigure $l -outline $normal"
    grid .$l -row $ypos -column 1
    incr ypos
}
```

Script Results

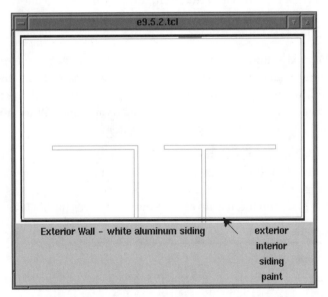

9.5.3 Focus

When a window manager is directing events to a particular item (window, widget, or canvas item), that window is said to have the *focus*.

Some events are always passed to an item that requests them, whether the item is defined as having focus or not. The cursor entering an item always generates an event, and a destroy event will always be transmitted to any applicable item. The keyboard events, however, are delivered only to the widget that currently has the focus.

The window manager controls the top-level focus. The default behavior for MS-Windows systems is to click a window to place the focus in a window. On Unix/X Window Systems, the window managers can be set to require a click or to place the focus automatically on the window where the cursor resides.

Within the Tcl application, the focus is in the top-level window, unless a widget explicitly demands the focus. Some widgets have default actions that acquire the focus: an entry widget, for instance, takes the focus when you click on it or tab to that widget. If you want to allow KeyPress events to be received in a widget that does not normally gain focus, you must add bindings to demand the focus.

The next example shows a label widget .1 with three events bound to it: Enter, Leave, and KeyPress. When the cursor enters the .1 widget, it acquires the focus, and all KeyPress events will be delivered to the script defined in the bind .1 <KeyPress> command. When the cursor leaves label .1, no events are passed to this item.

The label .12 shares the same -textvariable as label .1. When lvar is modified in response to an event on .1, it is reflected in .12. However, .12 never grabs the focus, as .1 does. The bind .12 <KeyPress> {append lvar "L2";} command has no effect, since .12 never has focus.

Example 9.5.3-1

Example Script

```
label .1 -width 40 -textvariable lvar -background gray80
label .12 -width 40 -textvariable lvar

pack .1
pack .12

bind .1 <KeyPress> {append lvar %A;}
bind .1 <Enter> {puts "IN"; focus .1}
bind .1 <Leave> {puts "Out"; focus .}
```

```
bind .12 <KeyPress> {append lvar "L2";}

puts "These events are valid on label .1: [bind .1]"
```

Script Output

```
These events are valid on label .1: <Leave> <Enter> <Key>
IN    # I moved the cursor into label .1, and I typed
        "Label .11 has focus"
```

Script Results

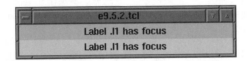

9.6 Creating a Widget

Now that we know how to create drawable items in a canvas and bind actions to events in that canvas, we can create our own widgets.

For example, suppose we want an MS-Windows/Netscape-style toolbar button that displays help information when the cursor hasn't moved for 2 seconds.

To create this we need to write a package that will create a canvas, draw something appropriate in that canvas, and bind scripts to the appropriate events.

Here is a specification for a toolbar button:

- Will be invoked as `toolbutton name ?-option value?`
- Required options will be

    `-bitmap bitmapName`

    `-command script`

    `-info infoText`

- Optional arguments will include

    `-height number`

    `-width number`

```
-foreground color
-background color
-highlight color
```

- Clicking the button with a left mouse button will invoke *script*.
- The button will default to 32×32 pixels.
- The button will default to medium gray color.
- The highlight color will default to light gray.
- The button background will become the highlight color when a cursor enters the button.
- The button background will return to normal color when the cursor leaves the button.
- The text in the info label will be displayed if the cursor rests within the canvas for 2 seconds with no movement.
- Any mouse movement will delete the info label.

This section will discuss building a package to fufill these requirements. The next example shows this package being used to display three simple tool buttons.

Notice the way the `after` command is used to schedule creating the information label. First, the `after cancel` command is invoked to cancel any existing `after` script for this button, and then `after` is used to schedule drawing the information label 2 seconds from now. This pair of actions occurs whenever a mouse motion event is received.

When the mouse leaves the button, any unprocessed `after` event is canceled.

When the pointer sits for 2 seconds, the call to `createInfo` is evaluated. Whenever there is a `<Motion>` event, the time to create an information label is moved 2 seconds into the future.

Also pay attention to the `namespace` commands. Because the `after` and `bind` scripts are evaluated in global scope, I've used the `namespace current` command to create full namespace names to define the scripts to be called when events occur. The `namespace current` command is used instead of just `::toolButton::` because this package could be placed inside another namespace.

Putting the scheduleInfo, cancelInfo, createInfo, and deleteInfo commands into a namespace protects these commands from possible collision with other commands and does not pollute the global space. Creating these procedures inside the namespace also allows them to create and share the associative arrays afters and binding without exposing these arrays to procedures executing outside this namespace.

Example 9.6-1

```
###############################################################
# proc toolbutton {toolButtonName args}--
#    Create a toolbutton icon that will evaluate a command when
#    clicked
#    and display an information label if the cursor rests on it
#
# Arguments
#    toolButtonName      The name of this toolbutton
#    args                A list of -flag value pairs
#
# Results
#    Creates a new toolbutton and returns the name to the
#    calling script
#    Throws an error if unrecognized arguments or required args
#    are missing.
#
proc toolbutton {toolButtonName args} {

    # These arguments are required.

    set reqOptions [list -command -info -bitmap]

    # Check that the required arguments are present
    # Throw an error if any are missing.

    foreach required $reqOptions {
        if {[lsearch -exact $args $required ] < 0} {
            error "toolbutton requires a $required option"
        }
    }

    # define defaults
    set height 32
    set width 32
```

```
set background gray80
set highlight gray90
set foreground black

#
# Step through the arguments.
# Confirm that each -option is valid, and
# set a variable for each option that is defined.
#    The variable for -foo is "foo".
#

set validOptions [list -bitmap -command -info -height \
    -width -foreground -background -highlight]

foreach {option val} $args {
    if {[lsearch $validOptions $option ] < 0} {
        error "Bad argument $option - \
        must be one of $validOptions"
    }
    set item [string range $option 1 end]
    eval [list set $item $val]
}

# Create the canvas for this toolbutton

canvas $toolButtonName -height $height -width $width \
    -background $background

# Place the bitmap in it.

$toolButtonName create bitmap [expr $height/2] \
    [expr $width/2] -bitmap $bitmap -foreground $foreground

# Bind the button click to evaluate the $command
#     script in global scope

bind $toolButtonName <ButtonPress-1> \
    "uplevel 0 [list $command]"

# Bind the background to change color when the
#     cursor enters

bind $toolButtonName <Enter> \
    "$toolButtonName configure -background $highlight"
```

```
    # Bind the background to change color when the cursor
    #  leaves. Cancel any pending display of an info label.

    bind $toolButtonName <Leave> "$toolButtonName \
        configure -background $background;\
        [namespace current]::toolButton::cancelInfo \
        $toolButtonName;"

    # Whenever the button moves, reset the Motion task.

    bind $toolButtonName <Motion> \
        "[list [namespace current]::toolButton::scheduleInfo \
        $toolButtonName $info ]"

    # And return the name

    return $toolButtonName
}

#
# The infoIdentifier, scheduleInfo, cancelInfo, createInfo
#  and deleteInfo procedures are created in the toolButton
#  namespace to
#  1) avoid polluting the global space.
#  2) make the  "afters" array of identifiers returned by the
#     after command private to these procedures.
#  3) make the "afters" array persistent
#  4) make the  "binding" array of identifiers returned by
#     the after command private to these procedures.
#  5) make the "binding" array persistent
#

namespace eval toolButton {

###############################################################
    # proc infoIdentifier {toolButtonName}--
    #    Convert a button path name into a string that can
    #    be used to identify the label.
    #    The label will be placed in the root window,
    #    independent of frames that may hold the toolButtons.
    #    This allows the labels to overlap other widgets
```

```
#     without causing the frame to resize itself.
#     Because of this, the label can only have one "."
#     in its name, and other "." are converted to "_"
#
# Arguments
#     toolButtonName   The full window name of a toolButton
#
# Results
#   Returns the modified string

proc infoIdentifier {toolButtonName} {
    regsub -all {\.} $toolButtonName "_" infoID
    return $infoID
}


################################################################
# proc cancelInfo {toolButtonName}--
#     Cancels the scheduled display of an Info label
# Arguments
#     toolButtonName   The name of the toolbutton
#
# Results
#   If this label was scheduled to be displayed,
#     it is disabled.

proc cancelInfo {toolButtonName} {
    variable afters
    if {[info exists afters($toolButtonName)]} {
        after cancel $afters($toolButtonName);
    }
}


################################################################
#     proc scheduleInfo {name info }--
#     Cancel any existing "after" scripts for this button.
#
# Arguments
```

```
#   name  The name of this toolbutton
#   info  The text to display in the  info label
#
# Results
#   Places an item in the "after" queue to be evaluated
#       2 seconds from now

proc scheduleInfo {toolButtonName info } {
    variable afters

    cancelInfo $toolButtonName

    set afters($toolButtonName) \
        [after 2000 [list \
            [namespace current]::createInfo \
        $toolButtonName $info ]]
}


#############################################################
#       proc createInfo { toolButtonName info}--
#    Creates an info label, and sets up bindings to
#    delete it.
#
# Arguments
#    toolButtonName  The name of the parent button
#    info            The information to display.
#
# Results
#    Creates and places a label.
#    Adds a script to the motion binding for the parent
#    button, and clears it when the motion occurs.

proc createInfo { toolButtonName info} {

    variable binding

    # Create a name for this label, and create the label

    set labelName ".toolbutton_[infoIdentifier \
        $toolButtonName]"
    label $labelName -text $info

    # Determine the location for this label.
    #
```

```
# winfo returns the geometry of the window within
#    its parent as WIDTHxHEIGHT+XOFFSET+YOFFSET
#    split at the + to separate out the X and Y
#    offsets.

set coordLst [split [winfo geometry \
    $toolButtonName] "+"]
set x [lindex $coordLst 1]
set y [lindex $coordLst 2]

# Place the label over the appropriate toolButton

place $labelName -x [expr $x+6] -y [expr $y+10]

# If this toolButton is close to the right margin
#    of the root window, the label won't be
#    completely displayed.
# In this case, the label must be moved to the
#    left to fit on the window.

# Update to make the label appear.  The $labelName
#    geometry is not valid until this update occurs.

update

# Get the width of the root window, and the width
#    of the $labelName label.
# If the X location + width goes over the edge,
#    move the label to the left until it fits.

set rootWidth [lindex [split [winfo geometry .] "x"] 0]
set labelWidth [lindex [split \
    [winfo geometry $labelName] "x"] 0]

if {[expr $x + $labelWidth] > $rootWidth} {
    set x [expr $rootWidth - $labelWidth]
    place $labelName -x $x -y [expr $y+10]
}

# Save the old event binding, and set a new one,
# that binds a Motion event to destroying the label

set binding($toolButtonName) \
    [bind $toolButtonName <Motion>]
```

```
    bind $toolButtonName <Motion> \
        "[namespace current]::deleteInfo $toolButtonName";

    bind $labelName <Motion> \
        "[namespace current]::deleteInfo $toolButtonName";
}


#############################################################
#       proc deleteInfo {toolButtonName}--
#    Deletes the label associated with this button, and
#    resets the binding to the original actions.
# Arguments
#    toolButtonName     The name of the parent button
#
# Results
#    No more label, and bindings as they were before the
#    mouse paused
#    on this button

proc deleteInfo {toolButtonName} {
    variable binding

    set labelName \
        ".toolbutton_[infoIdentifier $toolButtonName]"
    destroy $labelName;

    bind $toolButtonName <Motion> \
        $binding($toolButtonName);
    }
}
```

Example Script

```
frame .f
pack .f

toolbutton .f.b1 -info "B1 Message" -bitmap questhead \
        -command {puts "seeing head"}
pack .f.b1 -side left

toolbutton .f.b2 -info "B2 Message" -bitmap question \
```

```
         -command {incr counter}
pack .f.b2  -side left

toolbutton .f.b3 -info "B3 Message" -bitmap warning \
         -command {puts "COUNTER: $counter"} \
         -background #000000 -foreground #FFFFFF -highlight
#888888
pack .f.b3  -side left

set counter 0
```

Script Output

```
seeing head        # Clicked Head
COUNTER: 0         # Clicked question mark
COUNTER: 1         # Clicked question mark after clicking
exclamation
```

Script Results

Start Condition

After Mouse Is Idle

9.7 *The* image *Object*

Creating items like lines and arcs on a canvas is one way to generate a picture, but for some applications a rasterized image is more useful. There are two ways to create images in Tcl. The create bitmap canvas command will display a single color image on a canvas. The create image canvas command will display an image object on the canvas.

The canvas bitmap item is easy to use but is not as versatile as the image object. The previous tool button example uses the canvas bitmap command to map images onto the tool buttons.

The Tk image object is more versatile than the canvas bitmap item. You can use it to create simple bitmap images or full color images. The full color image objects can be shrunk, zoomed, subsampled, and moved from image object to image object. The image objects can be displayed in other widgets including buttons, labels, and text widgets.

The standard Tk distribution supports images defined in the X-Bitmap, GIF, Portable Pixmap, and Portable GrayMap formats. Some extensions exist that provide support for other formats such as JPEG and PNG. (See Chapter 13 for Jan Nijtmans's patch to add more image support to Tk.)

This section will explain how to create and use image objects.

9.7.1 The **image** Command

In order to create an image item on a canvas, you must first create an image object. The image command supports creating, deleting, and getting information about the image objects within the Tk interpreter.

The image create command creates an image object from a file or internal data and returns a handle for accessing that object.

Syntax: image create *type ?name? ?options?*

image create Create an image object of the desired type, and return a handle for referencing this object.

type The type of image that will be created. Tk versions 8.0 and 8.1 support:

- photo—a multicolor graphic.
- bitmap—a two-color graphic.

?name? The name for this image. If this is left out, the system will assign a name of the form imageX where X is a unique numeric value.

?options? These are options that are specific to the type of image being created. I'll discuss the appropriate options with the bitmap and photo.

An image can be deleted with the image delete command.

Syntax: `image delete` *name ?name?*

`image delete`   Delete the named image.

`name`   The handle returned by the `image create` command.

The `image` command can be used to get information about a single `image` or all the `images` that exist in the interpreter.

Syntax: `image height` *name*

Syntax: `image width` *name*

Syntax: `image type` *name*

`image height`   Return the height of the named `image`.

`image width`   Return the width of the named `image`.

`image type`   Return the type of the named `image`.

`name`   The handle returned by the `image create`.

Syntax: `image names`

`names`   Return a list of the image object names.

When an image is created with the `image create` command, a command with the same name as the `image` is also created. This image object command can be used to manipulate the object via its `cget` and `configure` subcommands. These commands behave in the same way as other widget `cget` and `configure` subcommands.

The configuration options that can be modified with the `configure` subcommand depend on the type of `image` created and are the same as the options available to that `image create` *type* command.

9.7.2 Bitmap Images

Bitmap images (which are different from a canvas `bitmap` item) are created with the command `image create bitmap`, as described before. The options supported for this command include:

-background *color*

>   The background color for this bitmap. If this is empty (the default), then background pixels will be transparent.

-foreground *color*

>   The foreground color for this image. The default is black.

-data *data*   The data that defines this image. This must be in the same format as an X Window System bitmap file.

-file *filename*

>   A file containing the X-Bitmap data.

The X Window System bitmap file is quite simple. It was designed to be included in C programs and looks like a piece of C code. The format is

```
#define name_width width
#define name_height height
static unsigned char name_bits[] = {
  data1, data2, ...
};
```

The good news is that this is simple and easy to construct. The bitmap program on a Unix system will let you construct an X-Bitmap file, or you can use the imagemagick or PBM utilities to convert an MS-Windows or Mac bitmap file to an X-Bitmap file.

9.7.3 Photo Images

The image data for a photo image may be PPM, PGM, or GIF. The data may be in binary form in a disk file or encoded as base64 data within the Tcl script.

Base64 encoding is a technique for converting binary data to printable ASCII with the least expansion. This format is used by all e-mail systems that support the MIME (multipurpose Internet mail extensions) protocol (which most modern mail programs do). Strange as it sounds, the most portable way to convert a file from binary to base64 encoding is to mail it to yourself, save the mail, and extract the data you want from the saved mail file.

If you are running on a Unix system, you may have the mmencode or mimencode program installed. These are part of the metamail MIME mail support.

The CD-ROM includes a Tcl script that will encode and decode base64 files. The script is named binary2b64.tcl and is in the examples/random directory. This script uses the b64tools.tcl package developed by Jan Wieck, which is also in that directory.

The image create photo command supports several options. These include:

-data *string*   The base64 encoded data that defines this image.

-file *filename*

A file that contains the image data in binary format.

-format *format*

The format for this image data. Tk will attempt to determine the type of image by default. The possible values for this option in version 8.0 are gif, pgm, and ppm.

As with the image create bitmap command, this command creates a new command with the same name as the new image, which can be used to manipulate the image via the *imageName* cget and *imageName* configure commands.

The photo type images support other subcommands, including:

Syntax: *imageName* copy *sourceImage ?options?*

copy   Copy the image data from *sourceImage* to the image *imageName*. Options include:

-from *x1 y1 x2 y2*

The area to copy from in the source image. The coordinates define opposing corners of a rectangle.

-to *x1 y1 x2 y2*

The area to copy to in the destination image.

-shrink   Shrink the image if necessary to fit the available space.

-zoom   Expand the image if necessary to fit the available space.

Syntax: *imageName* get *x y*

get   Return the value of the pixel at coordinates *x, y*. The color is returned as three integers, the red, green, and blue intensities.

Syntax: *imageName* put *data ?-to x1 y1 ?x2 y2??*

put   Put new pixel data into an image object.

data   The data is a string of color values, either as color names or in #rgb format. By default these pixels will be placed from the upper left corner, across each line, and then across the next line.

-to *x1 y1 x2 y2*

         Declares the location for the data to be placed. If only *x1, y1* are defined, then this is a starting point, and the edges of the image will be used as end points. If both *x1, y1* and *x2, y2* are defined, they define the opposing corners of a rectangle.

Example 9.7.3-1

Example Script

```
#
# Create a canvas

canvas .c -height 100 -width 300 -background white
pack .c

#
# This is an image created with xpaint, saved in gif format,
# and converted to base64 with metamail.

set img {
R01GODdhQAAwAKEAAP///wAAADz4NAD//ywAAAAAQAAwAAAC/
oSPqcvtD6OctNqLs16h+w+G
4kiWAWOm6hqi7AuLbijU9k3adHxyYt0BBoQjokfAm4GQQeawZBw6X8riFHq9sq
o/rZQY9aq4
NK3wPI1ufdilE/0Rj9m5rNcoT5Hd/
PIxb7IXZ9d1xOMh+Ne3CBhIZ+UX1DR52KNgguOGBtTo
eFkJBWqZIJojmlgKipp6uDoyABsrGxCr+sgC25FLO6DbW+kq8svr8bvbehtzXD
```

```
yclOw7+9rs
Cw1DJos9TQ1yrK2XnB3Nrb3r/f35EY4dskxtfk46rt5OLP/uGZ8+T8/
fSz+Hjtk+duSM3RvB
ZV8/
gsys3VI4TRyvYbXWBBQYjhXAJXz61GmEh4BEto8bQ5JkFewkyAMqU6VsSWKDzJ
k0a9q8
iTNnhQIAOw==
}

#
# Create an image from the img data

set i [image create photo -data $img]

#
# Now, create a displayable canvas image item from the image

.c create image 45 40 -image $i

#
# Create an image with no data,

set i2 [image create photo -height 50 -width 70]

#
# And copy data from the original image into it.

$i2 copy $i -from 1 1 50 40 -to 10 10 60 50

#
# Now display the image
.c create image 160 40 -image $i2

#
# Display some of the values in the new  image

for {set i 11} {$i < 30} {incr i} {
    for {set j 11} {$j < 15} {incr j} {
        puts -nonewline "   [$i2 get $j $i]"
    }
    puts ""
}

#
# And draw a horizontal line in it.
```

```
for {set i 20} {$i < 50} {incr i} {
    for {set j 30} {$j < 32} {incr j} {
        $i2 put #FFEF10 -to $i $j
    }
}
#
# This is the hourglass bitmap from the predefined bitmaps in
#  the Tk 8.0 distribution:  tk8.0/bitmaps/hourglass.bmp
set hourglassdata {
#define hourglass_width 19
#define hourglass_height 21
static unsigned char hourglass_bits[] = {
   0xff, 0xff, 0x07, 0x55, 0x55, 0x05, 0xa2, 0x2a, 0x03, 0x66,
0x15, 0x01,
   0xa2, 0x2a, 0x03, 0x66, 0x15, 0x01, 0xc2, 0x0a, 0x03, 0x46,
0x05, 0x01,
   0x82, 0x0a, 0x03, 0x06, 0x05, 0x01, 0x02, 0x03, 0x03, 0x86,
0x05, 0x01,
   0xc2, 0x0a, 0x03, 0x66, 0x15, 0x01, 0xa2, 0x2a, 0x03, 0x66,
0x15, 0x01,
   0xa2, 0x2a, 0x03, 0x66, 0x15, 0x01, 0xa2, 0x2a, 0x03, 0xff,
0xff, 0x07,
   0xab, 0xaa, 0x02};
}
#
# Create a bitmap image from the hourglass data
set bm [image create bitmap -data $hourglassdata]
#
# And create a displayable canvas image item from that image.
.c create image 260 40 -image $bm

#
# And label the images.
.c create text 44 80 -text "photo image 1"

.c create text 160 80 -text "copied and \nmodified"

.c create text 260 80 -text "bitmap image"
```

Script Output

```
255 255 255    255 255 255    255 255 255    255 255 255
255 255 255    255 255 255    255 255 255    255 255 255
  255 255 255    255 255 255    0 0 0    0 0 0
  255 255 255    255 255 255    0 0 0    0 0 0
  255 255 255    255 255 255    0 0 0    0 0 0
  255 255 255    255 255 255    0 0 0    0 0 0
  255 255 255    255 255 255    0 0 0    0 0 0
  255 255 255    255 255 255    0 0 0    0 0 0
...
```

Script Results

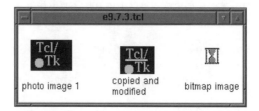

9.7.4 Revisiting the **toolbutton** Widget

The bitmaps used in the toolbutton example are all predefined in the Tk interpreter. If you have a bitmap of your own that you'd like to use, you'd have to define it in a data file using the X Window System bitmap format. For example, if the bitmap image is in a file named bitmap.xbm, then the toolbutton could be created with the command:

```
toolbutton .f.bFile -bitmap @bitmap.xbm ...
```

Tk has no method for defining canvas bitmap item data in a script.

Tk *does* allow you to define an image of type bitmap from data included in the script. The image command is the preferred way to deal with images on canvases.

Unfortunately, you can't access the predefined bitmaps with the image command, though you can load the data from the distribution (under the *TkDistribution*/bitmaps directory), as was just done in Example 9.7.3-1.

Following is a modified version of the toolbar procedure that uses an image instead of a bitmap and a script that creates its own bitmaps to display in the buttons. The code that executes within the toolButton namespace doesn't change.

The questhead, question, and warning bitmap data are taken from the files bitmaps/questhead.bmp, bitmaps/question.bmp, and bitmaps/warning.bmp, respectively.

The points to note in this version of the script are

- The -bitmap options are replaced with -image options.
- The -foreground option is not supported in the *canvasName* create image command but *is* supported as a subcommand of the image object.

Example 9.7.4-1

```
##################################################################
# proc toolbutton {name args}--
#     Create a toolbutton icon that will evaluate a command when
#         clicked
# Arguments
#     name      The name of this toolbutton
#     args      A list of -flag value pairs
#
# Results
#     Creates a new toolbutton and returns the name to the
#         calling script
#     Throws an error if unrecognized arguments or required
#         args are missing.
#
proc toolbutton {name args} {

    # These arguments are required.

    set reqOptions [list -command -info -image]

    # Check that the required arguments are present
    # Throw an error if any are missing.
```

```
foreach required $reqOptions {
    if {[lsearch -exact $args $required ] < 0} {
        error "toolbutton requires a $required option"
    }
}

# define defaults
set height 32
set width 32
set background gray80
set highlight gray90
set foreground black

#
# Step through the arguments.
# Confirm that each -option is valid, and
# set a variable for each option that is defined.
#    The variable for -foo is "foo".
#

set validOptions [list -image -command -info -height \
    -width -foreground -background -highlight]

foreach {option val} $args {
    if {[lsearch $validOptions $option ] < 0} {
        error "Bad argument $option - \
        must be one of $validOptions"
    }
    set item [string range $option 1 end]
    eval [list set $item $val]
}

# Set the foreground for the image

$image configure -foreground $foreground

# Create the canvas for this toolbutton

canvas $name -height $height -width $width \
    -background $background

# Place the image in it.
```

```
$name create image [expr $height/2] [expr $width/2] \
    -image $image

# Bind the button click to evaluate the command in
#    global scope

bind $name <ButtonPress-1> "uplevel 0 [list $command]"

# Bind the background to change color when the
#    cursor enters

bind $name <Enter> "$name configure -background $highlight"

# Bind the background to change color when the cursor
#  leaves. Cancel any pending display of an info label.

bind $name <Leave> "\
    $name {configure -background $background;\
    catch {after cancel \
        $[namespace current]::toolButton::afters($name) \
        };\
        "

# Whenever the button moves, reset the Motion task.

bind $name <Motion> "[list \
    [namespace current]::toolButton::scheduleInfo \
    $name $info ]"

# And return the name

return $name
}
```

Example Script

```
frame .f
pack .f

# The question/head from bitmaps/questhead.bm

set questhd [image create bitmap -data {
#define questhead_width 20
#define questhead_height 22
static unsigned char questhead_bits[] = {
```

```
    0xf8, 0x1f, 0x00, 0xac, 0x2a, 0x00, 0x56, 0x55, 0x00, 0xeb,
0xaf, 0x00,
    0xf5, 0x5f, 0x01, 0xfb, 0xbf, 0x00, 0x75, 0x5d, 0x01, 0xfb,
0xbe, 0x02,
    0x75, 0x5d, 0x05, 0xab, 0xbe, 0x0a, 0x55, 0x5f, 0x07, 0xab,
0xaf, 0x00,
    0xd6, 0x57, 0x01, 0xac, 0xab, 0x00, 0xd8, 0x57, 0x00, 0xb0,
0xaa, 0x00,
    0x50, 0x55, 0x00, 0xb0, 0x0b, 0x00, 0xd0, 0x17, 0x00, 0xb0,
0x0b, 0x00,
    0x58, 0x15, 0x00, 0xa8, 0x2a, 0x00};
}]

set question [image create bitmap -data {
#define question_width 17
#define question_height 27
static unsigned char question_bits[] = {
    0xf0, 0x0f, 0x00, 0x58, 0x15, 0x00, 0xac, 0x2a, 0x00, 0x56,
0x55, 0x00,
    0x2b, 0xa8, 0x00, 0x15, 0x50, 0x01, 0x0b, 0xa0, 0x00, 0x05,
0x60, 0x01,
    0x0b, 0xa0, 0x00, 0x05, 0x60, 0x01, 0x0b, 0xb0, 0x00, 0x00,
0x58, 0x01,
    0x00, 0xaf, 0x00, 0x80, 0x55, 0x00, 0xc0, 0x2a, 0x00, 0x40,
0x15, 0x00,
    0xc0, 0x02, 0x00, 0x40, 0x01, 0x00, 0xc0, 0x02, 0x00, 0x40,
0x01, 0x00,
    0xc0, 0x02, 0x00, 0x00, 0x00, 0x00, 0x80, 0x01, 0x00, 0xc0,
0x02, 0x00,
    0x40, 0x01, 0x00, 0xc0, 0x02, 0x00, 0x00, 0x01, 0x00};
}]

set warning [image create bitmap -data {
#define warning_width 6
#define warning_height 19
static unsigned char warning_bits[] = {
    0x0c, 0x16, 0x2b, 0x15, 0x2b, 0x15, 0x2b, 0x16, 0x0a, 0x16,
0x0a, 0x16,
    0x0a, 0x00, 0x00, 0x1e, 0x0a, 0x16, 0x0a};
}]

toolbutton .f.b1 -info "B1 Message" -image $questhd \
        -command {puts "seeing head"}
```

```
pack .f.b1 -side left

toolbutton .f.b2 -info "B2 Message" -image $question \
        -command {incr counter}
pack .f.b2  -side left

toolbutton .f.b3 -info "B3 Message" -image $warning \
        -command {puts "COUNTER: $counter"} \
        -background #000000 -foreground #FFFFFF \
        -highlight #888888
pack .f.b3  -side left

set counter 0
```

Script Output

```
seeing head       # Clicked Head
COUNTER: 0        # Clicked question mark
COUNTER: 1        # Clicked question mark after clicking
exclamation
```

Script Results

Start Condition	After Mouse Is Idle

As you can see, the results are the same with the -bitmap version and the -image version. The -image version of this widget needs more setup but is more versatile.

9.8 Bottom Line

- The canvas widget creates a drawing surface.
- The canvas widget returns a unique identifier whenever a drawable item is created.
- Drawable items may be associated with one or more tag strings.

- The coordinates of a drawable item can be accessed or modified with the *canvasName* coords command.

  Syntax: *canvasName* coords *tagOrId ?x1 y1? ... ?xn yn?*

- A drawable item can be moved on a canvas with the *canvasName* move command.

  Syntax: *canvasName* move *tagOrId xoffset yoffset*

- The space occupied by a drawable item is returned by the *canvasName* bbox command.

  Syntax: *canvasName* bbox *tagOrId*

- A list of items that match a search criterion is returned by the *canvasName* find command.

  Syntax: *canvasName* find *searchSpec*

- A drawable item's location in the display list can be modified with the *canvasName* raise command and *canvasName* lower command.

  Syntax: *canvasName* raise *tagOrId ?abovetagOrId?*

  Syntax: *canvasName* lower *tagOrId ?belowtagOrId?*

- A list of available fonts is returned with the font families command.

  Syntax: font families *?-displayof windowName?*

- The horizontal space necessary to display a string in a particular font is returned by the font measure command.

  Syntax: font measure *font ?-displayof windowName? text*

- The closest match to a requested font is returned by the font actual command.

  Syntax: font actual *font ?-displayof windowName?*

- Actions can be bound to events on a widget with the bind command.

  Syntax: bind *widgetName eventType script*

- Actions can be bound to events on a drawable item within a canvas widget with the *canvasName* bind command.

  Syntax: *canvasName* bind *tagOrId eventType script*

Two-color (`bitmap`) and multicolor (`photo`) images can be created with the image create command.

>**Syntax:** `image create` *type ?name? ?options?*

- Images can be deleted with the `image delete` command.

>**Syntax:** `image delete` *name ?name?*

- Information about an image is returned by the `image height`, `image width`, and `image type` commands.

>**Syntax:** `image height` *name*

>**Syntax:** `image width` *name*

>**Syntax:** `image type` *name*

- A list of images currently defined in a script is returned by the `image names` command.

>**Syntax:** `image names`

- Photo image pixel data can be copied from one image to another with the *imageName* `copy` command.

>**Syntax:** *imageName* `copy` *sourceImage ?options?*

- Photo image pixel data can be accessed or modified with the *imageName* `get` and *imageName* `put` commands.

>**Syntax:** *imageName* `get` *x y*

>**Syntax:** *imageName* `put` *data ?-to x1 y1 ?x2 y2??*

- The `canvas create bitmap` command and the `image create bitmap` command are not the same but can be used to achieve equivalent results.

canvas create bitmap	**image create bitmap**
Can access internal bitmaps	Can use data defined within a script
Can reference a data file via: `@filename`	Can reference a data file via: `-file`
Can modify foreground via:	Can modify foreground via:
cvsName `create bitmap \ -foreground $newcolor`	*imageHandle* `configure \ -foreground $newcolor`

The text *Widget and* html_library

The entry and label widgets are useful for applications with short prompts and short amounts of data to enter, applications that resemble filling out a form. However some applications need to allow the user to display, enter, or edit large amounts of text. These needs are supported by the text widget.

The text widget supports:

- emacs-style editing.
- scrollbars.
- multiple fonts in a single document.
- tagging a single character or multiple-character strings (in a similar manner to the way tags are applied to canvas objects).
- marking positions in the text.
- inserting other Tk widgets or images into the text display.
- binding events to a single character or a multiple-character string.

One of the packages built with the text widget is the html_library written by Stephen Uhler. This is not part of the Tcl/Tk distribution but is available via ftp at:

```
ftp.smli.com:/pub/tcl/html_library-0.3.tar.gz.
```

This extension will render html text and provides hooks for links and images.

This chapter introduces the text widget and the html library.

10.1 Overview of the text Widget

An application may create multiple text windows, which can be displayed in either a frame, a canvas, or another text widget.

The contents of a text widget are addressed by line and character location.

The text widget contents are maintained as a set of lists. Each list consists of the text string to display, along with any tags, marks, image annotations, and window annotations associated with this text string.

If the text string is longer than the width of the text widget, the widget can be configured either to wrap the text onto multiple lines (at word boundary, or at the last character that fits on the line) or to truncate the line. Note that allowing text to wrap to multiple lines will cause the number of lines on the display to be different from the number of text strings in the internal representation of the text. When referencing a location within the text widget, the line and character position refers to the internal representation of the text, which may not be what is displayed.

When a scrollbar is connected to the text widget, the user can modify which lines are displayed on the screen. This does not affect the contents of the text widget, and the line and character positions still reflect the internal representation of the text, not the displayed text. For example, if the user has scrolled to the bottom of a document and the top line displayed is the 50th line of the document, it is still referenced as line 50, not line 1.

A text string can have a tag associated with it. Tags in a text widget are similar to tags in the canvas object. You can apply zero or more tags to a line of text and apply a given tag to one or more lines of text. The tags will be discussed in more detail later in this chapter.

A text widget can also have marks associated with it. Marks are similar to tags, except that where tags are associated with a text string, a mark is associated with a location in the text. You can have only a single instance of any mark, but you can have multiple marks referring to a single location.

10.1.1 Text Location in the **text** Widget

The text widget does not allow you to place text at any location, the way a canvas widget does. A text widget "fills" from the top left, and you can address any position that has a character defined at that location. If a position outside the range of available lines and characters is requested, it will be mapped to the nearest location in the text widget that has a character defined.

The locations are addressed with index values that are formatted as a list:

position *?modifier1 modifier2...modifierN?*

The position field may be one of:

line.character

>The line and character that define a location in the internal representation of the text.

>Lines are numbered starting from 1 (to conform to the numbering style of other Unix applications), and character positions are numbered starting from 0 (to conform to the numbering style of C strings).

>The *character* field may be numeric or the word end. The end keyword indicates the position of the newline character that terminates a line.

@x.y

>The x and y parameters are in pixels. This index maps to the character with a bounding box that includes this pixel.

markID	The character just after the mark named *markID*.
tagID.`first`	The first occurrence of tag *tagID*.
tagID.`last`	The last occurrence of tag *tagID*.
windowName	The name of a window that was placed in this `text` widget with the `window create` widget command.
imageName	The name of an image that was placed in this `text` widget with the `image create` widget command.
`end`	The last character in the `text` widget.

The modifier field in an index may be one of:

`+`*num* `chars`
`−`*num* `chars`
`+`*num* `lines`
`−`*num* `lines`
	The `location` moves forward or backward by the defined number of characters or lines. The "+" symbol moves the `location` forward and the "−" symbol moves the `location` backward.

`linestart` `lineend`	The index refers to the beginning or end of the line that includes the *location* index. NOTE: {1.0 `lineend`} is equivalent to {1.`end`} and {1.0 `linestart`} is equivalent to {1.0}.
`wordstart` `wordend`	The index refers to the beginning or end of the word that includes the *location* index.

Index Examples

`0.0`	Not a valid index, line numbers start at 1. This will be mapped to the beginning of the text widget, index `1.0`.
{`.b wordend`}	If a letter follows window `.b`, this refers to the location just before the first space after the `.b` window. If window `.b` is at the end of a word, this refers to the location just after the space that follows window `.b`

`1.0 lineend`   This is not a valid index; it is not a list.

`[list mytag.first lineend -10c wordend]`
Sets the index to the end of the word that has a letter 10
character-positions from the end of the line that includes
the first reference to the tag `mytag`.

Note that the index is evaluated left to right;

- Find the tag `mytag`.
- Move to the end of the line.
- Count back 10 characters.
- Go to the end of the word.

10.1.2 Tag Overview

The `tag` used in a `text` widget is similar to the `tag` used with the canvas
object. A `tag` is a string of characters that can be used to identify a single
character or a text string. A tag can be attached to several text strings, and a
text string may have multiple tags associated with it.

The text string associated with a tag is defined by the tag's start and end
locations. Note that the tag is associated with a location, not the character
at a location. If the character at the location is deleted, the tag moves to the
location of the nearest character that was included in a tagged area. If all
the characters associated with a tag are deleted, the tag no longer exists.

Manipulating portions of text (setting fonts or colors, binding actions, etc.)
is done by identifying the text portion with a `tag` and then manipulating
the tagged text via the *textWidget* `tag` command.

For instance, the command *textName* `tag configure loud -font [times
24 bold]` will cause the text tagged with the tag `loud` to be drawn with large,
bold letters. All text tagged `loud` will be displayed in a large, bold font.

The `sel` tag is always defined in a `text` widget. It cannot be destroyed.
When characters in the text widget have been selected (by dragging the
cursor over them with the mouse button depressed), the `sel` tag will define

the start and end indices of the selected characters. The sel tag is configured to display the selected text in reverse video.

10.1.3 Mark Overview

Marks are associated with the spaces between the characters, instead of being associated with a character location. If the characters around a mark are deleted, the mark will be moved to stay next to the remaining characters. Marks are manipulated with the *textName* mark commands.

A mark identifies a single location in the text, not a range of locations.

A mark can be declared to have gravity. The gravity of a mark controls how the mark will be moved when new characters are inserted at a mark. The gravity may be one of:

left   The mark is treated as though it is attached to the character on the left, and any new characters are inserted to the right of the mark; thus the location of the mark on a line will not change.

right   The mark is treated as though it is attached to the character on the right, and new characters are inserted to the left of the mark. Thus, the location of the mark will be one greater character location every time a character is inserted.

Two marks are always defined:

insert   The location of the insertion cursor.

current   The location closest to the mouse location. Note that this is not updated if the mouse is moved with button one depressed (as in a drag operation).

10.1.4 Image Overview

Images created with the image create command (covered in Chapter 9) can be inserted into a text widget. The annotation that defines an image uses a single character location regardless of the height or width of the image.

Multiple copies of an image can be inserted into a text widget. Each time an image is inserted, a unique identifier will be returned that can be used to refer to this display of the image.

10.1.5 Window Overview

A Tk widget such as a button, canvas, or another text widget can be inserted into a text widget with the *textWidget* window create command.

Only a single copy of any widget can be inserted. If the same widget is used as the argument of two *textWidget* window create commands, the first occurrence of the widget will be deleted, and it will be inserted at the location defined in the second command.

10.2 *Creating a* text *Widget*

Text widgets are created the same way as other widgets, with a command that returns the specified widget name. Like other widgets, the text widget supports defining the height and width on the command line. Note that the unit for the height and width is the size of a character in the default font, rather than pixels. You can determine the font being used by a text widget with the configure or cget widget command. (See Section 8.4.)

Syntax: text *textName ?options?*

text   Create a text widget.

textName   The name for this text widget.

?options?   Some of the options supported by the text widget are:

-state *state* Defines the initial state for this widget. May be one of:

normal   The text widget will permit text to be edited.

disabled   The `text` widget will not permit text to be edited. This option creates a display-only version of the widget.

-tabs *tabList*

Defines the tab stops for this `text` widget. Tabs are defined as a location (in any screen distance format, as described in Chapter 9) and an optional modifier to define how to justify the text within the column.

The modifier may be one of:

left   Left justify the text.

right   Right justify the text.

center   Center the text.

numeric   Line up a decimal point, or the least significant digit at the tab location.

-wrap *style*   Defines how lines of text will wrap. May be one of:

none   Lines will not wrap. Characters that do not fit within the defined width are not displayed.

word   Lines will wrap on the space between words. The final space on a line will be displayed as a `newline`, rather than leave a trailing space on the line before the wrap. Words are not wrapped on hyphens.

char | Lines will wrap at the last location in the text widget regardless of the character. This is the default mode.

-spacing1 *distance*

Defines the extra blank space to leave above a line of text when it is displayed. If the line of text wraps to multiple lines when it is displayed, only the top line will have this space added.

-spacing2 *distance*

Defines the extra blank space to leave above lines that have been wrapped when they are displayed.

-spacing3 *distance*

Defines the extra blank space to leave below a line of text when it is displayed. If the line of text wraps to multiple lines when it is displayed, only the bottom line will have this space added.

Example 10.2-1

Example Script

```
# Create the text widget and pack it.
set txt  [text .t -height 12 -width 102 -background white \
              -tabs {2.5i right 3i left 5.8i numeric}]
pack $txt

# Insert several lines at the end location.  Each new line
# becomes the new last line in the widget.

$txt  insert end "The next lines demonstrate tabbed text\n"
$txt  insert end "\n"
$txt  insert end "noTab \t Right Justified \t Left \
    Justified \t Numeric\n"
$txt  insert end "\n"
```

```
$txt  insert end "line1 \t column1 \t column2 \t 1.0\n"
$txt  insert end "line2 \t column1 text \t column2\
    text \t 22.00\n"
$txt  insert end "line3 \t text in column1 \t text\
    for column2 \t 333.00\n"

# Insert a few lines at specific line locations.
#   To demonstrate some location examples

$txt  insert 1.0 "These lines are inserted last, but are\n"
$txt  insert 2.0 "inserted at the\n"
$txt  insert 2.end " beginning of the text widget\n"
$txt  insert {3.5 linestart} "so that they appear first.\n"
$txt  insert 4.0 "\n"
```

Script Results

```
┌──────────────────── e10_2_1.tcl ────────────────────┐
│These lines are inserted last, but are               │
│inserted at the beginning of the text widget         │
│so that they appear first.                           │
│                                                     │
│The next lines demonstrate tabbed text               │
│                                                     │
│noTab        Right Justified   Left Justified    Numeric │
│                                                     │
│line1              column1     column2               1.0 │
│line2         column1 text     column2 text        22.00 │
│line3      text in column1     text for column2   333.00 │
└─────────────────────────────────────────────────────┘
```

10.3 Text *Widget Subcommands*

The text widget has several subcommands. This section gives an overview of some of the available subcommands. See the online documentation for your version of Tk for more details and to see if other commands are implemented in the version you are using.

The dump subcommand provides detailed information about the contents of the text widget. Thus, it is very seldom used in actual programming. The dump subcommand will be used in the following discussion of the text widget as we examine how text strings, marks, and tags are handled by the text widget.

The dump subcommand returns a list of the text widget's contents between two index points. Each entry in the list consists of sets of three fields: identifier, data, and index. The identifier may have one of several values that will define the data that follows. The data field will contain different values depending on the value of the identifier. The index field will always be a value in line.char format.

The values of identifier and the associated data may be one of:

text The following data will be text to be displayed on the text widget. If there are multiple words in the text, the text will be grouped with curly braces.

tagon Denotes the start of a tagged section of text. The data associated with this identifier will be a tag name. The index will be the location at which the tagged text starts.

tagoff Denotes the end of a tagged section of text. The data associated with this identifier will be a tag name. The index will be the location at which the tagged text ends.

mark Denotes the location of a mark. The data associated with this identifier will be a mark name. The index will be the location to the right of the mark.

image Denotes the location of an image to be displayed in the text widget. The index will be the index of the character to the right of the image.

window Denotes the location of a window to be displayed in the text widget. The index will be the index of the character to the right of the window.

10.3.1 Inserting Text

The subcommand that inserts text into a text window is the insert subcommand. This command can be used to insert one or more lines of text with zero or more tags attached to each set of text.

Syntax: *textName* insert *index text* ?*tagList*? ?*moreText*? \
?*moreTagList*? ?...?

textName	The name of the text widget.
insert	Insert new text into this text widget.
index	The index at which to insert this text.
text	A string of text to insert. If this text includes embedded newlines (\n), then it will be inserted as multiple lines.
tagList	An optional list of tags to associate with the preceding text.

The following example creates a text widget, inserts three lines of text, and displays a formatted dump of the text widget contents.

Notice the foreach command with three arguments in a list to step through the dump output. The ability to use a list of arguments to a foreach command was added in Tcl revision 7.4. The foreach with a list of iterator variables is a useful construct for stepping through data formatted as sets of items, instead of as a list of lists. (See Section 8.8.1.1 for another example of this form of the foreach command.)

Example 10.3.1-1

Example Script

```
text .t -height 5 -width 70
pack .t

.t insert end "This text is tagged 'TAG1'.   " TAG1
.t insert end "This is on the same line, 'TAG2'\n" TAG2

.t insert end "The linefeed after 'TAG2' puts this on a new \
    line.\n"
.t insert 2.0 "Line 2 becomes line 3 when this is inserted at \
    2.0\n" INSERTED

set textDump [.t dump 1.0 end -all]

puts "[format "%-8s %-50s %6s\n" ID DATA INDEX]"
foreach {id data index} $textDump {
    puts "[format {%-8s %-50s %6s} $id $data $index]"
}
```

Script Output

ID	DATA	INDEX
tagon	TAG1	1.0
text	This text is tagged 'TAG1'.	1.0
tagoff	TAG1	1.29
tagon	TAG2	1.29
text	This is on the same line, 'TAG2'	1.29
tagoff	TAG2	2.0
tagon	INSERTED	2.0
text	Line 2 becomes line 3 when this is inserted at 2.0	2.0
tagoff	INSERTED	3.0
text	The linefeed after 'TAG2' puts this on a new line.	3.0
mark	insert	4.0
mark	current	4.0

Script Results

```
e10_3_1_1.tcl
This text is tagged 'TAG1'.   This is on the same line, 'TAG2'
Line 2 becomes line 3 when this is inserted at 2.0
The linefeed after 'TAG2' puts this on a new line.
```

In the previous example, all the lines are shorter than the width of the text widget. Since none of the lines wrap, the text is displayed on the same line as the internal representation.

The first line of the example inserted a line with the text This text is tagged 'TAG1'. at the end of the text widget. Since there was no text in the widget, the end was also the beginning at that point.

The dump shows that tag TAG1 starts at index 1.0 and ends at index 1.29. The text also starts at index 1.0.

Note that the second set of text is also inserted onto line 1. This is because the first set of inserted text did not have a newline character to mark it as terminating a line.

The second set of text has a newline character at the end, which causes the next line to be inserted at index 2.0.

However, the last `insert` command inserts text at location `2.0` and terminates that text with a `newline`, pushing the line that was at index `2.0` down to index `3.0`.

10.3.2 Searching Text

A script can search for text within a `text` widget using the *textName* `search` subcommand. This command will search forward or backward from an index point or search between two index points.

Syntax: *textName* `search` *?options? pattern startIndex ?end-Index?*

textName	The name of the `text` widget.
`search`	Search the contents of this `text` widget for text that matches a particular pattern.
?options?	Options for `search` include:

Search Direction

These are mutually exclusive options.

`-forwards`	The direction to search from the
`-backwards`	*startIndex*.

Search Style   These are mutually exclusive options.

`-exact`	Search for an exact match.
`-regexp`	Use regular expression rules to match the *pattern* to text.
`-nocase`	Ignore the case when comparing *pattern* to the text.

Other Options   These are not mutually exclusive options.

`-count` *varName*

The `-count` option must be followed by a variable name. If the search is successful,

> the number of characters matched will be placed in *varName*.

> -- Signifies that this is the last option. The next argument will be interpreted as a pattern, even if it starts with a "-", and would otherwise be interpreted as an option.

It's good style to use the "--" option whenever you use the search subcommand. This will ensure that your code will not generate an unexpected syntax error if it is used to search for a string starting with a "-".

Example 10.3.2-1

Example Script

```
text .t -height 5 -width 60
pack .t

# Insert some text

.t insert end "The search command can search using glob\
    rules (default)\n"
.t insert end "Or for an exact match (using -exact)\n"
.t insert end "Or for a regular expression (using -regexp)\n"

# "Exact" doesn't exist in this text, search will return ""

set pos [.t search -exact -count matchchars -- "Exact" 1.0 end]
puts "Position of 'Exact': $pos "

# "-exact" does exist.  This will match 6 characters

set pos \
    [.t search -exact -count matchchars -- "-exact" 1.0 end]
puts "Position of '-exact': $pos   matched $matchchars chars"

# This regular expression search also searches for "-e"
#   followed by any characters except a ")".
#   It will match to "-exact"

set pos [.t search -regexp -count matchchars -- {-e[^)]*} 1.0 end]
puts "Position of '-e\[^)]*': $pos   matched $matchchars chars"
```

```
# This is an error - the lack of the "--" argument causes the
#   search argument "-e[^)]*" to be treated as a flag.

set pos [.t search -regexp -count matchchars {-e[^)]*} 1.0 end]
puts "POS: $pos match: $matchchars"
```

Script Output

```
Position of 'Exact':
Position of '-exact': 2.29    matched 6 chars
Position of '-e[^)]*': 2.29    matched 6 chars
Error in startup script: bad switch "-e[^)]*": must be -
forward, -backward,
   -exact, -regexp, -nocase, -count, -elide, or --
   while executing
".t search -regexp -count matchchars {-e[^)]*} 1.0 end"
```

Script Results

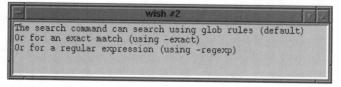

10.3.3 The mark Subcommands

The *textName* mark subcommands are used to manipulate marks in the text widget. Marks are used when you need to remember a particular location in the text. For instance, you can use marks to define an area of text to highlight, for a cut-and-paste operation, etc.

A mark is defined with the *textName* mark set command.

Syntax: *textName* mark set *markName index*

textName mark set

Set a mark in the text widget *textName*.

markName   The name to assign to this mark.

index   The index of the character to the right of the mark.

A mark can be removed with the *textName* mark unset command.

Syntax: *textName* mark unset *markName ?markName2? ?...? \
?markNameN?*

textName mark unset
> Remove a mark from the text widget *textName*.

markName　　　The name of the mark to remove.

You can get a list of all the marks defined in a text widget with the *text-Name* mark names command.

Syntax: *textName* mark names

textName mark names
> Return the names of all marks defined in text widget *textName*.

You can search for marks before or after a given index position with the *textName* mark next and *textName* mark previous commands.

Syntax: *textName* mark next *index*
Syntax: *textName* mark previous *index*

textName mark next

textName mark previous
> Return the name of the first mark after (next) or before (previous) the *index* location.

index
The index from which to start the search.

Example 10.3.3-1

Example Script

```
text .t -height 5 -width 60
pack .t

.t insert end "A mark will be set in this line,\n as shown by \
dump"

.t mark set demoMark 1.2

puts "The first mark is: [.t mark next 1.0]"
puts "The last mark is: [.t mark previous end]"
```

```
set textDump [.t dump 1.0 end -all]

puts "[format "%-8s %-50s %6s\n" ID DATA INDEX]"
foreach {id data index} $textDump {
    puts "[format {%-8s %-50s %6s} $id $data $index]"
}
```

Script Output

The first mark is: demoMark
The last mark is: current

ID	DATA	INDEX
text	A	1.0
mark	demoMark	1.2
text	mark will be set in this line,	1.2
text	as shown by dump	2.0
mark	insert	2.17
mark	current	2.17

Script Results

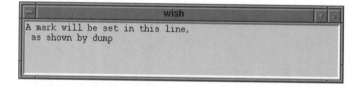

10.3.4 Tags

Many of the interesting things that can be done with a text widget are done with tags. Tags define text that is to be in different fonts, text that is bound to an event, text that should be displayed in different colors, etc.

10.3.4.1 Creating and Destroying Tags

Tags can be attached to text when the text is inserted, as shown in Example 10.3.1-1, or they can be added later with the *textName* tag add command. The *textName* tag remove command can be used to remove the tags from a specific set of characters, and the *textName* tag delete command can be used to remove all occurrences of a tag from a text widget.

Syntax: *textName* tag add *tagName startIndex1 ?end1?* \
?start2? ... ?endN?

textName   The text widget that will contain the tag.

tag add   Add a tag at the defined index points.

startIndex ?end?

        The tag will be attached to the character at *startIndex* and will contain all characters up to but not including the character at *end*. If the *end* is less than the *startIndex* or the *startIndex* does not refer to any character in the text widget, then no characters are tagged.

Syntax: *textName* tag remove *tagName startIndex1 ?end1?* \
?start2? ... ?endN?

textName   The text widget that contains the tag.

tag delete   Remove tag information for the named tags from characters in the ranges defined.

tagName   The names of tags to be removed.

startIndex ?end?

        The range of characters from which to remove the tag information.

Syntax: *textName* tag delete *tagName ?tagname2? ...* \
?tagNameN?

textName   The text widget that contains the tag.

tag delete   Delete all information about the tags named in this command.

tagName   The names of tags to be deleted.

10.3.4.2 Finding Tags

Your script can get a list of tags that have been defined at a particular location, a range of locations, or an entire text widget. You can also retrieve a list of locations that are associated with a tag.

Many tags can be defined for single location in a text file. For instance, the first character of a paragraph may be in a different font, tagged to show that it's the start of a keyword, and tagged as the first character after a pagebreak. You can get a list of the tags at a location with the tag names command.

Syntax: *textName* tag names *index*

textName   The text widget that contains the tags.

tag names   Return a list of all tags defined at *index*.

index   The index point to check for tags.

When you are processing the contents of a text widget, you may want to step through the widget looking at tags in the order in which they appear. The nextrange and prevrange commands will step through a text widget, returning the index points that fall within the requested range of characters.

Note that the prevrange and nextrange commands expect the start and end locations in the opposite order. For the prevrange command, startindex is greater than endindex, whereas for nextrange the endindex is greater than startindex.

Syntax: *textName* tag nextrange *tagName startIndex ?endIndex?*
Syntax: *textName* tag prevrange *tagName startIndex ?endIndex?*

textName   The text widget that contains the tags.

tag nextrange

      Return the first index defined after *startIndex* but before *endIndex*.

tag prevrange

      Return the first index defined before *startIndex* but after *endIndex*.

tagName   The name of the tag to search for.

startIndex endIndex

      The index points that defined the boundaries for the search.

Alternatively, you can get a list of all the index ranges that are tagged with a particular tag with the tag ranges command.

Syntax: *textName* tag ranges *tagName*

textName   The text widget that contains the tags.

tag ranges   Return a list of index ranges that have been tagged with *tagName*.

tagName   The name of the tag to search for.

Example 10.3.4.2-1

Example Script

```
text .t -height 5 -width 70
pack .t

.t insert end "Text can have multiple tags at any \
    given index.\n" T1
.t insert end "You can get a list of tags at an index \
    with 'tag names'.\n" T2
.t insert end "You can search the text with prevrange and \
    nextrange.\n" T3
.t insert end "You can get the ranges where a tag is \
    defined with 'ranges'" T4

.t tag add firstchar 1.0
.t tag add firstline 1.0 {1.0 lineend}
.t tag add firstpage 1.0 end

.t tag add secondline 2.0

.t tag add firstchar 2.0
.t tag add firstchar 3.0
.t tag add firstchar 4.0

puts "These tags are defined: \n    [.t tag names]"

puts "These tags are defined at index 1.0: [.t tag names 1.0]"

puts "Tag firstchar is defined for these ranges: \n\
    [.t tag ranges firstchar]"

puts "Tag T2 is defined for the range: \n    [.t tag ranges T2]"
```

```
puts "The first occurrence of firstchar after the start of\
    line 3 is: [.t tag nextrange firstchar 3.0]"

puts "The first occurrence of firstchar before the start of\
    line 3 is: [.t tag prevrange firstchar 3.0]"
```

Script Output

THESE Tags are defined:
**   sel T1 T2 T3 T4 firstchar firstline firstpage second-**
line
These tags are defined at index 1.0: T1 firstchar first-
line firstpage
Tag firstchar is defined for these ranges:
** 1.0 1.1 2.0 2.1 3.0 3.1 4.0 4.1**
Tag T2 is defined for the range:
**   2.0 3.0**
The first occurrence of firstchar after the start of line
3 is: 3.0 3.1
The first occurrence of firstchar before the start of line
3 is: 2.0 2.1

Script Results

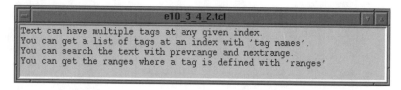

10.3.4.3 Using Tags

Tags are the interface into the text widget that allows you to bind actions to events on sections of text, set colors, set fonts, set margins, set line spacing, etc. This section will discuss a few of the things that can be done with tags and provide an example of how to use tags. The complete list of options you can set with a tag is in the online documentation.

An action can be bound to an event on a tagged area of text using the tag bind command.

Syntax: *textName* tag bind *tagName ?eventType? ?script?*

textName   The name of the text widget.

tag bind   Bind an action to an event occurring on the tagged section of text, or return the script to be evaluated when an event occurs.

tagName   The name of the tag that defines the range of characters that will accept an event.

?eventType?   If the *eventType* field is set, this defines the event that will trigger this action. The event types are the same as those defined for canvas events in Section 9.5.

script   The script to evaluate when this event occurs.

The display configuration of text can be modified with the tag configure command. The tag configure command will allow you to set many of the options that control a display, including:

-background *color*   The foreground and background colors for the text.
-foreground *color*

-font *fontID*   The font to use when displaying this text.

-justify *style*   How to justify text with this tag. May be left, right, or center.

-offset *pixels*   The vertical offset in pixels for this line from the base location for displaying text. A positive value raises the text above where it would otherwise be displayed, and a negative value lowers the text. This can be used to display subscripts and superscripts.

-lmargin1 *pixels*   The distance from the left and right edges to use as a
-lmargin2 *pixels*   margin. The rmargin value is a distance from the
-rmargin *pixels*   right edge of the text widget to treat as a right margin.

The `lmargin1` is a distance from the left edge to treat as a margin for display lines that have not wrapped, and `lmargin2` is a distance to use as a margin for lines that have wrapped.

`-underline` *boolean*   Specifies whether or not to underline characters.

The next example displays a few lines of text in several fonts and binds the creation of a label with more information to a button click on the word `tag`.

Example 10.3.4.3-1

Example Script

```
# Create and pack the text widget

text .t -height 5 -width 60
pack .t

# Insert some text with lots of tags.

.t insert end "T" {firstLetter} "he " {normal} "tag" \
    {code action}
.t insert end " command allows you to create displays\n"
.t insert end "with multiple fonts" {normal} "1" {superscript}
.t insert end "\n\n"
.t insert end "1" {superscript}
.t insert end "Tcl/Tk for Real Programmers,  " {italic} \
    "Clif Flynt, "  {bold}
.t insert end "Academic Press, 1998"

# Set the fonts for the various types of tagged text

.t tag configure italic -font {times 14 italic}
.t tag configure normal -font {times 14 roman}
.t tag configure bold -font {times 14 bold}

# Set font and offset to make superscript text

.t tag configure superscript -font {times 10 roman} -offset 5

# Set font for typewriter style font
```

```
.t tag configure code -font {courier 14 roman underline}

# Define a font to make a fancy first letter for a word

.t tag configure firstLetter -font {times 16 italic bold}

# Bind an action to the text tagged as "action".

.t tag bind {action} <Button-1> {
    label .l -text "See Chapter 10" -relief raised;
    place .l -x 50 -y 10 ;
}
```

Script Results

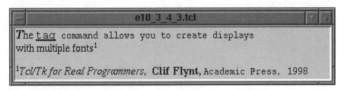

Script Results (after Clicking on `tag`)

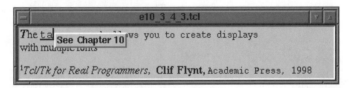

10.3.5 Inserting Images and Widgets into a **text** Widget

You can insert an image created with the `image create` command into a text widget with the *textName* `image create` command, and other Tk widgets can be inserted into a `text` widget with the `window create` command.

Syntax: *textName* `image create` *index ?options?*

textName `image create`

        Insert an image into a `text` widget.

index   The index at which to insert the image.

?options?   The options for the image create command include

    -image *handle*

        The image object handle returned when the Tk image object was created. (See Section 9.7.1.)

    -name *imageName*

        A name to use to refer to this image. A default name will be returned if this option is not present.

Syntax: *textName* window create   *index ?options?*

textName window create
    Insert a Tk widget into the text widget.

index   The index at which to insert the Tk widget.

?options?   The options for the window create command include

    -window *widgetName*

        The name given to this widget when it was created.

    -create *script*

        A script to evaluate to create the window if the -window option is not used.

The new image or widget will be inserted into the text at the requested index. Images and windows are inserted into the text widget just like another character. If they are inserted into an existing line, the height of the line will be increased to the size of the image. If you want to create a display with columnar format, you'll have to put the text and image into separate widgets and then place those widgets in the primary text widget.

Example 10.3.5-1

Example Script

```
set logo {
R0lGODdhKwBAAKUAAP////r6+vX19e3t7fPz8+jo6Obm5uDg4NXV1aurq56e
nnV1dcjIyOLi4ufn/5T09Ovr6+zs7OHh4Xt7e1JSUsXFxX9/f2FhYeTk5I+P
```

```
j3Jycn19fbW1tUVFRWtra5mZmY2Njd/f38LCwvHx8ZycnPf39wAAAAAAAAA
AAAAAAAAAAAAAAAAAAAAAAAAAAAAAAAAAAAAAAAAAAAAAAAAAAAAAAAAAAAA
AAAAAAAAAAAAAAAAAAAAAAAAAAAAAACwAAAAKwBAAAAG/kCAcEgsEgOC
pGAgMDqLyCRhQC0YDtgDIsFNKL7fxKH5NAq84LR6zU4UlNNqIZtk2+94tiCA
zvv/CgkAfICFeIIAfXYLYAuMhmoIQopsDGAN1pBpB5N4AwyODg8NmpudbAsM
Awqpq6VpBkIIiw0NjJ+PjayFBUIHiwygDA65uxBLhQO+wKwOoI0JexERCMV3
ygC/eQ5pCwkBEhMUFBWAZNrAxF/eAhLj4xbmy3cLzrkD7u8XgN9CBtuNMBh4
Ny5DGnsKuKVBBKAAQDADxL3TsCHNAGL1noUZ4hCPwgUH8o3bFwjis0xgJAlx
dSfTggISC2YoEODArTucVubRiIHg/rgJEyIMSKWQTU4ALPMk4OBzXIcCAzxg
sgYmls4/CT40pXBBgM2ibHoJEcBPa1MQZxRoZIMNAFmsZn2GGIrSTtu3f8x+
iFlglh8ybv8wusCVg8QPBqjqGYL3kALCFkK8q0DJTj8hhPJQIVxBMtddfhgO
qqxmAYEIWjsX3IK1CGk1A7R2OCBi5IhqflQOed2ogNYLvn8O4G1qSGZ6wYGb
nUAAkO7ReRZAYKp83IehrRn7WYCBqQWY4zhgD02k8SIEki1EHFcBguI1os1b
Tr+eAgn3WANoD12BgnqJFdiU335+HDDBf+Og8wdgSdGTwAQXxOZfAwrmwaBg
CnxQ3Uzj/v01RIOWPVYdBRMU8N4aBHy43RgfPFUbBR8I+EdbINo1wVP5hJDA
ibBxJNgBWjXgTomGtNXRHwZWMNAHuAEiFgD/FFKBkvZVxMsQFfoxUzyQWJUN
IACU8EUiuoSBx1FZ3gEAK2SG0Yd8YKAJhiB9eNHHmgoI8QieX7zFZ5xYgjEI
n0KkseYCeuZZaJ95VqabX4EEAMZbYo65kaBp1NHGEJAKgqkahKKxpp1kwcmQ
InxWeqcXiKIhpp14tjnnboamWukXt5bgaq64wkfrK5BcRhywdpAxLLFrNHEc
sgtCx6w8cLZxrB/K4NUFFgZAxcQeUSghQBxUDFDAuAZckYUWDQgoS0AS+pXh
7rtOBAEAOw==
```
```
}

# Create the image we'll use for this example

set img [image create photo -data $logo]

# And create and display the primary text widget

text .t -height 14 -width 60
pack .t

#
# Insert some lines into the text widget.
#

.t insert 1.0 \
    "This is a line with an image () in the middle of it.\n"
.t insert end \
    "As you can see it makes a large space between the\n"
.t insert end \
    "line with the image, and the line below it.\n\n"
```

```
# Find the close parenthesis, and place the image
#    just before it.

set closeParenLocation [.t search ")" 1.0]
.t image create $closeParenLocation -image $img

# Create a new text widget for columnar text.

text .t2 -height 5 -width 40 -relief flat

# Insert some prose.

.t2 insert end "This is a separate text widget with\n"
.t2 insert end "a few lines of text in it that will\n"
.t2 insert end "be placed next to another copy of the \n"
.t2 insert end "image.  This is more aesthetically \n"
.t2 insert end "pleasing."

# Place the new window and image side by side in the
#    primary text widget.

.t window create end -window .t2
.t image create end -image $img
```

Script Results

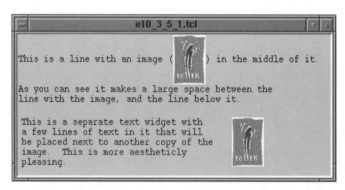

10.4 HTML Display Package

HTML is currently the most portable protocol for distributing formatted text, and the odds are good that HTML will continue to be important for the next few years. The text widget tags make it possible to use the text widget to display HTML text with little work.

Stephen Uhler wrote html_library, a library that will display HTML in a text widget. The html_library is a good example of what you can do with the text widget, so we'll look at it a bit. The HTML library is not a part of the standard Tk distribution. It is distributed as a standalone module (from ftp.smli.com /pub/tcl/html_library-0.3.tar.gz) and as part of the webtk 1.0 program available from http://sunscript .sun.com/TclTkCore/. In the webtk package, the HTML library code is in the file lib/dpackage.tcl.

10.4.1 Displaying Text

Using the html_library package to display text is very simple:

1. Source the html_library code.
2. Create a text widget to contain the displayed HTML text.
3. Map the text widget to the display with pack, place, or grid.
4. Initialize the HTML library by calling HMinit_win *textName*.
5. Display your HTML text by calling HMparse_html "HMrender *textName*."

The following example shows a text window being used to display some HTML text and a dump of the first couple of lines.

Note how the tags are used to define the indenting and fonts.

Example 10.4.1-1

Example Script

```
source "html_library.tcl"
text .t -height 6 -width 50
pack .t
HMinit_win .t
```

```
set txt {
<HTML><BODY>
    Test HTML
    <P><B>Bold Text</B>
    <P><I>Italics</I>
</BODY></HTML>
}

HMparse_html $txt "HMrender .t"

set textDump [.t dump 1.0 4.0 -all]

puts "[format "%-8s %-50s %6s\n" ID DATA INDEX]"
foreach {id data index} $textDump {
    puts "[format {%-8s %-50s %6s} $id $data $index]"
}
```

Script Output

ID	DATA	INDEX
mark	current	1.0
tagon		1.0
tagon	indent0	1.0
tagon	font:times:14:medium:r	1.0
text	Test HTML	1.0
tagoff	indent0	1.10
tagoff		1.10
tagon	space	1.10
text	{\n}	1.10
text	{\n}	2.0
tagoff	space	3.0
tagoff	font:times:14:medium:r	3.0
tagon		3.0
tagon	indent0	3.0
tagon	font:times:14:bold:r	3.0
text	Bold Text	3.0
tagoff	font:times:14:bold:r	3.9
tagoff	indent0	3.9
tagoff		3.9
tagon	font:times:14:medium:r	3.9
tagon	space	3.9
text	{\n}	3.9

Script Results

10.4.2 Using html_library Callbacks: Loading Images and Hypertext Links

In order to display an image, the html_library needs an image widget handle. If the library tried to create the image it would need code to handle all of different methods for obtaining image data, and the odds are good that the technique you need for your application wouldn't be supported.

To get around this problem, the html_library calls a procedure that you supply (HMset_image) to get an image handle. This technique makes the library versatile. Your script can use whatever method is necessary to acquire the image data: load it from the Web, extract it from a database, code it into the script, etc.

The requirements for handling hypertext links are similar. A browser will download a hypertext link from a remote site, a hypertext online help will load help files, and a hypertext GUI to a database engine might generate SQL queries. When a user clicks on a hypertext link, the html_library invokes the user-supplied procedure HMlink_callback to process the request.

Note that you must source html_library.tcl before you define your callback procedures. There are dummy versions of HMset_image and HMlink_callback in the html_library package that will override your functions if your script defines these procedures before it sources the html_library.tcl script.

One of the requirements of event-driven GUI programming is that procedures must return quickly. When the script is evaluating a procedure, it isn't evaluating the event loop to see if the user has clicked a button (perhaps the CANCEL button!). In particular, if the procedure acquiring image data is waiting for data to be read from a remote site, you can't even use update to force the event loop to run.

Therefore, the html_library package was designed to allow the script retrieving an image to return immediately and to use another procedure in the html_library to display the image when it is ready.

The following flowchart shows control flow when the html_library code encounters an <IMG> tag. Notice that the creation of the image need not be connected to the flow that initiated the image creation (the HMset_image procedure). The procedure that invokes HMgot_image can be invoked by an outside event, such as a socket being closed.

When HMset_image is called, it is passed a handle that identifies this image to the html_library. When the application script calls HMgot_image, it includes this handle and the image object handle of the new image object so that the html_library code knows which <IMG> tag is associated with this image object.

Syntax: HMset_image *win handle src*

HMset_image	Create an image widget from the appropriate data, and transfer that image back to the html_library by calling HMgot_image.
win	The name of the text widget that will ultimately receive the image.
handle	A handle provided by the html_library script that must be included with the image handle when HMgot_image is invoked.
src	The textual description of the image source. This is the contents of the SRC="XXX" field.

html_library   application script

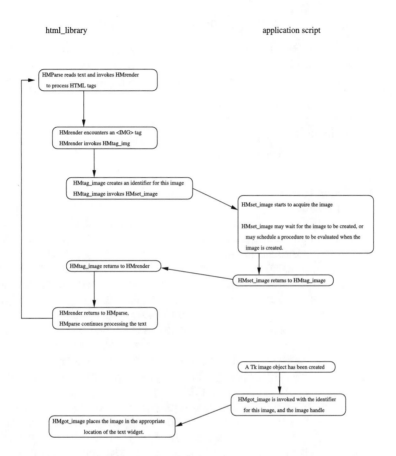

Syntax: HMgot_image *handle image*

HMgot_image   Maps an image widget handle into a text in the location
               defined by data associated with *handle*.

handle   The value that was passed to HMset_image as a argument.

image   The image handle returned by an image create command.

The next example displays the Tcl feather logo. In this example, the HMset_image call is done as a hardcoded image creation. In an actual application, this would be code to parse the src parameter, etc.

Example 10.4.2-1

Example Script

```
source html_library.tcl

set logo {
```
```
R01GODdhKwBAAKUAAP////r6+vX19e3t7fPz8+jo6Obm5uDg4NXV1aurq56e
nnV1dcjIyOLi4ufn/5T09Ovr6+zs7OHh4Xt7e1JSUsXFxX9/f2FhYeTk5I+P
j3Jycn19fbW1tUVFRWtra5mZmY2Njd/f38LCwvHx8ZycnPf39wAAAAAAAAAA
AAAAAAAAAAAAAAAAAAAAAAAAAAAAAAAAAAAAAAAAAAAAAAAAAAAAAAAAAAAAA
AAAAAAAAAAAAAAAAAAAAAAAAAAAAAACwAAAAAKwBAAAAG/kCAcEgsEgOC
pGAgMDqLyCRhQC0YDtgDIsFNKL7fxKH5NAq84LR6zU4UlNNqqIZtk2+94tiCA
zvv/CgkAfICFeIIAfXYLYAuMhmoIQopsDGANlpBpB5N4AwyODg8NmpudbAsM
Awqpq6VpBkIIiw0NjJ+PjayFBUIHiwygDA65uxBLhQO+wKwOoI0JexERCMV3
ygC/eQ5pCwkBEhMUFBWAZNrAxF/eAhLj4xbmy3cLzrkD7u8XgN9CBtuNMBh4
Ny5DGnsKuKVBBKAAQDADxL3TsCHNAGL1noUZ4hCPwgUH8o3bFwjis0xgJAlx
dSfTggISC2YoEODArTucVubRiIHg/rgJEyIMSKWQTU4ALPMk4OBzXIcCAzxg
sgYmls4/CT40pXBBgM2ibHoJEcBPa1MQZxRoZIMNAFmsZn2GGIrSTtu3f8x+
iFlglh8ybv8wusCVg8QPBqjqGYL3kALCFkK8q0DJTj8hhPJQIVxBMtddfhgO
qqxmAYEIWjsX3IK1CGk1A7R2OCBi5IhqflQOed2ogNYLvn8O4G1qSGZ6wYGb
nUAAkO7ReRZAYKp83IehrRn7WYCBqQWY4zhgD02k8SIEki1EHFcBguI1os1b
Tr+eAgn3WANoD12BgnqJFdiU335+HDDBf+Og8wdgSdGTwAQXxOZfAwrmwaBg
CnxQ3Uzj/v01RIOWPVYdBRMU8N4aBHy43RgfPFUbBR8I+EdbINo1wVP5hJDA
ibBxJNgBWjXgTomGtNXRHwZWMNAHuAEiFgD/FFKBkvZVxMsQFfoxUzyQWJUN
IACU8EUiuoSBx1FZ3gEAK2SG0Yd8YKAJhiB9eNHHmgoI8QieX7zFZ5xYgjEI
n0KkseYCeuZZaJ95VqabX4EEAMZbYo65kaBp1NHGEJAKgqkahKKxpp1kwcmQ
InxWeqcXiKIhpp14tjnnboamWukXt5bgaq64wkfrK5BcRhywdpAxLLFrNHEc
sgtCx6w8cLZxrB/K4NUFFgZAxcQeUSghQBxUDFDAuAZckYUWDQgoS0AS+pXh
7rtOBAEAOw==
```
```
}

set HTMLtxt {
<HTML>
<HEAD>
<TITLE>Example of Embedded image</TITLE></HEAD>
    <BODY>
```

```
    <IMG src=logo>
    </BODY>
</HTML>
}

###############################################################
# proc HMset_image {win handle src}--
#    Acquire image data, create a Tcl image object,
#    and return the image handle.
#
# Arguments
#    win        The text window in which the html is rendered.
#    handle     A handle to return to the html library with
#               the image handle
#    src        The description of the image from:
#               <IMG src=XX>
#
# Results
#    This example creates a hard-coded image. and then invokes
#    HMgot_image with the handle for that image.


proc HMset_image {win handle src} {
    global logo
    puts "HMset_image was invoked with WIN: \
        $win HANDLE: $handle SRC: $src"

    # In a real application this would parse the src, and load the
    #  appropriate image data.

    set img [image create photo -data $logo]

    HMgot_image $handle $img

    return ""
}
text .t -height 6 -width 50
pack .t
HMinit_win .t

HMparse_html $HTMLtxt "HMrender .t"
```

Script Output

HMset_image was invoked with WIN: .t HANDLE: .t.7 SRC: logo

Script Results

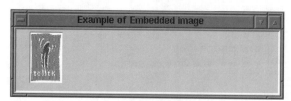

The **html_library** uses a technique similar to the image callback procedures to resolve hypertext links. When a user clicks on a hypertext link, a user-supplied procedure named **HMlink_callback** is invoked with the name of the **text** window and the contents of the **href=value** field.

Syntax: HMlink_callback *win href*

HMlink_callback

> A procedure that is called from the **html_library** package when a user clicks on an <A href=*value*> field.

win   The **text** widget in which the new text can be rendered.

href   The hypertext reference.

The next example shows an **HMlink_callback** that will display the HTML text contained in a Tcl variable. In a browser application, the **HMlink_callback** procedure would download the requested URL, and in a Help application it would load the requested help file.

Example 10.4.2-2

```
##############################################################
# proc HMlink_callback {win href}--
#    This procedure is invoked when a user selects a hypertext
#    link in the HTML display.
#
#    In an actual browser, the href field would contain the URL of
#    the HTML page to retrieve.  In this example, it contains the
#    name of a Tcl variable.
```

```
#
# Arguments
#   win       The window in which the new page will be displayed
#   href      The hypertext reference.
# Results
#
proc HMlink_callback {win href} {
    global HTMLText2 HTMLText3
    puts "HMlink_callback was invoked with win: $win href: $href"

    # Clear the window

    HMreset_win $win

    # Display new text
    #   - href will be substituted to the name of a text string,
    #       and "set varName" returns the contents of a variable.
    #       "[set $href]" could also be written as "[subst $$href]"

    HMparse_html [set $href] "HMrender $win"
}
```

Example Script

```
source html_library.tcl

# Define three sets of simple HTML text to display

# This is the first text to display.  It is an Unordered List of
#   hypertext links to the other two sets of HTML text.

set HTMLText1 {
<HTML>
<HEAD><TITLE> Initial Text </TITLE></HEAD>
<BODY>
<UL>
<LI>
  <A href=HTMLText2> Clicking this line will select text 2.</A>
<LI>
  <A href=HTMLText3> Clicking this line will select text 3.</A>
<UL>
</BODY> </HTML>
}

# This text will be displayed if the user selects the
```

```
#     top line in the list.

set HTMLText2 {
<HTML>

<HEAD><TITLE> Initial Text </TITLE></HEAD>
<BODY>
    <CENTER>This is text 2.</CENTER>
</BODY> </HTML>
}

# This text will be displayed if the user selects the
#     bottom line in the list.

set HTMLText3 {
<HTML>
<HEAD><TITLE> Initial Text </TITLE></HEAD>
<BODY>
    <CENTER>This is text 3.</CENTER>
</BODY> </HTML>
}

# Create the text window for this display

text .t -height 5 -width 60 -background white
pack .t

# Initialize the html_library package and display the text.
HMinit_win .t
HMparse_html $HTMLText1 "HMrender .t"
```

Before Clicking a Hypertext Link

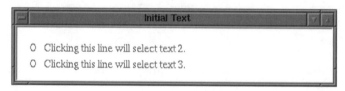

After Clicking Top Hypertext Link

Script Output

HMlink_callback was invoked with win: .t href: Text2

10.4.3 Extending the `html_library` package

The 0.3 revision of the `html_library.tcl` package supports HTML version 2.0. It supports forms, but not tables.

However, the package is designed so you can easily add support for other tags. In this section, we'll add support for a simple table to show how this package can be extended.

The `html_library` package works by using a set of regular expression statements to turn a hypertext tag into a command to be evaluated. The naming convention for the commands is to merge the HTML tag identifier (converted to lowercase) into the name of a procedure.

Syntax: HMtag_*htmlTag window param text*

HMtag_*htmlTag*

    The procedure to invoke when *htmlTag* is evaluated in the HTML text.

window   The text widget that will receive the text.

param   Any parameters that may be included with the HTML tag.

text   The name of the variable that contains the text in the calling procedure. This procedure must use upvar to gain access to the text. The text may be modified in this procedure as necessary before it is inserted into the text window by the calling procedure.

To add simple support for tables, we'll create five procedures. For the sake of brevity (and because it's not often used), there is no procedure to handle the </TR> tag.

Syntax: HMtag_table *window param text*

- This will be called when a <TABLE> tag is evaluated, defining the start of a table.

  This procedure will create a new text widget for the table, initialize the global state variables, set the row and column counters to 0, etc.

Syntax: HMtag_/table *window param text*

- This will be called when a </TABLE> tag is evaluated, marking the end of data for a table.

  This procedure will insert the text widget that contains the table into the main text widget and set the tab stops to make the entries line up in columns.

Syntax: HMtag_tr *window param text*

- This will be called when a <TR> tag is evaluated. This tag denotes the start of a new table row.

  This procedure increments the row counter and resets the column counter to 0.

Syntax: HMtag_td *window param text*

- This will be called when a <TD> tag marking the beginning of the text for a cell in the table is encountered.

  This procedure places a tab character at the beginning of the text, and sets a tag that describes the row and column for this text.

Syntax: HMtag_/td *window param text*

- This will be called when a </TD> tag marking the end of the text in a table cell is encountered.

  This procedure increments the column marker so that the next entry goes into the next column, and keeps track of the maximum number of columns.

The next example uses all of the features of the html_library we've discussed. It includes a hypertext link in the first set of display text to load a new page with a table.

This example follows the convention used in the html_library package for creating a global state array named HM*widgetName* to hold the information about the current values in the text widget. The html_library package was written before the namespace commands became available in Tcl, so it follows the older convention of keeping state information in specially named global variables, instead of within the namespace.

Notice that the procedures that need to interact with the global state array use the upvar #0 HM$win var command to map array HM*windowName* (in global scope) onto the variable var (in the local procedure scope).

This is similar to the C language technique of using a pointer to a structure to access one of several structures with a single set of code.

Example 10.4.3-1

html_tableProcedures.tcl

```
source html_library.tcl

set HMtable(unique) 0

##############################################################
# proc HMtag_table {win param text}--
#     Process the <TABLE> tag - Called from html_library
#     Creates a new text widget to hold the table
#     Creates HM.WindowName state variables with default values
#     Sets HM.win(divert) to point to the new window so that
#        all text being processed is directed to the table text
#        widget.
#
# Arguments
#   win           The window that will hold everything
#   param         Any parameters in the <TABLE ...> tag
#   text          The name of a variable with associated text
# Results
#
#
```

```
proc HMtag_table {win param text} {
    global HMtable

    upvar #0 HM$win var

    # Define a unique name for the text widget
    #    that will contain this table

    set newTable .txt_$HMtable(unique)

    # Divert output to the new window.

    set var(divert) $newTable

    # Make a new global state variable for the new text widget
    upvar #0 HM$newTable newvar

    # and initialize it

    HMinit_state $newTable
    set newvar(family) times
    set newvar(size) 12
    set newvar(weight) normal
    set newvar(style) roman
    set newvar(indent) 0
    set newvar(stop) 0
    set newvar(S_insert) end
    set newvar(oldWindow) $win

    # Create the new text widget

    text $newTable -width [expr [$win cget -width] -2] \
        -background white

    # Set the row and column descriptors.

    set HMtable(row) 0
    set HMtable(column) 0
    set HMtable(maxCol) 0

    # increment the unique number pointer so that the next
    # table will get a new text widget name.

    incr HMtable(unique)
}
```

```
##############################################################
# proc HMtag_/table {win param text}--
#     Process the </TABLE> tag
#     This procedure resets the window to receive text to the
#     master window.
# Arguments
#
#   table     The window that holds the table
#   param     Any parameters in the </TABLE ...> tag
#   text      The name of a variable with associated text
#
# Results
#   Maps the new window into the master text window.
#   Sets tab locations in new window
#
proc HMtag_/table {table param text} {
    global HMtable

    # Set the var pointer for the table text widget
    upvar #0 HM$table var

    # Set the win and var variables to point to the master text
    # widget, instead of the table text widget.
    set win $var(oldWindow)
    upvar #0 HM$win var

    # unset var(divert) so that text will no longer be diverted
    # to the table window
    unset var(divert)

    # Reset the height of the table text widget to match the
    # number of rows actually used  and  insert it into the
    # master text widget

    $table configure -height $HMtable(row) -font $var(xfont)
    $win window create $var(S_insert) -window $table

    # The next pieces of code set the tab stops to define
    #  the columns in the table.

    # First determine the widest entry in each column.

    # Initialize the sizes for the columns to 0

    for {set j 0} {$j < $HMtable(maxCol)} {incr j} {
```

```
        set colSize($j) 0;
}

# Get the list of tags - to make the loop faster

set alltags [$table tag names]

# Check the width of the contents of each cell.
# use the font measure command to get width in pixels.
# This provides a font-independant value.

for {set i 0} {$i <= $HMtable(row)} {incr i} {
    for {set j 0} {$j < $HMtable(maxCol)} {incr j} {

    # A cell may be blank.
    # Check for a tag before proceeding

        if {[lsearch $alltags tbl.$i.$j] != -1} {
            set range [$table tag ranges tbl.$i.$j]

            # Get the size of the text associated with this
            # cell. check to see if it's longer than
            # previous longest text in this column
            set line [$table get [lindex $range 0] \
                    [lindex $range 1]]
            set len [font measure  $var(xfont) $line ]

            if {$len > $colSize($j) } {
                set colSize($j) $len
            }

            # Delete the trailing \n that was added by
            # html_lib.tcl.
            $table delete "[lindex $range 0] lineend"
        }
    }
}

# Determine the grid width of the parent window.  If the
#  window is gridded the tab stops are set in terms of
#  grid units, not pixels.

set gridWidth [lindex [wm grid .] 2]
if {$gridWidth == ""} {set gridWidth 1}

# Define the tab stops to the maximum
```

```
#     size for each column.
#
# The pad value of 8 is to separate the columns

set tabStops 0;
set totl 0;

for {set j 1} {$j < $HMtable(maxCol)} {incr j} {
    set wid [expr ($colSize($j) + 8)/$gridWidth]
    lappend tabStops [expr $wid + $totl]
    incr totl $wid
}

# and set the tab stops.

$table configure -tabs $tabStops

# Wipe the first character - a bare (and useless) newline.

$table delete 1.0
}
############################################################
# proc HMtag_tr {win param text}--
#    Process the <TR> tag
#    This begins a new row by setting the row and column values.
# Arguments
#
#    win             The window that holds the table
#    param     Any parameters in the </TR ...> tag
#    text      The name of a variable with associated text
#
# Results
#    Increments the row position.
#    Sets the column to 0.
#
 proc HMtag_tr {win param text} {
    global HMtable
    incr HMtable(row)
    set HMtable(column) 0
}
############################################################
# proc HMtag_td {win param text}--
```

```
#       Process the <TD> tag
# Arguments
#
#   win             The window that holds the table
#   param       Any parameters in the <TD ...> tag
#   text        The name of a variable with associated text
#
# Results
#   Sets a tag for the start of this table entry to be used to
#   set tab positions
#
proc HMtag_td {win param text} {

    global HMtable
    upvar $text t

    set t "\t[string trim $t]"

    upvar #0 HM$win var
    set var(Ttab) tbl.$HMtable(row).$HMtable(column)
}

#############################################################
# proc HMtag_/td {win param text}--
#
# Arguments
#
#   win     The window that holds the table
#   param       Any parameters in the </TD ...> tag
#   text        The name of a variable with associated text
#
# Results
#   Increments the column position.
#   If there are more columns in this table row than in previous
#       rows, set the max column

proc HMtag_/td {win param text} {
    global HMtable

    incr HMtable(column)
    if {$HMtable(column) > $HMtable(maxCol)} {
        set HMtable(maxCol) $HMtable(column)
    }
```

```
}

############################################################
# proc HMlink_callback {win href}--
#    This proc is called by the html_library code to parse a
#       hypertext reference.
#
# Arguments
#    win       The text window that is used by the html_library to
#              display the text
#    href      A hypertext reference to use for the next hyper-
#              text.
#
# Results
#    This example simply replaces the contents of the display
#    with hardcoded new text.

proc HMlink_callback {win href} {
    global newHTMLtxt

    puts "HMlink_callback was invoked with WIN: $win HREF: \
        $href"

    # Clear the old contents from the window.

    HMreset_win $win

    # Display the new text.

    HMparse_html $newHTMLtxt "HMrender $win"
}

############################################################
# proc HMset_image {win handle src}--
#    Acquire image data, create a Tcl image object,
#       and return the image handle.
#
# Arguments
#    win       The text window in which the html is rendered.
#    handle    A handle to return to the html library with the
#    image handle
#    src       The description of the image from: <IMG src=XX>
#
```

```
# Results
#    This example creates a hardcoded image. and then invokes
#    HMgot_image with the handle for that image.

proc HMset_image {win handle src} {
    global logo
    puts "HMset_image was invoked with WIN: $win HANDLE: \
        $handle SRC: $src"

    # In a real application this would parse the src, and load
    # the appropriate image data.

    set img [image create photo -data $logo]

    HMgot_image $handle $img

    return ""
}

####### End of procedure definitions ****
#
# Define the image and HTML text data
#

set logo {
```

```
R0lGODdhKwBAAKUAAP////r6+vX19e3t7fPz8+jo6Obm5uDg4NXV1aurq56en
nV1dcjIyOLi4ufn5/T09Ovr6+zs7OHh4Xt7e1JSUsXFxX9/f2FhYeTk5I+Pj
3Jycn19fbW1tUVFRWtra5mZmY2Njd/f38LCwvHx8Zycnf39wAAAAAAAAAAAA
AAAAAAAAAAAAAAAAAAAAAAAAAAAAAAAAAAAAAAAAAAAAAAAAAAAAAAAAAAAAA
AAAAAAAAAAAAAAAAAAAAAAAACwAAAAAKwBAAAG/kCAcEgsEgOCpGAgM
DqLyCRhQC0YDtgDIsFNKL7fxKH5NAq84LR6zU4UlNNqIZtk2+94tiCAzvv/
CgkAfICFeIIAfXYYLYAuMhmoIQopsDGANlpBpB5N4AwyODg8NmpudbAsMAwqp
q6VpBkIIiw0NjJ+PjayFBUIHiwygDA65uxBLhQO+wKwOoI0JexERCMV3ygC/
eQ5pCwkBEhMUFBWAZNrAxF/eAhLj4xbmy3cLzrkD7u8XgN9CBtuNMBh4Ny5DGn
sKuKVBBKAAQDADxL3TsCHNAGL1noUZ4hCPwgUH8o3bFwjis0xgJAlxdSfTqgIS
C2YoEODArTucVubRiIHg/rgJEyIMSKWQTU5A4LPMk40BzXCxcCAzxgsgYmls4/
CT40pXBBgM2ibHoJEcBPa1MQZxRoZIMNAfmsZn2GGIrSTtu3f8x+iFlg1h8byv
8wusCVg8QPBqgjqGYL3kALCFkK8q0DJTj8hhPJQIVxBMtddfhgOqqxmAYEIWjsX
3IK1CGk1A7R2OCBi5IhqfLQOed2ogNYLvn804G1qSGZ6wYGbnUAAkO7ReRZAYK
p83IehrRn7WYCBqQWY4zhgD02k8SIEki1EHFcBguI1os1bTr+eAgn3WANoD12B
gnqqJFdiU335+HDDBf+Og8wdgSdGTwAQXxOZfAwrmwaBgCnxQ3Uzj/v01RIOWP
VYdBRMU8N4aBHy43RgfPFUbBR8I+EdbINo1wVP5hJDAibBxJNgBWjXgTomGtNX
RHwZWMNAHuAEiFgD/FFKBkvZVxMsQFfoxUzyQWJUNIACU8EUiuoSBx1FZ3gEA
K2SG0Yd8YKAJhiB9eNHHmgoI8QieX7zFZ5xYgjEIn0KkseYCeuZZaJ95VqabX4
```

EEAMZbYo65kaBp1NHGEJAKgqkahKKxpp1kwcmQInxWeqcXiKIhpp14tjnnboam
WukXt5bgaq64wkfrK5BcRhywdpAxLLFrNHEcsgtCx6w8cLZxrB/K4NUFFgZAxc
QeUSghQBxUDFDAuAZckYUWDQgoS0AS+pXh7rtOBAEAOw==
}

```
set HTMLtxt {
<HTML>
<HEAD>
<TITLE>Example of HTML package</TITLE></HEAD>
<BODY>
<CENTER><H1>Tcl/Tk</H1></CENTER>
<B>Tcl/Tk</B> is a programming package for all your needs.  You
can use it for simple scripting, gluing applications together,
providing an interpreter in other applications, and as an
extensible interpreter.
<P>
<IMG src=logo>
<A HREF=DemoLink>Click This for a link</A>
</BODY>
</HTML>
}

set newHTMLtxt {
<HTML>
<HEAD>
<TITLE>Example of HTML package</TITLE></HEAD>
<BODY>
<CENTER><H2>HyperText Reference</H2></CENTER>
<CENTER><H4>This table shows some features of Tcl/Tk</H4></CEN-
TER>
<P>
<TABLE>
  <TR>
    <TD>Extensible</TD>
    <TD>Versatile</TD>
    <TD>Multi-Platform</TD>
  <TR>
    <TD>Supports Rapid Development</TD>
    <TD>Active User Community</TD>
    <TD>Many Extensions</TD>
  <TR>
```

```
   <TD>Development Tools available</TD>
   <TD>Graphics Support</TD>
   <TD>Internet Support</TD>
 <TR>
   <TD><B>Netscape</B> Plugin</TD>
   <TD><CODE>HTML</CODE> Display Library</TD>
   <TD><CODE>HTTP</CODE> Library</TD>
</TABLE>
<CENTER><IMG src=logo></CENTER>
</BODY>
</HTML>
}

#
# Set up the text window, and display the HTML text
#

text .t -height 22 -width 80 -background white
pack .t

HMinit_win .t

HMparse_html $HTMLtxt "HMrender .t"
```

Script Output

```
HMset_image was invoked with WIN: .t HANDLE: .t.14 SRC: logo
HMlink_callback was invoked with WIN: .t HREF: DemoLink
HMset_image was invoked with WIN: .t HANDLE: .t.18 SRC: logo
```

Script Results

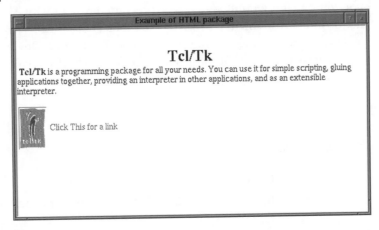

Script Results after Clicking Link

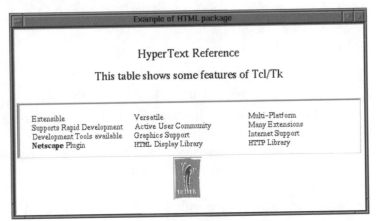

The previous example has hardcoded text and images in order to make an example that can be placed in the book. Your applications may use the `http:` package to download pages from a remote site, load pages from a disk, generate pages from database records, or whatever technique your program specifications require. See the bonus book chapter "Birthday Robot" for more info about the `http` package.

The ease with which HTML support is added to the text widget may make you think that it would be easy to write a full browser with Tk. Before you do too much work on that project, take a look at Steve Ball's plume browser at http://tcltk.anu.edu.au/1.0a1/ and read Mike Doyle and Hattie Schroeder's book *Web Applications in Tcl/Tk*. Much of the work that you'll need to do to create a browser has already been done.

10.5 Bottom Line

- The text widget can be used to display formatted text.
- The text widget can be configured to allow the user to edit text.
- The text widget supports:
  - Multiple fonts
  - Multiple colors for foreground and background
  - Varying margins
  - Varying line spacing
  - Binding actions to characters or strings
  - Including images and other Tk widgets in the text
- Locations in the text widget are identified as line and character positions. Only locations where text exists can be accessed.
- Lines that are longer than the display can wrap. If this occurs, then the line and character index points reflect the internal representation of the data, not the display.
- A text widget is created with the text command.

  Syntax: text *textName ?options?*

- Text is inserted into a text widget with the insert subcommand.

  Syntax: *textName* insert *index text ?tagList?* \
  ?moreText? ?moreTagList? ?...?

- An image is inserted into a text widget with the *textName* image create subcommand.

  Syntax: *textName* image create *index ?options?*

- A Tk widget can be inserted into a `text` widget with the `textName` `window create` subcommand.

  Syntax: `textName window create  index ?options?`

- Text is deleted from a `text` widget with the `delete` subcommand.

  Syntax: `textName delete startIndex ?endIndex?`

- You can search for patterns in a `text` widget with the `search` subcommand.

  Syntax: `textName search ?options? pattern startIndex ?endIndex?`

- A mark is placed with the `mark set` subcommand.

  Syntax: `textName mark set markName index`

- A mark is removed with the `mark unset` subcommand.

  Syntax: `textName mark unset markName ?markName2? ?...? ?markNameN?`

- You can get a list of marks with the `mark names` subcommand.

  Syntax: `textName mark names`

- You can iterate through the marks in a `text` widget with the `mark next` and `mark previous` subcommands.

  Syntax: `textName mark next index`

  Syntax: `textName mark previous index`

- You can add tags either in the `insert` subcommand or with the `tag add` subcommand.

  Syntax: `textName tag add  tagName startIndex1 ?end1? ?start2? ... ?endN?`

- You can remove a tag from a location with the `tag remove` subcommand.

  Syntax: `textName tag remove tagName startIndex1 ?end1? ?start2? ... ?endN?`

- You can remove all references to a tag with the `tag delete` subcommand.

> **Syntax:** *textName* tag delete *tagName ?tagname2? ... ?tagNameN?*

- You can get a list of tag names with the tag names subcommand.

> **Syntax:** *textName* tag names *index*

- You can iterate through tag locations with the tag nextrange and tag prevrange subcommands.

> **Syntax:** *textName* tag nextrange *tagName startIndex ?endIndex?*

> **Syntax:** *textName* tag prevrange *tagName startIndex ?endIndex?*

- You can bind an event to an action that occurs on a character or string with the tag bind subcommand.

> **Syntax:** *textName* tag bind *tagName ?eventType? ?script?*

- The html_library.tcl package provides a set of procedures that will render HTML into a text widget.

  - Images are inserted into the HTML document with the HMset_image and associated HMgot_image procedures.

  > **Syntax:** HMset_image *win handle src*

  > **Syntax:** HMgot_image *handle image*

  - Hypertext links are inserted with a user-supplied HMlink_callback procedure.

  > **Syntax:** HMlink_callback *win href*

Tk Megawidgets

The widgets described in Chapter 8 are relatively small and simple objects created to serve a single purpose. They are designed to be combined into larger and more complex user interfaces in your application.

Some complex user interface widgets are needed in many applications. For instance, any program that allows a user to save or read data from a disk file will need a file selection widget that supports browsing, and many applications require a listbox or text widget that displays a scrollbar when the number of lines displayed exceeds the widget height.

Tk supports merging several widgets into a larger widget that can be used again in other applications. These compound widget interfaces are commonly referred to as megawidgets.

The standard distribution of the Tk toolkit contains a few megawidgets, and many more megawidgets are supported in Tk extensions such as `tix` (`http://www.xpi.com/tix/index.html`), `wigwam` and `TkMegaWidget` (`http://www.neosoft.com`).

Megawidget packages can be created using only Tk or with C language extensions to the wish shell. In this chapter, we'll discuss the megawidgets included with the standard distribution, which are written in Tk, and methods for building your own megawidget libraries with Tk.

11.1 Standard Dialog Widgets

Several megawidgets are provided in the Tk 8.0 distribution to simplify writing applications. These widgets extend the functionality of the Tk interpreter and save the script writer from having to reinvent some wheels.

The implementation of these widgets varies among the platforms that Tcl supports. On the Unix platform, they are all implemented as .tcl scripts in the TK_LIBRARY directory. On Windows and Macintosh platforms, some of these widgets are supported by the OS, in which case Tk uses the native implementation. If you prefer to have your application use the Motif-style widgets instead of the native widgets, set the global variable tk_strictMotif to 1, and Tk will use the Unix scripts for these widgets instead of the native widgets.

* tk_optionMenu

  This menubutton widget displays the text of the selected item on the button.

  The widget creation command returns the name of the menu associated with the button name provided by the script.

Syntax: tk_optionMenu *buttonName varName val1 ?val2...valN?*

tk_optionMenu

        Create a menu from which to select an item.

buttonName   A name for the button to be created. This name must not belong to an existing widget. Once the tk_optionMenu call has returned, this name can be used to display the widget.

varName   The text variable to be associated with the menu. The selected value will be saved in this variable.

val1...N   The values that a user can select from on this menu. These values will be displayed on the button face.

Example

```
tk_optionMenu .button varName Val1 Val2 Val3
pack .button
```

- `tk_chooseColor`

  This color selector widget returns a properly formatted string that can be used for a color name. The string will be the red-blue-green value displayed in the **Selection** field.

  This widget creates a new window in the center of the screen and disables the other windows in the task that invoked it until interaction with this widget is complete.

Syntax: `tk_chooseColor`

Example

`tk_chooseColor`

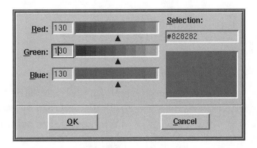

- `tk_getOpenFile`

  This file browser widget returns the name of a file that already exists. If the user types in a nonexistent file name, an error message dialog box is displayed, and the window focus is returned to the `tk_getOpenFile` window.

  This widget creates a new window on the screen and disables the other widgets in the task that invoked it until interaction with this widget is complete.

Syntax: tk_getOpenFile *?option value?*

tk_getOpenFile

> Create a file browsing widget to find an existing file.

?option value?

> The options supported by the tk_getOpenFile megawidget include:

> -defaultextension *extension*
>
> > The *extension* string will be appended to a file name entered by users if they do not provide an extension. The default is an empty string. This option is ignored on the Macintosh.

> -filetypes *patternList*
>
> > This list is used to create menu entries in the **Files of type:** menubutton. If file types are not supported by the platform that is evaluating the script, this option is ignored.

> -initialdir *directory*
>
> > The initial directory for the directory choice menubutton. Note that on the Macintosh the *General Controls* panel may be set to override application defaults, which will cause this option to be ignored.

> -initialfile *fileName*
>
> > Specifies a default file name to appear in the selection window.

> -parent *parentWindow*
>
> > Specifies the parent window for this widget. The widget will attempt to be placed over its parent but may be placed elsewhere by the window manager.

-title *titleString*

> The title for this window. The window may be displayed without a title bar by some window managers.

Example

```
set typeList {
{{Include Files} {.h}}
{{Object Files} {.o}}
{{Source Files} {.c}}
{{All Files} {.*}}
}
tk_getOpenFile -initialdir /usr/src/TCL/tk8.0/library \
    -filetypes $typeList
```

- tk_getSaveFile

  This file browser widget returns the name of a selected file. If the selected file already exists, users are prompted to confirm that they are willing to overwrite the file.

  This widget creates a new window that is identical to the window created by tk_getOpenFile.

Syntax: tk_getSaveFile *?option value?*

tk_getSaveFile

> Create a file-browsing widget to find an existing file or enter the name of a nonexistent file.

?option value?

> The tk_getSaveFile megawidget supports the same options as the tk_getOpenFile widget.

- tk_messageBox

  Creates a dialog window in one of several defined styles. Returns the name of the button that was clicked.

  This widget creates a new window that takes focus until interaction with this widget is complete.

Syntax: tk_messageBox *?option value?*

tk_messageBox

> Create a new window with a message and a set of buttons. When a button is clicked, the window is destroyed and the value of the button that was clicked is returned to the script that created this widget.

option value

> Options for this widget include:

> | | |
> |---|---|
> | *-message* | The message to display in the box. |
> | *-title* | The title to display in the window border. |
> | *-type* | The type of message box to create. The type of box will determine what buttons are created. The options are: |

> > abortretryignore
> >
> > > Displays three buttons: abort, retry, and ignore.
> >
> > | | |
> > |---|---|
> > | ok | Displays one button: ok. |
> > | okcancel | Displays two buttons: ok and cancel. |
> > | retrycancel | Displays two buttons: retry and cancel. |

yesno	Displays two buttons: yes and no.
yesnocancel	Displays three buttons: yes, no, and cancel.

Example

```
tk_messageBox -message "Continue Examples?" -type yesno
```

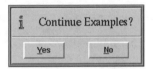

- tk_dialog

  This megawidget creates a message window with one or more buttons that are labeled with text provided in the command line. When the user clicks a button, the button position is returned. The first button is number "0." If the user destroys the window a "-1" is returned.

  This widget creates a new window in the center of the screen and disables the other windows in the task that invoked it until interaction with this widget is complete.

Syntax: tk_dialog *win title text bitmap default string1* \
    ?... stringN?

tk_dialog	Create a dialog box and wait until the user clicks a button or destroys the box.
win	The name for this dialog box widget.
title	A string to place in the border of the new window. Whether or not the window is displayed with a border depends on the window manager you are using.
text	The text to display in the message box.
bitmap	If this is not an empty string, it must be a bitmap object or bitmap file name (not an image object) to display.

default   A numeric value that describes the default button choice for this window. The buttons are numbered from 0.

string   The strings to place in the buttons.

Example

```
tk_dialog .box "Example Dialog" \
    "Who's on first? " \
    questhead 0 "Yes" "No" "Don't Know"
```

- tk_popup

This megawidget creates a popup menu window at a given location on the display (not constrained within the wish window). The menu appears with a tearoff entry and takes focus. Note that this is not a modal widget. The command after the tk_popup will be evaluated immediately; it will not wait for the user to select an item from this widget.

The following example shows the popup bound to a left button press to display a question based on the contents of a text widget.

Syntax: tk_popup *menu x y ?entry?*

tk_popup   Create a popup style menu somewhere on the display. This need not be within the Tcl/Tk application window.

menu   A previously defined menu object.

x y   The x and y coordinates for the menu in screen coordinates.

?entry?   A numeric value that defines a position in the menu. The defined position will be selected (active), and the menu will be placed with that entry at the x, y position requested.

Example

```
proc question {} {
    global var;
```

```
# Remove any existing .m menu.
# Use catch in case there is no previous .m menu.

catch {destroy .m}

# Create a menu for this popup selector

menu .m
.m add radiobutton \
-label "This dialog is from Abbot & Costello's \
    ''Who's on First?`` routine"\
    -variable var -value 1

.m add radiobutton \
    -label "This dialog is from _War_and_Peace_" \
    -variable var -value 2

.m add radiobutton -label \
    "This dialog is from Monty Python's Parrot sketch" \
    -variable var -value 3

# Get the size and location of this window with the "winfo"
#      command, which returns the geometry as
#      WIDTHxHEIGHT+XPOS+YPOS
# The scan command is similar to the C standard
#      library "sscanf" function.

scan [winfo geometry .]  "%dx%d+%d+%d" \
    width height xpos ypos

# Put the popup near the bottom, right hand
#      edge of the parent window.

tk_popup .m [expr $xpos + ($width/2) + 50 ] \
    [expr $ypos + $height - 40] 1
}
# Create a text window, display it, and insert some text
#      from a famous dialog.

text .t -height 12 -width 75
pack .t

set dialog {
    "C: Tell me the names of the ballplayers on this team.\n"
    "A: We have Who's on first,  What's on second, "
```

```
            "I Don't Know is on third.\n"
            "C: That's what I want to find out.\n"
            "   I want you to tell me the names of the fellows"
            "on the team.\n"
            "A: I'm telling you.  Who's on first, "
            "What's on second, I Don't\n"
            "   Know is on third --\n"
            "C: You know the fellows' names?\n"
            "A: Yes.\n"
            "C: Well, then who's playin' first.\n"
            "A: Yes.\n"
}
foreach line $dialog {
    .t insert end $line
}

# Bind the right button to a question about this dialog.

bind .t <Button-3> question
```

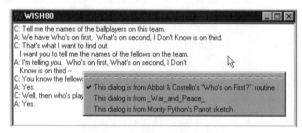

11.2 Megawidget Building Philosophy

The megawidgets included in the standard distribution are useful, but the odds are good that you'll end up needing to build your own widgets at some point.

Megawidget libraries can be constructed in a number of ways. All techniques have features that may make them better or worse for your application. One of the primary trade-offs is versatility and ease of use versus speed of construction. If you expect to be using the widget more than once, it may be worthwhile to take the extra time to design the widget library for versatility.

Here are a few points to consider when building your widget libraries.

11.2.1 Display in Application Window or Main Display

Many of the megawidgets included in the Tk distribution open their own windows on the primary display rather than being loaded into the application window. Some widgets are best handled as temporary top-level windows in the main display, and some are more useful when they can be packed into an application window.

A fallback position here is to design a widget to be loaded, and then have a wrapper that will create a new `toplevel` window and `pack` the widget into that window when you need a popup.

11.2.2 Modal versus Modeless Operation

Most of the megawidgets in the standard Tk distribution operate in a modal style, freezing any other activities until the user has completed an interaction with this widget. In some circumstances this is appropriate behavior, and in others it's not.

You should consider the applications in which your megawidget will be used and determine whether modal or modeless operation is required or whether script writers should be able to define the behavior when they create the widget.

11.2.3 Widget Access Conventions

Megawidgets can be built to mimic the behavior of the standard Tk widgets (as later examples in this chapter will do) or to follow their own conventions.

One method of constructing megawidgets is to return a name that can be used as a procedure to access the megawidget. This technique mimics the behavior of the standard widgets and can be implemented with the object-style technique introduced in Chapters 6 and 7.

Code using this technique would resemble:

```
set mega [newMegaWidget -option value]
$mega configure -newOption -newValue
```

Another method is for the widget creation command to return a handle that is used to identify the particular megawidget to procedures that will manipulate it.

Code using this technique would resemble:

```
set megaHandle [megaCreate -option value]
myMegaConfigureProc $megaHandle -newOption -newValue
```

11.2.4 Widget Frames

Most megawidgets have a parent frame that holds their subwidgets. This frame can be created by the megawidget creation command or provided by the calling procedure. If the frame is created by the widget creation command, calling script can provide the name (as names are given to Tk widgets) or the megawidget can generate its own unique name.

If you provide the parent frame for the megawidget (instead of just providing a name), you can have the megawidget display itself in that frame automatically. This is not a generally good technique. It restricts the usefulness of the widget to applications that have similar display requirements; however, it can be useful for widgets such as toolbar buttons that will always be displayed side by side in a frame.

11.2.5 Configuration

The default values you choose for a megawidget when you design it may not be what the next person to use the library needs. For instance, the dialog box that informs users that the nuclear reactor is about to explode and asks whether they would like do something about it should probably be in a bright color with big letters, rather than the usual dull gray with discrete letters.

Configuration options can be set in a state variable and applied when the widget is created, defined on the widget creation command line, or set in a `configure` procedure associated with the widget.

If you will be using many items in a megawidget library and want to keep the configuration consistent across the widgets, then a state variable will be easier to use. You can define the state values once and then just create the megawidgets. For an example of this style of megawidget library, look at the file `Widgets.tk` in the `TclTutor` package.

Note that this technique will make it very difficult to use different configuration options on widgets that share that state variable.

If you do not require consistency across the application, or if you don't expect multiple widgets in the same family to be used, you may find it simpler to set configuration options on the command line when you create the widget or provide a `configure` command with your megawidget set.

11.2.6 Access to Subwidgets

A megawidget can be designed in an opaque manner, so that the component widgets cannot be accessed, or in a transparent manner, so that the component widgets can be accessed and modified.

If the goal of this megawidget is to provide a uniform interface across all applications that use it, then the widget should be designed to restrict programmers from modifying the options of the subwidgets. The message box and file browsers that are provided by the OS platform are examples of this style of widget.

If the goal for this megawidget is to provide a tool for a wide variety of applications, then the megawidget should be designed to allow the application script writer access to the subwidgets. This allows the application writer to modify options such as background color and font.

This can be handled by a few techniques:

- *Naming convention.* The megawidget creation command returns a base name for the megawidget, and subwidgets are accessed as *base.label-Name*, *base.buttonOK*, etc. This is the simplest technique to implement, although it may be difficult to use if you nest megawidgets within other megawidgets.

- `subwidget` command. The megawidget package you design can include a `subwidget` command that will return the full name of a subwidget component of the megawidget. Code that uses this technique would resemble:

```
set buttonOK [$myMegaWidget subwidget buttonOK]
$buttonOK configure -text "A-OK"
```

- `subwidget option`. The widget procedures you create can accept (or require) a subwidget as an argument when they are invoked. Code that uses this technique would resemble:

```
$myMegawidget configure -subwidget buttonOK -text "A-OK"
```

11.2.7 Following Tk Conventions

As a general rule, the closer you follow the Tk conventions for names, options, and subcommands the easier it will be for script writers to use your megawidgets. If there are two equally good methods for creating the functionality you need, choose the one that mimics Tk.

11.3 Building a Megawidget Library

The first step in designing a megawidget is deciding what sets of conventions you'll follow. The actual conventions do not matter as much as consistently following the conventions. Consistency is one of the keys to creating a usable set of tools.

Configuration options, for example, should be processed in the same way for all the megawidgets in a family. Rather than duplicate the code that processes these options in each megawidget, the code should extracted and placed be in a library of procedures. This forces the megawidgets that use these conventions to be consistent, saves development time, and simplifies package maintenance.

This section will show how to create a library of procedures to manipulate the options for a megawidget. In Section 11.4 we'll use this library to build a scrollable listbox megawidget.

The conventions that we'll establish with this library are:

- A configuration option can be defined for the entire megawidget and it will be propagated to all appropriate subwidgets.
- A configuration option can be defined for a list of subwidgets by declaring those subwidgets in a `configure` command.
- A subwidget is identified by its window name. This may be a complete window path or just the final entity of the window path. For example, `.parentwindow.megawidget.subwidget` may be identified as `.parentwindow.megawidget.subwidget` or `.subwidget` or `subwidget`.
- Subwidget names may begin with ".", but the "." is not required.

The procedures that implement these conventions are created within a namespace, and all the procedure names are exported. Thus, megawidgets that use this library may import the commands into their namespace.

Two procedures are defined in this library: `makeOptionList` and `processOptions`. The `makeOptionList` procedure massages its input into a set of lists that the `processOptions` procedure can iterate through to set options in the subwidgets.

The `makeOptionList` procedure takes a list of arguments in the form

```
?subwidget1? ... ?subwidgetN? -option1 ?value1? ... \
    ?-optionN valueN?
```

and splits that into a list of subwidgets and a list of options. The contents of the subwidget list are checked against a list of valid subwidgets, and only valid subwidget names are placed in the list of subwidgets to be returned. If there are no valid subwidgets in the argument list, the procedure will return a subwidget list that contains all valid subwidgets.

Returning a list with all the valid subwidgets when no subwidgets are requested is perhaps not intuitive. This behavior allows all of the subwidgets to be modified when the megawidget `configure` command is invoked with no subwidget list.

The makeOptionList procedure ensures that all the subwidget names are valid and that they follow a regular pattern. This allows the code in processOptions to be simpler, since it doesn't need to do any argument validation. The convention for the subwidget names returned by makeOptionList is to strip all parent window names from the subwidget name and start the subwidget name with a period. For example, if makeOptionList is called with subwidget arguments of megawidget.sub1 sub2 .sub3 .badName, the returned list will be .sub1 .sub2 .sub3.

Two lists are returned by this procedure, so rather than use the common Tcl technique of returning the results of the procedure with the return command, this procedure gets the names of the variables for these lists from the command line. These names are mapped into the procedure's scope with the upvar command, as described in Chapter 6.

Syntax: makeOptionList *argList validSubwidgets* \
subwidgetVarName optionVarName

makeOptionList
> Splits a list of arguments into a list of subwidgets and options.

argList
> The list of arguments: first the subwidgets, then the options and values.

validSubwidgets
> A list of the valid subwidget names.

subwidgetVarName
> The name of the variable to receive the list of valid subwidgets to be configured. Note that this will be treated as a "call by reference" variable, and the variable in the calling procedure will be modified.

optionVarName
> The name of the variable to receive the list of options and values. Note that this will be treated as a "call by reference" variable, and the variable in the calling procedure will be modified.

The processOptions command will step through a list of options and a list of subwidgets and apply all the options to all the subwidgets.

If the option list is a single -option with no associated value, then this procedure will return a list of the values associated with that option for each of the widgets.

If the option list is a set of -option value pairs, then each of the -option value pairs will be applied to each of the subwidgets.

Syntax: processOptions *optionlist widgetlist ?parent?*

processOptions

> Steps through a list of subwidgets, either retrieving the values of configuration options or setting each option in the list to the requested value.

optionlist   A list of options and values or a single option to query.

widgetlist   The list of subwidgets to process. This list may be full window path names (e.g., .parent.megawidget.subwidget) or the subwidget names as returned by makeOptionList.

> If the full window path names are used, the *parent* argument must be unused or an empty string.

> If the *widgetlist* is in the form returned by makeOption-List, the *parent* argument must be defined.

parent   If present, this is the parent widget of the subwidgets.

The following code implements these two functions.

The processOptions procedure uses the catch command to process the configure subcommand for each of the subwidgets. This allows the script to attempt to set an option on all of the subwidgets without knowing which subwidgets will accept the value and which ones won't. For example, the scrollbar widget accepts a -background option but does not support a -foreground option.

Using the catch is what makes it possible to configure all the subwidgets in a megawidget with a single configure command. This makes the megawidget easier for script writers to use, since they can simply configure the -foreground to a color without needing to know which parts of the megawidget can accept a -foreground option and which ones can't. However, this technique also allows silent failures. This is not good, because silent failures make it difficult to track down problems in scripts.

As a compromise between ease of use and ease of debugging, the `process Options` procedure returns a list of the results of the `catch ... configure` calls. This is a list of success and failure codes (0 or 1) in the order of the widget and options.

If `processOptions` is called with a list of two options and two widgets, there will be four return codes in the list: the results of `widget1 -option1`, `widget2 -option1`, `widget1 -option2`, and `widget2 -option2`. Using this list, scripts that need to know what failed or succeeded can check the results, and scripts that simply need to set any valid option can ignore the return.

WidgetLib.tcl

```
package provide widgetLib 1.0

namespace eval widgetLib {
namespace export processOptions makeOptionList

#############################################################
# proc makeOptionList {argList validSubwidgets \
#                        subwidgetVarName optionVarName }
#    Split an argument list into a list of subwidgets and
#    options. Only include valid subwidgets
#    (those in the validSubwidgets list)
#
#    If no valid subwidgets exist in argList, set the
#       variable defined by subwidgetVarName to the
#       list  $validSubwidgets
#
# Arguments
#    argList:    The argument list
#            ?sub1? ?subX? -option1 ?val1? ?-option2 val2?
#    argList:    The argument list
#            ?sub1? ?subX? -option1 ?val1? ?-option2 val2? ...
#
```

```
#   validSubwidgets:     A list of subwidget names that are
#                        valid for the parent mega-widget
#
#   subwidgetVarName:    The name of the variable in the
#                        parent to receive the
#                        list of subwidgets
#
#   optionVarName:       The name of the variable in the parent
#                        to receive the list of options
# Results
#  Changes the values in the parent procedure of the
#  variables defined by $subwidgetVarName and $optionVarName.
#

    proc makeOptionList {argList validSubwidgets \
                     subwidgetReturn optionReturn } {

        # Upvar the pass-by-reference variables

        upvar $subwidgetReturn subwidgetList
        upvar $optionReturn optionList

        # Look for an element that starts with  a -.
        # All elements before the first -option are subwidgets,
        #  and all elements after that are options or
        #  option/value pairs
        # If the subwidget does not include a ".", prepend the
        #  name with a dot.

        set i 0
        while {[string first "-" [set arg \
              [lindex $argList $i]]] != 0} {
            if {[string first $arg $validSubwidgets] >= 0} {
                if {[string first "." $arg] != 0} {
                    set prepend "."
                } else {
                    set prepend ""
                }
                lappend subwidgetList ${prepend}${arg}
            }
            incr i
```

```
        }

        set optionList [lrange $argList $i end]

        # If there were no subwidgets in the arg list, then

        # return a list of all valid subwidgets, with dots
        # prepended as necessary.

        if {![info exists subwidgetList]} {
            foreach arg $validSubwidgets {
                if {[string first "." $arg] != 0} {
                    set prepend "."
                } else {
                    set prepend ""
                }
                lappend subwidgetList ${prepend}${arg}
            }
        }
    }

###############################################################
# proc processOptions {optionlist widgetlist {parent {}} }
#     Sets the options in the option list in each of the
#     widgets # in the widget list.
#
#     If parent is defined, then it is the parent of the
#     widgets, and it will be prepended to the widget names.
#
#     Expects widget names to start with "."
# Arguments
#   optionlist: A list of options in the form:
#               {-opt1 val1 -opt2 val2...}
#   widgetlist: A list of widgets to which these options
#               will be applied.
#   parent:     The parent widget for the widgets in the
#               widgetlist
#
# Results
#   Changes the configuration of the widgets.
#
```

```
proc processOptions {optionlist widgetlist {parent {}} } {

    set return ""

    # Loop through the options and widgets.
    # If an option is not valid for a widget, fail silently
    #    and continue processing

    foreach {option value} $optionlist {
        foreach widget $widgetlist {
            if {[string length $value] > 0} {
                lappend return \
                    [catch "$parent$widget \
                        configure $option\
                        $value"]
            } else {
                catch "$parent$widget configure \
                    $option " val
                lappend return $val
            }
        }
    }
    return $return
}
}
```

11.4 A Scrolling Listbox Megawidget

This section will show how a megawidget can be built using the two procedures described in Section 11.3 and the namespace and package
commands. We'll start out with a simple megawidget—a scrolling
listbox—and then use that megawidget to build a more complex megawidget that will take selected items from one scrolled listbox, place them
into another, and finally put a wrapper around the latter megawidget to
make a modal file selector.

11.4.1 `scrolledListBox` Description

The scrollable listbox megawidget that we'll be constructing will mimic the structure of the Tk widgets.

The package will be built with the support procedures in a namespace and a single procedure (`scrolledListBox`) in the global scope to create a `scrolledListBox` megawidget.

The `scrolledListBox` procedure will return the name of the new widget's parent frame and will create a procedure with that name in the global scope. This procedure will support several subcommands in the same manner as the Tk widgets.

The `scrolledListBox` procedure will accept any configuration values that are valid for the scrollbar or listbox and will pass these values to the scrollbar and listbox subwidgets. In addition, the `scrolledListBox` command will accept an option to define whether the scrollbar should be on the left or right side of the listbox.

Syntax: `scrolledListBox` *?frameName? ?-option value?*

`scrolledListBox`

> Create a scrolledListBox megawidget. Returns the name of the parent frame for this widget for use with the `pack`, `grid`, or `place` layout managers and creates a procedure with the same name to be used to interact with the mega-widget.

?frameName? An optional name for this widget. If this argument is not present the widget will be created as a unique child of the root frame, ".".

?-option value?

> Sets of configuration values that can be applied to the scrollbar or listbox.

The widget procedure created by the `scrolledListBox` command will accept the subcommands `configure`, `insert`, `delete`, `selection`, and `subwidget`.

The scrolledListBox widget configure subcommand is similar to the standard Tk configure command except that it will accept a subwidget argument. If the subwidget argument is supplied, then the configuration options will be applied only to those subwidgets. If no subwidget argument is supplied, then the configuration options will be applied to the entire widget and all the subwidgets.

Syntax: *scrolledListBoxName* configure *?subwidget?*
?-option? ?value?

scrolledListBoxName configure

Return the value of an option, or set an option, if a value is supplied.

subwidget   The name of a subwidget or subwidgets to be configured or queried. If the widget is being queried and multiple subwidget names are present, the return value will be a list of configurations in the order in which the subwidgets appear in the list.

NOTE: This field is different from standard widget usage.

-option   An option name. If multiple options are being set, there may be multiple *-option value* pairs. If the configuration is being queried, only one *-option* argument may be present.

value   The value to assign to a configuration option.

The insert and delete subcommands pass their arguments to the listbox subwidget with no further parsing. Thus, they exactly duplicate the behavior of the listbox subcommands.

Syntax: *scrolledListBoxName* insert *index string*

scrolledListBoxName insert

Inserts an item into the listbox at the requested index position.

index   The location in the list before which this entry will be inserted. Any index value appropriate for a listbox widget may be used.

string   The text to insert into that location of the listbox.

411

Syntax: *scrolledListBoxName* delete *first ?last?*

scrolledListBoxName delete
> Delete one or more items from the listbox.

first
> The index of the first item to delete. The listbox items are numbered from 0.

?last?
> The index of the last item in a range to delete. If this argument is not present, only the item identified by the *first* is deleted.

The selection subcommand returns the contents of the selected entries of the listbox. Note that the listbox curselection subcommand returns a list of the indices of selected items, whereas this selection returns a list of the contents.

Syntax: *scrolledListBoxName* selection

scrolledListBoxName selection
> Returns the text of the selected item or items from the listbox.

The subwidget subcommand returns the full path name of a subwidget of the scrolledListBox.

Syntax: *scrolledListBoxName* subwidget

scrolledListBoxName subwidget
> Returns the full name of a subwidget of this scrolledListBox.

subwidget
> The name of the subwidget to return. May be one of:
>
> *listbox*
> > The full name of the listbox widget.
>
> *scrollbar*
> > The full name of the scrollbar widget.

11.4.2 Using the scrolledListBox

The following is a simple example of how the scrolled listbox can be used. The widget creation command resembles that of a standard Tk widget.

Example 11.4.2-1

Example Script

```
# set the auto_path and declare that we require the
#   scrolledListBox package.
# The widget pkgIndex.tcl file is in the current directory

lappend auto_path .
package require widgets 1.0

# Create the scrolledListBox, three lines high, with a white
#   background
#  Note that the background is set for both the listbox and the
#   scrollbar

set sl1 [scrolledListBox -height 3 -background white ]

# Insert the items into the listbox.

foreach musketeer [list Athos Porthos Aramis d'Artagnan] {
    $sl1 insert end $musketeer
}

# And create a button to display the results.

button .report -text "Which Musketeer is selected" \
  -command {puts "[$sl1 selection] is selected "}

# Display the widgets

pack $sl1 -side top
pack .report -side top
```

Script Output

Aramis is selected   ;# Printed when the button is clicked

Script Results

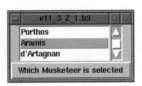

11.4.3 Implementing the Scrollable ListBox

The `scrolledListBox` widget is implemented using the same code pattern that was described for the Tree object in Chapter 7. There will be a library of general-purpose procedures in a generic namespace, a set of support procedures for the `scrolledListBox` in a private namespace, and a procedure to create the widget in the global scope.

The code to implement the `scrolledListBox` megawidget consists of a state variable and three procedures.

The state variable, `ScInfo`, exists within the `scrolledLB` namespace to hold information that needs to be maintained between evaluations of the scripts in this package. For the `scrolledListBox` package this information consists of the unique number used to create unique names for the `scrolledListBox` widgets when no name is provided in the creation command line.

The `scrolledListBox` megawidget consists of two pairs of procedures. In each pair, one procedure exists in the global scope and is used by the script writer. The other procedure exists in the `scrolledLB` namespace and is used to interact with the megawidget's components. This is the same pattern that was described in Chapter 7 for the procedures that create a tree object and implement its methods.

The first of these pairs of procedures creates a `scrolledListBox` widget.

The script writer will invoke `scrolledListBox` to create a new listbox-with-scrollbar. The `scrolledListBox` procedure calls `MakeScrolledListBox` to create the widget and return the name of the megawidget it created, which will also be the name of the procedure created to interact with this new megawidget.

Global Scope	scrolledLB Namespace
scrolledListBox	*MakeScrolledListBox*
Creates a new `scrolledListBox` widget.	Creates a frame with the name of the megawidget (*scrolledListBox-Name*).

Global Scope	scrolledLB Namespace
Calls `MakeScrolledListBox` to construct the frame and subwidgets.	Populates the frame with appropriate subwidgets.
	Creates a new procedure *scrolledListBoxName* to be used to interact with the megawidget.

After `MakeScrolledListBox` has created a frame to hold the subwidgets, it creates a procedure in the global scope with the same name as the frame. This new procedure is the global portion of the second pair of procedures. Script writers will use this procedure when they need to interact with the megawidget. This procedure will invoke `ScrolledListBoxProc` in the `scrolledLB` namespace to actually implement the widget commands.

Global Scope	scrolledLB Namespace
scrolledListBoxName	*ScrolledListBoxProc*
Accepts the `scrolledListBox` widget subcommands.	Performs the widget interactions requested by the widget subcommands.

The `MakeScrolledListBox` procedure needs to create a frame to hold the subwidgets that constitute this megawidget. That frame should have the same name as the megawidget. This lets us access the subwidgets as children of the parent megawidget.

However, there is a name conflict when you use the same name for both the megawidget and the frame that contains the megawidget components. The trick is that we want the megawidget to look like a Tk object, but the megawidgets in these examples are actually just a frame holding some subwidgets and a procedure to access the subwidgets.

For instance, if you construct a megawidget named .foo and create the subwidgets within a frame named .foo, you can't use .foo as the procedure name for the megawidget commands. The command name .foo is already in use by the frame .foo, and Tcl command and procedure names may not conflict.

There are several ways around this problem. You could use a naming convention that some string (for example, _frame) will be appended to the megawidget name to create the frame name. In this case, if you create a megawidget .foo, the frame would be .foo_frame, and the subwidgets would be addressed as .foo_frame.subwidget.

This solution to the problem makes it impossible to address subwidgets as children of the megawidget .foo, because they are actually children of the frame .foo_frame.

```
set widget [megawidget .foo]
#
# This won't work.
#
$widget.subwidget configure -option value
#
# This would work
#
$widget_frame.subwidget configure -option value
```

This set of code uses a different technique: it renames the frame widget command name to appear as though the frame were the child of the mega-widget. This creates a naming convention that makes the frame and subwidgets appear as children to the megawidget. This is the way the megawidget and subwidgets are related to each other logically, although it is not the way the megawidget is implemented.

MakeScrolledListBox creates a frame to hold the subwidgets and then renames the widget procedure associated with that frame before creating a new procedure with that name to be the procedure for the megawidget.

For example, if your script invokes scrolledListBox to create a scrolledListBox named .sl1, the MakeScrolledListBox command will create a frame named .sl1. After the scrollbar and listbox have been packed into the frame .sl1, it will rename the frame widget command from .sl1 to .sl1.fr. Since there is no longer a procedure named .sl1, the MakeScrolledListBox procedure can create a new procedure named .sl1 that will invoke ScrolledListBoxProc to process the megawidget commands.

We can do this because procedure names and window names are resolved from separate tables. When you create a frame .foo, the Tk interpreter creates a window named .foo and a procedure named .foo to access that window. You can rename the procedure .foo without affecting the window .foo.

Being able to disconnect the frame .sl1 from the procedure .sl1 allows us to duplicate the Tk convention of declaring a name for the megawidget and then using that name as the widget procedure. If we didn't rename the frame widget procedure, there would be no way to interact with the frame after we create a new procedure with that name.

11.4.4 The `scrolledListBox` Code

ScrolledList.tcl

```
package provide widgets 1.0

################################################################
# proc scrolledListBox {args}
#    Create a scrolledListBox megawidget
#    External entry point for creating a megawidget.
# Arguments
#   ?parentFrame?       A frame to use for the parent,
#                       If this is not provided, the mega widget
#                       is a child of the root frame (".").
#   ?-scrollposition left/right?
#                       The side of the listbox for the scrollbar
# Results
#   Creates a procedure with the megawidget name for processing
#     widget commands
#   Returns the name of the megawidget

proc scrolledListBox {args} {
    set newWidget [eval scrolledLB::MakeScrolledListBox $args]
    proc $newWidget {args} "
        return \[scrolledLB::ScrolledListBoxProc \
                $newWidget \$args]
    "

    return $newWidget
```

```
    }

namespace eval scrolledLB {

    # Force the load of the widgetLib package so that the
    #   procedures can be imported.

    package require widgetLib
    if {[info exists \
            auto_index(::widgetLib::processOptions)]} {
        eval $auto_index(::widgetLib::processOptions)
        namespace import widgetLib::*
    }



    variable ScInfo
    set ScInfo(unique) 0


############################################################
    # proc MakeScrolledListBox {args}
    #    Create a scrolledListBox megawidget
    # Arguments
    #    ?parentFrame?  A frame to use for the parent.
    #                    If this is not provided, the mega widget
    #                    is a child of the root frame (".").
    #    ?-scrollposition left/right?
    #                    The side of the listbox for the scrollbar
    # Results
    #    Returns the name of the parent frame for use as a
    #    megawidget

    proc MakeScrolledListBox {args} {
        variable ScInfo

        #
        # Set some defaults
        #
        set widgetName .scl_$ScInfo(unique)
        set scrollPosition right
        set height 4
```

```
#
# If the first argument is a window path, use that as
# the base name for this widget.
#

if {[string first "." [lindex $args 0]] == 0} {
    set widgetName [lindex $args 0]
    set args [lreplace $args 0 0]
}

#
# The -scrollposition option is specific to this
# megawidget. Look for that option, and set
# scrollPosition if it's defined.
# Wipe it from the arg list after finding it.
#

for {set i 0} {$i < [llength $args]} {incr i} {
    switch -- [string tolower [lindex $args $i]] {
    -sp -
    -scrollposition {
            set j [expr $i +1]

            set scrollPosition [string tolower \
                    [lindex $args $j]]
            set args [lreplace $args $i $j]
        }
    }
}

frame $widgetName

#
# Create the scrollbar and listbox.
#

scrollbar $widgetName.scroll -command \
        "$widgetName.list yview"

listbox $widgetName.list -height $height \
  -yscrollcommand "$widgetName.scroll set"
```

```
    if {[string first "r" $scrollPosition] == 0} {
        set listColumn 0
        set scrollColumn 1
    } {
        set listColumn 1
        set scrollColumn 0
    }

    grid $widgetName.scroll -row 0 -column $scrollColumn \
            -sticky ns
    grid $widgetName.list -row 0 -column $listColumn

    # We can't have two widgets with the same name.
    #  Rename the base frame procedure for this
    #  widget to $widgetName.fr so that we can use
    #  $widgetName as the widget procedure name
    #  for the megawidget.

    uplevel #0 rename $widgetName $widgetName.fr
    incr ScInfo(unique)

    proc $widgetName {args} " [namespace code\
      {return \[ScrolledListBoxProc $widgetName \$args]}] "

    #
    # Set any options that were defined in the command line.
    #

    processOptions $args [list .list .scroll .fr] \
        $widgetName

    return $widgetName
}


############################################################
#      proc ScrolledListBoxProc {widgetName methodArgs}
#    The master procedure for handling scrolledListBox
#    widget subcommands
# Arguments
#    widgetName:          The name of the scrolledListBox
#                         widget
#    methodArgs:          The rest of the command line
#                              arguments
#                         The first element must be the
```

```
#                           subcommand name Subsequent list
#                           elements depend on subcommand
#    configure - configure entire widget, or certain
#                subwidgets
#                (configure subwidgetList -option1 \
#                     val1 -option2 val2 ...)
#    insert    - add an item to listbox
#    delete    - delete an item from listbox
#    selection - Return a list of selected values from
#                the listbox.
#    subwidget - return the full pathname of a
#                requested subwidget
#
# Results
#    Evaluates a subcommand and returns a result if required.
#
proc ScrolledListBoxProc {widgetName methodArgs} {
    set subCommand [lindex $methodArgs 0]
    set cmdArgs [lrange $methodArgs 1 end]

    set validSubWidgets [list scroll list fr]

    switch -- $subCommand {
    configure {
            makeOptionList $cmdArgs $validSubWidgets \
                    subwidgetList options

            set rtn [processOptions $options \
                    $subwidgetList $widgetName]
            return $rtn
        }
    delete -
    insert {
            eval $widgetName.list $methodArgs
        }
    subwidget {
            switch [lindex $methodArgs 1] {
            listbox {
                    return $widgetName.list
```

```
                                        }
                             scrollbar {
                                      return $widgetName.scroll
                             }
                             default {
                                      error "bad subwidget: \
                                        [lindex $methodArgs 0] - \
                                        must be listbox or scrollbar"
                             }
                           }
                     }
            selection {
                      set lst [$widgetName.list curselection]
                      set itemlst ""
                      foreach l $lst {
                          lappend itemlst [$widgetName.list get $l]
                      }
                      return $itemlst
                }
            default {
                      error "bad command: $subCommand -\
                          must be configure delete\
                          insert selection or subwidget"
                }
            }
        }
    }
}
```

11.5 Incorporating a Megawidget into a Larger Megawidget

In this section, we'll create a larger megawidget that contains two of the scrolledListBox widgets, a label, a button, and an entry widget.

This megawidget will allow a user to define a filter to extract a subset of the entries from the first listbox for display in the second listbox. When the widget is queried, it will return the selected items in the filtered listbox or the selected items in the unfiltered listbox if nothing was selected in the filtered box.

The justification for this widget is that sometimes there are just too many items in a listbox for it to be easy to select the ones the user is interested in, but a simple filter could cut down the size to something manageable. This is similar to the effect that various file browsers get with the "filter" option, but it allows the user to see both the unfiltered list and the filtered list at the same time.

Like the `scrolledListBox`, this megawidget is implemented as a procedure for creating the widget in the global scope with support procedures maintained in a namespace scope.

There are some points to watch when using namespaces with Tk widgets. In particular, you should note the use of the `namespace code` construct for the button command string. When the command associated with a Tk widget is evaluated, it is evaluated in the global namespace. Since the `DoFilter` procedure is defined within a namespace, the button command string needs to include that namespace as part of the command string.

If we knew that the `FilteredList` widget would always be defined at a top level, we could just define the command string as `::FilteredList::DoFilter`, but just as the `scrolledListBox` megawidget is contained within the `filteredList` widget, the `filteredList` widget may be contained in a larger widget, as we'll show in the file browser megawidget example in the next section.

The `namespace code` command adds information to the script argument to define the current namespace. You can get the same effect by using the `namespace current` command to find the current namespace and `regsub` or `format` to modify a script to reflect the current namespace. Using the `namespace code` command is both simpler and guaranteed to continue working if anything should ever change in the Tcl namespace implementation.

Filtered.tcl

```
package provide widgets 1.0

package require widgets
```

```
##############################################################
# proc filteredList {args}--
#    Global entry point for creating a filteredList megawidget
# Arguments
#   Optional frame to parent the widget
#   Standard options for the subwidgets
#
# Results
#   Returns the name of the parent frame for use with
#   subcommands and geometry managers.
#
proc filteredList {args} {
    set newWidget [eval FilteredList::makeFilteredList $args]
    proc $newWidget {args} "return  \
        \[FilteredList::FilteredListProc $newWidget \$args]
    "
    return $newWidget
}

namespace eval FilteredList {

    # FilteredInfo is the static state variable with info
    #       about the widgets.

    variable FilteredInfo

    # Unique number to reduce naming conflicts.

    set FilteredInfo(unique) 0

    # widgetLib provides support procedures for this package.

    package require widgetLib
    if {[info exists \
                auto_index(::widgetLib::processOptions)]} {
        eval $auto_index(::widgetLib::processOptions)
        namespace import widgetLib::*
    }

    ##########################################################
    #     proc makeFilteredList {args}--
    #   Create a Filtered Listbox widget
    # Arguments
    #   Optional frame to parent the widget
```

```tcl
#    Standard options for the subwidgets
#
# Results
#    Returns the name of the parent frame for use with
#    subcommands and geometry managers.
#
proc makeFilteredList {args} {
    variable FilteredInfo

    set widgetName .sl_$FilteredInfo(unique)

    #
    # If the first argument is a window path, use that as
    # the base name for this widget.
    #
    if {[string first "." [lindex $args 0]] == 0} {
        set widgetName [lindex $args 0]
        set args [lreplace $args 0 0]
    }

    #
    # Create the holding frame
    #
    frame $widgetName
    incr FilteredInfo(unique)

    #
    # The prompt and entry label for a Filter pattern
    #
    label $widgetName.prompt -text "Filter:"
    entry $widgetName.srchField

    #
    # Create the complete listbox and label
    #
    label $widgetName.fullLabel -text "Full List"

    # eval is used to ungroup the items in the $args.
    #  The eval command splits the arguments into a
    # string, and then evaluates the string.
    #
```

```
#    If scrolledListBox were evaluated without the
#    'eval' command then scrolledListbox would be
#    invoked with two arguments, the
#     widgetName.fullList and a list of the values
#    in $args.
#
#    With the eval, it is invoked as N arguments,
#    and each element in $args is a separate
#    element in the arguments to scrolledListBox

eval scrolledListBox $widgetName.fullList $args

#
# Create a listbox and label for the entries in
#  fullList that match a Filter pattern
#

label $widgetName.filterLabel -text "Filtered List"

eval scrolledListBox $widgetName.filterList $args

#
# The code to run the filtering process must be run
#   in this namespace.
# The procedure to be run is DoFilter.
#
#  doFilter is a temporary variable which holds
#  the script that will be evaluated when the
#  <Filter> button is clicked, or the user presses the
#  <Return> in the entry widget.

set doFilter [namespace code "DoFilter \
    [$widgetName.fullList subwidget listbox] \
    $widgetName.srchField \
    [$widgetName.filterList subwidget listbox]"]

#
# Create a button to run the filter.
# And bind that filter to the <Return>
# event in the entry widget
#

button $widgetName.filter -text "Filter" \
        -command $doFilter
```

```
bind $widgetName.srchField <Return> $doFilter

#
# Place the widgets on the frame
#

grid $widgetName.prompt -row 0 -column 0
grid $widgetName.srchField -row 0 -column 1
grid $widgetName.filter -row 0 -column 2
grid $widgetName.fullList -row 2 -column 0 \
        -columnspan 2
grid $widgetName.fullLabel -row 1 -column 0 \
        -columnspan 2
grid $widgetName.filterLabel -row 1 -column 2
grid $widgetName.filterList -row 2 -column 2

#
# We need to rename the frame widget procedure to
#   another name because we'll be using the name of
#   the frame for the megawidget procedure.
# The frame name can be used with the pack/grid/etc
#   commands, and the new procedure name will work
#   to modify that frame.

uplevel #0 rename $widgetName $widgetName.fr

#
# Create the procedure that will provide an \
#   interface to this widget.
#

proc $widgetName {args} " return
    \[FilteredListProc $widgetName\$args] "

#
# Set any options that were defined in the command
# line in the various widgets.  Any creation option
# is extended to all subwidgets
#

processOptions $args [list .prompt .srchField \
 .fullLabel .fullList .filterLabel .filterList \
  .filter .fr] $widgetName
```

```
        return $widgetName
    }

    ##########################################################
    #     proc DoFilter {fullListbox entry filterListbox}--
    #    Filters a set of items from the fullListbox and
    #    places them in the filterListbox.
    #
    # Arguments
    #    fullListbox:    A path to the listbox with all the
    #                    entries
    #    entry           An entry widget that will contain the
    #                    filter pattern
    #    filterListbox   The listbox that will receive the
    #                    items that match the pattern
    #
    # Results
    #    Clears out old entries in filterListbox and
    #    Puts new matching entries in it.
    #
    proc DoFilter {fullListbox entry filterListbox} {
        variable FilteredInfo

        #
        # Get the pattern, and clear out old entries in
        #  the filterListbox
        #
        set pattern [$entry get]
        $filterListbox delete 0 end

        #
        # Loop through the contents of the complete list,
        #  and insert any that match the pattern into
        #  filterListbox

        foreach item [$fullListbox get 0 end] {
            if {[string match $pattern $item]} {
                $filterListbox insert end $item
            }
        }

    }
```

```
############################################################
#      proc FilteredListProc {widgetName methodArgs}--
#    The master procedure for handling FilteredList
#    widget subcommands
# Arguments
#   widgetName:       The name of the FilteredList widget
#   methodArgs:       The rest of the command line arguments
#                     The first element must be the
#                         subcommand name Subsequent list
#                         elements depend on subcommand
# Widget commands:
#   configure - configure entire widget, or certain
#                 subwidgets
#                 (configure subwidgetList -option1 val1 \
#                     -option2 val2 ...)
#   insert    - add an item to fullList
#   delete    - delete an item from fullList
#   selection - Return a list of selected values in the
#                 filter listbox or a list from the full
#                 listbox if nothing is selected
#                 in the filter listbox, or an empty return
#                 if nothing is selected in either box.
#
#   subwidget - return the full pathname of a requested
#                 subwidget
# Results
#   Evaluates the command and returns a result if
#   required.
#
proc FilteredListProc {widgetName methodArgs} {
    variable FilteredInfo
    #
    # Extract the first list entry from methodArgs. It
    # will be the subcommand to evaluate.
    #
    # Make a new list without the subcommand, which
    # is the arguments associated with this command.
    #
    set subCommand [lindex $methodArgs 0]
    set cmdArgs [lrange $methodArgs 1 end]
```

```
# Set up a list of valid subwidget names.

set validSubList [list prompt srchField filterLabel \
  fullLabel fr\ fullList filter filterList]

#
# Evaluate the code appropriate to this subcommand.
#

switch -- $subCommand {
configure {
        #
        # makeOptionList will split the command arg
        # list into a set of subwidgets and options.
        # If there are no subwidgets in the cmdArgs,
        # then it will return a list of all valid
        # subwidgets.

         makeOptionList $cmdArgs $validSubList \
                subwidgetList options

         #
         # Set the options in the appropriate subwidgets
         #

         set rtn [processOptions $options \
                $subwidgetList $widgetName]
         return $rtn
    }
delete -
insert {
        #
        # Add or delete an item from the full list
        # listbox. arguments as defined for the
        # listbox
        #

        eval $widgetName.fullList $methodArgs
    }
subwidget {
        set subwidget [lindex $cmdArgs 0]
        if {[string first $subwidget $validSubList]\
                >= 0} {
```

```
                 return $widgetName.$subwidget
             } else {
                error "bad subwidget: $subwidget -\
                    must be one of:\  $validSubList"
             }
          }
       selection {

             # If something is selected in the filter
             # listbox, return that item/items text.
             set l1 [eval $widgetName.filterList selection]

             # Else, check for items selected in the full
             # listbox.
             if {$l1 == ""} {set l1 \
                 [eval $widgetName.fullList selection]
             }
             return $l1
          }
       default {
             # Should not be here, this is an error
             set methods {insert configure delete selection}
             error "Bad method: $subCommand\n use $methods"
          }
       }
     }
   }
}
```

11.6 *Making a Modal Megawidget: The* grab *Command*

In this section we'll take the filteredList megawidget we just developed and make a modal file selection widget. This widget is far from the last word in file selection widgets, but it makes a good example of how a modal widget can be constructed.

This widget is implemented as a single procedure that creates and displays the megawidget and returns the results of the user interaction when that interaction is complete. The condition for completion is that the user has either clicked the QUIT button, clicked the OK button, or destroyed the widget using a window manager command.

This widget introduces the grab command that hasn't been used in previous examples. The grab command allows your application to examine and control how mouse and keyboard events are reported to the windows on your display.

By default, whenever a cursor enters or leaves a widget, an Enter or Leave event is generated. When the cursor enters a widget, that widget is said to have focus, and all keystroke and button events will be reported to that widget. By using the grab command, you can declare that all keyboard and mouse events will go to a particular widget regardless of the location of the cursor. This requires a user to perform a set of interactions before your program releases the grab. Once the grab is released, the focus will follow the cursor and mouse and keyboard events will be distributed normally.

The grab command has several subcommands that let you determine whether other grabs are already in place (in which case your program should save that state and restore it when it's done) and set a new state.

You can learn what window is currently grabbing events with the grab current command.

Syntax: grab current *?window?*

grab current   Returns a list of the windows that are currently grabbing events.

window   If *window* is defined and a child of *window* has grabbed events, then that child will be returned, or an empty string. If *window* is not defined, then all windows in the application that have grabbed events will be reported.

A window can grab either all the events for that application or all events for the entire system. The default mode is to grab only events for the current application. If you need to grab events for the entire system, this can be done with the -global flag when a grab is requested.

If a grab is in effect, you can determine whether it is for a local (default) or global scope with the grab status command.

Syntax: grab status *window*

grab status   Returns the status of a grab on the defined window. The return will be one of:

    local   The window is in local (default) mode. Only events destined for this application will be routed to this window.

    global   The window is in global mode. All events in the system will be routed to this window.

    empty string

         There is no grab in effect for this window.

window   The window for which status will be returned.

You can declare that all events will go to a window with the grab or grab set command. These commands behave identically.

Syntax: grab ?set? *?-global?* *window*

grab set   Set a window to grab keyboard and mouse events.

-global   Grab all events for the system. By default, only events that are generated while this application has the focus will be directed to this window.

window   The window that is to receive the events.

Once all the events in the system are directed to the modal widget, the widget has to know when the interaction is complete. We can force the Tcl interpreter to wait until the user has performed an interaction with the tkwait command. This command will wait until a particular event has occurred. The event may be a variable being modified (perhaps by a button press), a change in the visibility of a window, or a window being destroyed.

Syntax: tkwait *EventType name*

tkwait   Wait for an event to occur.

EventType A name describing the type of event that may occur. The contents of *name* depend on which type of event has occurred.

       Valid events are:

       variable *varName*

           Causes tkwait to wait until the variable named in *varName* changes value.

       visibility *windowName*

           Causes tkwait to wait until the window named in *windowName* either becomes visible or is hidden.

       window *windowName*

           Causes tkwait to wait until the window named in *windowName* is destroyed.

The next example shows how the filtered listbox megawidget can be used to create a modal file selection megawidget.

Example 11.6-1

```
lappend auto_path "."
package require widgets

package provide widgets 1.0

################################################################
# proc getFileList {directory}--
#    Returns a list of selected files from the requested
#    directory.
# Arguments
#   directory      The directory to return a list of files from
#
```

```
# Results
#    Creates a new window and grabs focus until user
#    interacts with it.
#    Returns a list of the selected files, or an empty list if :
#                no files are selected,
#                'QUIT' button is clicked
#                window is destroyed.
#
proc getFileList {directory} {
    global popup_File_Global_Var

    # Find an unused, unique name for a toplevel window.
    #  winfo children returns a list of child windows.

    set unique 0
    set childlist [winfo children .]
    while {[lsearch $childlist .dirList_$unique] != -1} {
        incr unique
    }

    # Create the new toplevel window that will hold this
    #    widget
    set win [toplevel .dirList_$unique]

    # Create the widget as a child of the $win window
    #  And configure the listboxes for multiple selections

    set fl [filteredList $win.fl1 -scrollposition left]
    $fl configure filterList -selectmode multiple
    $fl configure fullList -selectmode multiple

    # And fill the full list

    foreach file [glob -nocomplain $directory/*] {
        $fl insert end [file tail $file]
    }

    # Pack the filteredList megawidget at the top of the
    # new window

    pack $fl -side top

    #
    # Create the buttons in a frame of their own, and pack them
    #
```

```
set bframe [frame $win.buttons]

set quit [button $bframe.quit -text "QUIT" -command\
  {set popup_File_Global_Var(ret) ""}]

set ok [button $bframe.ok -text "OK" -command " \
        set popup_File_Global_Var(ret) \[$f1 selection\]
    "]

pack $quit -side left
pack $ok -side left
pack $bframe -side bottom

#
# bind the destroy event to setting the trigger variable,
# so we can exit properly if the window is destroyed by
# the window manager.
#

bind $win <Destroy> {set popup_File_Global_Var(ret) ""}

#
# The following code is adapted from dialog.tcl in the
# tk library. It sets the focus of the window manager
# on the new window, and waits for the value of
# popup_File_Global_Var(ret) to change.
#
# When the user clicks a button, or destroys the window,
# it will set the value of popup_File_Global_Var(ret),
# and processing will continue

# Set a grab and claim the focus.

set oldFocus [focus]
set oldGrab [grab current $win]

if {$oldGrab != ""} {
    set grabStatus [grab status $oldGrab]
}

grab $win
focus $win

# Wait for the user to respond, then restore the focus
# and return the index of the selected button. Restore
# the focus before deleting the window, since otherwise
# the window manager may take the focus away so we can't
```

```
# redirect it.  Finally, restore any grab that was in
# effect.

tkwait variable popup_File_Global_Var(ret)
catch {focus $oldFocus}
catch {
        # It's possible that the window has already been
        # destroyed, hence this "catch".  Delete the
        # <Destroy> handler so that popup_File_Global_Var(ret)
        # doesn't get reset by it.

        bind $win <Destroy> {}
        destroy $win
    }
    if {$oldGrab != ""} {
        if {$grabStatus == "global"} {
            grab -global $oldGrab
        } {
            grab $oldGrab
        }
    }
    return $popup_File_Global_Var(ret)
}
```

Example Script

```
# The widgets pkgIndex.tcl file is in the current directory
# in this example.

lappend auto_path "."

# Include the widgets package to get the
#    getFileList megawidget.

package require widgets

# Create a label and entry widget to get a base directory path

set dirFrame [frame .f1]
label $dirFrame.l1 -text "base directory: "
entry $dirFrame.e1 -textvariable directory

# Create buttons to invoke the getFileList widget.
set buttonFrame [frame .f2]

button $buttonFrame.b1 -text "Select Files" \
    -command {set filelist [getFileList $directory]}
```

```
# The selected files will be displayed in a label widget
#  with the -textvariable defined as the filelist returned
#  from the getFileList widget.

set selFrame [frame .sel]
set selectVal [label $selFrame.selected \
        -textvariable filelist -width 40]
set selectLabel [label $selFrame.label -text \
        "Selected files:"]

# and pack everything

pack $dirFrame.l1 -side left
pack $dirFrame.e1 -side right
pack $dirFrame -side top

pack $selFrame -side top
pack $selectVal -side right
pack $selectLabel -side left

pack $buttonFrame -side top
pack $buttonFrame.b1 -side left
```

Script Results

Initial Window

File Selection Window, after Selections

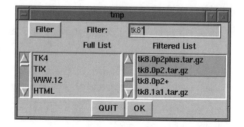

Initial Window, after OK Button Clicked

11.7 A Different Technique for Building Megawidgets

The previous examples have been for megawidgets that you build from scratch following a pattern.

Jeffrey Hobbs, jeff.hobbs@acm.org, has automated much of this in his `widget` package. His package will allow you to create easily a megawidget that uses a `subwidget` command or a naming convention to access the subwidgets. The subwidgets can be configured by accessing them as individual widgets, using either the name returned with the `subwidget` command or the subwidget naming convention to access the subwidgets. Configuration options that are related to the entire megawidget can be processed via the megawidget widget procedure, a procedure with the same name as that given to the megawidget.

You need only write the code to arrange the subwidgets to create a simple megawidget with this package. Optionally, you can add procedures to handle configuration options specific to your megawidget, special initialization, or widget destruction.

This package is on the CD-ROM, with documentation and examples in the `widget.tcl` and `TOUR.tcl` programs. If you wish to use the package, you should read that documentation. This section will give you an overview and an example of how it works.

To use this package to create a megawidget you must:

1. Invoke `widget create` to generate the widget creation procedure in the global scope and initialize the state variables.

2. Provide a `construct` procedure in the namespace for this class of mega-widget. This namespace must be a child namespace of the `::Widget` namespace.

3. If the megawidget has options that are specific to the entire megawidget, rather than the subwidgets, provide a `configure` procedure within this megawidget's namespace.

4. If there are special initializations that need to be done before the widget is displayed, provide an `init` procedure within the megawidget namespace.

5. If you need to do any special operations when the megawidget is destroyed, provide a `destruct` procedure in the megawidget namespace.

In addition, if this megawidget will be included in a package, you must write dummy megawidget creation commands so that `pkg_mkIndex` will index those procedures. The widget package generates the code for a megawidget at run time, thus the actual megawidget creation commands do not exist when `pkg_mkIndex` is evaluated. If you create a dummy creation command, the dummy will be entered into the `pkgIndex.tcl` file, where it will be read by the `package require` command. When the script is evaluated the dummy is replaced by the actual megawidget creation command.

The `widget create` command is the workhorse of this package. It takes several options that describe the megawidget being created.

Syntax: `widget create -options`

`widget create`

> Generate a procedure to construct a megawidget. The procedure will be generated in the global namespace.

`-options` The options for this command include:

> `-type ?type?` The type of megawidget to create. The possible values for type are:

`frame`	Return a frame that can be displayed with one of the layout managers (`pack`, `place`, or `grid`).
`toplevel`	Return a top-level window that can be displayed outside the application window.

`-components` *list*

The components of this megawidget. Each component is defined in a list with these fields:

`type`	The type of widget this will be: `button`, `label`, etc.
`name`	The name for this widget.
`args`	A list of arguments that will be appended to the widget creation line when this widget is created. This is where arguments defining the relationship between a scrollbar and its target widget can be placed.

The next example creates a megawidget that consists of a prompt and an entry widget. By default, the prompt will be on the left of the entry widget, but it can be configured to be on the right (to demonstrate using the `configure` command).

In most megawidgets created with this `widget` command, the layout of the individual widgets would be done in the `construct` procedure. Because this widget allows the user to define the layout of the prompt and entry widgets, that functionality is placed in a separate procedure that can be invoked from either the `construct` command or the `configure` command.

Example 11.7-1

```
#
# The widget index file is in the current directory in this
# example.

lappend auto_path "."

# Uncomment these lines if this will be in a package.
# The dummy procedure will be indexed by pkg_mkIndex

# package provide PromptEntry 1.0
# PromptEntry args {}

# Generate the PromptEntry megawidget creation command

widget create PromptEntry -type frame \
    -components { {label prompt} {entry entry} } \
    -options { {-side Side side left} }

# The support functions for the PromptEntry megawidget

namespace eval ::Widget::PromptEntry {

################################################################
#   proc construct {w}--
#     Called when a PromptEntry megawidget is created to handle
#     widget specific initializations.
# Arguments
#   w          The window name for this megawidget.
#
# Results
#   calls layout to specify the locations of the subwidgets.
#
  proc construct {w} {
    layout $w
```

```
    }
############################################################
#   proc layout {w}--
#     sets the location of the subwidgets
# Arguments
#   w          The window name for this megawidget.
#
# Results
#   packs the prompt and entry subwidgets in the locations
#     defined by the -side option

  proc layout {w} {
      upvar \#0 [namespace current]::$w data

      if {[string match $data(-side) right]} {
          pack $data(prompt) -side right
          pack $data(entry) -side left
      } else {
          pack $data(prompt) -side left
          pack $data(entry) -side right
      }
  }

############################################################
#   proc configure {w args}--
#     Process configuration commands that are specific to the
#       PromptEntry megawidget.
# Arguments
#   w                  The window name for this megawidget.
#   args                A list of key/value pairs.
#
# Results
#   Will either set the -side option to the requested value and
#     rearrange the window, or generate an error.
#
  proc configure {w args} {
      upvar \#0 [namespace current]::$w data

      foreach {key val} $args {
          switch -- $key {
              "-side" {
                  set data(-side) $val
```

```
                    layout $w
                }
                default {
                    error "bad option - use -side"
                }
            }
        }
    }
}
```

Example Script

```
# Create the widget and pack it.
set userInput [PromptEntry .pe]
pack $userInput

# Configure the base widget (the frame) to have a raised
#   relief, with a 5 pixel border.

$userInput configure -relief raised -borderwidth 5

# Use the subwidget command to access the entry subwidget
# and change its width to 40 characters.

[.pe subwidget entry] configure -width 40

# Use the naming convention to set the background color to
#   white, and define a textvariable for this widget.

$userInput.entry configure -background white \
        -textvariable peValue

# Use the subwidget command to set the text for the
#   prompt

[$userInput subwidget prompt] configure -text "Enter Text: "

# The results label will echo the contents of the entry widget
#   to demonstrate the widget behavior.
label .results -textvariable peValue -background gray80

pack .results
```

Script Results

11.8 Bottom Line

- This chapter has described the megawidgets included in the Tk distribution and shown how megawidgets can be constructed using Tk without any C language extensions.

- The megawidgets included in the Tk distribution are:

  Syntax: `tk_optionMenu buttonName varName val1 \`
  `?val2...valN?`

  Syntax: `tk_chooseColor`

  Syntax: `tk_getOpenFile`

  Syntax: `tk_getSaveFile`

  Syntax: `tk_messageBox ?option value?`

  Syntax: `tk_dialog win title text bitmap default \`
  `string1 ?... stringN?`

  Syntax: `tk_popup menu x y ?entry?`

- A Tk window can be declared to be the recipient of all keyboard and mouse events with the `grab` command.

  Syntax: `grab set ?-global? window`

- A Tk script can be made to wait for an event to occur with the `tkwait` command.

  Syntax: `tkwait EventType name`

- You can determine what windows (if any) have grabbed events with the `grab current` command.

  Syntax: `grab current` *?window?*

- You can determine whether a window that is grabbing events is grabbing them for the local task or all tasks with the `grab status` command.

  Syntax: `grab status` *window*

- You can construct your own megawidgets by providing a wrapper procedure that arranges widgets within a frame.

- The name of a frame can be disassociated from the name of the procedure used to configure the frame.

- Megawidgets can be built using namespaces to conceal the internal structure of the megawidget.

- Megawidgets can be nested within other megawidgets to support more complex interactions.

- A megawidget can be made modal with the `grab`, `focus`, and `tkwait` commands.

CHAPTER 12 — *Writing a Tcl Extension*

One of the greatest strengths of the Tcl package is the ease with which it can be extended. By adding your own extensions to the interpreter you can:

- Use compiled code to perform algorithms that are too computation-intensive for an interpreted language.
- Add support for devices or data formats that are not currently supported by Tcl.
- Create a rapid prototyping interpreter for an existing C language library.
- Add Tk graphics to an existing application or set of libraries.
- Create a script-driven validation test suite for an application.

Extensions can be linked with the Tcl library to create a new `tclsh` or `wish` interpreter, or they can be loaded into a running `tclsh`. Note that support for loading binary objects into a running `tclsh` requires a version of the Tcl library that is more recent than 7.5 and an operating system that supports dynamic run-time libraries. Microsoft Windows, Macintosh OS, Linux, and many flavors of Unix support this capability.

Whether you are building a new `tclsh` or a loadable binary package, and whether you are linking to an existing library or are writing your own functions, the steps to follow are the same. This chapter will describe the components of an extension, step through creating a simple Tcl extension, discuss how to move data between the Tcl interpreter and your C language functions, and discuss how to handle complex data such as structures.

In Tcl version 8.0 a major modification was introduced to the Tcl internals. Prior to this (Tcl 7.3, 7.4, 7.5, and 7.6), all data was stored internally as a string. When a script needed to perform a math operation, the data was converted from string to native format (integer, long, float, double, etc.), the operation was performed, and then the native format data was converted back to a string to be returned to the script. This procedure caused Tcl scripts to run rather slowly.

With Tcl revision 8.0 and later, the data is stored internally in a `Tcl_Obj` structure. The `Tcl_Obj` structure contains a string representation of the data and a native representation of the data. The two representations are kept in sync in a *lazy* manner; the native and string representations are calculated when needed and retained as long as they are valid.

This change to the Tcl interpreter helped speed up the Tcl interpreter, but it causes some problems for extension writers. Most of the Tcl library functions that interface with data now come in two forms, one to deal with old-style string data and one to deal with new-style `Tcl_Obj` data.

If you are writing a new extension, you can use all of the new `Tcl_Obj`-oriented commands (which have the word `Obj` in their names). If you need to link with an earlier version of Tcl (for instance, if you need to use an extension that exists only for Tcl 7.5), you will need to use the older version of the commands.

This chapter will cover both sets of commands. If you don't need to be able to link with an older version of Tcl, it is recommended that you use the `Tcl_Obj` objects for your data and the Tcl_Obj API to interface with the interpreter.

12.1 Overview

This section will provide an overview of how to construct an extension, first from the functional viewpoint of what functionality is required in an extension and how the parts work together and then from the structural viewpoint of how the pieces should be assembled.

12.1.1 Functional Overview of an Extension

An extension must perform these actions:

- Initialize any persistent data structures.
- Register new commands in the Tcl interpreter.
- Accept data from the Tcl interpreter.
- Process the new commands.
- Return results to the calling scripts.
- Return status to the calling scripts.

Your extension must include an initialization function that will be called by the Tcl interpreter when the extension is loaded into the interpreter. The code that performs the initialization will depend on your application.

The interface between the Tcl library and an extension is provided by several functions. On Windows systems these are documented under the **Tcl Library Procedures** entry in the **Tcl Help** menu. On Unix systems, they are documented in files named `Tcl_*.3` in the doc directory. On the Macintosh these functions are documented under the **HTML DOCS** folder. Read those entries for more details on these commands.

12.1.2 Data Types

The interface to the Tcl library includes several data types that are specific to Tcl. The ones we'll be dealing with include:

`Tcl_Interp *` A pointer to a Tcl interpreter state structure.

`Tcl_ObjCmdProc *`

> A pointer to a function that will accept Tcl objects as arguments.

`Tcl_CmdProc *`

> A pointer to a function that will accept strings as arguments.

`ClientData` A one-word value that is passed to functions but is never used by the Tcl interpreter. This allows functions to use data that is specific to the application, not the interpreter. For instance, this argument could be used to pass a pointer to a database record, or a window object, or a C++ `this` pointer.

12.1.3 Registering New Commands with the Interpreter

You register a new command with the Tcl interpreter by calling a function that will insert the name of the new command into the Tcl command hash table and associate that name with a pointer to a function that will implement the command.

There are two functions that can be invoked to register a new command with the Tcl interpreter. One will register the new command as a function that can use Tcl objects, and the other will register the new command as a function that requires string arguments. Extensions that are to be linked with versions of Tcl more recent than 8.0 should create Tcl object-based functions rather than string-based functions.

Syntax: int **Tcl_CreateObjCommand** *(interp, cmdName, func, clientData, deleteFunc)*

Syntax: int **Tcl_CreateCommand** *(interp, cmdName, func, clientData, deleteFunc)*

`Tcl_CreateObjCommand`

> These functions register a new command with the Tcl interpreter. These actions are performed within the Tcl interpreter:
>
> - Register *cmdName* with the Tcl interpreter.
> - Define `clientData` data for the command.

- Define the function to call when the command is evaluated.
- Define the command to call when the command is destroyed.

Tcl_CreateCommand

> This is the pre-8.0 version of this command. It will still work with 8.0 and newer interpreters but will create an extension that does not run as fast as an extension that uses Tcl_CreateObjCommand.

Tcl_Interp *interp

> This is a pointer to the Tcl interpreter. It is required by all commands that need to interact with the interpreter state.

> Your extensions will probably just pass this pointer to Tcl library functions that require a Tcl interpreter pointer.

> Your code should not attempt to manipulate any components of the interpreter structure directly.

char *cmdName

> The name of the new command, as a NULL-terminated string.

Tcl_ObjCmdProc *func

> The function to call when cmdName is encountered in a script.

ClientData clientData

> A value that will be passed to func when the interpreter encounters cmdName and calls func.

> The ClientData type is a word, which on most machines is the size of a pointer. You can allocate memory and use this pointer to pass an arbitrarily large data structure to a function.

Tcl_CmdDeleteProc *deleteFunc

> A pointer to a function to call when the command is deleted. If the command has some persistent data object

associated with it, this function should free that memory. If you have no special processing, set this pointer to NULL, and the Tcl interpreter will not register a command deletion procedure.

These commands will return TCL_OK to indicate success or TCL_ERROR to indicate a failure. These are defined in the file tcl.h, which should be #included in your source.

12.1.4 Transferring Data from a Tcl Script to a C Language Extension

When a command is evaluated the interpreter needs to pass data from the script to the function. The Tcl interpreter handles this with a technique similar to that used by the C language for receiving command line parameters. The function that implements the C command receives an integer argument count and an array of pointers to the Tcl script arguments.

For example, if you register a command foo with the interpreter as

```
Tcl_CreateObjCommand(interp, "foo", fooCmd, NULL, NULL);
```

and later write a script command

```
foo one 1 two 2
```

then fooCmd will be passed an argument count of 4 and an argument list that contains one, 1, two, and 2.

When the Tcl interpreter evaluates the Tcl command that is associated with a function in your extension, it will invoke that function with a defined set of arguments. If you are using Tcl 8.0 or newer and register your command using Tcl_CreateObjCommand, the Tcl command arguments will be passed to your function as an array of objects. If you are using an older version of Tcl or register your command using the Tcl_CreateCommand function, the arguments will be passed as an array of strings.

The function prototype for the C function that implements the Tcl command will take one of these two forms:

Syntax: int **func**(*clientData, interp, objc, objv*)
Syntax: int **func**(*clientData, interp, argc, argv*)

func   The function to be called when *cmdName* is evaluated.

ClientData *clientData*
              This is the value that was defined when the command was registered with the interpreter.

Tcl_Interp *interp*
              A pointer to the Tcl interpreter. It will be passed to Tcl library commands that need to interact with the interpreter state.

int *objc*   The count of objects being passed as arguments.

Tcl_Obj *objv[]*
              An array of Tcl Objects that were the arguments to the Tcl command in the script.

int *argc*   In pre-8.0 versions of Tcl, this is the count of argument strings being passed to this function.

char *argv[]* Versions of Tcl prior to 8.0 used strings instead of objects for arguments. The objects are much more efficient and should be used unless you have compelling reasons for maintaining compatibility with older code.

If you are using Tcl version 8.0 or newer and register the command with the Tcl_CreateObjCommand function, your function must accept an array of object pointers. If you are using a version of Tcl older than 8.0, your function must accept arguments as an array of char pointers. In either case, the third argument will be an integer that describes the number of arguments in the array.

Your function may return either TCL_OK, TCL_ERROR, TCL_RETURN, TCL_BREAK, or TCL_CONTINUE. The most frequently used codes are TCL_OK and TCL_ERROR.

The TCL_BREAK, TCL_RETURN, and TCL_CONTINUE are used for building program flow control commands such as looping or branching commands. Since Tcl already includes a complete set of the standard looping and branching commands, if you think you need to implement a new flow control command, you may want to look at your application very closely to see if you've missed an existing command that you could use.

12.1.5 Data Representation

Once your function has been called, you'll need to convert the data to the format your function can use.

In order to convert the data, you need to know a little about how the Tcl interpreter stores data internally.

In versions of Tcl earlier than 8.0, all data was stored as strings. Whenever data was needed in another format, it needed to be converted at that point, and the native format of the data was discarded when that use was finished.

With versions of Tcl that pass the arguments as strings, you can convert the data from the Tcl script to native (int, float, etc.) format with the standard library calls `sscanf`, `atof`, `atol`, `strtod`, `strtol`, `strtoul`, etc.

As of Tcl 8.0, the Tcl interpreter stores data in `Tcl_Obj` structures. The `Tcl_Obj` structure stores its data in two forms: a string representation and a native representation. The data in a `Tcl_Obj` object is accessed via a set of function calls that will be discussed later in this section.

It is not necessary to know the details of the `Tcl_Obj` structure implementation, because all interactions with a Tcl object will be done via Tcl library functions, but you will understand the function calls better if you understand the design of the `Tcl_Obj` structure.

The two primary design features of the Tcl object are the structure's dual-ported nature (the string and native representations of the data) and the interpreter's use of references to objects rather than copies of objects.

A `Tcl_Obj` structure maintains a string representation of the data as well as the native representation. The conversion between these two representations of the data (the dual nature of the object) is handled in a *lazy* manner. The data is converted between formats only when necessary. When one representation of the data is modified, the other representation is deleted to indicate that it must be regenerated when needed again.

For example, in the commands:

`set x 12` The Tcl interpreter creates an object and assigns the string representation to "12".

```
puts "The value of X is: $x"
```
> The `puts` command does not require a conversion to native mode, so the string representation of $x is displayed and no conversion to integer is made.

```
incr x 2
```
> The string representation of the data in the $x object is now converted to native (integer) representation, and the value 2 is added to it. The old string representation is cleared to show that the native representation is valid.

```
set y [expr $x+2]
```
> When $x is accessed by the `expr` command, the object's native representation is used. After the addition is performed, a new object is created to hold the result. There is no need to convert the integer representation of x into a string, so it will be left blank.
>
> This new object is assigned to the variable y, with a native representation (integer) but no string representation defined.

```
puts "The value of Y is: $y"
```
> When the `puts` is evaluated, the Tcl script needs a string representation of the object, the integer is then converted to a string, and the string representation is saved for future use.

If the value of $x were only displayed and never used for a calculation (as a report generator would treat the value), it would never be converted to integer format. Similarly, if the value of $y were never displayed (simply used in other calculations), the conversion to a string would never be made. Since most applications deal with data in native or string representation in batches, this *lazy* conversion increases the speed of the Tcl interpreter.

The reference counts associated with Tcl objects allow the Tcl interpreter to maintain pointers to objects, instead of making copies of any objects that are referenced in more than one location. This lets the interpreter maintain a smaller number of objects than would otherwise be necessary.

When an object is created, it is assigned a reference count of 0.

When a Tcl object is referenced by other objects the reference counter is incremented. The reference counter will be incremented by one when a variable is declared as the -textvariable for a label or passed as an argument to a procedure. When an object that references another Tcl object is destroyed (with the unset command or by destroying an associated widget), the reference count for the associated object is decremented by one. If the reference count becomes 0 or less, the object is deleted and its memory is returned to the heap.

12.1.6 Obtaining the Data

Since arguments are passed to your function in an array of pointers, the function can access data as argument[0], argument[1], etc.

For example, if you register your command using the Tcl_CreateCommand function, you could print out the arguments to a function with code like this:

```
int myFunc(ClientData data, Tcl_Interp *interp, int argc,
    char **argv) {
    int i;
    for (i=0; i<argc; i++) {
        printf("argument %d is %s\n", i, argv[i]);
    }
}
```

More recent versions of Tcl pass the data as an array of pointers to Tcl objects. In that case you need to use the Tcl conversion functions to extract either the string or native representation of the data.

Syntax: int **Tcl_GetIntFromObj** *(interp, objPtr, intPtr)*

Tcl_GetIntFromObj
> Retrieve an integer from the object.

Tcl_Interp *interp*
> A pointer to the Tcl interpreter.

Tcl_Obj *objPtr*
> A pointer to the object that contains an integer.

int *intPtr*   A pointer to the integer that will receive this data.

Syntax: int **Tcl_GetDoubleFromObj** *(interp, objPtr, doublePtr)*

Tcl_GetDoubleFromObj
> Retrieve a double from the object.

Tcl_Interp *interp*
> A pointer to the Tcl interpreter.

Tcl_Obj *objPtr*
> A pointer to the object that contains a double.

Double *doublePtr*
> A pointer to the double that will receive this data.

The Tcl_GetIntFromObj and Tcl_GetDoubleFromObj functions return a TCL_OK if they successfully extract a numeric value from the object or TCL_ERROR if they cannot generate a numeric value for this object. (For instance, if the object contains an alphabetic string, there is no integer or floating-point equivalent.)

Tcl data is always available as a string. When you need to get the string representation of an object's data, you use the Tcl_GetStringFromObj command.

Syntax: char ***Tcl_GetStringFromObj** *(objPtr, lengthPtr)*

Tcl_GetStringFromObj
> Retrieve a byte string from the object.

Tcl_Obj *objPtr*
> A pointer to the object that contains a string.

int *lengthPtr*
> A pointer to an int that will receive the number of characters in this data. If this value is NULL, the length will not be returned.

Note that the Tcl_GetStringFromObj function does not follow the format of the previous Get functions. It returns the requested data as a char pointer rather than returning a status. Since the data is always available in a string format, this command can fail only if the object pointer is invalid, in which case the program has other problems and will probably crash.

The `Tcl_GetStringFromObj` command can place the number of valid bytes in the `char` pointer in an integer pointer (`lengthPtr`). The data in a string may be binary data (accessed via the Tcl `binary` command, for instance), in which case the length pointer is necessary to track the number of bytes in the string.

12.1.7 Returning Results

The function implementing a Tcl command can return results to a script in several ways:

1. Return a single value as the result.
2. Return a list of values as the result.
3. Modify the contents of a script variable named as an argument.
4. Modify the contents of a known script variable.

In Tcl earlier than 8.0, since all variables were maintained as strings, a function could create an ASCII string to return with the `sprintf` command or could modify data in an existing string with the standard string library commands.

In Tcl 8.0 and more recent versions, you need to create a new object to return or modify the contents of an existing object.

You can create a new object with one of these commands:

Syntax: `Tcl_Obj *`**`Tcl_NewIntObj`** *(intValue)*

Syntax: `Tcl_Obj *`**`Tcl_NewDoubleObj`** *(doubleValue)*

Syntax: `Tcl_Obj *`**`Tcl_NewStringObj`** *(bytes, length)*

`Tcl_NewIntObj`
> Create a new Tcl object with an integer value.

`Tcl_NewDoubleObj`
> Create a new Tcl object with a double value.

`Tcl_NewStringObj`
> Create a new Tcl object from a byte string.

intValue   The integer to assign to the new object.

doubleValue   The double to assign to the new object.

bytes   An array of bytes to copy to the new object.

length   The number of bytes to copy to the new object. If this is a negative value, all the bytes up to the first NULL byte will be copied.

You can modify the contents of an object by changing either the natural or string representation with these commands:

Syntax: void **Tcl_SetIntObj** *(objPtr, intValue)*

Tcl_SetIntObj

Set the value of the integer representation of an object. If the object was not already an integer type, it will be converted to one if possible.

Tcl_Obj *objPtr*

A pointer to the object that will contain the integer.

int *intValue* The integer to assign to this object.

Syntax: void **Tcl_SetDoubleObj** *(objPtr, doubleValue)*

Tcl_SetDoubleObj

Set the value of the integer representation of an object. If the object was not already a double type, it will be converted to one if possible.

Tcl_Obj *objPtr*

A pointer to the object that will contain the double.

double *doubleValue*

The double to assign to this object.

An object's string representation can be modified in several ways, either completely replacing one byte string with a new byte string, appending a single string, appending a string from another object, or appending a list of strings.

Syntax: void **Tcl_SetStringObj** *(objPtr, bytes, length)*
Syntax: void **Tcl_AppendToObj** *(objPtr, bytes, length)*

Syntax: void **Tcl_AppendObjToObj** *(objPtr, appendObjPtr)*
Syntax: void **Tcl_AppendStringsToObj** *(objPtr, string, ...,*
NULL)

Tcl_SetStringObj

>   Redefine the string value of an object.

Tcl_AppendToObj

>   Append a string to the string representation of the data in an object.

Tcl_AppendObjectToObj

>   Append the string representation of the value of one object to the string currently in an object.

Tcl_AppendStringsToObj

>   Append one or more strings to the string currently in an object.

Tcl_Obj *objPtr*

>   A pointer to the object that contains the string.

bytes   An array of bytes to copy to the object.

length   The number of bytes to copy to the new object. If this is a negative value, all the bytes up to the first NULL byte will be copied.

appendObjPtr A pointer to an object that contains a string to be appended.

string   A NULL-terminated string of characters. You may not use a binary string with the Tcl_AppendStringsToObj command.

If you desire to have your function return a value to the script as the result of evaluating the command (which is how most functions return their results), you call a function that sets the return to be a particular object. This object is generally one that is created within the function (thus has a reference count of 0). If the return value from the function is assigned to a variable, the object's reference count will be incremented; otherwise, the object will be deleted.

Syntax: void **Tcl_SetObjResult** *(interp, objPtr)*
Syntax: void **Tcl_SetResult** *(interp, string, freeProc)*

Tcl_SetObjResult

> Makes the Tcl interpreter point to *objPtr* as the result of this function. If this function has already had a result object defined, that object will be replaced by the object pointed to by objPtr. This function should be used with Tcl 8.0 and more recent versions.

Tcl_SetResult

> Copies the string into the result string for this function, replacing any previous string that was there. This function is for use with pre-8.0 versions of Tcl.

Tcl_Interp *interp*

> A pointer to the Tcl interpreter.

Tcl_Obj *objPtr*

> A pointer to the object that will become the result.

char *string*

> A string to copy to the object.

freeProc

> The name of a procedure to call to free the memory associated with the string when this object is destroyed. Must be one of:
>
> TCL_STATIC The string was defined in static memory and will remain constant.
>
> TCL_DYNAMIC The memory for the string was allocated with a call to Tcl_Alloc. It will be returned to the Tcl memory pool.
>
> TCL_VOLATILE The string was allocated from a nonpersistent area of memory (probably declared on the call stack) and may change when the function exits. In this case, the Tcl interpreter will allocate a safe space for the string and copy the memory contents.

12.1.8 Returning Status to the Script

When a function returns execution control to the Tcl interpreter, it must return its status. The status should be either TCL_OK or TCL_ERROR. If the function returns TCL_OK, the object defined by Tcl_SetObjResult will be returned to the script, and script will continue execution.

If the function returns TCL_ERROR, an error will be generated, and unless your script is trapping errors with the catch command, the execution will stop and error messages will be returned.

By default, the error messages returned will be the Tcl call stack leading to the Tcl command that caused the error. You may want to add other information to this, such as why a file write failed, what database seek didn't return a value, or what socket can no longer be contacted.

You can add more information to that message by invoking the function Tcl_AddErrorInfo, Tcl_SetErrorCode, Tcl_AddObjErrorInfo, or Tcl_SetObjErrorCode.

Syntax: void **Tcl_AddObjErrorInfo** *(interp, message, length)*
Syntax: void **Tcl_AddErrorInfo** *(interp, message)*
Syntax: void **Tcl_SetObjErrorCode** *(interp, objPtr)*
Syntax: void **Tcl_SetErrorCode** *(interp, element1,*
        element2...NULL)

Tcl_AddObjErrorInfo

> Append additional text to the information object. This information object can be accessed within the Tcl script as the global variable errorInfo.

Tcl_AddErrorInfo

> Append additional text to the information to be returned to the script. This function should be used with versions of Tcl before 8.0.

Tcl_SetObjErrorCode

> Set the errorCode global variable to the value contained in the Tcl object. If the object contains a list, the list values are concatenated together to form the return. By default errorCode will be NONE.

Tcl_SetErrorCode

>Set the errorCode global variable to the value of the concatenated strings.

Tcl_Interp *interp

>A pointer to the Tcl interpreter.

char *message

>The message to append to the errorInfo global variable. This string will have a newline appended to it.

Tcl_Obj *objPtr

>A pointer to the object that will contain the error code.

char *element

>A NULL-terminated ASCII string representation of a portion of the error code.

If a system error occurs, your function can invoke Tcl_PosixError to set the errorCode variable from the C language global errno. The behavior of this command varies slightly for different platforms. You should check the online documentation for your platform and Tcl revision before using it.

12.1.9 Dealing with Persistent Data

There are circumstances in which an extension needs to maintain a copy of some persistent data separate from the script that is being evaluated, while allowing the script to describe the piece of data with which it needs to interact. For instance, a file pointer must be maintained until the file is closed, and a Tcl script may have several files open simultaneously, accessing one file and then another.

If your extension's data requirements are simple, it may be sufficient to allocate an array of items and assign them to scripts as necessary. For instance, if you write an extension that interfaces with a particular piece of hardware and there will never be more than one of these devices on a system, you may declare the control structure as a static global in your C code.

For more complex situations, the Tcl library includes functions that let you use a Tcl hash table to store key and value pairs. Your extension can allocate memory for a data structure, define a key to identify that structure, and then place a pointer to the structure in the hash table, to be accessed with the key. The key may be an alphanumeric string that can be returned to the Tcl script. When a Tcl script needs to access the data, it passes the key back to the extension code, which then retrieves the data from the hash table.

The Tcl hash table consists of a `Tcl_HashTable` structure that is allocated by your extension code and `Tcl_HashEntry` structures that are created as necessary to hold Key/Value pairs.

You must initialize the hash table before using it with the functions that access hash table entries. Once the table is initialized, your code can add, access, or delete items from the hash table.

Syntax: void **Tcl_InitHashTable** *(tablePtr, keyType)*

Tcl_InitHashTable
> Initializes the hash table.

Tcl_HashTable *tablePtr*
> A pointer to the `Tcl_HashTable` structure. The space for this structure must be allocated before calling `Tcl_Init-HashTable`.

int *keyType*   A Tcl hash table can use one of three different types of keys to access the data saved in the hash table. The acceptable values for *keyType* are:

> TCL_STRING_KEYS
>> The hash table will use a NULL-terminated string as the key. This is the most commonly used type of hash key. The string representation of a Tcl_Obj object can be used as the key, which makes it simple to pass a value from a script to the Tcl hash table functions.

TCL_ONE_WORD_KEYS

>The hash table will use a single word value as the key. Note that if the word is a pointer, the value of the pointer is used as the key, not the data that the pointer references.

positiveInteger

>If a positive integer is used as the *keyType*, then the key will be an array of the number of integers described. This allows complex binary data constructs to be used as keys. Note that the constructs used as keys must be the same size.

Once a hash table has been initialized, the Tcl_CreateHashEntry, Tcl_FindHashEntry, and Tcl_DeleteHashEntry commands can be used to create, query, or remove entries from the hash table.

Syntax: Tcl_HashEntry *__Tcl_CreateHashEntry__ *(tablePtr, key, newPtr)*
Syntax: Tcl_HashEntry *__Tcl_FindHashEntry__ *(tablePtr, key)*
Syntax: void __Tcl_DeleteHashEntry__ *(entryPtr)*

Tcl_CreateHashEntry

>Allocates and initializes a new Tcl_HashEntry object for the requested key. If there was a previous entry with this key, then newPtr is set to NULL.

Tcl_FindHashEntry

>This function returns a pointer to the Tcl_HashEntry object that is associated with the key value. If that key does not exist in this hash table, this function returns NULL.

Tcl_DeleteHashEntry

>This removes a hash table entry from the table. After this function has been called, Tcl_FindHashEntry will return a NULL if used with this key. This does not destroy data associated with the hash entry. Your functions that interact with the hash table must do that.

Tcl_HashTable *tablePtr
> A pointer to a Tcl hash table. This table must be initialized by Tcl_InitHashTable before being used by these commands.

char *key

> The key that defines this entry. This value must be one of the types described in the Tcl_InitHashTable call.

int *newPtr

> This value will be 1 if a new entry was created and 0 if a key with this value already existed.

Tcl_HashEntry *entryPtr
> A pointer to a hash table entry.

A Tcl_HashEntry contains the key value that identifies it and a Client-Data data object. The ClientData type is a word-sized object. On most modern machines, this is the same size as a pointer, which allows you to allocate an arbitrary data space and place the pointer to that space in a Tcl_HashEntry.

You can manipulate a Tcl_HashEntry object with the Tcl_SetHashValue and Tcl_GetHashValue commands.

Syntax: ClientData **TclGetHashValue** (entryPtr)
Syntax: void **TclSetHashValue** (entryPtr, value)

TclGetHashValue
> Retrieve the data from a Tcl_HashEntry.

TclSetHashValue
> Set the value of the data in a Tcl_HashEntry.

Tcl_HashEntry *entryPtr
> A pointer to a hash table entry.

ClientData value
> The value to be placed in the clientData field of the Tcl_HashEntry.

Here is a code snippet that will create a hash table, add an entry, and retrieve the data.

Example 12.1.9-1

Example Snippet

```
void hashSnippet () {
    Tcl_HashTable *hashTable;
    Tcl_HashEntry *firstEntry, *secondEntry;
    int isNew;
    char *insertData, *retrievedData;
    char *key;

    key = "myKey";
    insertData = "This is data in the hash table";

    /* Allocate the space and initialize the hash table */

    hashTable = (Tcl_HashTable *)
            malloc(sizeof(Tcl_HashTable));
    Tcl_InitHashTable(hashTable, TCL_STRING_KEYS);

    /* Get a hash Entry for the key, and confirm it is a
     * new key
     */

    firstEntry = Tcl_CreateHashEntry(hashTable, key, &isNew);
    if (isNew == 0) {
        printf("Bad key - this key already exists!");
        return;
    }

    /* Define the value for this entry.              */
    Tcl_SetHashValue(firstEntry, insertData);

    /* -----------------------------------------------------
     * At this point, the data has been placed in the hash
     * table. In an actual application, these sections of
     * code would be in separate functions.
     * -----------------------------------------------------*/
    /* Retrieve the hash entry with the key.     */

    secondEntry = Tcl_FindHashEntry(hashTable, key);
        if (secondEntry == (Tcl_HashEntry *) NULL) {
        printf("Failed to find %s\n", key);
        return;
```

```
    }

    /* Extract the data from the hash entry      */
    retrievedData = (char *)Tcl_GetHashValue(secondEntry);

    /* Display the data, just to prove a point    */
    printf("Retrieved this string from hashTable: \n%s\n",
        retrievedData);
}
```

Snippet Output

```
Retrieved this string from hashTable:
This is data in the hash table
```

12.2 Building an Extension

The bulk of your extension may be a library of code that has already been developed and tested, a library that you need to test and validate, or a set of code that you will write for this specific extension. In each of these cases, you'll use the functions described above to connect the application code to the interpreter.

The next step is the mechanics of constructing the extension.

12.2.1 Structural Overview of an Extension

An extension consists of one or more source code files, one or more include files, and a makefile. The source code files must contain a function with initialization code and that function must conform to the naming conventions described in the Section 12.2.2.

The source code files will include at least one function that adds new commands to the interpreter and at least one function to implement the new commands.

A common structure is to create two files: one with the initialization function that adds the new commands to the interpreter and a second file with the functions that implement the new commands.

All code that uses functions from the Tcl library will need to include `tcl.h`. The `tcl.h` file has all the function prototypes, `#define`, data definitions, etc. that are required to interact with the Tcl library functions.

12.2.2 Naming Conventions

There are a few naming conventions involved with writing a Tcl extension. Some of these are required in order to interact with the Tcl interpreter, and some are recommended in order to conform to the appearance of other Tcl extensions. If you write your extension to conform to the recommended standards, it will be easier for your extension to be used (and extended) by others.

These conventions are describe in the *Tcl/Tk Engineering Manual*, which is on the CD-ROM included with this book. This can also be acquired via FTP from `mirror.neosoft.com` as `/usr/ftp/archive0/tcl/mirror/ftp.smli .com/docs/engManual.tar.Z`. Before you start writing an extension, I recommend you read the engineering manual. It may save you some rewrites.

Function Name	Description
`ExtName_Init`	This function is required. It initializes an extension by creating any persistent data objects and registering new commands with the Tcl interpreter.
	This entry point is used to initialize the extension when a DLL (Dynamic Link Library) or shared library is loaded.
	The capitalization is important. For example, for an extension named `ext` the `Init` function would be `Ext_Init`.
`ExtName_AppInit`	This function is called to initialize a stand-alone `tclsh` interpreter with the extension compiled into it.

Function Name	Description
extName_command *NameCmd*	These entry points are optional, but this is the naming convention used for the C code that will be invoked when the command `commandName` is evaluated by a Tcl script.

Files	Description
extNameInt.h	This file is required. It will contain the `#include` statements, `#define` statements, data structure definitions, and function prototypes that are used by the code in this extension. This is for the package's internal use. This file will be included by all the extension code files.
extNameInit.c	This file is required. It will contain the *ExtName_Init* function. If your application is simple, it may also include the C language functions that implement the extension.
extNameCmd.c	This file is optional. If the code to interface between Tcl and the C code is large, you may want to separate the code that creates the new commands in the Tcl interpreter from the *extNameInit.c* file and place that code in a separate file.
extNameCmdAL.c *extNameCmdMZ.c*	These files are optional. If you have a truly large extension, it can make the code easier to follow if you split the functions that implement the commands into smaller files. One convention used for this is to put the commands that start

Files	Description
	with the letter A through some other letter in one file and those that start with a character after the breakpoint letter in another file.
extNameCommand.c	These files are optional. If your extension has commands that accept a number of subcommands, or if the command is implemented with several functions, it can make the code easier to follow if you split the functions that implement a command into a separate file. Thus, the functions that implement command `foo` would be in `extFoo.c`, while those that implement command `bar` would be in `extBar.c`
extName.dll *libextName.so* *extName.shlb* *extName.sl* *extNameCFM68K.shl*	A file in one of these formats will be created for your extension when you have completed compiling your extension.
	The Tcl interpreter will use the `extName` part of the extension to find the default *ExtName_Init* function.
	If you can't follow this naming convention for the extension file, you can force the Tcl interpreter to find the initialization function by declaring the extension name in the `load` command like this:
	`load wrongname.dll myextension`
	Not following the naming convention for the extension file will make it impossible to use `pkg_mkIndex` to construct a `tclIndex` file, but you can build the index line with a text editor if necessary.

12.3 An Example

This section will construct a simple extension that will demonstrate the mechanisms discussed in this chapter. On the CD-ROM you'll find the demo code, the example extension packages from Sun, and a dummyTclExtension kit with a Tcl script that will create a skeleton extension similar to the demo extension.

This example follows the coding standards in the *Tcl/Tk Engineering Manual*, which is included on the CD-ROM. In places where the manual doesn't define a standard, I'll note that this convention is mine, not the Tcl standard. Otherwise, the naming conventions etc. are those defined by the Tcl community.

This demo extension doesn't perform any calculations. It just shows how an extension can be constructed and how to acquire and return data using the hash functions.

The demo package implements one Tcl command and five subcommands within that command.

The subcommands are debug, create, get, destroy, and set.

Syntax: demo debug *level*

demo debug	Sets a static global variable in the C code that turns on or off internal debug output.
level	The level to assign to this variable. A value of zero will disable the debugging output, and a nonzero value will enable that output.

Syntax: demo create *key raw_message*

demo create	Create a hash table entry.
key	The key for this hash table entry.
raw_message	The string to assign to this hash.

Syntax: demo get *key*

demo get   Retrieves the value of an entry from the hash table and returns the string saved with that key.

key   The key for the entry to return.

Syntax: demo destroy *key*

demo destroy   Deletes an entry in the hash table.

key   The key that identifies which entry to delete.

Syntax: demo set *arrayName index Value*

demo set   An example of how to set the values in an associative array. It sets the requested index to the requested value and sets the index alpha of the array to the value NewValue. The index alpha and value NewValue are hard-coded in the procedure Demo_SetCmd.

                This subcommand executes the C code equivalent of

```
set arrayName(index) Value
set arrayName(alpha) "NewValue"
```

                The command will return the string "NewValue".

arrayName   The name of a Tcl array. It need not exist before calling this subcommand.

index   An index into the array. This index will have Value assigned to it.

Value   The value to assign to *arrayName(index)*.

The demo extension is arranged in the style of a large package with many commands, to show how the functionality can be split across files and functions. It consists of these files:

demoInt.h   This include file has the definitions for the structures used by this extension and the function prototypes of the functions that are defined in demoInit.c, demoCmd.c, and demoDemo.c.

demoInit.c   This file contains the `Demo_Init` function.

DemoCmd.c   This file contains the `Demo_Cmd` function, which is invoked when a `demo` `Tcl` command is evaluated in a script.

                  This file also includes the descriptions of the subcommands associated with the `demo` command.

demoDemo.c   This file contains the functions that implement the `demo` subcommands.

12.3.1 `demoInt.h`

The `demoInt.h` include file will be included by all the source files in the `demo` extension. It includes the version number information for this extension, the include files that will be used by other functions, some magic for Microsoft VC++, definition of data structures used by the `demo` extension, and the function prototypes.

Example 12.3.1-1
_____

demoInt.h

```
/*
 * demoInt.h --
 *
 *       Declarations used by the demotcl extension
 *
 */

#ifndef _DEMOINT
#define _DEMOINT

/* 1
 * Declare the #includes that will be used by this extension
 */

#include <tcl.h>
#include <string.h>

/* 2
 * Define the version number.
```

```
 * Note: VERSION is defined as a string, not integer.
 */

#define DEMO_VERSION "1.0"

/* 3
 * VC++ has an alternate entry point called
 * DllMain, so we need to rename our entry point.
 */

#if defined(__WIN32__)
#    define WIN32_LEAN_AND_MEAN
#    include <windows.h>
#    undef WIN32_LEAN_AND_MEAN
#    if defined(_MSC_VER)
#        define EXPORT(a,b) __declspec(dllexport) a b
#        define DllEntryPoint DllMain
#    else
#        if defined(__BORLANDC__)
#            define EXPORT(a,b) a _export b
#        else
#            define EXPORT(a,b) a b
#        endif
#    endif
#else
#    define EXPORT(a,b) a b
#endif

/* 4
 *   The CmdReturn structure is used by the subroutines to
 *    pass back a success/failure code and a Tcl_Obj result.
 *
 *   This is not an official Tcl standard return type. I
 *   find this works well with commands that accept subcommands.
 */
typedef struct cmd_return {
  int status;
  Tcl_Obj *object;
} CmdReturn;
```

```
/* 5
 * Function Prototypes for the commands that actually do the
 * processing.
 * Two macros are used in these prototypes:
 *
 * EXTERN EXPORT is for functions that must interact with the
 *      Microsoft or Borland C++ DLL loader.
 * ANSI_ARGS is defined in tcl.h
 *      ANSI_ARGS returns an empty string for non-ANSI C
 *      compilers, and returns its arguments for ANSI C
 *      compilers.
 */

EXTERN EXPORT(int,Demo_Init) _ANSI_ARGS_ ((Tcl_Interp *));
EXTERN EXPORT(int,Demo_Cmd) _ANSI_ARGS_
        ((ClientData, Tcl_Interp *, int, Tcl_Obj **));

CmdReturn *demo_GetCmd _ANSI_ARGS_ ((ClientData,
        Tcl_Interp *, int, Tcl_Obj **));
CmdReturn *demo_SetCmd _ANSI_ARGS_ ((ClientData,
        Tcl_Interp *, int, Tcl_Obj **));
CmdReturn *demo_SendCmd _ANSI_ARGS_ ((ClientData,
        Tcl_Interp *, int, Tcl_Obj **));
CmdReturn *demo_CreateCmd _ANSI_ARGS_ ((ClientData,
        Tcl_Interp *, int, Tcl_Obj **));
CmdReturn *demo_DestroyCmd _ANSI_ARGS_ ((ClientData,
        Tcl_Interp *, int, Tcl_Obj **));
void demo_InitHashTable _ANSI_ARGS_ (());

#define debugprt  if (demoDebugPrint>0) printf
/* End _DEMOINT */
#endif
```

1. The demoInt.h file has the #include definitions that will be used by the source code files in the demo package. If the extension requires several include files, this convention makes it easier to maintain the list of include files.

2. The DEMO_VERSION string will be used in the Demo_Init function to define the script global variable demo_version. All packages should include a *packageName*_version variable definition. Defining this variable allows scripts to check the version of the package they have loaded.

3. There are some conventions that Microsoft VC++ demands for code that will be dynamically loaded. If your extension will need to compile only on Unix or Macintosh, you may delete this section and simplify the function prototypes.

4. The CmdReturn structure is not a part of the Tcl standard. I use it to allow functions that implement subcommands to return both a status and a Tcl_Obj to the function that implements the primary command. The status field will be assigned the value TCL_OK or TCL_ERROR. The object field may be NULL if the function has no return or a pointer to a Tcl Object.

   If you find another convention more suited to your needs, feel free to use that instead.

5. The function prototypes for the functions in the source code files. All of the functions defined in the source code files should also be defined here.

12.3.2 `demoInit.c`

The demoInit.c file is one of the required files in an extension. At a minimum this file must define the Demo_Init function, as shown (and discussed) next:

Example 12.3.2-1
_____

demoInit.c

```
#include "demoInt.h"

/* CVS Revision Tag */
#define DEMOINIT_REVISION "$Revision: 1.2 $"
/*
 *------------------------------------------------------------
 *
 * Demo_Init
 *
 *      Called from demo_AppInit() if this is a standalone
 *      shell, r when the package is loaded if compiled
 *      into a binary package.
 *
 */
```

```
 * Results:
 *       A standard Tcl result.
 *
 * Side effects:
 *       Creates a hash table.
 *       Adds new commands
 *       Creates new Tcl global variables for demo_version and
 *           demoInit_revision.
 *
 *-----------------------------------------------------------------
 */

int Demo_Init(Tcl_Interp *interp) {
  /* interp         Current interpreter. */

  /* 1
   * If this application will need to save any
   * data in a hash table initialize the hash table.

   */

  Demo_InitHashTable ();

  /* 2
   * Call Tcl_CreateCommand for commands defined by this
   * extension
   */

  Tcl_CreateObjCommand(interp, "demo", Demo_Cmd,
      (ClientData) NULL, NULL);

  /* 3
   * Define the package for pkg_mkIndex to index
   */

  Tcl_PkgProvide(interp, "demo", DEMO_VERSION);

  /* 4
   * Define the version for this package
   */

  Tcl_SetVar((Tcl_Interp *) interp, "demo_version",
          DEMO_VERSION, TCL_GLOBAL_ONLY);
```

```
/* 5
 * Not a requirement.  I like to make the source code
 * revision available as a Tcl variable.
 * It's easier to track bugs when you can track all the
 * revisions of all the files in a release.
 */

Tcl_SetVar((Tcl_Interp *) interp, "demoInit_revision",
        DEMOINIT_REVISION, TCL_GLOBAL_ONLY);
/* 6
 */
return TCL_OK;
}
```

1. Tcl allows any package to create its own hash table database to store and retrieve arbitrary data. If a package needs to share persistent information with scripts, you will probably need to save that data in a hash table and return a key to the script to identify which data is being referenced. The hash table will be discussed in more detail with the functions that actually interact with the table.

2. The `Tcl_CreateObjCommand` function creates a Tcl command `demo` and declares that the function `Demo_Cmd` is to be called when this command is evaluated.

3. The `Tcl_PkgProvide` command declares that this package is named `demo`, and it is the revision defined by DEMO_VERSION. DEMO_VERSION is `#defined` in `demoInt.h`.

4. This `Tcl_SetVar` command defines a global Tcl variable `demo_version` as the version number of this package. This definition allows a script to check the version number of the `demo` package that was loaded.

5. This is not part of the Tcl standard. My preference is to include the source control revision string in each module to make it easy to determine just what versions of all the code were linked into a package. I've found this particularly important when I'm in a crunch phase of a project and making several releases a day to testers who are trying to tell me what behavior was seen on what version of the code.

6. Finally, return TCL_OK. None of these function calls should fail.

12.3.3 `demoCmd.c`

The `demoCmd.c` file is where most of your extension code will exist. For small extensions this file will contain all the code that implements your package functionality.

The `Demo_Cmd` function introduces a couple of new Tcl library functions.

The `Tcl_GetIndexFromObj` function searches a list of words for a target word. This function will return the index of the word that either exactly matches the target word or is a unique abbreviation of the target word. This function is used in this example to extract a subcommand from a list of valid subcommands.

Syntax: int **Tcl_GetIndexFromObj** *(interp, objPtr, tblPtr, msg, flags, indexPtr)*

Tcl_GetIndexFromObj

> Tcl_GetIndexFromObj sets *indexPtr* to the offset into *tablePtr* of the entry that matches the string representation of the data in *objPtr*. An item in *tablePtr* is defined as a match if it is either an exact match to a string in the table or a unique abbreviation for a string in the table.
>
> This function returns TCL_OK if it finds a match or TCL_ERROR if no match can found. If Tcl_GetIndexFromObj fails, it will set an error message in the interpreter's result object.

interp A pointer to the Tcl interpreter.

tablePtr A pointer to a NULL-terminated list of strings to be searched for a match.

msg A string that will be included in an error message to explain what was being looked up if *Tcl_GetIndexFromObj* fails. The error message will resemble

bad *msg* "*string*": must be *tableStrings*

msg The string defined in the msg argument

string The string representation of the data in objPtr

tableStrings

> The strings defined in *tablePtr*

flags
: The *flags* argument allows the calling code to define what matches are acceptable. If this flag is TCL_EXACT, only exact matches will be returned, rather than allowing abbreviations.

indexPtr
: A pointer to the integer that will receive the index of the matching field.

The demoCmd.c file contains the C functions that are called when demo commands are evaluated in the Tcl script. In a larger package with several commands, this file would contain several entry points.

Example 12.3.3-1

demoCmd.c

```
#include "demoInt.h"

/* 1
 * Define the sub commands
 *
 * These strings define the subcommands that the demo command
 * supports.
 *
 * To add a new subcommand, add the new subcommand string,
 * #define, and entry in cmdDefinition.
 *
 * Note: Order is important.
 *
 * These are the subcommands that will be recognized
 *
 */

static char *subcommands[] = {
        "create", "set", "get", "debug", "destroy", NULL};

/* 2
 * These #defines define the positions of the subcommands.
 * You can use enum if you are certain your compiler will
 * provide the same numbers as this.
 */
```

```
#define M_create  0
#define M_set     1
#define M_get     2
#define M_debug   3
#define M_destroy  4

/* 3
 * The cmdDefinition structure describes the minimum and
 *  maximum number of expected arguments for the subcommand
 * (including cmd and subcommand names), and a usage message
 * to return if the argument count is outside the expected
 * range.
 */

typedef struct cmd_Def {
   char *usage;
   int   minArgCnt;
   int   maxArgCnt;
   } cmdDefinition;

static cmdDefinition definitions[5] = {
    {"create key raw_message", 4 , 4},
    {"set arrayName index Value", 5, 5},
    {"get key ", 3, 3},
    {"debug level", 3, 3},
    {"destroy key", 3,3}
};

/* 4
 * If demoDebugPrint != 0, then debugprt will print debugging
 * info.  This value is set with the subcommand debug.
 */

int demoDebugPrint = 0;

/* 5
 *-----------------------------------------------------------------
 *
 * Demo_Cmd --
 *
 *      Demo_Cmd is invoked to process the "demo" Tcl command.
 *      It will parse a subcommand, and perform the requested
 *         action.
 *
```

```
 * Results:
 *      A standard Tcl result.
 *
 * Side effects:
 *
 *-----------------------------------------------------------
 */

int Demo_Cmd(ClientData demo,
             Tcl_Interp *interp,
             int objc,
             Tcl_Obj *objv[]) {

    /* ClientData demo;            /* Not used. */
    /* Tcl_Interp *interp;          /* Current interpreter. */
    /* int objc;                    /* Number of arguments. */
    /* Tcl_Obj *CONST objv[];      /* Argument objects. */

    int cmdnum;
    int result;
    Tcl_Obj *returnValue;
    CmdReturn *returnStruct;
    ClientData info;

    /*
     * Initialize the return value
     */

    returnValue = NULL;
    returnStruct = NULL;

    /* 6
     *  Check that we have at least a subcommand,
     *  else return an Error and the usage message
     */

    if (objc < 2) {
        Tcl_WrongNumArgs(interp, 1, objv,
                "subcommand ?options?");
        return TCL_ERROR;
    }

    /* 7
     * Find this demo subcommand in the list of subcommands.
```

```
 * Tcl_GetIndexFromObj returns the offset of the recognized
 * string, which is used to index into the command
 * definitions table.
 * /

result = Tcl_GetIndexFromObj(interp, objv[1], subcommands,
                             "subcommand", TCL_EXACT, &cmdnum);

/* 8
 * If the result is not TCL_OK, then the error message is
 * already in the Tcl Interpreter, this code can
 * immediately return.
 */

if (result != TCL_OK) {
    return TCL_ERROR;
}

/* 9
 *  Check that the argument count matches what's expected
 * for this Subcommand.
 */

if ((objc < definitions[cmdnum].minArgCnt) ||
    (objc > definitions[cmdnum].maxArgCnt) ) {
    Tcl_WrongNumArgs(interp, 1, objv,
                     definitions[cmdnum].usage);
    return TCL_ERROR;
}

result = TCL_OK;

/* 10
 * The subcommand is recognized, and has a valid number of
 * arguments Process the command.
 */

switch (cmdnum) {
    case M_debug: {
            char *tmp;
            tmp = Tcl_GetStringFromObj(objv[2], NULL);
            if (TCL_OK !=
                Tcl_GetInt(interp, tmp, &demoDebugPrint)) {
                    return (TCL_ERROR);
```

```
            }
            break;
    }
    case M_destroy: {
            returnStruct =
                Demo_DestroyCmd((ClientData) &info,
                        interp, objc, objv);
            break;
    }
    case M_create:  {
            returnStruct =
                Demo_CreateCmd((ClientData) &info,
                        interp, objc, objv);
            break;
    }
    case M_get:             {
            returnStruct =
                Demo_GetCmd((ClientData) &info,
                        interp, objc, objv);
            break;
    }
    case M_set:             {
            returnStruct =
                Demo_SetCmd((ClientData) &info,
                        interp, objc, objv);
            break;
    }
    default:                {
            char error[80];
            sprintf(error,
                "Bad sub-command %s.  Has no switch entry",
                Tcl_GetStringFromObj(objv[1], NULL));
            returnValue = Tcl_NewStringObj(error, -1);
            result = TCL_ERROR;
    }
}

/* 11
 * Extract an object to return from returnStruc.
 * returnStruct will be NULL if the processing is done
```

```
 * in this function and no other function is called.
 */

if (returnStruct != NULL) {
    returnValue = returnStruct->object;
    result = returnStruct->status;
    free (returnStruct);
}

/* 12
 * Set the return value and return the status
 */

if (returnValue != NULL) {
    Tcl_SetObjResult(interp, returnValue);
}

return result;
}
```

1. This array of strings will be passed to the `Tcl_GetIndexFromObj` function that will identify a valid subcommand from this list.

2. These `#defines` create a set of textual identifiers for the positions of the subcommands in the list. They will be used in a `switch` command in the main code to select which function to call to implement the subcommands.

3. The `cmdDefinition` structure is one that I prefer. It is not part of the official Tcl coding standards. It is strongly recommended that functions check their arguments and return a usage message if the arguments do not at least match the expected count. This can be done in each function that implements a subcommand, or in the function that implements the main command. I prefer to use this table to define the maximum and minimum number of arguments expected and the error message to return if the number of arguments received is not within that range.

4. There is a `#define` macro used to define `debugprt` in `demoInt.h`. This will reference the `demoDebugPrint` global variable. This is not part of the official Tcl coding standards. I find it convenient to use `printf` for some levels of debugging.

5. This is the standard header for a C function in a Tcl extension, as recommended in the *Tcl/Tk Engineering Manual*.

6. If there are not at least two arguments, then this command wasn't called with the required subcommand argument.

7. The `Tcl_GetIndexFromObj` call will set the `cmdnum` variable to the index of the subcommand in the list, if there is a match.

8. If the `Tcl_GetIndexFromObj` call returned `TCL_ERROR`, it will have set an error return as a side effect. If the return value is not `TCL_OK`, this function can do any required cleanup and return a `TCL_ERROR` status. The interface with Tcl interpreter is already taken care of.

9. This section of code is not part of the official Tcl coding standard. The tests can be done here or in the individual functions that will be called from the `switch` statement. The call to `Tcl_WrongNumArgs` sets the return value for this function to a standard error message and leaves the interface with the interpreter ready for this function return.

10. When the execution has reached this point, all syntactical checks have been completed. The subcommand processing can be done in this function, as is done for the `demo debug` command, or another function can be called, as is done for the other subcommands.

    The functions that implement the commands are named using the naming convention `Demo_subcommandCmd`.

    Note that this `switch` statement does not require a default case statement. This code will be evaluated only if the `Tcl_GetIndexFromObj` function returned a valid index. This code should not be called with an unexpected value in normal operation.

    However, most code will require maintenance at some point in its life cycle. If a new command were added, the tables updated, and the switch statement not changed, a silent error could be introduced to the extension. Including the default case protects against that failure mode.

11. The `CmdReturn` structure is not part of the official Tcl coding style. I find it useful to return both status and an object from a function, and this works. You may prefer to transfer the status and object with C variables passed as pointers in the function argument list.

12. The `returnValue` is tracked separately from the `returnStruct` so that subcommands processed within this function as well as external functions can set the integer result code and `returnStruct` object to return values to the calling script.

12.3.4 `demoDemo.c`

The `demoDemo.c` file has the functions that implement the subcommands of the `demo` command. The naming convention is that the first `demo` indicates this is part of the `demo` package, and the second `Demo` indicates that this file implements the `demo` command. If there were a `foo` command in this `demo` package, it would be implemented in the file `demoFoo.c`.

Most of these functions will be called from `demoCmd.c`. The exception is the `Demo_InitHashTable` function, which is called from `Demo_Init`. This function is included in this file to allow the hash table pointer (`demo_hashtbl`) to be a `static` global and keep all references to it within this file.

12.3.4.1 `Demo_InitHashTable`

This function simply initializes the Tcl hash table and defines the keys to be NULL-terminated strings.

Example: 12.3.4.1-1

Demo_InitHashTable

```
#include "demoInt.h"
static Tcl_HashTable *demo_hashtblPtr;
extern int demoDebugPrint;

/*-------------------------------------------------------------
* void Demo_InitHashTable ()--
*     Initialize a hash table.
*     If your application does not need a hash table, this may be
*     deleted.
*
* Arguments
*    NONE
*
* Results
*    Initializes the hash table to accept STRING keys
*
* Side Effects:
*    None
-------------------------------------------------------------*/
```

```
void Demo_InitHashTable () {
    demo_hashtblPtr = (Tcl_HashTable *)
            malloc(sizeof(Tcl_HashTable));
    Tcl_InitHashTable(demo_hashtblPtr, TCL_STRING_KEYS);
}
```

12.3.4.2 `Demo_CreateCmd`

This function implements the `create` subcommand. `Demo_CreateCmd` is the first function we've discussed that checks arguments for more than syntactic correctness and needs to return status messages other than syntax messages provided by the Tcl interpreter.

This function uses both the `Tcl_AddObjErrorInfo` and the `Tcl_Add-ErrorInfo` function to demonstrate how each can be used. The error messages are appended to the return value for `Demo_CreateCmd` in the order in which the error functions are called.

The `Tcl_SetErrorCode` function concatenates the string arguments into the Tcl script global variable `errorCode`. It adds spaces as required to maintain the arguments as separate words in the `errorCode` variable.

Example: 12.3.4.2-1

Demo_CreateCmd

```
/*------------------------------------------------------------
* CmdReturn *Demo_CreateCmd ()--
*     Demonstrates creating a hash entry.
*     Creates a hash entry for Key, with value String
* Arguments
*     objv[0]:    "demo"
*     objv[1]:    "create"
*     objv[2]:    hash Key
*     objv[3]:    String
*
* Results
*   Creates a new hash entry.  Sets error if entry already
*   exists.
*
* Side Effects:
*   None
```

```
---------------------------------------------------------------*/
CmdReturn *Demo_CreateCmd (ClientData info,
                          Tcl_Interp *interp,
                          int objc,
                          Tcl_Obj *objv[]) {
    Tcl_HashEntry *hashEntryPtr;
    CmdReturn *returnStructPtr;
    char *returnCharPtr;
    char *tmpString;
    Tcl_Obj *returnObjPtr;

    char *hashEntryContentsPtr;
    char *hashKeyPtr;
    int  isNew;
    int length;

    /* 1
     * Print that the function was called for debugging
     */

    debugprt("Demo_CreateCmd called with %d args\n", objc);

    /* 2
     * Allocate the space and initialize the return structure.
     */

    returnStructPtr = (CmdReturn *) malloc(sizeof (CmdReturn));
    returnStructPtr->status = TCL_OK;
    returnCharPtr = NULL;
    returnObjPtr  = NULL;

    /* 3
     * Extract the string representation of the object
     * argument, and use that as a key into the hash table.
     *
     * If this entry already exists, complain.
     */

    hashKeyPtr   = Tcl_GetStringFromObj(objv[2], NULL);
    hashEntryPtr = Tcl_CreateHashEntry(demo_hashtblPtr,
            hashKeyPtr, &isNew);

    if (!isNew) {
    char errString[80];
```

```
    sprintf(errString,
        "Hashed object named \"%s\" already exists.\n",
        hashKeyPtr);

    /* 4
     * Both of these strings will be added to the Tcl script
     *  global variable errorInfo
     */

    Tcl_AddErrorInfo(interp, "error in Demo_CreateCmd");
    Tcl_AddObjErrorInfo(interp, errString,
            strlen(errString));

    /* 5
     * This SetErrorCode command will set the Tcl script
     *  variable errorCode to "5 5 5"
     */

    Tcl_SetErrorCode(interp, "5", "5", "5", (char *) NULL);

    /*
     * This defines the return string for this subcommand
     */

    Tcl_AppendResult(interp, "Hashed object named \"",
        hashKeyPtr, "\" already exists.", (char *) NULL);

    returnStructPtr->status = TCL_ERROR;
    goto done;
}

/* 6
 * If we are here, then the key is unused.
 * Get the string representation from the object,
 *  and make a copy that can be placed into the hash table.
 */

tmpString = Tcl_GetStringFromObj(objv[3], &length);
hashEntryContentsPtr = (char *) malloc(length+1);
strcpy(hashEntryContentsPtr, tmpString);

debugprt("setting: %s\n", hashEntryContentsPtr);
Tcl_SetHashValue(hashEntryPtr, hashEntryContentsPtr);
```

```
    /* 7
     * Set the return values, cleanup and return
     */
done:
    if ((returnObjPtr == NULL) && (returnCharPtr != NULL)) {
        returnObjPtr = Tcl_NewStringObj(returnCharPtr, -1);
    }

    returnStructPtr->object = returnObjPtr;
    if (returnCharPtr != NULL) {free(returnCharPtr);}

    return returnStructPtr;
    }
```

1. This is not a part of the Tcl standard. I find that in many circumstances I need to generate execution traces to track down the sorts of bugs that show up once every three weeks of continuous operation. Thus, I like to be able to enable an output message whenever a function is entered.

2. The returnStructPtr is initialized in each of the functions that process the subcommands. It will be freed in the Demo_Cmd function after this function returns.

3. If the hashKeyPtr already exists, then isNew will be set to zero, and a pointer to the previous hashEntryPtr will be returned. If your code sets the value of this entry with a Tcl_SetHashValue call, the old data will be lost.

4. Note that the sprintf call in this example is error prone. If the key is more than 37 characters, it will overflow the 80 characters allocated for errString. A robust application would count the characters, allocate space for the string, invoke Tcl_AddError to copy the error message to the error return, and then free the string.

   Each time Tcl_AddError or Tcl_AddObjError is called, it will append the argument followed by a newline to the end of the global script variable errorInfo.

5. The Tcl_SetErrorCode function will add a space between the arguments to force each of them to be a word. Thus, you cannot use this function to concatenate fields of a multiple-digit error return into a single numeric return.

6. Note that the string data in the third argument to the create subcommand is copied to another area of memory before being inserted into the hash table. The argument object is a temporary object that will be destroyed, along with its data, when the demo create command is fully evaluated.

   The Tcl_HashEntry structure accepts a pointer as the data to store. It retains the pointer, rather than copying the data to a new place. Thus, if the string pointer returned from the Tcl_GetStringFromObj(objv[3],... call were used as the data in the Tcl_SetHashValue call, the string would be destroyed when the command completed, and the data in those memory locations could become corrupted

7. All of the functions that implement the demo subcommands use a flow model of testing values, setting failure values if necessary, and using a goto to exit the function. This can also be done using a structured programming flow but becomes complex and difficult to follow when there are multiple tests.

12.3.4.3 Demo_GetCmd

The Demo_GetCmd will return the string that was inserted into the hash table with a demo create command.

This function follows the same flow as the Demo_CreateCmd function.

Example: 12.3.4.3-1

Demo_GetCmd

```
/*-------------------------------------------------------------
* CmdReturn *Demo_GetCmd ()--
*     Demonstrates retrieving a value from a hash table.
*     Returns the value of the requested item in the hash table
*
* Arguments
*    objv[0]:    "demo"
*    objv[1]:    "get"
*    objv[2]:    hash Key
*
* Results
*    No changes to hash table.  Returns saved value, or sets error.
*
* Side Effects:
```

```
 *    None
------------------------------------------------------------*/
CmdReturn *Demo_GetCmd (ClientData info,
                        Tcl_Interp *interp,
                        int objc,
                        Tcl_Obj *objv[]) {
    Tcl_HashEntry *hashEntryPtr;
    CmdReturn *returnStructPtr;
    char *returnCharPtr;
    Tcl_Obj *returnObjPtr;

    char *hashKeyPtr;

    debugprt("Demo_GetCmd called with %d args\n", objc);

    /*
     * Allocate the space and initialize the return structure.
     */

    returnStructPtr = (CmdReturn *) malloc(sizeof (CmdReturn));
    returnStructPtr->status = TCL_OK;
    returnStructPtr->object = NULL;
    returnCharPtr = NULL;
    returnObjPtr   = NULL;

    /*
     * Get the key from the argument
     * and attempt to extract that entry from the hashtable.
     * If the returned entry pointer is NULL, this key is not in
     * the table.
     */

    hashKeyPtr = Tcl_GetStringFromObj(objv[2], NULL);

    hashEntryPtr = Tcl_FindHashEntry(demo_hashtblPtr,
        hashKeyPtr);

    if (hashEntryPtr == (Tcl_HashEntry *) NULL) {
        char errString[80];
        Tcl_Obj *errCodePtr;

        /* 1
         * Define an error code from an integer, and
         * set errorCode.
         */
        errCodePtr = Tcl_NewIntObj(554);
```

```
        Tcl_SetObjErrorCode(interp, errCodePtr);

        /*
         * This string will be placed in the global variable
         * errorInfo
         */

        sprintf(errString,
            "Hash object \"%s\" does not exist.", hashKeyPtr);
        Tcl_AddErrorInfo(interp, errString);

        /*
         * This string will be returned as the result of the
           command.
         */

        Tcl_AppendResult(interp,
                "can not find hashed object named \"",
                hashKeyPtr, "\"", (char *) NULL);
        returnStructPtr->status = TCL_ERROR;
        goto done;
    }
    /* 2
     * If we got here, then the search was successful and we can
     *  extract the data value from the hash entry and return it.
     */

    returnCharPtr = (char *)Tcl_GetHashValue(hashEntryPtr);

    debugprt("returnString: %s\n", returnCharPtr);

done:
    if ((returnObjPtr == NULL) && (returnCharPtr != NULL)) {
        returnObjPtr = Tcl_NewStringObj(returnCharPtr, -1);
    }

    returnStructPtr->object = returnObjPtr;
    if (returnCharPtr != NULL) {free(returnCharPtr);}

    return returnStructPtr;
}
```

1. Demo_GetCmd uses the Tcl_SetObjErrorCode function to set the global script variable errorCode. This function assigns the errCodePtr to the error code. It does not make a copy of the object.

2. The character pointer returnCharPtr will be set to point to the string that was stored in the hash table. This is not a copy of the data. The data is copied when returnObjPtr is created with the Tcl_NewStringObj(returnCharPtr, -1) function.

12.3.4.4 Demo_DestroyCmd

The Demo_DestroyCmd function will remove an item from the hash table and release the memory associated with it. This example uses yet another technique for setting the error returns. The default behavior is to set the global script variable errorInfo with the same string as the function return and to set the errorCode value to NONE. This function simply allows that to happen.

Example 12.3.4.4-1

Demo_DestroyCmd

```
/*----------------------------------------------------------
* CmdReturn *Demo_DestroyCmd ()--
*     Demonstrate destroying an entry in the hash table.
* Arguments
*    objv[0]:     "demo"
*    objv[1]:     "destroy"
*    objv[2]:     hash Key
*
* Results
*    Deletes the hash table entry and frees the memory
*    associated with the hash object being stored.
*
* Side Effects:
*    None
----------------------------------------------------------*/
CmdReturn *Demo_DestroyCmd (ClientData info,
                        Tcl_Interp *interp,
                        int objc,
                        Tcl_Obj *objv[]) {
    Tcl_HashEntry *hashEntryPtr;
```

```
        CmdReturn *returnStructPtr;
        char *returnCharPtr;
        Tcl_Obj *returnObjPtr;

        char *hashEntryContentsPtr;
        char *hashKeyPtr;

        debugprt("Demo_DestroyCmd called with %d args\n", objc);

        /*
         * Allocate the space and initialize the return structure.
         */

        returnStructPtr = (CmdReturn *) malloc(sizeof (CmdReturn));
        returnStructPtr->status = TCL_OK;
        returnStructPtr->object = NULL;
        returnCharPtr = NULL;
        returnObjPtr    = NULL;

        /*
         * Extract the string representation from the argument, and
         * use it as a key into the hash table.
         */

        hashKeyPtr = Tcl_GetStringFromObj(objv[2], NULL);
        hashEntryPtr = Tcl_FindHashEntry(demo_hashtblPtr,
                        hashKeyPtr);

        /* 1
         * If the hashEntryPtr returns NULL, then this key is not in
         *  the table.  Return an error.
         */

        if (hashEntryPtr == (Tcl_HashEntry *) NULL) {
            /*
             * Tcl_AppendResult sets the return for this command.
             * The script global variable errorInfo will also be
             * set to  this string.
             * The script global variable errorCode will be set to
             * "NONE"
             */

            Tcl_AppendResult(interp,
                    "cannot find hashed object named \"",
```

```
                hashKeyPtr, "\"", (char *) NULL);
        returnStructPtr->status = TCL_ERROR;
        goto done;
    }

    /* 2
     * Retrieve the pointer to the data saved in the hash table
     *  and free it.  Then delete the hash table entry.
     */

    hashEntryContentsPtr =
        (char *)Tcl_GetHashValue(hashEntryPtr);
    free(hashEntryContentsPtr);

    Tcl_DeleteHashEntry(hashEntryPtr);
done:
    if ((returnObjPtr == NULL) && (returnCharPtr != NULL)) {
        returnObjPtr = Tcl_NewStringObj(returnCharPtr, -1);
    }

    returnStructPtr->object = returnObjPtr;
    if (returnCharPtr != NULL) {free(returnCharPtr);}

    return returnStructPtr;
}
```

1. This function allows the interpreter to set the errorInfo and errorCode values. The string cannot find hashed object... will be returned as the result of the command and will also be placed in the errorInfo variable.

2. The data saved in the hash table is the pointer to the string that was created in the Demo_CreateCmd function. Once the Tcl_HashEntry pointer is destroyed, that pointer will be an orphan unless there is other code that references it. In this example, there is no other code using the pointer, so the memory must be released.

12.3.4.5 Demo_SetCmd

The Demo_SetCmd demonstrates creating or modifying an array variable in the calling script. By default, the variable will be set in the scope of the command that calls the demo set command. If demo set is called from within a procedure, the variable will exist only while that procedure is being evaluated. The Tcl interpreter will take care of releasing the variable when the procedure completes.

`Demo_SetCmd` uses the `Tcl_ObjSetVar2` function to set the value of the array variable. The `Tcl_ObjSetVar2` and `Tcl_ObjGetVar2` functions allow C code to get or set the value of a Tcl script variable.

`Tcl_ObjSetVar2` and `Tcl_ObjGetVar2` are the functions called by the Tcl interpreter to access variables in a script. Any behavior that the Tcl interpreter supports for scripts is also supported for C code that is using these functions.

You can modify the behavior of these commands with the *flags* argument. By default, the behavior is as follows:

- When accessing an existing variable, the `Tcl_ObjGetVar2` command first tries to find a variable in the local procedure scope. If that fails, it looks for a variable defined with the `variable` command in the current namespace. Finally, it looks in the global scope.

- The `Tcl_ObjSetVar2` function will overwrite the existing value of a variable by default. The default is not to append the new data to an existing variable.

- When referencing an array, the array name and index are referenced in separate objects. By default, you cannot reference an array item with an object that has a string representation of name(index).

Syntax: Tcl_Obj *`Tcl_ObjSetVar2` *(interp, id1Ptr, id2Ptr, newValPtr, flags)*

Syntax: Tcl_Obj *`Tcl_ObjGetVar2` *(interp, id1Ptr, id2Ptr, flags)*

Syntax: char *`Tcl_SetVar2` *(interp, name1, name2, newstring, flags)*

Syntax: char *`Tcl_GetVar2` *(interp, name2, name1, flags)*

Tcl_ObjSetVar2

> Creates or modifies a Tcl variable. The value of the referenced variable will be set to the value of the *newValPtr* object. The Tcl_Obj pointer will be a pointer to the new object.

This may not be a pointer to *newValPtr* if events triggered by accessing the *newValPtr* modify the contents of *newValPtr*. This can occur if you are using the trace command to observe a variable. See the discussion on using trace in Section 15.1 and read about the trace command in your online help to see how this can happen.

Tcl_ObjGetVar2

Returns a Tcl object containing a value for the variable identified by the string values in *id1Ptr* and *id2Ptr*.

Tcl_SetVar2   Creates or modifies a script variable. The value of the referenced variable will be set to *newstring*. This function returns a char * pointer to the new value.

This function is for use with versions of Tcl older than 8.0.

Tcl_GetVar2   Returns the string value for the variable or array reference identified by the string values in *name1* and *name2*.

This function is for use with versions of Tcl older than 8.0.

Tcl_Interp *interp*

A pointer to the Tcl interpreter.

Tcl_Obj *id1Ptr*

An object that contains the name of a Tcl variable. This may be either a simple variable or an array name.

Tcl_Obj *id2Ptr*

If this is not NULL, it contains the index of an array variable. If this is not NULL, then *id1Ptr* **must** contain the name of an array variable.

char *name1*   A string that references either a simple Tcl string variable or the name of an associative array.

char *name2*   If this is not NULL, it is the index of an array variable. If this is not NULL, then *name1* **must** contain the name of an array variable.

`Tcl_Obj *newValPtr`

A pointer to an object with the new value to be assigned to the variable described by *id1Ptr* and *id2Ptr*.

`char *newstring`

A string that contains the new value to be assigned to the variable described by *name1* and *name2*.

`int flags`
The *flags* parameter can be used to tune the behavior of these commands. The value of flags is a bitmap composed of the logical OR of these fields:

TCL_GLOBAL_ONLY

Setting this flag causes the variable name to be referenced only in the global scope, not a namespace or local procedure scope. If both this and the TCL_NAMESPACE_ONLY flags are set, this flag is ignored.

TCL_NAMESPACE_ONLY

Setting this flag causes the variable to be referenced only in the current namespace scope, not in the current local procedure scope. This flag overrides TCL_GLOBAL_ONLY.

TCL_LEAVE_ERR_MSG

This flag causes an error message to be placed in the interpreter's result object if the command fails. If this is not set, no error message will be left.

TCL_APPEND_VALUE

If this flag is set, the new value will be appended to the existing value, instead of overwriting it.

TCL_LIST_ELEMENT

If this flag is set, the new data will be converted into a valid list element before being appended to the existing data.

TCL_PARSE_PART1

> If this flag is set and the *id1Ptr* object contains a string defining an array element (*arrayName(index)*), then this will be used to reference the array index, rather than using the value in *id2Ptr* as the index.

Example 12.3.4.5-1

Demo_SetCmd

```
/*-----------------------------------------------------------
* CmdReturn *Demo_SetCmd ()--
*    Demonstrates setting an array to a value
* Arguments
*    objv[0]:     "demo"
*    objv[1]:     "set"
*    objv[2]:     arrayName
*    objv[3]:     Index
*    objv[4]:     Value
*
* Results
*    Sets arrayName(Index) to the Value
*    Also sets arrayName(alpha) to the string "NewValue".
*    Returns the string "NewValue"
*
* Side Effects:
*    None
-----------------------------------------------------------*/
CmdReturn *Demo_SetCmd (ClientData info,
                        Tcl_Interp *interp,
                        int objc,
                        Tcl_Obj *objv[]) {
    Tcl_Obj *returnObjPtr;
    Tcl_Obj *indexObjPtr;
    Tcl_Obj *arrayObjPtr;
    Tcl_Obj *valueObjPtr;
    CmdReturn *returnStructPtr;

    debugprt("Demo_SetCmd called with %d args\n", objc);
```

```
/*
 * Allocate the space and initialize the return structure.
 */

returnStructPtr = (CmdReturn *) malloc(sizeof (CmdReturn));
returnStructPtr->status = TCL_OK;
returnObjPtr    = NULL;

/* 1
 * Use Tcl_ObjSetVar2 to set the array element "Index" to
 * "Value"
 */

arrayObjPtr = objv[2];
Tcl_ObjSetVar2(interp, arrayObjPtr, objv[3], objv[4], 0);

/* 2
 * Create two new objects to set a value for index "alpha"
 * in the array.
 */

indexObjPtr = Tcl_NewStringObj("alpha", -1);
valueObjPtr = Tcl_NewStringObj("NewValue", -1);
returnObjPtr = Tcl_ObjSetVar2(interp, arrayObjPtr,
        indexObjPtr, valueObjPtr, 0);

returnStructPtr->status = TCL_OK;
returnStructPtr->object = returnObjPtr;

/* 3
 * Delete the temporary objects by reducing their RefCount
 *   The object manager will free them, and associated
 *   memory when  the reference count becomes 0.
 */

Tcl_DecrRefCount(indexObjPtr);

/* 4
 *  Don't delete valueObjPtr - it's the returnObjPtr
 *  object. The task will core dump if you clear it,
 *   and then use it.
 *   Tcl_DecrRefCount(valueObjPtr);
 */
```

```
    return(returnStructPtr);
    }
```

1. This code implements the equivalent of set *arrayName(Index) Value*.

2. This section of code implements the equivalent of
   set *arrayName*(alpha) NewValue.
   The value assigned to returnObjPtr is a pointer to valueObjPtr,
   because there is no extra processing attached to the valueObjPtr variable.

3. Note that you should use the Tcl_DecrRefCount function to free Tcl
   objects. Do not use the free function.

4. The valueObjPtr is also created in this function. A pointer to this object
   will be returned by the Tcl_ObjSetVar2 call, but the reference count for
   this object is not incremented.

   Since this object is being returned as the returnObjPtr, the reference
   count should not be decremented. If a pointer to this object is passed to
   Tcl_DecrRefCount, the object will be destroyed, and returnObjPtr will
   point to a nonexistent object. When the Tcl interpreter tries to process
   the nonexistent object, it will not do anything pleasant.

12.4 Complex Data

If you need to handle complex data (such as a structure) in your extension,
there are some options.

1. You can define the structure in your Tcl script as a list of values and pass
   that list to extension code to parse into a structure.

2. You can use an associative array in the Tcl script, where each index into
   the associative array is a field in the structure.

3. You can create a function that will accept the values for a structure in
   list or array format, parse them into a structure, place that structure in a
   hash table, and return a key to the Tcl script for future use.

The following code snippet shows how a Tcl associative array can be used
to pass a structure into a C code extension. The code expects to be called
with the name of an array that has the appropriate indices set. The indices
of the array must have the same names as the fields of the structure.

Example 12.4-1

Using an Associative Array to Define a Structure

. . .

```
Tcl_Obj      *indexPtr;
Tcl_Obj      *structElementPtr;

struct demo {
    int      firstInt;
    char     *secondString;
    double   thirdFloat;
} demoStruct;

/* The names of the fields to be used as array indices */

char *fields[] = {"firstInt", "secondString",
                  "thirdFloat", NULL };
/*
 * Create an object that can be used with Tcl_ObjGetVar2
 * to find the object identified with the array and
 * index names
 */

indexPtr = Tcl_NewStringObj(fields[0], -1);

/*
 * Loop through the elements in the structure/ indices of
 * the array.
 */

for (i=0; i<3; i++) {

    /*
     * Set the index object to reference the field
     * being processed.
     */

    Tcl_SetStringObj (indexPtr, fields[i], -1);

            /*
     * Get the object identified as arrayName(index)
     * If that value is NULL, there is no
     * arrayName(index): complain.
     */

    structElementPtr =
```

```
                    Tcl_ObjGetVar2(interp, objv[2], indexPtr, 0);

          if (structElementPtr == NULL) {
             Tcl_AppendResult(interp,
                   "Array Index \"", fields[i],
                   "\" is not defined ", (char *) NULL);
             returnStructPtr->status = TCL_ERROR;
             goto done;
          }

          /*
           * This is a strange way to determine which structure
           * element is being processed, but it works in the loop.
           *
           * If an illegal value is in the object, the error
           *  return will be set automatically by the interpreter.
           */

          switch (i) {
          case 0: {
                     int t;
                     if (TCL_OK !=
                         Tcl_GetIntFromObj(interp,
                                structElementPtr, &t)) {
                            returnStructPtr->status = TCL_ERROR;
                            goto done;
                     } else {
                         demoStruct.firstInt = t;
                     }
                 break;
                 }
          case 1: {
                     char *t;
                     if (NULL == (t =
                         Tcl_GetStringFromObj(structElementPtr,
                                NULL))) {
                            returnStructPtr->status = TCL_ERROR;
                            goto done;
                     } else {
                         demoStruct.secondString=
                              (char *)malloc(strlen(t)+1);
                         strcpy(demoStruct.secondString, t);
```

```
                    }
                break;
                }
        case 2: {
                    double t;
                    if (TCL_OK !=
                        Tcl_GetDoubleFromObj(interp,
                                structElementPtr, &t)) {
                            returnStructPtr->status = TCL_ERROR;
                            goto done;
                    } else {
                        demoStruct.thirdFloat = t;
                    }
                break;
                }
            }
        }
printf("demoStruct assigned values: \n %d\n %s\n %f\n",
    demoStruct.firstInt, demoStruct.secondString,
    demoStruct.thirdFloat);

...
```

Example Script

```
set struct(firstInt) "12"
set struct(secondString) "Testing"
set struct(thirdFloat) "34.56"

demo arraystr struct
```

Script Output

```
demoStruct assigned values:
 12
 Testing
 34.560000
```

The next example demonstrates a pair of functions that use a list to define the elements of a structure and save the structure in a hash table. These functions implement two new subcommands in the demo extension: demo liststr *key list* and demo getstr *key*.

These functions introduce the Tcl list object. A Tcl list object is an object that contains a set of pointers to other objects. There are several commands in the Tcl library API to manipulate the list object. This example will introduce only a few that are necessary for this application.

Syntax: int **Tcl_ListObjLength** *(interp, listPtr, lengthPtr)*

Tcl_ListObjLength

> Places the length of the list (the number of list elements, not the string length) in the *lengthPtr* argument. This function returns either TCL_OK or TCL_ERROR.

Tcl_Interp *interp*

> A pointer to the Tcl interpreter.

Tcl_Obj *listPtr*

> A pointer to the list object.

int *lengthPtr*

> A pointer to the integer that will receive the length of this list.

Syntax: int **Tcl_ListObjIndex** *(interp, listPtr, index, elementPtr)*

Tcl_ListObjIndex

> Places a pointer to the object identified by the *index* argument in the *elementPtr* variable. This function returns either TCL_OK or TCL_ERROR.

Tcl_Interp *interp*

> A pointer to the Tcl interpreter.

Tcl_Obj *listPtr*

> A pointer to the list object.

int *index*   The index of the list element to return.

Tcl_Obj **elementPtr*

> The address of a pointer to a Tcl_Obj that will be set to point to the Tcl_Obj that is referenced by *index*.

Syntax: Tcl_Obj* **Tcl_NewListObj** *(count, objv)*

`Tcl_NewListObj`

> Returns a pointer to a new `Tcl_Obj` that is a list object pointing to each of the objects in the *objv* array of objects.

`int count`   The number of objects defined in the *objv* array of objects.

`Tcl_Obj *objv[]`

> An array of pointers to Tcl objects that will be included in this list.

Example 12.4-2

List to Structure Example

```
/*------------------------------------------------------------
* CmdReturn *Demo_ListstrCmd (ClientData info--
*    Accepts a key and a list of data items that will be used to
*    fill a  pre-defined structure.
*    The newly filled structure pointer is saved in a hash
*    table, referenced by 'key_Value'.
*
* Arguments:
*    objv[0] "demo"
*    objv[1] "liststr"
*    objv[2] key_Value
*    objv[3] structure_List
*
* Results:
*    Places a structure pointer in the hash table.
*
* Side Effects:
*    None
------------------------------------------------------------*/
CmdReturn *Demo_ListstrCmd (ClientData info,
                            Tcl_Interp *interp,
                            int objc,
                            Tcl_Obj *objv[]) {
    Tcl_HashEntry *hashEntryPtr;
    CmdReturn *returnStructPtr;
    char *returnCharPtr;
    Tcl_Obj *returnObjPtr;
    Tcl_Obj *listElementPtr;
```

```
        int listlen;
        int  isNew;
        int length;
        char *tmpString;
        int i;
        char *hashEntryContentsPtr;
        char *hashKeyPtr;

        struct demo {
            int     firstInt;
            char    *secondString;
            double  thirdFloat;
        } *demoStruct;

        debugprt("Demo_ListstrCmd called with %d args\n", objc);

        /*
         * Allocate the space and initialize the return structure.
         */

        returnStructPtr = (CmdReturn *) malloc(sizeof (CmdReturn));
        returnStructPtr->status = TCL_OK;
        returnStructPtr->object = NULL;
        returnCharPtr = NULL;
        returnObjPtr   = NULL;

        /*
         * Allocate space for the structure
         */

        demoStruct = (struct demo *) malloc(sizeof (struct demo));

        /*
         * Get the length of the list, then step through it.
         */

        Tcl_ListObjLength(interp, objv[3], &listlen);

        for(i=0; i< listlen; i++) {

            /*
             * Extract a list element from the list pointer
             */

            Tcl_ListObjIndex(interp, objv[3], i, &listElementPtr);
            debugprt("Position: %d : Value: %s\n",
                i, Tcl_GetStringFromObj(listElementPtr, NULL));
```

```
/*
 * A strange way to determine which structure element
 * is being processed, but it works in the loop.
 * If an illegal value is in the object, the error
 * return will be set automatically by the interpreter.
 */
switch (i) {
case 0: {
            int t;
            if (TCL_OK !=
                Tcl_GetIntFromObj(interp,
                        listElementPtr, &t)) {
                    returnStructPtr->status = TCL_ERROR;
                    goto done;
            } else {
                demoStruct->firstInt = t;
            }
        break;
        }
case 1: {
            char *t;
            if (NULL == (t =
                Tcl_GetStringFromObj(listElementPtr,
                        NULL))) {
                    returnStructPtr->status = TCL_ERROR;
                    goto done;
            } else {
                demoStruct->secondString=
                    (char *)malloc(strlen(t)+1);
                strcpy(demoStruct->secondString, t);
            }
        break;
        }
case 2: {
            double t;
            if (TCL_OK !=
                Tcl_GetDoubleFromObj(interp,
                        listElementPtr, &t)) {
                    returnStructPtr->status = TCL_ERROR;
                    goto done;
```

```
                } else {
                    demoStruct->thirdFloat = t;
                }
            break;
            }
    }
}
/*
 * Extract the string representation of the object
 * argument, and use that as a key into the hash table.
 *
 * If this entry already exists, complain.
 */

hashKeyPtr = Tcl_GetStringFromObj(objv[2], NULL);
hashEntryPtr = Tcl_CreateHashEntry(demo_hashtblPtr,
        hashKeyPtr, &isNew);

if (!isNew) {
    char errString[80];

    sprintf(errString,
        "Hashed object named \"%s\" already exists.\n",
        hashKeyPtr);

    /*
     * Both of these strings will be added to the Tcl
     * script global variable errorInfo
     */
    Tcl_AddObjErrorInfo(interp, errString,
            strlen(errString));
    Tcl_AddErrorInfo(interp, "error in Demo_CreateCmd");

    /*
     * This SetErrorCode command will set the Tcl script
     *  variable errorCode to "5 5 5"
     */

    Tcl_SetErrorCode(interp, "5", "5", "5", (char *) NULL);

    /*
     * This defines the return string for this subcommand
     */
```

```
            Tcl_AppendResult(interp, "Hashed object named \"",
                    hashKeyPtr, "\" already exists.", (char *) NULL);

            returnStructPtr->status = TCL_ERROR;
            goto done;
        }

        /*
         * If we are here, then the key is unused.
         * Get the string representation from the object,
         *  and make a copy that can be placed into the hash table.
         */

        tmpString = Tcl_GetStringFromObj(objv[3], &length);
        hashEntryContentsPtr = (char *) malloc(length+1);
        strcpy(hashEntryContentsPtr, tmpString);

        debugprt("setting: %s\n", hashEntryContentsPtr);
        Tcl_SetHashValue(hashEntryPtr, demoStruct);
done:
        if ((returnObjPtr == NULL) && (returnCharPtr != NULL)) {
            returnObjPtr = Tcl_NewStringObj(returnCharPtr, -1);
        }

        returnStructPtr->object = returnObjPtr;
        if (returnCharPtr != NULL) {free(returnCharPtr);}

        return returnStructPtr;
}

/*------------------------------------------------------------
 * CmdReturn *Demo_GetstrCmd ()--
 *     Demonstrates retrieving a structure pointer from a hash
 *     table, and stuffing that into a list.
 *
 * Arguments
 *     objv[0]:    "demo"
 *     objv[1]:    "getstr"
 *     objv[2]:    hash_Key
 *
 * Results
 *    No changes to hash table.  Returns saved value, or sets
error.
 *
```

```
* Side Effects:
*    None
-------------------------------------------------------------*/
CmdReturn *Demo_GetstrCmd (ClientData info,
                          Tcl_Interp *interp,
                          int objc,
                          Tcl_Obj *objv[]) {
    Tcl_HashEntry *hashEntryPtr;
    CmdReturn *returnStructPtr;
    char *returnCharPtr;
    Tcl_Obj *returnObjPtr;
    Tcl_Obj *listPtrPtr[3];

    char *hashKeyPtr;

    struct demo {
        int     firstInt;
        char    *secondString;
        double  thirdFloat;
    } *demoStruct;

    debugprt("Demo_GetCmd called with %d args\n", objc);

    /*
     * Allocate the space and initialize the return structure.
     */

    returnStructPtr = (CmdReturn *) malloc(sizeof (CmdReturn));
    returnStructPtr->status = TCL_OK;
    returnStructPtr->object = NULL;
    returnCharPtr = NULL;
    returnObjPtr  = NULL;

    /*
     * Get the key from the argument
     * And attempt to extract that entry from the hashtable.
     * If the returned entry pointer is NULL, this key is not
     * in the table.
     */

    hashKeyPtr = Tcl_GetStringFromObj(objv[2], NULL);

    hashEntryPtr = Tcl_FindHashEntry(demo_hashtblPtr,
            hashKeyPtr);
```

```
    if (hashEntryPtr == (Tcl_HashEntry *) NULL) {
        char errString[80];
        Tcl_Obj *errCodePtr;

        /*
         * This string will be returned as the result of the
         * command.
         */

        Tcl_AppendResult(interp,
                "can not find hashed object named \"",
                hashKeyPtr, "\"", (char *) NULL);
        returnStructPtr->status = TCL_ERROR;
        goto done;
    }
    /*
     * If we got here, then the search was successful and we
     *  can extract the data value from the hash entry and
     *  return it.
     */

    demoStruct = (struct demo *)Tcl_GetHashValue(hashEntryPtr);

    /*
     * Create three objects with the values from the structure,
     * and then merge them into a list object.
     *
     * Return the list object.
     */

    listPtrPtr[0] = Tcl_NewIntObj(demoStruct->firstInt);
    listPtrPtr[1] =
         Tcl_NewStringObj(demoStruct->secondString, -1);
    listPtrPtr[2] =
         Tcl_NewDoubleObj((double) demoStruct->thirdFloat);

    returnObjPtr = Tcl_NewListObj(3, listPtrPtr);

    debugprt("returnString: %s\n", returnCharPtr);

done:
    if ((returnObjPtr == NULL) && (returnCharPtr != NULL)) {
        returnObjPtr = Tcl_NewStringObj(returnCharPtr, -1);
    }
```

```
        returnStructPtr->object = returnObjPtr;
        if (returnCharPtr != NULL) {free(returnCharPtr);}

        return returnStructPtr;
}
```

Example Script

```
% demo liststr key1 [list 12 "this is a test" 34.56]
% demo getstr key1
12 {this is a test} 34.56
```

12.5 Bottom Line

- A Tcl extension can be built for several purposes, including:
  - Adding graphics to an existing library.
  - Adding new features to a Tcl interpreter.
  - Creating a rapid prototyping interpreter from a library.
  - Creating a script-driven test package for a library.
- A Tcl extension must include:
  - *ExtName*_Init function.
  - A code to implement each new Tcl command.
- A Tcl extension should also include:
  - An include file named *extName*Int.h.
  - A makefile.
- A Tcl extension may include other files as necessary to make it a maintainable, modular set of code.
- New Tcl commands are defined with the Tcl_CreateObjCommand or Tcl_CreateCommand commands.

    Syntax: int **Tcl_CreateObjCommand** *(interp, cmdName, func, clientData, deleteFunc)*

    Syntax: int **Tcl_CreateCommand** *(interp, cmdName, func, clientData, deleteFunc)*

- The C function that is associated with the new Tcl command created by `Tcl_Create...Command` should have a function prototype that resembles:

      int **func**(*clientData, interp, objc, objv*)

- You can get a native or a string representation from a Tcl Object with the `Tcl_GetIntFromObj`, `Tcl_GetDoubleFromObj`, or `Tcl_GetStringFromObj`.

    Syntax: int **Tcl_GetIntFromObj** (*interp, objPtr,*
         intPtr)

    Syntax: int **Tcl_GetDoubleFromObj** (*interp, objPtr,*
         doublePtr)

    Syntax: char *__Tcl_GetStringFromObj__ (*objPtr, lengthPtr*)

- You can create a new object with one of these functions:

    Syntax: Tcl_Obj *__Tcl_NewIntObj__ (*intValue*)

    Syntax: Tcl_Obj *__Tcl_NewDoubleObj__ (*doubleValue*)

    Syntax: Tcl_Obj *__Tcl_NewStringObj__ (*bytes, length*)

- You can modify the contents of an object with one of these functions:

    Syntax: void **Tcl_SetIntObj** (*objPtr, intValue*)

    Syntax: void **Tcl_SetDoubleObj** (*objPtr, doubleValue*)

    Syntax: void **Tcl_SetStringObj** (*objPtr, bytes, length*)

    Syntax: void **Tcl_AppendToObj** (*objPtr, bytes, length*)

    Syntax: void **Tcl_AppendObjToObj** (*objPtr, appendObjPtr*)

    Syntax: void **Tcl_AppendStringsToObj** (*objPtr, string,*
         ..., NULL)

- The results of a function are returned to the calling script with the functions `Tcl_SetObjResult` and `Tcl_SetResult`.

    Syntax: void **Tcl_SetObjResult** (*interp, objPtr*)

    Syntax: void **Tcl_SetResult** (*interp, string, freeProc*)

- The status of a function is returned to the calling script with the functions `Tcl_AddObjErrorInfo`, `Tcl_AddErrorInfo`, `Tcl_SetObjErrorCode`, and `Tcl_SetErrorCode`, which set the error-Code and errorInfo global Tcl variables.

Syntax: void **Tcl_AddObjErrorInfo** *(interp, message, length)*

Syntax: void **Tcl_AddErrorInfo** *(interp, message)*

Syntax: void **Tcl_SetObjErrorCode** *(interp, objPtr)*

Syntax: void **Tcl_SetErrorCode** *(interp, element1, element2...NULL)*

- Tcl provides an interface to fast hash table database functions to allow tasks to save and retrieve arbitrary data based on keys.

- A hash table must be initialized with the Tcl_InitHashTable function.

  Syntax: void **Tcl_InitHashTable** *(tablePtr, keyType)*

- Hash table entries may be manipulated with these functions:

  Syntax: Tcl_HashEntry ***Tcl_CreateHashEntry** *(tablePtr, key, newPtr)*

  Syntax: Tcl_HashEntry ***Tcl_FindHashEntry** *(tablePtr, key)*

  Syntax: void **Tcl_DeleteHashEntry** *(entryPtr)*

- Data may be retrieved or deposited in a Tcl_HashEntry with these functions:

  Syntax: ClientData **TclGetHashValue** *(entryPtr)*

  Syntax: void **TclSetHashValue** *(entryPtr, value)*

- A match to a string can be found in an array of strings with the Tcl_GetIndexFromObj function.

  Syntax: int **Tcl_GetIndexFromObj** *(interp, objPtr, tblPtr, msg, flags, indexPtr)*

- The contents of Tcl variables can be accessed with these functions:

  Syntax: Tcl_Obj ***Tcl_ObjGetVar2** *(interp, id1Ptr, id2Ptr, flags)*

  Syntax: char ***Tcl_GetVar2** *(interp, name2, name1, flags)*

- The contents of Tcl script variables can be set with these functions:

Syntax: Tcl_Obj *`Tcl_ObjSetVar2` *(interp, id1Ptr, id2Ptr, newValPtr, flags)*

Syntax: char *`Tcl_SetVar2` *(interp, name1, name2, ne string, flags)*

- A Tcl list is implemented with a Tcl object that contains an array of pointers to the elements of the list.

- You can create a Tcl list within a C function with the `Tcl_NewListObj` function.

  Syntax: Tcl_Obj* `Tcl_NewListObj` *(count, objv)*

- You can get the length of a list with the `Tcl_ListObjLength` function.

  Syntax: int `Tcl_ListObjLength` *(interp, listPtr, lengthPtr)*

- You can retrieve the list element from a particular index in a list with the `Tcl_ListObjIndex` function.

  Syntax: int `Tcl_ListObjIndex` *(interp, listPtr, index, elementPtr*

Extensions and Packages

The previous chapters described building Tcl packages and C language extensions to Tcl. Using these techniques, you can create almost any application you need.

In many cases your applications will need features that have already been developed. You can save time by using existing extensions and packages for these features. Using existing extensions not only saves you development time but also reduces your maintenance and testing time.

This chapter provides an overview of a few extensions and packages. Unfortunately, it isn't large enough to cover all of the extensions and packages written for Tcl. The Tcl FAQ (frequently asked question) lists over 700 extensions, and more are being written every day. Before you write your own extension, check to see if one has already been written.

The primary archive for Tcl extensions and packages is `http://www.neosoft.com`. The search engine at Neosoft will let you scan for a particular extension. Most extensions are also announced in `comp.lang.tcl` or `comp.lang.tcl.announce`. You can use the DejaNews PowerSearch engine (`http://www.dejanews.com/home_ps.shtml`) to limit your search to those newsgroups. Finally, many of the extensions are described in the Tcl/Tk FAQ (`http://www.purl.org/NET/Tcl-FAQ`).

Although extensions can save you a great deal of development time, there are some points to consider when using extensions and packages.

- *Extensions tend to lag behind the Tcl core.* Most of these packages are developed by Tcl advocates who work in their spare time to maintain the packages. It can take weeks or months before they have time to update their package after a major change to the Tcl internals. In particular, the change from Tcl 7.6 to Tcl 8.0 introduced some API changes requiring enough rewriting that many extensions have not yet been ported beyond revision 7.6.

- *Not all extensions are available on all platforms.* Many packages were developed before Tcl was available on Macintosh and Windows platforms, and they may have some Unix-specific code in them. As I'm writing this book, several packages are being ported to other platforms. The extension descriptions list home pages where you can find out whether a package has been ported since this book was published.

- *Not all extensions are available at all sites.* Installing extensions takes time, and keeping multiple versions of libraries and extensions consistent can create problems for system administrators. Thus, the more extensions your application requires, the harder it may be for users to install your application.

  If you are writing an application for in-house use (and your system administrators will install the extensions you need), this is not a problem. But if you write an application you'd like to see used throughout your company or distributed across the net, the more extensions it requires, the less likely someone is to be willing to try it.

  If you need an extension, by all means use it. However, if you can limit a package to core Tcl or a single extension, you should do so.

- *Packages written in Tcl are more easily distributed than extensions written in C.* Whereas many sites may not have an extension, any site that is interested in running your Tcl application can run Tcl packages. You can include the Tcl packages your script needs with the distribution and install them with your application. For example, the HTML library discussed in Chapter 10 has been included in several other packages, including TclTutor, SurfIt, and webtk.

This chapter will introduce these extensions:

[incr Tcl] The previous chapters have shown how object-oriented techniques can be used with pure Tcl. The [incr Tcl] is a true object-oriented extension of the Tcl core. It supports classes, private, public, and protected scopes, constructors, destructors, and inheritance.

expect Expect automates procedures that have a character-based interaction.

TclX This is a collection of new Tcl commands that support system access and reduce the amount of code you need to write. Many of the TclX features have been integrated into the more recent versions of Tcl.

VS This package includes a database, a GUI form generator, and a report generator. It's easy to set up and use and well suited to tasks that don't require a relational database server.

SybTcl SybTcl provides an interface to a Sybase database server.

OraTcl OraTcl provides an interface to an Oracle database server.

BLT A set of Tcl and Tk extensions that include support for treating numeric lists as high-speed vectors and creating graphs and bar charts.

Img, dash-patch

These extensions increase Tk's graphics and imaging capabilities. The dash-patch provides speedup and feature enhancements to the canvas widget, and the Img extension adds support for more image file formats to the Tcl image object.

13.1 [incr Tcl]

Language	C
Primary Site	http://www.tcltk.com/itcl/
Contact	mmclennan@lucent.com, Michael McLennan
Tcl Revision Supported	Tcl: 7.3-8.0 Tk: 3.6-8.0
Supported Platforms	Unix, MS Windows, Mac 68K, Mac PowerPC
Mailing List	itcl-request@tcltk.com. with a subject of: subscribe
Other Book References	Tcl/Tk Tools

[Incr Tcl] is to Tcl what C++ is to C, right down to the pun for the name. It extends the base Tcl language with support for:

- Namespaces.
- Class definition with:
    - Public, private, and protected class methods.
    - Public, private, and protected data.
    - Inheritance.
    - Constructors.
    - Destructors.
- Variables attached to a class rather than a class instance.

The namespace commands were first introduced into Tcl by [incr Tcl]. The [incr Tcl] namespace command has same basic format as the namespace command in Tcl 8.0. One difference is that [incr Tcl] allows you to define items in a namespace to be completely private. A pure Tcl script can always access items in a Tcl namespace using the complete name of the item.

In previous chapters, I showed how you could use subsets of object-oriented programming techniques with Tcl. With [incr Tcl] you can do *real* object-oriented programming.

The following example is adapted from the [incr Tcl] introduction (itcl-intro/itcl/tree/tree2.itcl). It implements a tree structure, similar to that developed in Chapters 5 and 6 of this book.

The class command defines the Tree class with the private data members key, value, parent, and children.

The class methods are defined with the method command and can be defined either in line (as the methods add, clear, and parent are defined) or similarly to function prototypes (as the get method is defined). When a method is defined as a function prototype, the code that implements the method can be placed later in the script or in a separate file.

Example 13.1-1

```
class Tree {
    private variable key ""
    private variable value ""
    private variable parent ""
    private variable children ""

    constructor {n v} {
        set key $n
        set value $v
    }
    destructor {
        clear
    }

    method add {obj} {
        $obj parent $this
        lappend children $obj
    }
    method clear {} {
        if {$children != ""} {
            eval delete object $children
        }
        set children {}
    }
    method parent {pobj} {
        set parent $pobj
    }
```

```
    public method get {option}

    method contents {} {
        return $children
    }
}

body Tree::get {{option -value}} {
        switch -- $option {
            -key    { return $key }
            -value  { return $value }
            -parent { return $parent }
        }
        error "bad option \"$option\""
    }
```

Example Script

```
#
# Create a Tree
#
Tree topNode key0 Value0

#
# Add two children
#
topNode add [Tree childNode1 key1 Value1]
topNode add [Tree childNode2 key2 Value2]

#
# Display some values from the tree.
#
puts "topNode's children are: [topNode contents]"
puts "Value associated with childNode1 is \
    [childNode1 get -value]"
puts "Parent of childNode2 is: [childNode2 get -parent]"
```

Script Output

```
topNode's children are: childNode1 childNode2
Value associated with childNode1 is Value1
Parent of childNode2 is: ::topNode
```

13.2 Expect

Language	`C`
Primary Site	`http://expect.nist.gov/`
Contact	`libes@nist.gov`, Don Libes
Tcl Revision Supported	`Tcl: 7.3-8.0p2 Tk: 3.6-8.0p2`
Supported Platforms	`Unix`
Unofficially Supported Platforms	`Windows NT: http://bmrc.berkeley.edu/ people/chaffee/expectnt.html`
Other Book References	`Exploring Expect, Tcl/Tk Tools`

Expect adds commands to Tcl that make it easy to write scripts to interact with programs that use a character-based interface. This includes programs such as telnet and FTP that use a prompt/command type interface or even keyboard-driven spreadsheet packages such as `sc`.

Expect can be used for tasks ranging from changing passwords on remote systems to converting an interactive hardware diagnostics package into an automated test system. When you link the `expect` extension with the `Tk` libraries, you get an interpreter (`expectk`) that is ideal for adding a GUI to dialog-based programs.

There are three indispensable new commands in `expect`:

Syntax: `spawn` *options commandName commandArgs*

`spawn`	Starts a new process and connects the process's `stdin` and `stdout` to the `expect` interpreter.
options	The `spawn` command supports several options, including

	`-noecho`	The spawn will echo the command line and arguments unless this option is set.
	`-open` *fileID*	The `-open` option lets you process the input from a file handle (returned by

open) instead of executing a new program. This allows you to use an `expect` script to evaluate program output from a file as well as directly controlling a program.

`commandName commandArgs`

The name of the process to start and the command line arguments.

Syntax: `expect   ?-option? pattern1 action1 ?-option?\`
`                pattern2 action2 ...`

`expect`

Scan the input for one of several patterns. When a `pattern` is recognized, evaluate the associated `action`.

`-option`

Options that will control the matching are:

`-exact`

Match the pattern exactly.

`-re`

Use regular expression rules to match this pattern.

`-glob`

Use glob rules to match this pattern.

`pattern`

A pattern to match in the output from the spawned program.

`action`

A script to be evaluated when a pattern is matched.

Syntax: `exp_send string`

`exp_send`

Sends `string` to the slave process.

`string`

The string to be transmitted to the slave process. Note that a newline is *not* appended to this text.

When `expect` finds a string that matches a pattern, it stores information about the match in the associative array `expect_out`. This array contains several indices, including:

`expect_out(buffer)`

All characters up to and including the characters that matched a pattern.

`expect_out(0,string)`

> The characters that matched an exact, glob, or regular expression pattern.

`expect_out(#,string)`

> The indices `(1,string)-(9,string)` will contain the characters that match regular expressions within parentheses. The characters that match the first expression within parentheses are assigned to `expect_out(1,string)`, the characters that match the next parenthetical expression are assigned to `expect_out(2,string)`, etc.

The following example shows how a tedious set of interactions with an archie server can be automated. An archie server will return a list of anonymous FTP sites that contain a requested file. The example initiates a telnet session to an archie server, sets several configuration options, and searches for a pattern that is supplied on the command line.

When a new task is spawned, a variable named `spawn_id` is created in the current scope to reference the task. If the `spawn` command is evaluated within a procedure, then `spawn_id` should be defined as a global variable to allow other expect commands to access it.

In the following example, note the `timeout` and `eof` patterns in the `expect` commands. If a pattern is not recognized within a defined length of time, the `timeout` action will be evaluated. If the connection to the spawned process is closed, the `eof` action will be evaluated. This is similar to the behavior of the `default` pattern in the `switch` command. As with the `default` option, you don't *need* to check for the `timeout` and `eof` conditions, but you will eventually regret it if you don't.

Example 13.2-1

```
#!/usr/local/bin/expect5.26

set globalList [list spawn_id timeout archExp]

###############################################################
# proc archieCmd {cmd}--
#     Sends a command to the archie server,
#     watches for timeout or eof conditions.
```

```
#
# Arguments
#   cmd          A command (with newline character) to send to\
                 the server.
#
# Results
#   An archie command is evaluated at the server.
#
proc archieCmd {cmd} {
    global globalList;   eval "global $globalList"

    #
    # There should be an "archie>" prompt in the buffer, check
    # that it's there, then send the command.
    #

    expect {
            "archie>"     {
                          exp_send "$cmd"
                          }
            timeout       {
                          puts "Timeout: no 'archie>' prompt"
                          return -1
            }
            eof           {
                          puts "telnet died"
                          return -1
            }
    }

    return 0
}

############################################################
# proc doSearch {}--
#     Perform an archie search for the requested pattern.
#
# Arguments
#   NONE
#
```

```
# Results
#   Logs into the archie server,
#   configures the server
#   performs the search
#   logs out of server.
#
proc doSearch {searchString} {
    global globalList;  eval "global $globalList"

    #
    # Spawn a telnet session to the remote site.
    #
    exp_spawn telnet $archExp(site)

    #
    # Expect a login prompt, and send the loginid "archie" when
    #  it appears.
    # Complain if unknown, unreachable, timeout or eof occurs.
    #
    expect {
            "login:"    {
                        exp_send "archie\n"
            }
            "unknown"   {
                        return "No Path to $archExp(site)"
            }
            "unreachable" {
                        return "No Path to $archExp(site)"
            }
            timeout     {
                        return "Timeout connecting to \
                                $archExp(site)"
            }
            eof         {
                        return "telnet died"
            }
    }
    #
```

```tcl
    # Set the configuration options
    #

    if {[archieCmd "unset pager\n"]} {
        return "failed cmd: unset pager\n"
    }

    foreach config [list maxhits sortby search] {
        set cmd "set $config $archExp($config)\n"
        if {[archieCmd $cmd]} {
            return "failed cmd: $cmd"
        }
    }

    #
    # Search for the requested pattern
    #

    if {[archieCmd "prog $searchString\n"]} {
        return "failed cmd: prog $searchString\n"
    }

    # The timeout value is set long because it may take a while
    # for the archie server to perform the search and display
    # the results.
    # Three minutes seems like a while to me.

    set timeout 180

    #
    # We're done, exit the archie server
    #

    if {[archieCmd "quit\n"]} {
        return "failed cmd: quit\n"
    }
    return "Search Successful"
}
#
# Set the defaults for the archie configuration options
#
set archExp(maxhits) 5
set archExp(sortby) time
```

```
set archExp(site) archie.rutgers.edu
set archExp(search) sub

set status [doSearch $argv]
puts "$status"
```

Example Use

```
$> # Search for sites that archive expect
$> expect example.exp expect
```

Script Output

```
exp_spawn telnet archie.rutgers.edu
Trying 165.230.4.73...
Connected to archie.rutgers.edu.
Escape character is '^]'.

UNIX(r) System V Release 4.0 (dogbert.rutgers.edu)

login: archie
Last login: Sat May 30 21:01:42 from tr33-d50.msen.ne
Sun Microsystems Inc.   SunOS 5.5.1    Generic May 1996
------------------ Network Services --------------------

                 Welcome to Archie!
                 Vers 3.5

# Bunyip Information Systems, Inc., 1993, 1994, 1995

# Terminal type set to `xterm 24 80'.
# `erase' character is `^?'.
# `search' (type string) has the value `exact'.
archie> unset pager
archie> set maxhits 5
archie> set sortby time
archie> set search sub
archie> prog expect
# Search type: sub.
working...

Host ftp.fu-berlin.de   (160.45.10.6)
Last updated 06:49  3 Oct 1997

    Location: /unix/linux/mirrors/debian/hamm/hamm/binary-
i386/devel
```

```
       FILE    -rw-rw-r--           81160  08:57 21 Apr 1997
expect5.22-dev_5.22.0-1.deb

Host ftp.cs.us.es        (150.214.141.158)
Last updated 14:37   2 Mar 1998
...
archie> quit
# Bye.
Connection closed by foreign host.
Search Successful
```

13.3 TclX

Language	C
Primary Site	http://www.neosoft.com/tclx
Contact	markd@grizzly.com, Mark Diekhans
Tcl Revision Supported	Tcl: 7.3-8.0.3 Tk: 3.6-8.0.3
Supported Platforms	Unix, Windows NT, Windows 95
Other Book References	Tcl/Tk Tools

The TclX extension is designed to give the Tcl programmer more access to operating system functions and to make large programming tasks easier. TclX contains a large number of new commands. Many of the best features of Tcl (sockets, time and date, random numbers, associative arrays, and more) were introduced in TclX. There are still many features provided by TclX that are not in the Tcl core.

TclX features include:

- Extended file system interaction commands.
- Extended looping constructs.
- Extended string manipulation commands.
- Extended list manipulation commands.

- Keyed lists.
- Debugging commands.
- Performance profiling commands.
- System library interface commands.
- Network information commands.
- Message catalogs for multiple language support (compliant with X/Open Portability Guide).
- Help.
- Packages.

Using TclX can help you in three ways:

- TclX gives you access to operating system functions that are not supported by the Tcl core. Using the core Tcl, you would need to write stand-alone C programs (or your own extensions) to gain access to these.
- TclX scripts are smaller than pure Tcl scripts, because TclX has built-in constructs that you would otherwise need to write as procedures.
- TclX commands run faster than the equivalent function written as a Tcl procedure, because the TclX command is written in C and compiled instead of being interpreted.

The example shows a procedure that will walk down a directory tree and scan all files with names that match a pattern for a string. It will return lists of files that contain and files that do not contain that string. You may want to compare the code for addDirToTree in Section 5.7 with this example to see how much code can be saved by using the for_recursive_glob command.

This example uses two features from TclX: the for_recursive_glob looping construct and the scanfile file and text manipulation commands.

Syntax: for_recursive_glob *var dirlist globlist code*

for_recursive_glob

                Recursively loops through the directories in a list looking for files that match one of a list of glob patterns. When a file matching the pattern is found, the script defined in *code* is evaluated with the variable *var* set to the name of the file that matched the pattern.

var	The name of a variable that will receive the name of each matching file.
dirlist	A list of directories to search for files that match the *globlist* patterns.
globlist	A list of glob patterns that will be used to match file names.
code	A script to evaluate whenever a file name matches one of the patterns in *globlist*.

Syntax: scancontext create

scancontext create

Create a new scan context for use with the scanfile command. Returns a *contextHandle*.

Syntax: scanmatch *contextHandle* ?*regexp*? *code*

scanmatch	Associate a regular expression and script with the *contextHandle* returned by scancontext create.
regexp	A regular expression to scan for. If this is blank, the script is assigned as the default script to evaluate when no other expression is matched.
code	A script to evaluate when the *regexp* is matched.

When a regular expression defined with scanmatch is recognized, information about the match is stored in the associative array variable matchInfo, which is visible to the code script. The matchInfo variable has several indices with information about the match.

Syntax: scanfile *contexthandle* *fileId*

scanfile	Scan a file for lines that match one of the regular expressions defined in a context handle. If a line matches a regular expression, the associated script is evaluated.

Example 13.3-1

Example Script

```tcl
#!/usr/local/bin/tcl

proc scanTreeForString {topDir pattern matchString \
        filesWith filesWithout} {
    upvar $filesWith with
    upvar $filesWithout without

    set with ""

    #
    # Create a scan context for the files that will be scanned.
    #
    set sc [scancontext create]

    #
    # Add an action to take when the pattern is recognized
    #  in a file. If the pattern is recognized, append the
    #  file name to the list of files containing the pattern
    #  and break out of the scanning loop. Without the "break",
    #  scanfile would process each occurrence of the text that
    #  matches the regular expression.

    scanmatch $sc "$matchString" {
        lappend with [file tail $filename]
        break;
    }

    #
    # Process all the files below $topDir that match the
    # pattern
    #

    for_recursive_glob filename $topDir $pattern {

        set fl [open $filename RDONLY]
        scanfile $sc $fl
        close $fl

        # If there were no lines match the $matchString,
        # there will be no $filename in the list "with".
```

```
            # In that case, add $filename to the list of files
            # without the $matchString.

            if {[lsearch $with [file tail $filename]] < 0} {
                lappend without [file tail $filename]
            }
        }
    }
    #
    # Clean up and leave
    #
    scancontext delete $sc
}

scanTreeForString /usr/src/TCL/tcl8.0 *.c Tcl_Obj hasObj noObj

puts "These files have 'Tcl_Obj' in them: $hasObj"
puts "These files do not: $noObj"
```

Example Script

```
scanTreeForString /usr/src/TCL/tcl8.0 *.c Tcl_Obj hasObj noObj

puts "These files have 'Tcl_Obj' in them: $hasObj\n"
puts "These files do not: $noObj"
```

Script Output

```
These files have 'Tcl_Obj' in them: tclUnixFCmd.c
tclUnixPipe.c tclBasic.c tclBinary.c tclClock.c tclCmdAH.c
tclCmdIL.c tclCmdMZ.c tclCompExpr.c tclCompile.c tclExecute.c
tclFCmd.c tclHistory.c tclIO.c tclIOCmd.c tclIOUtil.c
tclIndexObj.c tclInterp.c tclListObj.c tclMain.c tclNamesp.c
tclObj.c tclParse.c tclProc.c tclStringObj.c tclTest.c
tclTestObj.c tclTimer.c tclUtil.c tclVar.c tclWinFCmd.c
tclWinPipe.c tclWinReg.c tclMacBOAMain.c tclMacChan.c
tclMacFCmd.c tclMacLibrary.c tclMacResource.c

These files do not: tclAppInit.c tclLoadAix.c tclLoadAout.c
tclLoadDl.c tclLoadDld.c tclLoadNext.c tclLoadOSF.c
tclLoadShl.c tclMtherr.c tclUnixChan.c tclUnixEvent.c
tclUnixFile.c tclUnixInit.c tclUnixNotfy.c tclUnixSock.c
tclUnixTest.c tclUnixTime.c tclXtTest.c panic.c regexp.c
...
```

13.4 VS Package

Language	`Tcl`
Primary Site	`http://www.neosoft.com`
Original Author	Steve Wahle
Contact	`VSdb: river@ibm.net`, Rick Enos
Tcl Revision Supported	`Tcl: 7.3-7.6 Tk: 3.6-4.2`
Supported Platforms	`Unix`

There are three utilities in the VS suite.

`VSdb`	A small database package.
`VSform`	A forms-based GUI generator.
`VSrpt`	A report-generating package.

These packages are written in pure Tcl and can be easily merged into an application. You can use one or all of the packages; they do not require each other. The `VSform` package, as a stand-alone, is a good tool for creating forms-based graphical interfaces to older pieces of code, and the `VSdb` package is fine for personal or small business database requirements.

The packages are documented with README files and short examples.

The next example creates an address book database. It supports adding entries to the database and can search on substrings in the name field.

VSdb and VSform Example

Example Script

```
source TclVSdb.tcl
source TkVSform.tcl

#
# Database access procedures that will be invoked by the buttons.
#
```

```
#
# Add an item to the database.
#
proc AddItem {} {
    global item db fields
    set frow [dbNewRow db addr]

    foreach field $fields {
        set db(addr,$field) $item($field)
    }
    dbPutRow db addr
}

#
# Clear all the displayed fields
#

proc ClearItems {} {
    global item fields
    foreach field $fields {
        set item($field) ""
    }
}

#
# Search for a substring in the name field.  Display the first
#  database entry that matches the substring.
#

proc SearchName {} {
    global item fields db

    set rowNumber [dbuSearchString db addr name $item(name)]
    dbGetRow db addr [lindex $rowNumber 0]

    foreach field $fields {
        set item($field) $db(addr,$field)
    }
}

#
# Define the fields for this database.
#  If the database does not exist, create it.
#
```

```
set fields "name street city state zip email web phone"
if {![file exists addr.idx]} {
    dbCreate . db addr $fields
    dbClose db
}

dbOpen . db

#
# Define the GUI form for the address book.
# The command format is:
# formLABEL FORMID STATE TEXT TEXTVARIABLE ELEMENT WIDTH
#   TK-OPTIONS
# formENTRY FORMID STATE TEXTVARIABLE ELEMENT WIDTH CMD
#   CMDARGS TK-OPTIONS
# formBUTTON FORMID STATE TEXT CMD CMDARGS TK-OPTIONS

formBEGIN f "Address Book" "+20+20" "" MAIN
  formGROUP f
    formNEWLINE f
      formLABEL f "" "NAME: "
      formENTRY f "" item name 30
    formNEWLINE f
      formLABEL f "" "STREET: "
      formENTRY f "" item street 30
    formNEWLINE f
      formLABEL f "" "CITY: "
      formENTRY f "" item city 18
      formLABEL f "" "STATE: "
      formENTRY f "" item state  4
      formLABEL f "" "ZIP: "
      formENTRY f "" item zip  12
    formNEWLINE f
      formLABEL f "" "PHONE: "
      formENTRY f "" item phone 15
      formLABEL f "" "EMAIL: "
      formENTRY f "" item email 20
      formLABEL f "" "WEB: "
      formENTRY f "" item web 20
    formNEWLINE f
      set fadd [formBUTTON f "" "Add Item" "AddItem"]
      set fclear [formBUTTON f "" "Clear Screen" "ClearItems"]
```

```
        set fsearch [formBUTTON f "" "Search for Name" \
                    "SearchName"]
        set fexit [formBUTTON f "" "EXIT" "formDIE f; dbClose db; \
                    exit"]
formEND f on $fexit
```

Script Results

13.5 Sybtcl and Oratcl

Language	C
Primary Site	http://www.neosoft.com
Contact	tpoindex@nyx.net, Tom Poindexter
Tcl Revision Supported	Tcl: 7.3-8.0 Tk: 3.6-8.0
Supported Platforms	Unix, Windows NT, Windows 95

Sybtcl and Oratcl are Tcl interfaces to the Sybase and Oracle database libraries. These packages allow you to use Tcl to write programs that interact with a database server.

In general, these two packages follow the same style of interaction with the Tcl interpreter and the database libraries. This consistency makes it easy to convert an application from one brand of database server to another.

The packages maintain the flavor of the C library for their respective servers. Hence, there are some optimized database access techniques that are available in one extension that are not available in the other.

Both of the packages support these primitive functions:

Function	Sybase	Oracle
Connect to Server	`sybconnect id \` `password`	`oraconnect` `id/password@server`
Send SQL to Server	`sybsql $handle \` `$sqlString`	`orasql $cursor \` `$sqlString`
Fetch Rows	`sybnext $handle`	`orafetch $cursor`
Close Connection	`sybclose $handle`	`oralogoff \` `$logon_connection`

Information Variables	Sybase	Oracle
Status Number	`$sybmsg(dberr)`	`$oramsg(dberr)`
Status Message	`$sybmsg(errortxt)`	`$oramsg(errortxt)`

The following example scripts show how a simple `Sybtcl` or `Oratcl` script can connect to a book database with rows for titles and authors.

Sybtcl and Oratcl: Database Access

Database Contents

The Three Musketeers	Alexandre Dumas
Great Expectations	Charles Dickens
Tcl/Tk for Real Programmers	Clif Flynt

Sybtcl Script

```
set handle [sybconnect $id $password]
sybsql $handle "select * from titles"
set row [sybnext $handle]
while {$sybnext(nextrow) == "REG_ROW"} {
    puts "column 1 = [lindex $row 0]"
    puts "column 2 = [lindex $row 1]"
    set row [sybnext $handle]
}
```

Oratcl Script

```
set lda [oralogon $id/$pass@server]
set cursor [oraopen $lda]
```

```
orasql $cursor "select * from titles"
while {[set row [orafetch $cursor]] != ""} {
    puts "column 1 = [lindex $row 0]"
    puts "column 2 = [lindex $row 1]"
}
```

Script Output

```
column 1 = The Three Musketeers
column 2 = Alexandre Dumas
column 1 = Great Expectations
column 2 = Charles Dickens
column 1 = Tcl/Tk for Real Programmers
column 2 = Clif Flynt
```

13.6 BLT

Language	C
Primary Site	http://www.tcltk.com/blt/
Contact	gah@lucent.com, George A. Howlett
Tcl Revision Supported	Tcl: 7.5-7.6p2 Tk: 4.1-4.2p2
Supported Platforms	Unix
Other Book References	Tcl/Tk Tools

BLT adds several useful new graphical features to Tk, including:

- Commands to draw graphs and bar charts:
- Commands to manipulate vectors of numeric data
- Commands to manage widget layout in a tabular fashion.
- Commands to better integrate with the X server.
- Commands to manipulate bitmaps.
- Drag-and-drop support.

The BLT extension introduced a tabular layout manager named table to Tk. The table commands were merged into the core Tk interpreter as the grid layout manager in version 4.1.

The BLT graphing commands let you easily construct and customize graphs and bar charts. The vector support is integrated with graph and bar chart support to improve the graphing performance. If you've spent any time converting data from a report into a format for other graphing programs, you'll enjoy having a full interpreter available to process your input. This makes data presentation tasks much simpler.

BLT widgets follow the same conventions as the primitive Tk widgets. When a new graph or bar chart widget is created, a new command is created to interact with that widget.

Syntax: barchart *widgetName ?options?*
Syntax: graph *widgetName ?options?*

barchart　　　　Create a bar chart widget.

graph　　　　　Create a graph widget.

widgetName　　A name for this widget. This name should follow the standard Tk naming convention.

options　　　　The widget appearance can be configured with the usual -height and -width options, as well as widget-specific options such as:

-title *text*　　A title for the graph.

-plotbackground *color*
　　　　　　　　　The color of the graph background.

-invertxy　　　　Invert the X and Y axes.

The data to be displayed on a graph is grouped in *graph elements*. A graph element describes the data to be plotted on an axis, the appearance of the plot, and information for the graph legend. A graph element's data may be defined as a single point of data, a list, or with a BLT vector. If the data are defined using a vector, the graph will automatically update when the vector contents are modified.

Syntax: *widgetName* create element *elementName* *?options?*

widgetName create element

> Create a graph element that will contain data to be graphed.

name

> An identifying string for this element. This is a descriptive name. It need not follow Tk naming conventions.

options

> The options for the element creation command include:
>
> -xdata *?value?*
>
>> Defines the data to plot along the X axis. The argument for this option may be a single value, a Tcl list of numbers, or the name of a previously defined BLT vector.
>
> -ydata *?value?*
>
>> Defines the data to plot along the Y axis. The argument for this option may be a single value, a Tcl list of numbers, or the name of a previously defined BLT vector.
>
> -background *color*
>
>> The background color for the plotted data points.
>
> -foreground *color*
>
>> The background color for the plotted data points.
>
> -label *text* The label to use to describe this data in the graph legend.

The next example generates a bar chart of the page hits reported by the Apache hypertext transfer protocol (HTTP) server. It creates BLT vectors as new pages appear in the data. As you can see, most of the code deals with extracting the information to be graphed from the report. Having the data extraction and graphing tool in a single package makes generating plots like this easier than reformatting the data with one program and visualizing it with another.

BLT: Activity Log Bar Chart

Example Script

```
#!/usr/local/blt/bin/bltwish4.2

# create a barchart, titled "Downloads"
#    display bars for a given day side by side
# Display the graph widget.

barchart .html -title Downloads -width 600 -height 300 \
        -barmode aligned

# Place the legend on the top.

.html legend configure -position top

# Configure the X axis to display just the third week of
# January. (24'th - 32'nd days of the mounth)

.html axis configure x -min 24 -max 32

pack .html

# Define a list of colors used to select contrasting colors
# for the bars

set colors [list black red green yellow orange blue purple]

# Make the vectors 32 days long because vectors count from 0
# while days of the months count from 1.

set days 32

# Vector x will be the x axis variable.

vector x($days)

while {![eof stdin]} {

    # Data is read in from stdin.
    # Read lines, and skip any short ones immediately.

    set len [gets stdin line]
    if {$len > 4}  {

    # A log entry resembles this:

    # tarantula.av.pa-x.dec.com - - [01/Jan/1998:04:18:19 \
    # -0500] www.msen.com "GET /~clif/TclTutor.html HTTP/1.0"
```

547

```
# 304 - "-"  "Web21 CustomCrawl bert@web21.com"

    # Treat the log line as a space delimited list, and
    #  split it into fields.  This is not completely
    #  accurate, but will work for the first several
    #  fields (all that this program uses.)

     set lst [split $line]

    # Field 9 is the status.  If this isn't 200,
    #  the browser made an unacceptable request (wanted
    #  an unavailable page).
    # No need to process those entries.

    if {[lindex $lst 9] != 200} {continue}

    # The date format is: [31/Jan/1998:15:07:47 -0500]
    #  The inner lindex returns [31/Jan/1998:15:07:47
    #  The split at ":" converts to: [31/Jan/1998 15 07 47
    #  The outer lindex grabs the date field: [31/Jan/1998
    #  The string trim removes the "["

     set date [string trim [lindex \
            [split [lindex $lst 3] :] 0] "\["]

    #"clock scan" recognizes "31 Jan 1998" but not \
    # "31/Jan/1998" regsub out the "/", then use the \
    # clock scan and format commands to convert this to a
    # julian date (day of the year)

    regsub -all "/" $date " " date
    set day [string trimleft [clock format \
            [clock scan $date] -format %j] 0]
    set x($day) $day

    # The seventh field is the page requested.
    #   The form is: "/~clif/TclTutor.html"
    #   file tail returns the filename: "TclTutor.html"
    # The regsub converts various punctuation marks to "_"
    #   to keep the Tcl parser happy

    set name [file tail [lindex $lst 7]]
    regsub -all -- {[\."-:]}  $name  "_" id

    #
    # If we've already seen this page, increment the days
```

```
#  page count. This is done with "expr" instead of
#  "incr" because the vectors store their data as
#  floating point numbers, and incr will only deal with
#  integers.

if {[info exists $id]} {
      set ${id}($day) [expr $$(id}($day) +1]
} else {
    # This is a new page.
    # Create a new vector for this page, and assign
    #   the hit count to 1

    vector ${id}($days)
      set ${id}($day) 1

    # Select the next color from the list, and
    #   rotate the list

    set c [lindex $colors 0]
    set colors [lreplace $colors 0 0]
    lappend colors $c

    # Create a new element in this barchart.
    # The x position will be the x vector.
    # The height of the bars (ydata) is the newly
    #       created vector.
    # The color is set to the new contrasting color
    # The label for the legend is the page name.

    .html element create $id -xdata x -ydata $id \
            -background $c -foreground $c -label $name
  }
 }

}
```

Script Results

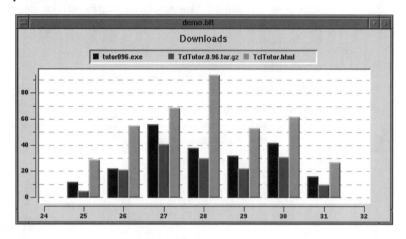

13.7 Graphics Extensions: Img and Dash-Patch

Language	C
Primary Site	http://home.wxs.nl/~nijtmans/
Contact	Jan.Nijtmans@wxs.nl, Jan Nijtmans
Tcl Revision Supported	Tcl: 7.6p2-8.1 Tk: 4.2p2-8.1
Supported Platforms	Unix, MS Windows 95, MS Windows NT

The dash-patch is not actually an extension, it's a set of patches (to be applied with Larry Wall's `patch` program) to the standard Tcl distribution that extend and improve the functionality of the canvas widget.

This set of patches has many features, including:

- Use the `Tcl_Obj` Tcl library calls, instead of the pre-8.0 string-based Tcl library calls in the canvas C code. This improves the performance of the canvas widget.

- Mark Weissman's patch for using hash tables to track canvas items. This improves the performance of canvas widgets with a large number of displayed items.
- Tom Phelp's *elide* patch (required for TkMan 2.0).
- John Ellson's *Tkspline* patch, which provides more smoothing methods for lines and polygons.
- Support for more styles of dashed and dotted lines.

Img adds support for BMP, XBM, XPM, GIF (with transparency), PNG, JPEG, TIFF, and postscript images to the Tk image object (described in Chapter 9). You must have the libtiff, libpng, and libjpg libraries available on your system to read TIFF, PNG, or JPEG image files. These libraries are all public domain and easily acquired.

The TIFF library code is archived at ftp://ftp.sgi.com/graphics/tiff/. The PNG library is archived at ftp://ftp.uu.net/graphics/png and on CompuServe, Lib 20 (PNG SUPPORT) at GO GRAPHSUP. The archive site for the JPEG library software is ftp://ftp.uu.net/graphics/jpeg.

13.8 Bottom Line

- There are many extensions to enhance the base Tcl/Tk functionality.
- Not all extensions are available for all platforms and all Tcl revisions.
- Tcl extensions tend to lag behind the core Tcl releases.
- The primary archive for Tcl code is http://www.neosoft.com.
- Extensions are frequently announced in comp.lang.tcl or comp.lang.tcl.announce.
- Many frequently used extensions are mentioned in the FAQ.

Programming Tools

One of the tricks to getting your job done efficiently is having the right tools for the job. There are plenty of tools available for developing Tcl applications.

This chapter will provide a quick description of several tools that are in use in the Tcl community. It's not a complete listing of tools. If the tool you need is not mentioned here, try checking the Neosoft search engine at `http://www.neosoft.com`, the Scriptics Resource Center at `http://www.scriptics.com/resource/`, the announcements in `comp.lang.tcl`, or the FAQs at `http://www.purl.org/NET/Tcl-FAQ`.

Tools for Tcl are rapidly changing and improving. This chapter discusses the versions of the tools that were available in July 1998. New versions of many of these packages will be available before the book and CD-ROM are published.

By the time you read this book, the commercial products from Scriptics and ICEM will be released. These packages will provide the Tcl developer with high-quality, commercially supported tools.

The Scriptics TclPro development suite will be a full development package including a GUI-based debugger, a static code checker, a wrapper tool for creating self-extracting Tcl applications, and a byte-code compiler that will produce machine-independent Tcl object code. This chapter will discuss the first set of tools, the TclPro Debugger, Wrapper, and Compiler.

Version 2.0 of the ICEM Tcl Compiler will support multiple back ends, allowing it to generate machine-independent Tcl object code, Java code, or C code.

In this chapter I'll briefly cover:

Code formatters

frink   Reformats code into a standard style for easy comprehension.

tcl_cruncher   Reformats code into a style that optimizes for interpreter efficiency. This program also does some syntax checking.

Code checkers

tclCheck   Checks for balanced brackets, braces, and parentheses.

tcl_lint   Checks for syntax errors, unset or nonexistent variables, incorrect procedure calls, and more.

tclparse   Checks for syntax errors, missing dollar signs, and other errors.

Debuggers

Don Libes's Debugger

         This is a text-oriented package with support for setting breakpoints, examining data, etc.

tuba   This is a GUI-based package with multiple windows for both Tcl and Tk.

TdDebug   This GUI-based package can attach itself to an already running Tk application.

Scriptics TclPro Debugger

         This is a full-featured, GUI-based package from Scriptics that can debug remote or embedded applications as well as those on the local host.

GUI generators

SpecTcl   SpecTcl creates a GUI skeleton for a Tk program.

Spynergy   The Spynergy GUI builder is integrated with the Spynergy interactive Web tools. This package helps you build HTTP robots, clients, and servers quickly and easily.

Tcl compilers

ICEM Tcl Compiler

The ICEM Tcl Compiler translates Tcl code into C code to improve performance.

Jan Nijtmans's plus-patch

This patch applies some minor bug fixes, extends the shared library support, and makes it possible to convert Tcl scripts into executables that can run when Tcl is not installed.

Scriptics TclPro Compiler

TclPro Compiler converts Tcl scripts into Tcl bytecode files.

Tcl extension generators

swig   SWIG creates Tcl extensions by reading the function and data definitions from an include file.

Packaging tools

Scriptics TclPro Wrapper

The Scriptics Wrapper converts a set of Tcl scripts and associated files (which may include an interpreter) into a single executable file.

14.1 Code Formatters

There are two reasons for reformatting Tcl code: to make the code more comprehensible and to make the program run faster.

14.1.1 Reformatting for Comprehension: `frink`

Despite our best efforts, after several hours of refining our understanding of the problem (i.e., hacking code), we usually end up with badly formatted code. Incorrectly formatted code can hide errors caused by misplaced braces. Reformatting the code can frequently help you find those errors.

The `frink` package will reformat a Tcl script to make it more comprehensible, and the `tcl_cruncher` will reformat a Tcl script to run faster.

Language	C
Primary Site	`ftp://catless.ncl.ac.uk/pub/frink.tar.gz`
Contact	`Lindsay.Marshall@newcastle.ac.uk`
Tcl Revision Supported	`Tcl: 7.3-8.1 Tk: 3.6-8.1`
Supported Platforms	`Unix`

`Frink` will convert your script to a format that closely resembles the recommended style for Tcl scripts described in the *Tcl Style Guide*. As added benefits, frink will check the script for syntactic errors while it's reformatting it, and the reformatted script will run faster.

`Frink` supports several command line options to define how the code will be formatted.

`-a`   Put spaces around -command code in { } and "". (default = OFF)

`-A`   Turn off processing of `expr` calls.

`-b`   Add braces (see manual page for details). (default = OFF)

`-B`   Turn off processing of code with `bind` calls.

`-c #`   Set further indent for continuations to #. (default = 2)

`-C`   Turn OFF processing of code with `catch` calls.

`-d`   Remove braces in certain (safe) circumstances. (default = OFF)

`-e`   Produce `else`. (default = OFF)

`-E`   Optimize string comparisons. Use at your own risk. (default = OFF)

-g   Indent switch cases. (default = OFF)

-h   Print this message.

-i #   Set indent for each level to #. (default = 4)

-j   Remove nonessential blank lines. (default = OFF)

-k   Remove nonessential braces.

-m   Minimize the code by removing redundant spacing. (default = OFF)

-n   Do not generate tab characters. (default = OFF, use tabs)

-P   Turn off processing of time command. (default = OFF)

-r   Remove comments. (default = OFF)

-s c   Format according to style "c:"

-S   Don't preserve end-of-line comments. (default = OFF)

-t #   Set tabstops every # characters. (default = 8)

-T   Produce then. (default = OFF)

-u   It is safe to remove brackets from elseif conditions.

-v   Put { } around variable names where appropriate.

-w #   Set line length. (default = 80)

-W   Halt on warnings as well as errors.

-x   Produce "xf style" continuations.

-z   Do not put a single space before the \ character on continuations.

-V   The current version number.

-X   Recognize TclX constructs.

Frink is distributed as source code with a configure file for Posix-style systems. You can compile and link this program under Microsoft Visual C++ 5.0 with this procedure:

1. Get a copy of Gnu getopt.c and getopt.h. (I found a good copy in the Gnu C library and as part of the Gnu m4 distribution.)

2. Copy `getopt.c` and `getopt.h` to the frink source code directory.

3. Within `Visual C++` create a **Win32 Console Application**. (**File - New - Projects**)

4. Add the files. (**Project - Add To Project - Files**)

5. Build all.

14.1.2 Reformatting for Speed: `tcl_cruncher`

Because Tcl is an interpreted language, you can get some speed improvement by reformatting your code. This effect is more pronounced in the versions of Tcl prior to Tcl 8.0.

Language	C
Primary Site	`ftp://hplyot.obspm.fr:/tcl/tcl_cruncher*`
Contact	`l@demailly.com`
Tcl Revision Supported	`Tcl: 7.3-8.1 Tk: 3.6-8.1`
Supported Platforms	`Unix`

`Tcl_cruncher` reformats the code into a less human-readable but more machine-friendly format, removing line feeds and extra spaces. This reformatting can provide a factor of two speed improvement.

The options of `tcl_cruncher`:

`-c`   Checks only.

`-s`   No warnings.

`-1`   Keep first comments.

`-t`   Show script tree.

`-d`   Define a command definition file for commands not defined within the `tcl_cruncher` parser.

The command definition file lets you extend `tcl_cruncher` by linking a new command syntax to that of a known command.

For example, if you have an extension with a command `foo` that takes two arguments (as `set` does), you can add the line

```
foo set
```

to the definition file, and `tcl_cruncher` will be able to check all `foo` commands for valid syntax.

`Tcl_cruncher` is distributed as source code with a `Makefile` for Posix-style systems. Version 1.11 uses some Unix-specific `#include` constructs and doesn't compile easily under Windows.

14.2 Code Checkers

One of the drawbacks of interpreted languages compared with compiled languages is that the program can run for months without evaluating a line of code that has a syntax error. This situation is most likely to occur in exception-handling code, since that's the code least often exercised. A syntax error in this code can cause your program to do something catastrophic while attempting to recover from a minor problem.

There are several code checkers that will examine your script for syntax errors, and more (including the Scriptics TclPro Checker) are being developed. Although none of these are perfect (Tcl has too many ways to confuse such programs), these will catch many bugs before you run your code.

14.2.1 tclCheck

Language	C
Primary Site	ftp://catless.ncl.ac.uk/pub/tclCheck.tar.gz
Contact	Lindsay.Marshall@newcastle.ac.uk
Tcl Revision Supported	Tcl: 7.3-8.1 Tk: 3.6-8.1
Supported Platforms	Unix

This program checks for matching parentheses, braces, and brackets. Most Tcl syntax errors are caused by miscounting or mismatching these items.

TclCheck (and frink) can save you hours of time you'd otherwise spend staring at your code and counting braces.

TclCheck is distributed as C source code with a Makefile. Like frink, it will compile under Windows if you get a copy of Gnu getopt.c to link with it.

14.2.2 ICE Tcl_lint

Language	executable
Primary Site	http://icemcfd.com/tcl/ice.html
Contact	tcl@icemcfd.com
Tcl Revision Supported	Tcl: 7.3-8.1 Tk: 3.6-8.1
Supported Platforms	DEC OSF1 V4.0, HP-UX 9.01, 10.0, IBM AIX 3.2, 4.0, 4.1, Slackware Linux 2.3.30 (ELF), SGI IRIX 5.X and above, Sparc Solaris 5.3 and up, Windows NT 4.0 and Win95.

The tcl_lint program is part of the ICEM Tcl compiler package. It can be licensed without charge for the preceding platforms.

This program uses the same sophisticated parser as the ICEM Tcl compiler and does an excellent job of detecting many different types of errors, including:

- Parsing errors.
- Unset or nonexistent variables.
- Incorrect usage of built-in and user-defined procedures.
- Possibly illegal arithmetic statements.
- A control command with an empty body.
- A nonparsable statement.
- Using a routine that has an implicit return in a command substitution.

The next example has the following errors, which are detected by tcl_lint:

- this_does_not_yet_exist has no value to be returned by set.
- Both expr statements are illegal.

- Both invocations of procedure foo are incorrect.
- The unset x in the second definition of foo tries to unset a variable that does not exist.
- The invocation of twoargs in the second definition of foo is incorrect.
- Incorrect usage of lappend.

Example 14.2.2-1

Example Script

```
proc upper_level {} {
    set this_does_not_yet_exist
     proc twoargs {a b} {
        puts $a$b
    }

    expr 5+"a"
    expr {5+"a"}
    proc foo {a} {} {
        upvar $a x
        set x 5
    }
    foo
    foo bar of this and that

    proc foo {a} {
        catch {unset x}
        list [twoargs 1 2 3 4]
    }

    catch {lappend}
}
```

tcl_lint Output

In proc "foo":

file "has_bugs_1.tcl" line 33.
At or near: "catch {unset x}"

--- ERROR ---: unset or undeclared Variable "x".
file "has_bugs_1.tcl" line 33.
At or near: "unset x"

```
--- ERROR ---: Illegal # args to proc "twoargs" = 4.
Usage : "twoargs arg arg "
file "has_bugs_1.tcl" line 34.
At or near: "list [twoargs 1 2 3 4]"

In proc "upper_level":
--- ERROR ---: unset or undeclared Variable
"this_does_not_yet_exist".--
-
WARNING ---: User should check to ensure
"this_does_not_yet_exist" exists at
this point.
file "has_bugs_1.tcl" line 16.
At or near: "set this_does_not_yet_exist"

--- ERROR ---: Illegal # args to proc "lappend" = 0.
Usage : "lappend varName ?value ...?"

Finished with compilation!
```

14.2.3 tclparse

Language	C++
Primary Site	http://www.informatik.uni-stuttgart.de/ ipvr/swlab/sopra/tclsyntax/tclparse-HomeEngl.html
Contact	07031760536-002@t-online.de
Tcl Revision Supported	Tcl: 7.3-8.1 Tk: 3.6-8.1
Supported Platforms	Unix

Tclparse checks for a large number of programming errors, including incorrect number of arguments, missing quotes and braces, mistakes in variable names, mistakes in command names, and a missing dollar sign in front of a variable name.

Tclparse is distributed as C++ source code with a Makefile. It compiles cleanly with gcc but not with VC++ 4.0.

The `tclparse` program generates the following output from the script in Example 14.2.2-1:

Example 14.2.3-1

TclParse output

```
TCLPARSE V3.00beta
>> loading information from '/usr/home/clif/.tclparse.vars' (1
bytes)
>> processing file 'has_bugs.tcl' (342 bytes)
ERROR    ( line 2 ) - unknown variable:
'this_does_not_yet_exist'
----------------------------------------
1 proc upper_level {} {
2     set this_does_not_yet_exist
3      proc twoargs {a b} {
4         puts $a$b
5      }
6
7     expr 5+"a"
----------------------------------------
ERROR    ( line 9 ) - wrong # args: should be 'proc name args
body'
----------------------------------------
6
7     expr 5+"a"
8     expr {5+"a"}
9     proc foo {a} {} {
10         upvar $a x
11         set x 5
12     }
----------------------------------------
ERROR    ( line 13 ) - unknown command 'foo'
----------------------------------------
10         upvar $a x
11         set x 5
12     }
13     foo
14     foo bar of this and that
15
16     proc foo {a} {
```

```
----------------------------------------
ERROR   ( line 17 ) - unknown variable 'x'
----------------------------------------
14      foo bar of this and that
15
16      proc foo {a} {
17          catch {unset x}
18          list [twoargs 1 2 3 4]
19      }
20

----------------------------------------
ERROR   ( line 18 ) - called '3' with too many arguments
----------------------------------------
15
16      proc foo {a} {
17          catch {unset x}
18          list [twoargs 1 2 3 4]
19      }
20
21      catch {lappend}
----------------------------------------
ERROR   ( line 21 ) - wrong # args: should be 'lappend varName
?value value ...?'
----------------------------------------
18          list [twoargs 1 2 3 4]
19      }
20
21      catch {lappend}
22 }
23
24
----------------------------------------
>> processing of file 'has_bugs.tcl' complete
>> done!
```

14.3 Debugging

Again, despite our best efforts, we spend a lot of time debugging code.

There are many debuggers that aren't covered here, some of which are tailored to work with specific Tcl extensions. If the debuggers described here don't meet your requirements, use the search engine at the Scriptics Resource Center (http://www.scriptics.com/resource/) or Neosoft (http://www.neosoft.com).

14.3.1 debug

Language	C
Primary Site	http://expect.nist.gov/
Contact	libes@nist.gov
Tcl Revision Supported	Tcl: 7.3-8.0p2 Tk: 3.6-8.0p2
Supported Platforms	Unix
Other Book References	Exploring Expect

This text-oriented debugger is distributed by Don Libes as part of the expect extension. The code for the debugger is in the files Dbg.c, Dbg.h, and Dbg_cf.h. With a little tweaking you can merge this debugger into other extensions.

This extension adds a debug command to the Tcl language. The command-debug 1 allows you to interact with the debugger; the command debug 0 turns the debugger off.

This debugger supports stepping into or over procedures and viewing the stack. This debugger supports setting breakpoints that stop on a given line and breakpoints with a command to evaluate when the breakpoint is hit.

The complete Tcl interpreter is available for use while in the debugger mode, so you can use normal Tcl commands to view or modify variables, load new procedures, etc.

The online help lists the available commands in this debugger:

```
% debug 1
dbg1.3> h
s [#]         step into procedure
n [#]         step over procedure
N [#]         step over procedures, commands, and arguments
c             continue
r             continue until return to caller
u [#]         move scope up level
d [#]         move scope down level
              go to absolute frame if # is prefaced by "#"
w             show stack ("where")
w -w [#]      show/set width
w -c [0|1]    show/set compress
b             show breakpoints
b [-r regexp-pattern] [if expr] [then command]
b [-g glob-pattern]   [if expr] [then command]
              if pattern given, break if command resembles
pattern
              if expr given, break if expr true
              if command given, execute command at break-
point
b -#          delete breakpoint
b -           delete all breakpoints
```

While in the debugging mode, the normal prompt resembles Dbg2.3>, where the digit 2 represents the current stack level and the 3 represents the number of interactive commands that have been executed.

In the sample debugging session shown next, the optional patterns and if/then statements are used with the break command to display the contents of the variable 1st when the breakpoint is encountered.

Example 14.3.1-1

Example Script

```
% cat test.tcl

proc addList {1st} {
    set total 0;
    foreach num $1st {
```

```
        set total [expr $total + $num]
    }
    return $total
}

proc mean {lst} {
    set sum [addList $lst]
    set count [llength $lst]
    set mean [expr $sum / $count]
    return $mean
}

set lst [list 2 4 6 8]
puts "Mean $lst : [mean $lst]"
```

Debugging Session

```
$>  expect
expect1.1> debug 1
0
expect1.2> source test.tcl
dbg1.1> b -g "*set count*" if {[llength $lst] < 10} then {puts
"LIST: $lst"}
0
dbg1.2> c
LIST: 2 4 6 8
3: set count [llength $lst]
dbg3.4> w
 0: expect
*1: mean {2 4 6 8}
 3: set {count} {4}
dbg3.5> n 2
3: set mean [expr $sum / $count]
dbg3.6> w
 0: expect
*1: mean {2 4 6 8}
 3: set {mean} {5}
dbg3.7> c
Mean 2 4 6 8 : 5
```

14.3.2 Graphic Debuggers

There are several GUI-oriented debuggers available for Tcl, ranging from the commercial debugger from Scriptics to freeware offerings.

14.3.2.1 Tuba

Language	`Tcl/C++`
Primary Site	`http://www.doitnow.com/~iliad/Tcl/tuba/`
Contact	`iliad@doitnow.com`
Tcl Revision Supported	`Tcl: 8.0-8.1 Tk: 8.0-8.1`
Supported Platforms	`Unix, Windows NT, Windows 95`

This package uses multiple windows to display the code being debugged; allow the user to display and modify variable contents; step into or through procedures; and set breakpoints by line, procedure, or when a variable is set. The GUI is very friendly and includes balloon popups to describe the tool buttons.

Tuba includes an extended `update` command and some parsing code to enable it to control the code being debugged. These functions are written in both C++ and Tcl. The Tcl code and the C++ libraries have the same functionality, but the compiled code runs much faster. If you cannot compile the C++ libraries, the Tcl libraries are acceptably fast.

The first image to follow shows the main window and file selection window. The second image shows the source code window with a variable monitor window displayed on top of it.

14.3.2.2 TdChoose/TdDebug

Language	`Tcl`
Primary Site	`http://www.neosoft.com`
Contact	`david.dougherty@amd.com`

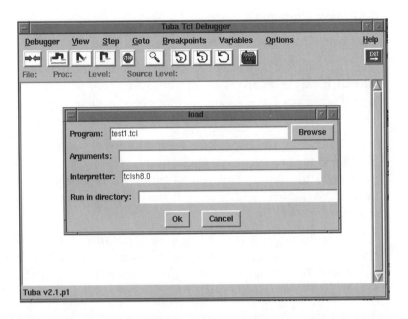

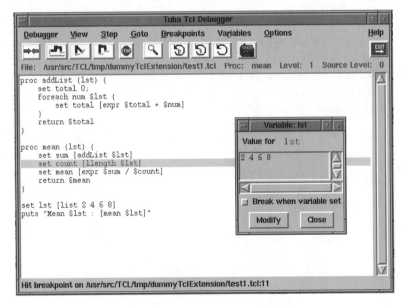

Tcl Revision Supported	`Tcl: 7.3-8.0 Tk: 3.6-8.0`
Supported Platforms	`Unix`

The TdDebug package (originally developed by Gregor Schmid) is unique in that it can be attached to an already running `wish` program. This is useful when you have a program that's been running for several days and suddenly goes into a strange state and needs to be examined.

With TdChoose, you choose the wish interpreter you want to debug and then select the procedures you wish to observe. Tcl commands are added to your code to invoke the debug window once a selected procedure is entered. A search field makes it easy to select procedures in large programs.

While the debugger is controlling your application, you can step through the procedure, insert breakpoints, or continue execution with a user-specified delay. The debugger updates the **variables** window and displays the result as each line is evaluated.

You can also enter a line of Tcl code to evaluate in the program's current scope. This line of code can modify variables, change program flow, etc.

TdDebug supports an extensive configuration file that lets you define the colors for the widgets and highlighting. There are various useful controls for the appearance and detail of the information in the debug window. Additional features are available if the wish interpreter contains `Tix` or `BLT` extensions.

The following images show a portion of a debugging session for a GUI that calculates the mean value from a list of numbers.

Example 14.3.2.2-1

Example Script

```
proc addList {lst} {
    set total 0;
    foreach num $lst {
        set total [expr $total + $num]
    }
    return $total
```

```
}
proc mean {lst} {
    set sum [addList $lst]
    set count [llength $lst]
    set mean [expr $sum / $count]
    return $mean
}
set lst [list 2 4 6 8]
entry .list -textvar lst
label .mean -textvar mean
button .go -text "Calculate mean" -command \
    {set mean [mean $lst]}
pack .list
pack .mean
pack .go
```

The application being debugged is displayed in the upper left corner. The upper right-hand corner shows the TdChoose window, which allows the user to select the application to debug and which procedures within that application to examine. The window labeled TDebug-Backtrace shows the current stack. The window labeled TDebug-Widget-Hierarchy shows the names and types of this application's widgets.

The bottom window shows the code currently being evaluated and the values of the local variables. I typed the command in the Eval entry widget to initialize the total variable to a bogus value, as shown in the Variables scrollbox.

14.3.2.3 Scriptics TclPro Debugger

Language	executable
Primary Site	http://www.scriptics.com
Contact	sales@scriptics.com
Tcl Revision Supported	Tcl: 7.6-8.0 Tk: 4.2-8.0
Supported Platforms	Unix, Windows NT, Windows 95

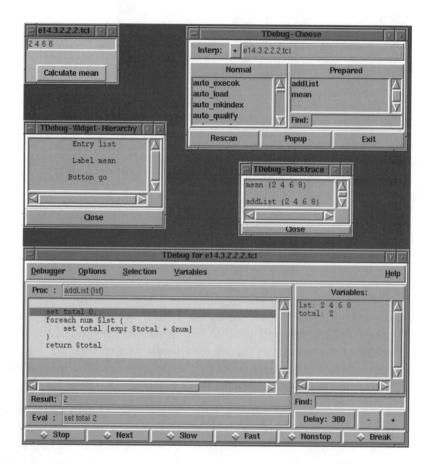

The Scriptics TclPro Debugger is part of the TclPro development suite. TclPro Debugger can be used to debug local, embedded, and remote applications written in either straight Tcl or [incr Tcl].

When a program is loaded into TclPro Debugger, it is checked for correctness. If TclPro Debugger finds a syntax error, it will display a window with a description of the error and mark the offending line in the main window.

The main window of the TclPro Debugger displays the contents of the local variables, the stack, the code being evaluated, and the visible breakpoints. You can open other windows to display all breakpoints, display variables being watched, select procedures to display in the main window, or enter commands that can be evaluated at different procedure scopes in the stack.

TclPro Debugger supports stepping into, over, or out of Tcl procedures; setting breakpoints on lines of Tcl code; setting variable breakpoints that stop execution when a variable is set; viewing variable data; and viewing the Tcl stack.

When the evaluation is halted at a breakpoint you can step up and down through the Tcl call stack to examine the program state. TclPro Debugger also displays the "hidden" stack levels such as the uplevel that occurs when the script associated with a button is evaluated.

In order to use the debugger with remote or embedded applications, you must add a small amount of initialization code to your application. Once this is done, a remote application can be debugged just like a local application.

The following image shows TclPro Debugger examining the application shown in Example 14.3.2.2-1. Line 4 is currently being evaluated, and there is a breakpoint set at line 10. The Stack Frame display in the main window shows that this procedure was entered from a button press. The display in the **Eval Console** window shows the variable total being set to 4 before the loop started.

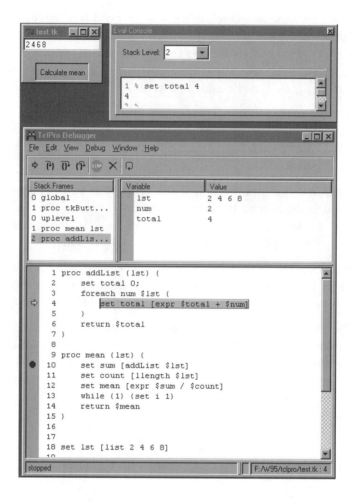

14.4 GUI Generators

If you are developing a GUI-intensive application, you can spend a lot of time rearranging the widgets trying to get the appearance you want. Alternatively, you can use one of the GUI generator programs to create a GUI skeleton that you can populate with your application code.

Again, there are other GUI builders available. You should check the Neosoft archives or comp.lang.tcl to see if other generators may suit your needs better than these.

14.4.1 SpecTcl

Language	`Tcl`
Primary Site	`http://sunscript.sun.com/products/spec-tcl.html`
Contact	`Not officially supported`
Tcl Revision Supported	`Tcl: 7.6-8.1 Tk: 4.2-8.1`
Supported Platforms	`Unix, Windows NT, Windows 95, Mac`

`SpecTcl` can generate the "skeleton" of a GUI program. It lets you position any of the standard Tcl widgets within a grid, define the properties for the widgets, test the appearance of the GUI, and save the GUI description and the Tcl (or Java) code.

The Tk tutorial chapters discussed several of the widget properties that can be defined when a widget is created or with the `configure` subcommand. Double clicking on a widget within `SpecTcl` will open a window that displays all of a widget's properties and allows you to modify them.

The following image shows SpecTcl creating a GUI similar to the one used for demonstrating the debuggers. The toolbuttons along the left side select the Tcl widget to be inserted into the GUI. The toolbuttons along the top allow you to set options that are likely to be consistent among your widgets, such as foreground color, background color, and font. The window displaying the button properties was placed over the main window for this image.

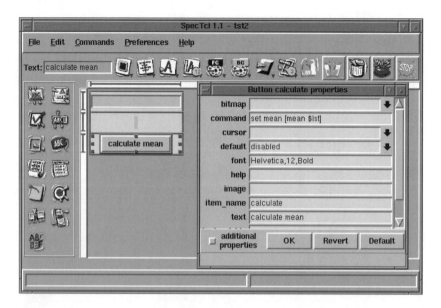

This session resulted in the following code. Adding the procedure definitions for main and addList completes the application.

Example 14.4.1-1

Generated Code

```
#! /bin/sh
# the next line restarts using wish \
exec wish "$0" "$@"

# interface generated by SpecTcl version 1.1 from /tmp/test.ui
#   root     is the parent window for this user interface

proc test_ui {root args} {

        # this treats "." as a special case

        if {$root == "."} {
            set base ""
        } else {
            set base $root
        }
```

```tcl
        entry $base.values \
                -textvariable lst

        label $base.mean \
                -textvariable mean

        button $base.calculate \
                -command {set mean [mean $lst]} \
                -text {calculate mean}

        # Geometry management

        grid $base.values -in $root      -row 1 -column 1
        grid $base.mean -in $root        -row 2 -column 1
        grid $base.calculate -in $root   -row 3 -column 1

        # Resize behavior management

        grid rowconfigure $root 1 -weight 0 -minsize 30
        grid rowconfigure $root 2 -weight 0 -minsize 30
        grid rowconfigure $root 3 -weight 0 -minsize 30
        grid columnconfigure $root 1 -weight 0 -minsize 30
# additional interface code
# end additional interface code

}

# Allow interface to be run "stand-alone" for testing

catch {
    if [info exists embed_args] {
        # we are running in the plugin
        test_ui .
    } else {
        # we are running in stand-alone mode
        if {$argv0 == [info script]} {
            wm title . "Testing test_ui"
            test_ui .
        }
    }
}
```

14.4.2 Spynergy

Eolas.com sells the Spynergy Toolkit for developing Web-based Tcl/Tk applications with a GUI builder that helps you take advantage of the toolkit.

Language	`Tcl`
Primary Site	`http://eolas.com`
Contact	`info@eolas.com`
Tcl Revision Supported	`Tcl: 7.4-8.1 Tk: 4.0-8.1`
Supported Platforms	Unix, Windows, Macintosh
Other Books	*Interactive Web Applications with Tcl/Tk*

The Spynergy Web Developer provides the Tcl programmer with an easy-to-use pure-Tcl/Tk tool for rapidly building dynamic applet-based content to either integrate into your Web pages or run as a stand-alone application. It uses the freely redistributable Spynergy Toolkit to enable you to build sophisticated applications with a minimum of effort.

The Spynergy toolkit includes:

- A highly customizable graphical development environment.
- A visual drag-and-drop graphical applet builder.
- Easy reuse of user-built application component objects.
- An integrated database engine.
- A powerful remote procedure call (RPC) facility.
- Public key authentication capability.
- Demonstration source code.
- Documentation in HTML format.

14.5 Tcl Compilers

There are some problems using Tcl in the commercial world. One is that you need to distribute the source code for your scripts. Another is that users must have the proper version of Tcl installed to run your script.

These compilers generate Tcl bytecode files or complete executable programs. Shipping bytecode files will hide your source, and shipping an executable program allows the user to execute your application without having to install a Tcl interpreter and libraries.

14.5.1 ICEM Tcl Compiler

Language	`executable`
Primary Site	`http://icemcfd.com/tcl/ice.html`
Contact	`tcl@icemcfd.com`
Tcl Revision Supported	`Tcl: 7.4-8.0 Tk: 4.0-8.0`
Supported Platforms	DEC `OSF1 V4.0`, HP-UX `9.01, 10.0`, IBM `AIX 3.2, 4.0, 4.1`, Slackware `Linux 2.3.30 (ELF)`, SGI `IRIX 5.X` and above, Sparc `Solaris 5.3` and up, `Windows NT 4.0` and `Win95`

Interpreted code is fast to develop but runs slowly, whereas compiled code runs quickly but is slow to develop. The ICE Tcl compiler helps you get the best of both worlds.

The compiler comes in two varieties. The version 1.3 compiler compiles Tcl 7.X scripts into C. This can speed up your 7.X script by factors between 5 and 15 depending on the script. The C output is compiled and linked with Tcl libraries to create an executable. The compiled C code produced by the 1.3 compiler is about 50% faster than the byte interpreted Tcl 8.0 code.

The version 2.0 compiler (under development during 1998) will be able to generate Tcl object code, Java code, or C object code and will perform compiler optimizations including *constant folding*, *subexpression elimination*, and *loop unrolling*.

14.5.2 Plus-Patch

Language	`C`
Primary Site	`http://home.wxs.nl/~nijtmans/`

Contact	`Jan.Nijtmans@wxs.nl`
Tcl Revision Supported	`Tcl: 7.6p2-8.1 Tk: 4.2p2-8.1`
Supported Platforms	`Unix, MS-Windows 95, MS-Windows NT`

The plus-patch lets you develop your script in Tcl/Tk and then create an executable object for distribution. It does this by creating a C language wrapper around the script so that you can compile the wrapper and link it with the Tcl/Tk initialization files and libraries.

The executable is not small, but not many GUI programs *are* small. Converting a script to an executable with this package is fast and easy.

The procedure to create a stand-alone application is:

1. Download the plus-patch. You may download either the patches or the complete Tcl/Tk distribution with the patches installed. The complete code is supplied as zip files and as gzipped tar files.

2. If you downloaded the patch kit, apply it to your Tcl/Tk distribution. If you downloaded the complete code with patches applied, unpack the distribution.

3. Compile the patched code. Use the same procedure as for a standard Tcl distribution:

    Cd to the appropriate directory for your OS (`win` or `unix`).

    Follow the instructions in the README file in that directory.

4. Create and debug your Tcl/Tk application.

5. Run `tcl2c` to create a C language wrapper around the Tcl script. The command line will resemble:

    ```
    tcl2c -o myFile.c -tk myFile.tk
    ```

6. Compile and link the new .c file with the Tcl-plus libraries. Under Unix this can be done with a command such as:

    ```
    cc myFile.c /usr/local/lib/libtk8.0.a \
         /usr/local/lib/tcl
    8.0.a \-L/usr/X11R6/lib \
         -lX11 -lsocket -lm -ldl
    ```

Under Windows you can modify the Makefile in the win directory (Makefile.vc for Microsoft Visual C++ or Makefile.bc for Borland C++). The Makefile contains entries to convert the hello.tcl example script into hello.exe. If you change the entries for hello to the name of your program, you can make your package using this Makefile.

If you are using VC++ 5.0, you can use the Visual C++ 5.0 development tools included with the tcl81a2plus.exe distribution.

The hello.tcl script is supplied with the plus-patch kit to demonstrate how an executable can be built.

The tcl2c program turns your Tcl script into a set of data definitions within a new C module. This module includes a main entry point that initializes the Tcl interpreter and then executes your script using a series of Tcl_Eval function calls to pass the script lines to the interpreter.

14.5.3 Scriptics TclPro Compiler

Language	executable
Primary Site	http://www.scriptics.com
Contact	sales@scriptics.com
Tcl Revision Supported	Tcl: 8.0.3 Tk: 8.0.3
Supported Platforms	Unix, Windows NT, Windows 95

The Scriptics TclPro Compiler will turn a Tcl script into a set of Tcl bytecodes that can load and run on any platform. The bytecode files can be read with an extension that is part of the TclPro package. This extension may be distributed by developers but is not part of the standard Tcl 8.0.3 release.

The bytecode files run faster than a pure script program (since there is no need for the just-in-time compilation) and are effective in concealing your program.

In the first beta release of TclPro Compiler the bytecode file may be slightly larger than the original script file. The bytecode file is generated as an ASCII representation of the binary bytecodes. The official release of the Tcl Compiler will produce smaller files.

14.6 Packaging Tools

One of the other problems with distributing Tcl packages and applications has been associated with installation. Some packages require that users modify a Makefile to define where the libraries and interpreter are stored on their system. Other packages have a start-up script that will either query the user or search in known places for libraries and interpreters.

Jan Nijtmans's plus-patch provides one solution to that problem by linking a Tcl script with the libraries and interpreters to create a single file executable.

This technique has problems if your application requires several files, rather than a single script.

TclTutor uses the plus-patch and tcl2c to create an installation program that moves the TclTutor program, lesson files, etc. into an installation directory. This works fairly well, but experience shows about 1 in 500 users misinstall the program.

14.6.1 Scriptics TclPro Wrapper

Language	executable
Primary Site	http://www.scriptics.com
Contact	sales@scriptics.com
Tcl Revision Supported	Tcl: 8.0.3 Tk: 8.0.3
Supported Platforms	Unix, Windows NT, Windows 95

The Scriptics TclPro Wrapper combines a set of Tcl script files, Tcl bytecode files, images, etc. into a single executable file that combines the functionality of an archive and an application. You can even include your own tclsh (or wish) interpreter and libraries in this executable file.

You can declare one script file within the bundle of files combined by TclPro Wrapper to be evaluated by the Tcl interpreter. This file may be evaluated by the interpreter included in the bundle or by an interpreter already resident on the user's system. The other files in the bundle can be accessed as though they were in the directory with the script being evaluated and can be accessed with the open and source command, as image files, etc.

This is a clean way to package a set of scripts and their associated files. It solves the installation problems that have plagued Tcl developers over the years.

14.7 Tcl Extension Generator: SWIG

Language	C++
Primary Site	http://www.swig.org swig.html
Contact	beazley@cs.utah.edu
Tcl Revision Supported	Tcl: 7.3-8.1 Tk: 3.6-8.1
Supported Platforms	Unix (gcc), Windows 95 or NT, Mac (PowerPC)

Chapter 12 of this book describes how to build a Tcl extension. Although the Tcl interface is very easy to work with, building an extension around a large library can mean writing a lot of code.

The SWIG (Simplified Wrapper and Interface Generator) program can read a slightly modified include file and generate the Tcl interface code to link with the library.

SWIG will create Tcl commands that can access pointers and structures, as well as the standard Tcl data types. With a command line option, SWIG can put the new commands into a private namespace.

SWIG can generate interfaces for almost any data construct. The package is very rich and complete.

The following example demonstrates how easily an extension can be created with SWIG. This example shows a subset of what SWIG can do.

If you have an image analysis library, it would probably have a function to translate points from one location to another. The function and data definitions in the include file might resemble this:

```
typedef struct point_s {
    float x;
    float y;
} point;

int translatePoint(float xOffset, float yOffset,
    point *original, point *translated);
```

To convert the structure and function definition into a SWIG definition file, you would add these items to a .h file:

- A module definition name.

    ```
    %module three_d
    ```

- An optional command to generate the AppInit function.

    ```
    %include tclsh.i
    ```

- Inline code for the include files that will be required to compile the wrapper.

    ```
    %{
    #include "imageOps.h"
    %}
    ```

- Dummy constructor–destructor functions for structures for which SWIG should create interfaces.

When this is done, the definition file would resemble:

```
%module imageOps
%include tclsh.i
%{
#include "imageOps.h"
%}
typedef struct point_s {
    float x;
    float y;
    point();
    ~point();
```

```
} point;

int translatePoint(float xOffset, float yOffset,
        point *original, point *translated);
```

This input is all SWIG needs to generate code to create the structures and invoke the translatePoint function.

The last steps in creating a new extension are compiling the wrapper and linking with the Tcl libraries:

```
$>   swig imageOps.i
$>   cc imageOps_wrap.c -limageOps -ltcl -ldl -lm
```

When this is done, you are ready to write scripts to use the new commands.

The new extension has these new commands:

Syntax: new_point

new_point   Create a new point structure, and return the handle for this structure.

Syntax: point_x_set *pointHandle value*
Syntax: point_y_set *pointHandle value*

point_*member*_set
           Sets the value of the member field of the point structure.

pointHandle
           The handle returned by the new_point command.

value   The value to assign to this member of the structure.

Syntax: point_x_get *pointHandle*
Syntax: point_y_get *pointHandle*

point_*member*_get
           Returns the value of the member member of the point structure.

pointHandle   The handle returned by the new_point command.

Syntax: delete_point *pointHandle*

delete_point   Destroys the point structure referenced by the handle.

pointHandle   The handle returned by the new_point command.

Syntax: translatePoint *xOffset yOffset originalPoint translatedPoint*

translatePoint

> Translates a point by xOffset and yOffset distances and puts the new values into the provided structure.

xOffset   The distance to translate in the X direction.

yOffset   The distance to translate in the Y direction.

originalPoint

> The handle returned by new_point with the location of the point to translate.

translatedPoint

> The handle returned by new_point. The results of the translation will be placed in this structure.

A script to use these new commands would resemble the following:

Example 14.7-1

Example Script

```
#
# Define the original point

set original [new_point]
point_x_set $original 100.0
point_y_set $original 200.0

#
# Create a point for the results

set translated [new_point]
#
# Perform the translation

translatePoint  50 -50 $original $translated

#
```

```
# Display the results:

puts "translated position is:\
    [point_x_get $translated] [point_y_get $translated]"
```

Script Output

translated position is: 150.0 150.0

14.8 Bottom Line

- There are many tools available to help you develop Tcl/Tk applications.
- Information about tools and extensions can be found in: http://www.neosoft.com, http://www.scriptics.com/resource/, the announcements in the newsgroup comp.lang.tcl, and the FAQs at http://www.purl.org/NET/Tcl-FAQ
- You can reformat your Tcl code with frink or tcl_cruncher.
- You can check your code for syntax errors with tclCheck, tcl_lint, and tclparse.
- You can debug Tcl scripts with debug, tuba, TdDebug, and TclPro Debugger.
- You can shorten your GUI development time with the GUI generators SpecTcl and Spynergy.
- You can convert scripts to executable binary code with the ICEM compiler, Jan Nijtmans's plus-patch, or the TclPro Compiler.
- You can develop extensions quickly with the SWIG extension generator.

Tips and Techniques

Every language has its strengths and weaknesses, and every programmer develops ways to take advantage of the strengths and work around the weaknesses. This chapter will cover some of the ways you can use Tcl more effectively to accomplish your tasks.

This chapter will discuss debugging, some common mistakes, some techniques to make your code more maintainable, and a bunch of odds and ends that haven't been covered in previous chapters.

15.1 Debugging Techniques

The debuggers discussed in Chapter 14 are very useful tools but are not the only way to debug code. Tcl has some features that make it easy to debug code without a debugger.

Because of the interpreted nature of Tcl, you may find it easier to do much of your debugging without a debugger. Since there is no separate compilation stage in Tcl, you can easily add a few debugging lines and rerun your test.

Here are a few techniques for debugging code without a debugger.

Examine variables when they are accessed with the `trace` command.

Sometimes you know that variable `foo` has an invalid value by the time it's used in procedure `bar`. You know the value of `foo` was valid when it was set in procedure `baz` and *something* changed the value but you don't know what.

The `trace` command will let you evaluate a script whenever the variable `foo` is accessed. This makes it easy to track which procedures are using (and changing) variables.

Syntax: `trace variable` *name operations command*

`trace variable`	Puts a `trace` on a variable that will cause a procedure to be evaluated whenever the variable is accessed.
name	The name of the variable to be traced.
operations	Whenever a selected operation on the variable occurs, the *command* will be evaluated. `Operation` may be one of:

	`r`	Evaluate the command whenever the variable is read.
	`w`	Evaluate the command whenever the variable is written.
	`u`	Evaluate the command whenever the variable is unset.

command	A command to evaluate when the variable is accessed. The command will be invoked with three arguments:

	`name1`	The name of the variable.
	`index`	If the variable is an associative array, this will be the index of the associative array. If the variable is a scalar variable, this will be an empty string.
	`operation`	A single letter to denote the operation that triggered this evaluation.

The following example shows how the `trace` command can be used with a procedure (`traceProc`) to display part of the call stack and the new value when a variable is modified.

If you find yourself using traces frequently, you may want to examine the `OAT` extension and `TclProp` package from the University of Minnesota (`http://www.cs.umn.edu/research/GIMME/tclprop.html`). The `OAT` extension enhances the `trace` command, allowing all Tcl and Tk objects (such as widgets) to be traced. The `TclProp` package (among other features) lets you watch for variables being changed with a single line command instead of needing to declare a script.

Example 15.1-1

```
#
# The procedure to invoke from trace
#

proc traceProc {varName index operation} {
    upvar $varName var
    set lvl [info level]
    incr lvl -1;
    puts "Variable $varName is being modified in:
        '[info level $lvl]'"
    if {$lvl > 1} {
        incr lvl -1;
        puts "    Which was invoked from: '[info level $lvl]'"
    }
    puts "The current value of $varName is: $var\n"
}
```

Example Script

```
#
# A procedure to modify the traced Variable
#

proc modifyVariable {newVal} {
    global tracedVariable
    set tracedVariable $newVal
}
#
```

```
# A procedure to call the variable changing procedure,
#   to demonstrate getting information further up the
#   call stack.
#

proc otherProc {newVal} {
    modifyVariable $newVal
}

#
# A variable to watch.
#

global tracedVariable

#
# Create a trace on the tracedVariable variable
#
trace variable tracedVariable w traceProc

# Now, modify the variable, twice within procedures,
# and once from the global scope.

# This will modify the variable two levels deep
# in the call stack.

otherProc One

# This will modify the variable one level down the call stack.

modifyVariable Two

# Notice that the change from global scope reports itself as
# coming from the 'traceproc' command

set tracedVariable Three
```

Script Output

Variable tracedVariable is being modified in:
**   'modifyVariable One'**
**   Which was invoked from: 'otherProc One'**
The current value of tracedVariable is: One

Variable tracedVariable is being modified in:
**   'modifyVariable Two'**

```
The current value of tracedVariable is: Two

Variable tracedVariable is being modified in:
        'traceProc tracedVariable {} w'
The current value of tracedVariable is: Three
```

Generate a call stack with the `info level` command.

Sometimes a bug appears in a procedure that is invoked with bad arguments. In order to fix the bug, you need to know which code invoked the procedure. You can learn this with the `info level` command.

Syntax: info level *?levelValue?*

info level   If invoked with no *levelValue* argument, info level returns the stack level that is currently being evaluated.

If invoked with a *levelValue* argument, info level returns the name and arguments of the procedure at that stack level.

levelValue   If *levelValue* is a positive value, it represents the level in the procedure stack to return. If it is a negative value, it represents a stack location relative to the current position in the stack.

In Example 15.1-4, the bit 8 test contains code that will display the procedure call stack.

Run a script in interactive mode.

You can invoke a script from a `tclsh` or `wish` interpreter with the `source` command. When a script is invoked with `source` command, the interpreter returns you to the interactive prompt instead of exiting on an error.

If your script requires command line arguments, you can set the `argv` and `argc` variables before you source the script, as shown in the example below. The example shows a simple debugging session that tries to open a nonexistent file, and then evaluates the procedure that would be called if a valid file name were provided.

Example 15.1-2

Example Script

```
proc processLineProcedure {line} {
    puts "Processing ``$line''"
}

puts "There are $argc arguments to this script"
puts "The arguments are: $argv"

set fileName [lindex $argv 0]
set infile [open $fileName "r"]

while {![eof $infile]} {
    set len [gets $infile line]
    if {$len > 0} {
        processLineProcedure $line
    }
}
```

Debugging Session

```
%> tclsh
%   set argv [list badFileName -option value]
badFileName -option value
%   set argc 3
3
%   source e15_1_2.tcl
There are 3 arguments to this script
The arguments are: badFileName -option value
couldn't open "badFileName": no such file or directory
%   set errorInfo
couldn't open "badFileName": no such file or directory
    while executing
"open $fileName "r""
    (file "e15_1_2.tcl" line 9)
    invoked from within
"source e15_1_2.tcl"
%   processLineProcedure "This is a first Line from a file"
Processing This is a first Line from a file
%
```

Use `puts` to print the value of variables or lines that are to be evaluated.
This technique may not be elegant, but it works in all environments. You may need to print the data to a file instead of the screen if you are trying to debug an application that runs for a long time, does something strange, recovers, and continues running.

Some of the variants on using `puts` to track program flow and variables include:

- A conditional `puts` in a procedure.

  This technique is useful while you are in the latter stages of debugging a system. With this technique you can leave your debugging code in place, while confirming the behavior without the extra output.

Example 15.1-3

```
proc debugPuts {args} {
    global DEBUG

    if { [info exists DEBUG] && $DEBUG } {
        puts "$args"
    }
}
```

- A bitmapped conditional.

  A bitmap can be used to control how much information is printed while the script is running.

  This is another technique that is useful when you don't always want to see a lot of output, but for tracking down some bugs, you need all the help you can get.

  The next example shows a procedure that will print different amounts of information depending on the value of `stateArray(debugLevel)`.

  If bit 8 is set, a call stack is displayed. Note that a positive (absolute) level is used for the `info level` command rather than a negative (relative) level. This is a workaround for the fact that Tcl generates an error when you try to access level 0 via a relative level offset but will accept 0 as an absolute level.

  For example, a procedure that is called from the global level is at level 1 (as returned by `[info level]`). If the `info level` command is invoked within that procedure as `info level -1` Tcl will generate an error, but if the `info level` command is invoked as `info level 0` Tcl will return the procedure name and argument that invoked the procedure.

Example 15.1-4

```
proc debugPuts {args} {
    global stateArray

    # If lower bit set, print the message(s)

    if {$stateArray(debugLevel) & 1} {
        puts "DEBUG Message: $args"
    }

    # If bit two is set, print the proc name and args that
    #    invoked debugPuts

    if {$stateArray(debugLevel) & 2} {
        set level [info level]
    incr level -1;
    puts "DEBUG Invoked from:: [info level $level]"
    }

    # If bit four is set, print the contents of stateArray

    if {$stateArray(debugLevel) & 4} {
    foreach index [array names stateArray] {
       puts "DEBUG: stateArray($index): $stateArray($index)"
    }
    }

    # If bit 8 is set, print the call stack

    if {$stateArray(debugLevel) & 8} {
        set level [info level]
    for {set l 1} {$l < $level} {incr l} {
        puts "DEBUG CallStack $l: [info level $l]"
    }
    }
}
```

Example Script

```
proc topProc {arg1 arg2} {
    lowerProc three four five
}
```

```
proc lowerProc {args} {
    debugPuts "Message from a proc called from a proc"
}

set stateArray(debugLevel) 15

topProc one two
```

Script Output

```
DEBUG Message: {Message from a proc called from a proc}
DEBUG Invoked from:: lowerProc three four five
DEBUG: stateArray(debugLevel): 15
DEBUG CallStack 1: topProc one two
DEBUG CallStack 2: lowerProc three four five
```

Printing every line.

To debug some nasty problems, you may want to display each line before it's evaluated. Sometimes, seeing the line with the substitutions done makes the script's behavior obvious.

You can modify your script to display each line beofre executing it by duplicating each line of code and adding a string resembling

```
puts "WILL EVAL:
```

to the beginning of the duplicated line, and a close quote to the end of the line. This modification is easily done with an editor that supports macros (like Emacs) or you can modify your script with another Tcl script.

The caveat with this technique is to be careful that you don't accidentally perform an action within your puts. For example:

Example 15.1-5

```
# This will evaluate the modifyDatabase procedure.
#   It will print the status return, not the procedure call.

puts "WILL EVAL set status [modifyDatabase $newData]"

# This prints the command and the value of newData

puts "WILL EVAL: set status \[modifyDatabase $newData\]"

set status [modifyDatabase $newData]
```

Extract portions of your script for unit testing.

Since Tcl does not have a separate compilation stage, unit testing can be more easily performed in Tcl than in languages such as C that might need to have more of the program infrastructure in place in order to link a test program.

Create a new window (using the `toplevel` command) to interact with your application.

When using the `wish` interpreter, you can open a new top-level window to interact with your script. This window can give you all the facilities that you'd get from running a script in an interactive wish interpreter.

The next example shows a procedure that opens a new window. This procedure can be invoked by a button, as shown in the following application code snippet. The graphic shows this debugging window being used to debug the `radiobutton` example from Chapter 8 (Example 8.8.1.1-1).

Example 15.1-6
___

Debugging Window

```
# Create a window to use to interact with the running script

proc makeInteractionWindow {} {

    # Create a toplevel window to hold these widgets
    set topWindow [toplevel .topInteraction]

    # Create an entry widget for commands to execute,
    #       and a label for the entry widget

    set cmdLabel [label $topWindow.cmdLabel -text "Command"]
    set cmd [entry $topWindow.cmd -textvariable cmdString \
        -width 60]
    grid $cmdLabel -row 0 -column 0
    grid $cmd -row 0 -column 1 -columnspan 3

    # Create a scrolling text window for the command output,

    set output [text $topWindow.output -height 5 -width 60 \
        -relief raised]
    set outputLabel [label $topWindow.outputLabel \
        -text "Command Result"]
    set sb [scrollbar $topWindow.sb -command "$output yview"]
    $output configure -yscrollcommand "$sb set"
```

```
    grid $outputLabel -row 1 -column 0
    grid $output -row 1 -column 1 -columnspan 3
    grid $sb -row 1 -column 4 -sticky ns

    # Create buttons to clear the command,
    #    execute the command and
    #    close the toplevel window.

    set clear [button $topWindow.clear -text "Clear Command" \
            -command { set cmdString "" }]
    # The command for the $go button is placed in quotes to
    #    allow "$output" to be replaced by the actual output
    #    window name. "$output see end" scrolls the window to
    #    the bottom after each command (to display the command
    #    output).

    set go [button $topWindow.go -text "Do Command" \
        -command "$output insert end \"\[uplevel #0 \
                \[list eval \$cmdString\]\n\]\"; \
                $output see end; \
                "]

    set close [button $topWindow.close -text "Close" \
        -command "destroy $topWindow"]

    grid $clear -row 2 -column 1
    grid $go    -row 2 -column 2
    grid $close -row 2 -column 3

    # bind the Return key in the command entry widget to
    #    behave the same as clicking the $go button.
    #    NOTE: <Enter> is the "cursor enters widget"
    #    event, NOT the Enter key

    bind $cmd "<Return>" "$go invoke"
}
```

Application

```
# Initialize application
# ...
#

if {[lsearch $argv -debug] != -1} {
    button .debugging -text "Open InteractionWindow" \
```

```
        -command makeInteractionWindow
}
```

Script Results

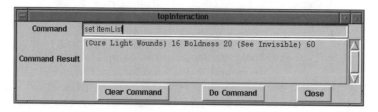

Use a second **wish** interpreter for remote debugging.

The send command allows you to send a command from one wish interpreter to another. The command will be evaluated in the target interpreter and the results will be returned to the source interpreter.

This feature lets you use one wish interpreter in interactive mode to debug a script running in another interpreter. You can display variables, evaluate procedures, load new procedures, etc.

Syntax: send *interp cmd*

send   Send a command to another wish interpreter, and return the results of that command.

interp   The name of the destination interpreter. You can get a list of the wish interpreters currently running on a system with the winfo interps command.

cmd   A command to be evaluated in the destination interpreter. Remember to enclose the cmd string in curly braces if you want substitutions to be performed in the destination interpreter, not the source interpreter.

All of the preceding techniques can be done in a remote interpreter using the send command. You can print out data, invoke procedures, check the state of the after queue, or even source new versions of procedures.

Note that using the send command on a Unix system requires that you use xauth security (or build wish with a reduced security). Under Windows, versions of Tk prior to 8.1 do not support the send command.

15.2 Tcl as a Glue Language: The exec Command

Although almost any application can be written in Tcl, not all applications *should* be written in Tcl. Some applications should be written using Tcl with an extension, and some should be written as stand-alone programs using Tcl as a glue language to join the programs together.

Scripting languages are extremely useful for applications that require gluing several pieces of functionality into a new application. They are less well suited to creating base functionality such as

- Arithmetic-based algorithms (generating checksums or compressing files).
- Large data applications (subsampling images).
- Controlling hardware (device drivers).

Tcl/Tk's strength is how easy it makes merging several libraries and stand-alone programs into a complex application. This merging can be done by creating new Tcl extensions or by using Tcl to glue several stand-alone programs into a new application.

If the functionality you need involves several functions and is available in an existing library, it's probably best to make a Tcl extension wrapper to access the library. See Chapter 12 on writing extensions and Chapter 14 on the SWIG package for automating creating extensions from libraries.

The extensions you create can either be linked into a new interpreter or merged at run time with the load command. Note that you can use the load command only if your operating system supports dynamically loaded libraries (.so under Linux and Solaris, .dll under Windows).

If a stand-alone application or two exist that do a subset of what you need, you can use these existing applications with a Tcl script to control and extend them to perform the tasks you need done.

Many applications are best written using Tcl code for some functionality, an extension or two, and invoking stand-alone programs when necessary. For example, I use a Tk script to control the PPP connections on my Unix system. It uses the BLT extension to create an activity bar chart, invokes several stand-alone programs to initiate PPP connections and monitor the activity, and has some Tcl code that tracks the number of connection hours.

The caveat with calling stand-alone programs from your script is that it can limit the portability of the script. For instance, a script that uses ps to monitor active processes and display the top CPU users will require different ps arguments for BSD and System V–based Unixes and won't run at all on a Macintosh or Windows platform.

The command that lets you merge existing stand-alone programs into a new application is the exec command. The exec command will invoke new programs in a subprocess and return the program output to the Tcl interpreter as the result of the command. If the subtask exits with a nonzero status (an error status), then the exec command will generate an error. You can invoke a single program with the exec command, or a series of commands where the output of one program becomes the input to the next program with the Unix pipe symbol (|).

The argument to the exec command is either an exec option, a command to execute as a subprocess, an argument for the commands, or a pipeline descriptor.

Syntax: exec *?-options? arg1 ?arg2...argn?*

exec	Execute arguments in a subproccess.
-options	The exec command supports two options:

-keepnewline

> Normally, a trailing newline character is deleted from the program output returned by the exec command. If this argument is set, the trailing newline is retained.

--

> Denotes the last option. All subsequent arguments will be treated as subprocess program names or arguments.

arg　　　　These arguments can be either a program name, a program argument, or a pipeline descriptor. There are many pipeline descriptors. Some of the commonly used ones are:

|　　Separates distinct programs in the command line. The standard output of the program on the left side of the pipe symbol (|) will be used as the standard input for the program on the right of the pipe symbol.

<fileName　　The first program in the list will use the contents of fileName as the standard input.

>fileName　　The standard output from the last program in the list will be written to *fileName*.

The following examples create compressed archives of files in a directory under Unix or Windows using the exec command.

Example 15.2-1

Creating a Gzipped Tar Archive under Unix

```
# This script is called with the name of a directory to
#   archive as the first argument in the command line,
#   and the name of the archive as the second argument.

set directory [lindex $argv 0]
set archive [lindex $argv 1]

# Get a list of the files to include in the archive.

set fllst [glob $directory/*]

# Create the tar archive, and gzip it.

eval exec tar -cvf $archive $fllst
exec gzip $archive
```

Example 15.2-2

Creating a Zip Archive under Windows

```
# This script is called with the name of a directory to
```

```
#    archive as the first argument in the command line,
#    and the name of the archive as the second argument.
set directory [lindex $argv 0]
set zipfile [lindex $argv 1]

# The file "distfiles" will contain a list of files for
#    this archive.
set outfl [open distfiles "w"]

# Get a list of the files to include in the archive.
set fllst [glob $directory/*]

# And write that list into the contents file, one
#    filename per line
foreach fl $fllst {
  puts $outfl "$fl"
}
close $outfl

# Execute the winzip program to make an archive.
eval "exec C:/winzip/winzip32.exe -a $zipfile @distfiles"
```

15.3 Common Mistakes

There are several common mistakes programmers make as they learn Tcl. Cameron Laird has collected many of these from the questions and answers posted in comp.lang.tcl, at http://Starbase.NeoSoft.COM/ ~claird/comp.lang.tcl/fmm.html). This section is a sampling of common errors not yet discussed in the previous chapters.

Problems using the exec command.

The previous description of the exec command looks straightforward, but there are some common mistakes people make trying to use the exec command.

- The tclsh shell is not the Unix shell.

  Many problems appear when people try to use shell expansions or shell escapes with the exec command.

For example, the wrong way to write the `exec tar...` command in the previous example would be:

```
exec tar -cvf $archive $directory/*
```

In this case, the `tclsh` shell would substitute the name of the directory (for example, `foo`) for `$directory` and would pass that string (`foo/*`) to the `tar` program. The `tar` program would fail to identify any file named "*" in that directory. When you type a command with a "*" at the shell prompt (or in a sh script), the shell automatically expands the * to the list of files. Under Tcl, this expansion is done by the `glob` command.

In the same way, if you try to group an argument to `exec` with single quotes it will fail. The single quote has meaning to the Unix shell interpreter (disable substitutions) but is just another character to the Tcl interpreter.

- The `tclsh` shell is not `COMMAND.COM`.

  This is the Windows equivalent of the previous mistake. Remember that the `DIR`, `COPY`, and `DEL` commands are part of `COMMAND.COM`, not stand-alone programs. You can't get a directory within a Tcl script with a command like:

  ```
  # Won't work
  set filelist [exec dir C:*.*]
  ```

  There is no `DIR.EXE` or `DIR.COM` for the Tcl shell to execute.

  The best workaround for this is to use the Tcl `glob`, `file copy`, `file delete`, and `file rename` commands. Another workaround (if you really need the `DIR` output) is to `exec` the `COMMAND.COM` program with the `/C` option. This option tells the `COMMAND.COM` program to evaluate the string after the `/C` as though it had been typed in at a command prompt.

  ```
  # This will get a list of files
  set filelist [glob C:/*.*]

  # This will get the output of the dir command
  set filelist [exec COMMAND.COM /C dir C:*.*]
  ```

  Note that `filelist` will contain all the output from the `DIR`, not just a list of the files.

- A Tcl list is passed as a single argument to a procedure.

Notice the `eval` in the `eval exec tar -cvf $archive $fllst` line in the previous Unix example. If you simply used

```
# won't work.
exec tar -cvf $archive $fllst
```

The contents of `fllst` would be passed as a single argument to the `exec` command, which would pass them as a single argument to the `tar` program. Since there is no file named `file1 file2 file3..`, this results in an error.

The `eval` command concatenates all of the arguments into one string and then evaluates that string. This changes the list from a single argument to as many arguments as there are file names in the list.

- `exec cd $newDirectory` is probably *not* what you want.

  The change directory command is a part of a shell. It changes the current directory within the shell. It's not an external program. Use the built-in `Tcl` command `cd` if you want to change the working directory for your script.

Calculating the time: Numbers in Tcl.

Numbers in Tcl can be represented in octal, decimal, or hexadecimal. The base of a number is determined by the first (or first two) digits.

If the first digit is not a 0, then the number is interpreted as a decimal number.

If the first digit is a 0 and the second character is x, then the number is interpreted as a hexadecimal number.

If the first digit is a 0 and the second digit is between 1 and 7, then the number is interpreted as an octal number.

If the first digit is a 0 and the second digit is 8 or 9, then this is an error.

In versions of Tcl without the `clock` command, it was common to split a time or date string and try to do calculations on the parts of the time. This would work most of the time. Note that at 08:00 the command

```
set minutes [expr [lindex [split $time ":"] 0]*60]
```

will generate an error, since `08` is not a valid octal number.

If you need to convert a time/date to seconds in versions of Tcl more recent than 7.5, you should use the `clock format` and `clock scan` commands.

If you need to process time and date in an older version of Tcl, or if you are reading data that may have leading zeros (the number of cents in a commercial transaction, for instance), use the `string trimleft` command to remove the leading zeros. In the following example, note the test for an empty string. If the initial value is `000`, `string trimleft` will remove all the zeros, leaving an empty string. An empty string will generate an error if you try to use it in a calculation.

```
set value [getNumberWithLeadingZeros]
set value [string trimleft $value "0"]
if {$value == ""} {set value 0}
```

`lappend`, `append`, and `incr` are the only Tcl commands that modify an argument.

The commands `lreplace`, `string`, and `expr` all return a new value without modifying the argument.

```
# This WON'T remove the first list entry
lreplace $list 0 0 ""

# This WILL remove the first list entry
set list [lreplace $list 0 0 ""]

# This WON'T shorten the string
string range $myString 5 end

# This WILL shorten the string
set myString [string range $myString 5 end]

# This WON'T change the value of counter
expr $counter + 1

# These commands WILL change the value of counter
set counter [expr $counter + 1]
incr counter
```

The `incr` command works with integers.

Some commands (for example, commands that return locations and widths of objects on a canvas) return float values that `incr` won't handle.

You can convert a floating-point number to an integer with the `expr round` and `expr int` commands, or you can use the `expr` command to increment a variable.

Remember that you must reassign the new value to the variable when using the `expr` command.

```
set variable [expr $variable+1]
```

The upvar command takes a name, not a value.

When you invoke a procedure that uses the `upvar` command, you must pass the variable name, not the $*varName*.

```
proc useUpvar {variableName} {
    upvar $variableName localVariable

    set localVariable 0
}

# This will set the value of x to 0
useUpvar x

# This will not change the value of x
useUpvar $x
```

Changes to widgets do not appear until the event loop is processed.

If your `wish` script is making many modifications to the display within a procedure, you may need to add the `update` command to the looping. This will not only update the screen and show the progress but also scan for user input (like someone clicking an abort button).

This is discussed in more detail in Chapter 8.

15.4 Coding Tips and Techniques

There are many ways to write a program. Some techniques work better with a particular language than others. Here are some techniques that work well with Tcl.

Use the interpreter to parse input.

Tcl is one of the very few languages that provides the script writer with access to a parse engine. This can save you time (and help you write more robust code) in several ways.

- Use procedures instead of `switch` statements to parse input.

  If you are accustomed to C programming, you are used to constructs like this:

```
while {[gets stdin cmdLine]} {
    set cmd [lindex $cmdLine 0]
    switch $cmd {
        "cmd1"        {cmd1Procedure $cmdLine}
        "cmd2"        {cmd2Procedure $cmdLine}

        ...

    }
}
```

  Whenever you add a new command using a `switch` statement, you need to add a new pattern to the `switch` command.

  In Tcl, you can write a loop to parse input like this:

```
while {[gets stdin cmdLine]} {
    set cmd [lindex $cmdLine 0]
    set cmdName [format "%sProcedure" $cmd]

    # Confirm that the command exists before trying to eval it.
    if {[info command $cmdName] != ""} {
        eval $cmdName $cmdLine
    }
}
```

  When the requirements change and you need to add a new command, you simply add a new procedure without changing the command parsing code.

- Use the `info complete` command to match quotes, braces, and brackets.

  The `info complete` command will return a 1 if a command is complete and a 0 if there are opening quotes, braces, or brackets without the appropriate closing quotes, braces, or brackets.

The `info complete` is designed to determine whether a Tcl command has unmatched quotes, braces, or brackets, but it can be used to test any line of text that may include nested braces, etc.

- Use `eval` to set command line arguments.

  Again, if you are familiar with C, you are familiar with parsing command line arguments using code that resembles this:

```
foreach arg $argv {
    switch $arg -- {
        "-alpha"        {set alphaMode 1}
        "-debug"        {set debugMode 1}
        ...
    }
}
```

When you need to add a new command line option, you need to add new code to the switch statement.

In Tcl, you can write code that resembles this:

```
foreach arg $argv {
    set varName [format "%sMode" $arg]
    eval set $varName 1
}
```

With this example, adding new options does not require changing the parse code.

Alternatively, if you have more complex command line requirements, you can use a first-letter convention to define how an argument should be processed. For example:

-SvarName Value

> Set the variable *varName* to *Value*.

-Aindex Value

> Set the state array *index* to *Value*.

The code to parse this style of command line would resemble this:

```
foreach {arg value} $argv {
    set type [string range $arg 1 1]
    set name [string range $arg 2 end]
    switch $type {
```

```
   "A"        {
         eval set stateArray($name) $value
   }
   "S"     {
         eval set $name $value
   }
   default {
       error "Unrecognized option: $arg"
   }
 }
}
```

With this style of command line parsing, you can set any variable from the command line without changing any code.

Note that this technique will not generate an error if you misspell the index or variable name in the command line. The error will be silent and evaluating the script may produce unexpected results, because the command line initialized a variable that is never used.

One method of protecting against this failure mode is to set default values for all the parameters that may be set from a command line and allow only existing variables and array indices to be modified.

Code to do this would resemble:

```
proc setDefaults {} {
    global stateArray

    set stateArray(firstIndex) 1
    set stateArray(secondIndex) 2
    # ...
}

foreach {arg value} $argv {
    set type [string range $arg 1 1]
    set name [string range $arg 2 end]

    switch $type {
      "A"        {
                if {[info exists stateArray($name)]} {
                    eval set stateArray($name) $value
                } else {
```

```
                    puts "$name is an invalid index"
                    puts "Use one of [array names stateArray]"
            }
        }
        "S"   {
                if {[info exists $name]} {
                    eval set $name $value
                } else {
                    puts "$name is an invalid variable name"
                }
        }
        default {
            error "Unrecognized option: $arg"
        }
    }
}
```

Use a single array for global variables.

Rather than use simple variables for global variables, group all the shared variables that a set of procedures will need in a single array variable.

This technique reduces the possibility of variable name collisions when you merge sets of code and makes it easy to add new variables when necessary without requiring changes to the global commands in all the procedures that will use the new value.

```
# Don't use this technique

proc initializeParameters {
    global height width linecolor
    set height 100
    set width 200
    set linecolor blue
}

# Use this technique
proc initializeParameters {
    global globalParams
    set globalParams(height) 100
    set globalParams(width) 200
    set globalParams(linecolor) blue
}
```

Using a single associative array lets you save the program's state with a loop resembling this:

```
foreach index [array names myStateArray] {
    puts $saveFile \
        "set myStateArray($index) {$myStateArray($index)}"
}
```

Saving the state in a data-driven loop allows you to add new indices to the state variable without needing to modify the save and restore state functions. Note that when the myStateArray values are saved as Tcl commands, the restore state function is simply source *saveFileName*.

Declare globals in a single location.

If you use more than a few global variables, it can become difficult to keep all the procedures that use them in sync as new variables are added.

The names of the global variables can be kept in a single global list, and that list can be evaluated to set the global variables.

```
set globalList {errorInfo errorCode argv argc stateArray1 \
stateArray2}

proc someProcedure {args} {
    global globalList ; eval global $globalList
}
```

Generate a GUI from data, not from code.

Some parts of a GUI need to be generated from code, but others can be generated on the fly from lists. For example, a menu can be generated with a set of commands like this:

```
set cmdButton [menubutton .cmdButton -text "Select cmds" \
    -menu .cmdButton.mnu]
set cmdMenu [menu $cmdButton.mnu]

$cmdMenu add command -label {Selection One} -command ProcOne
$cmdMenu add command -label {Selection Two} -command ProcTwo
```

Or, a menu could be generated with a loop and a list like this:

```
set cmdMenuList [list \
    {Selection One} {procOne} {Selection Two} {procTwo}]

set cmdButton [menubutton .cmdButton -text "Select cmds" \
```

```
              -menu  .cmdButton.mnu]
set cmdMenu [menu $cmdButton.mnu]

foreach {label cmd} $cmdMenuList {
    $cmdMenu add command -label $label -command $cmd
}
```

If there are more than three items in the menu, the list-driven code is smaller. The list-driven code is also simpler to maintain, because the list of labels and commands is more tightly localized. Finally, if the list can be generated at run time from other data, it can reduce the amount of code that needs to be modified when the program needs to be changed.

Handling platform-specific code.

Tcl has excellent multiple platform support. In many circumstances you can use built-in Tcl commands that are identical across all platforms. However, sometimes there are spots where you need to write platform-specific code. For instance, in TclTutor, you can click on a word to get online help. Under Unix, this is done using exec to run TkMan as a subprocess. Under Windows, it is done using exec to run winhlp32.exe.

The tcl_platform(platform) array variable (discussed in Chapter 4) contains the name of the platform where your code is being evaluated. Once you've determined the platform, there are several options for evaluating platform-specific code:

- Place platform-specific scripts in a variable, and evaluate the contents of the variable in the mainline code.

  This works well when the platform-specific script is short.

```
switch $tcl_platform(platform) {
    "unix"     {
                 set helpString "TkMan $topic"
    }
    "win"      {
                 set helpString "winhlp32 -k$topic $helpFile"
    }
}

...

if {[userRequestsHelp]} {eval exec $helpString}
```

- Place platform-specific code within `tcl_platform(platform)` test.
  - If the platform-specific code is more complex, you may prefer to put a script within the test, like this:

```
if {[userRequestsHelp]} {
    switch $tcl_platform(platform) {
        "unix"      {
            exec TkMan $topic
        }
        "win"       {
            exec winhlp32 -k$topic $helpFile
        }
    }
}
```

  ...

  - If there are large amounts of platform-specific code, those scripts can be placed in separate files and loaded at run time.

```
# A platform-specific procedure named HelpProc is defined in
# each of these script files.

switch $tcl_platform(platform) {
    "unix"  {
            source "unix_Procedures.tcl"
    }
    "win"   {
            source "win_Procedures.tcl"
    }
    "mac"   {
            source "mac_Procedures.tcl"
    }
}

if {[userRequestsHelp]} {HelpProc}
```

15.5 Bottom Line

This chapter has discussed several tricks, techniques, and tips for writing efficient and maintainable Tcl scripts. These include:

- You can use other wish interpreters or new windows to debug a wish application.
- Some applications should be written as separate programs, invoked with `exec`, rather than as extensions or Tcl scripts.
- The Tcl interpreter is not the Unix command shell or COMMAND.COM.
- Be aware of possible leading zeros in numbers.
- Most Tcl commands do not modify the contents of their arguments. `append`, `lappend`, and `incr` are the exceptions.
- Use the Tcl interpreter to parse data whenever possible rather than writing new code to parse data.
- Use a single global array for shared data instead of many variables. If you must use many variables, group them into a global list and evaluate that list to declare the globals in procedures.

Introduction to the CD-ROM

The CD-ROM supplied with *Tcl/Tk for Real Programmers* is more than just an extension of the book. The CD-ROM includes the usual examples from the book and code distributions and also additional tutorials, development tools, Tcl extensions, extra documentation, and a full extra bonus book.

For the beginner, the tutorials will get you programming in just a few hours. For the experienced user, the development tools will help you to program better and faster. Finally, the chapters with case studies discussing how Tcl/Tk is used in the real world will help advanced users see how to apply Tcl/Tk to their needs.

The material on the CD-ROM makes *Tcl/Tk for Real Programmers* truly a one-stop shopping spree for anyone interested in learning Tcl/Tk.

The three most recent Tcl and Tk interpreter distributions are on the CD-ROM, ready for installation on a Mac, Windows, or Unix machine.

The tutorials on the CD-ROM will help you learn the basics of Tcl/Tk quickly. There are HTML-based tutorials from the Net, some discussions of Tcl tricks from `comp.lang.tcl`, and a copy of TclTutor, a computer-aided instruction package. If you find that one tutorial doesn't explain something the way you'd like, look at the others. With several different authors presenting the same material from different angles you'll be certain to find one that explains what you need to know.

The bonus book chapters discuss how Tcl and Tk have been used in the real world, how to build extensions with C++ libraries, and how to use Tcl/Tk to build Web, e-mail, news robots and more.

I'm very grateful to the authors of those chapters for letting me include their work with this book.

A.1 How Do I Find Those Extra Goodies?

The CD-ROM contains an index.htm file at the top level. If you point your browser at that file (`file:/cdrom/index.htm`) you can browse the bonus chapters and README files from the packages distributed on the CD-ROM.

In order to install the packages, you'll need to know the directory layout. See Appendix B for instructions on installing the Tcl/Tk distributions. See Appendices C and D for instructions on installing the extensions and packages. Finally, see Appendix E for information about accessing the Real World Tcl chapters and the tutorials.

The CD-ROM contains the following directories:

bsd_bin   Selected distributions compiled under BSD/OS 3.0 Unix. Ready to install from `tar.gz` files.

devel   The latest distributions for the development tools discussed in Chapter 14.

docco   Additional Tcl documentation: the Tcl coding conventions documents supported by Sun and Scriptics, and Paul Raines' Tcl/Tk Reference Guide.

examples   Subdirectories for each of the chapters in *Tcl/Tk for Real Programmers*. The examples from each chapter are in these subdirectories.

extensns   The latest distributions of the extensions discussed in Chapter 13.

lin_bin   Selected distributions compiled under RedHat 5.0 Linux. Ready to install from `tar.gz` files.

packages   Tcl script packages such as the HTML library discussed in Chapter 10 and the megaWidget package discussed in Chapter 11.

realwrld   The *Real World Tcl* chapters, arranged in subdirectories by author name.

tcl_dist   Tcl and Tk distributions for Unix, Macintosh, and Windows platforms. Revisions 7.6, 8.0, and 8.1 are included.

tcltutor   TclTutor distributions for Macintosh-, MS-Windows-, and Unix-based computers.

tutorls   Several Tcl tutorials, including some HTML tutorials, and some text discussions of aspects of Tcl.

win_bin   Windows binaries of some of the tools discussed in the book.

A.2 Acknowledgments

The *Tcl/Tk for Real Programmers* book could not have existed without a lot of help from my friends, and for the CD-ROM I'm even more indebted to a number of folks who contributed their work.

For allowing me to include their tutorials I'm indebted to: Will Morse, Robert Hill, Alexandre Ferrieux, Bill Ho, Lakshmi Sastry, Jean-Claude Wipple, Donal K. Fellows, and Ernest Friedman-Hill.

For allowing me to include their descriptions on how Tcl can be applied in the Real World, I'm indebted to: David Beazley, Christopher Nelson, Donal K. Fellows, Carsten Zerbst, Doug Hughes, and Andreas Kupries.

For allowing me to include their extensions, packages, code, and extra documentation, I'm indebted to: David Dougherty, Jan Nijtmans, David Beazley, Don Libes, Stephen Uhler, Jon Stump, Raymond Johnson, Ioi Lam, Allan Pratt, Lindsay Marshall, Laurent Demailly, Stephan Weiss, Heiko Grossmann, Stefan Schreyjak, Michael McLennan, Mark Diekhans, Steve Wahle, Rick Enos, Tom Poindexter, George A. Howlett, Jeffrey Hobbs, John Ousterhout, and Paul Raines.

Installing Tcl/Tk Distributions

The CD-ROM contains distributions for revisions 7.6 (patchlevel 2), 8.0 (patchlevel 2) and 8.1 (release alpha 2) for the Macintosh, Unix, Windows 95 and Windows NT systems.

The distributions for the Macintosh and Windows systems are pre-compiled and can be quickly installed from the distribution files. For Unix systems, the Tcl and Tk interpreters are distributed as source code. In order to install them, you'll need a C compiler on your system.

To make some folks' lives a little simpler I've compiled the Tcl and Tk distributions under BSD/OS 3.0 Unix and RedHat 5.0 Linux, and made a gzipped tar file (`.tgz`) that can be extracted into the `/usr/local` directory.

The 8.0 release on the CD-ROM is the most recent stable release of Tcl/Tk. Unless you have a compelling reason to use 7.6 (you want the Motif style interface instead of native look-and-feel on Windows and Macs) or 8.1 (you need the Unicode support), you should install the 8.0 release.

The examples below will all assume 8.0. If you want to install 7.6 or 8.1, just change the numbers.

B.1 Installing Tcl/Tk on a Macintosh

The Tcl/Tk distribution for the Macintosh is created as a self-extracting BinHex archive. Installing Tcl/Tk from this file is a two-step process.

The first step is to convert the packed file into an installation file using the Aladdin Systems StuffIt Expander package. The StuffIt Expander program is distributed with Netscape and can be obtained from http://www.aladdinsys.com.

The second step is to run the installation program to perform the Tcl/Tk installation.

To unpack the distribution using the StuffIt Expander follow these steps:

1. Place the *Tcl/Tk for Real Programmers* CD-ROM in the CD-ROM drive and confirm that it creates an icon on your screen when it loads.

2. Start the StuffIt Expander program by double-clicking the Expander icon.

3. Click the **File** menu in the upper-left corner of your screen.

4. Click the **Expand** menu option from that menu. Clicking the **Expand** option will bring up a file browsing window to select the installation file. Select the file to extract with the sequence:

   - Select the **desktop**
   - Double-click the name of the CD-ROM
   - Double-click **tcl_dist**
   - Double-click **MAC**
   - Double-click **8.0**

At this point the window will resemble:

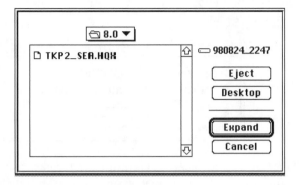

5. Double-click the entry **TKP2_SEA.HQX.**

At this point the window will resemble:

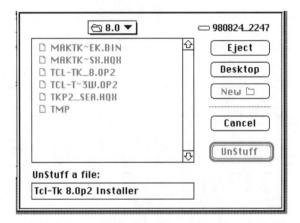

6. Click the **Desktop** button. The contents of the desktop will appear in the window, and the **Unstuff** button will no longer be grayed out.

7. Click the **Unstuff** button, or press the **Return** key.

8. StuffIt Expander will now convert the distribution file to an executable program on your desktop area. As it unpacks, you'll see a window that resembles this:

9. When StuffIt Expander has completed the expansion of the distribution file, there will be a new icon on your desktop that resembles this:

10. Click the **Tcl-Tk Installer** icon. This starts the Tcl/Tk installation.

11. The first window you'll see will have the Tcl/Tk license agreement.

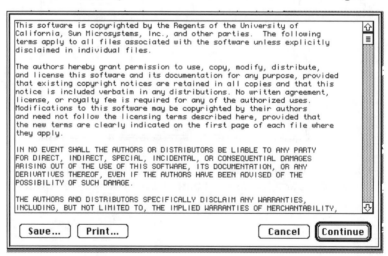

12. Click the **Continue** button.

13. The next screen allows you to select for a PowerPC or a Motorola 680x0-based Macintosh.

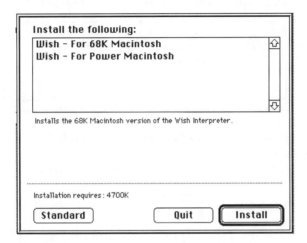

Click on the selection, which describes your system. If your Macintosh is more than a few years old, it is probably a 680x0-based system. If it is new, it is probably a Power PC-based system.

After you've selected your system, click the **Install** button.

14. The next window will allow you to select where you'd like to place the Tcl/Tk package.

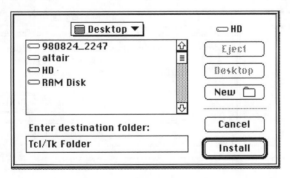

After you've selected the workspace for Tcl/Tk (perhaps the main desktop) click the **Install** button.

15. Your Macintosh may need to be rebooted after the Tcl/Tk package is installed. If a reboot is required, you will be given the opportunity to abort the installation if you do not wish to reboot.

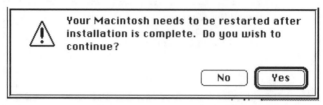

16. If you click **No**, the installation will be aborted, and the windows will disappear.

    If you click the **Yes** option Tcl/Tk will be installed on your Macintosh.

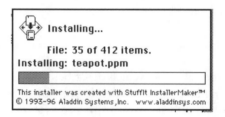

17. If your Macintosh needs to be rebooted after the installation is complete, you'll be prompted with this window:

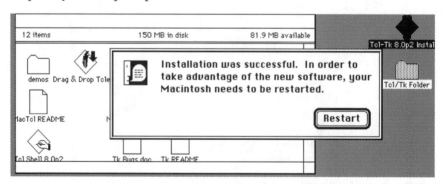

After your system has rebooted, there will be an icon for **Tcl/Tk Folder** in the workspace you selected for the installation.

You can now drag the **Tcl-Tk Installer** icon to the trash bin. You won't need it again.

When the **Tcl/Tk Folder** icon is opened, you'll see a window that resembles this:

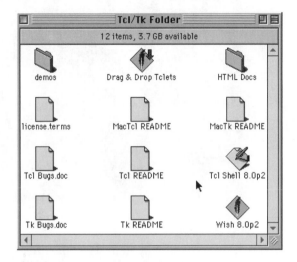

When you double-click the **Wish** icon, it will open two windows: an image window and a command window. You can use these windows to create wish programs, as described in Chapter 2.

B.2 Installing Tcl/Tk on Windows 95 or Windows NT

The Tcl/Tk distribution Microsoft Windows platforms is a self-extracting installation file created with InstallShield.

To install Tcl/Tk:

1. Place the *Tcl/Tk for Real Programmers* CD-ROM in the CD-ROM drive. The rest of these instructions assume that this is drive D.

2. Select **Start** and then **Run** from the Windows task button.

3. Enter or browse to `D:\tcl_dist\win\8.0\tcl80p2.exe` and run that program.

4. Your video display will turn blue, and you'll see a window resembling this in the center:

Click the **Next >** button.

5. The next window will allow you to select the directory for your Tcl/Tk installation. If you expect to be working with Tcl from DOS windows or .bat files, you may prefer to put the Tcl files in a directory with a simpler (shorter) path like `C:\tcl` instead of under `Program Files`.

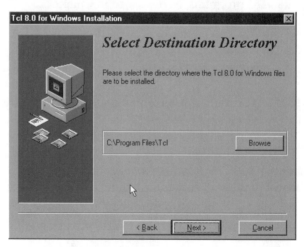

Once you have selected the destination directory, click **Next >**.

6. The next screen allows you to configure the Tcl installation to fit within your available disk space.

   The minimal installation will not install the documentation pages or demos. This installation requires a bit over one-half megabyte of disk space.

   The custom installation allows you to select or deselect:

   - Tcl Run Time Files

   - Example Scripts

   - Help Files

   - Header and Library Files

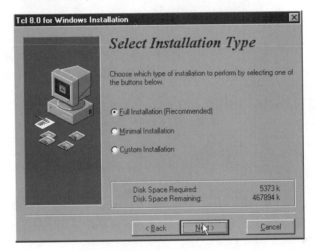

Unless you have a serious shortage of disk space, select the Full Installation, and click **Next >**.

7. The next screen gives you a chance to change your mind. You can back up to any of the previous screens and change the data.

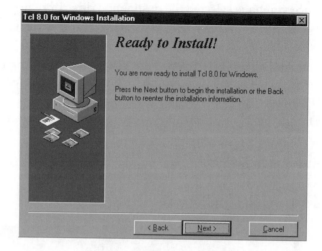

When all the selections are right, click **Next >**.

8. As Tcl is installed you'll see the familiar progress bar and running list of installed files.

9. When the installation is complete, it will be announced by a window that resembles this:

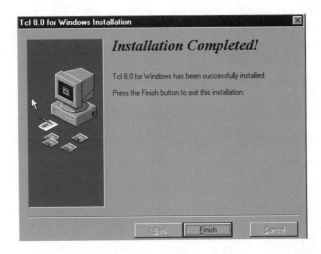

10. The last step of the Tcl installation creates a program group that resembles this:

and adds an entry for **Tcl** to the **Start - Programs -** menu item.

B.3 Installing Tcl/Tk on Unix/Linux Systems

The standard method for installing Tcl/Tk on a Unix or Linux system is to compile the code.

If you can use binaries compiled for a BSD/OS 3.0 or RedHat 5.0 Linux system you'll find pre-compiled binaries on the CD-ROM, ready to install in /usr/local. (Skip to B.3.3).

B.3.1 Compiling Tcl/Tk

To compile the Tcl/Tk distributions, you'll need:

- a C compiler (gcc is good, even the portable C compiler will work)
- gunzip (to uncompress the distribution)
- tar (to unpack the distribution)

You must compile the Tcl distribution before you can compile the Tk distribution.

1. Mount the *Tcl/Tk for Real Programmers* CD-ROM (I'll assume it's mounted on /cdrom).

2. Create a parent directory for the distributions, if necessary. I prefer to keep all the Tcl distributions under /usr/src/TCL instead of just /usr/src

3. Change to the parent directory for this distribution.

```
$> cd /usr/src/TCL
```

4. Unpack the distributions.

   (Note that true tar uses -xvof, while pax-based tar does not use the -o flag, and some modern tar programs do not require the dash.)

```
$> gzcat /cdrom/tcl_dist/unix/8.0/tcl8.0p2.tar.gz | tar -xvf -
$> gzcat /cdrom/tcl_dist/unix/8.0/tk8.0p2.tar.gz | tar -xvf -
```

5. Change to the distribution/unix directory.
```
$> cd tcl8.0/unix
```

6. Run configure to examine your system and create a Makefile.

```
$> configure
```

You can get a list of options to set when configure is run with the -help flag:

```
$> configure -help
Usage: configure [options] [host]
Options: [defaults in brackets after descriptions]
```

```
Configuration:
  --cache-file=FILE       cache test results in FILE
  --help                  print this message
  --no-create             do not create output files
  --quiet, --silent       do not print `checking...' messages
  --version               print the version of autoconf
                           that created configure
Directory and file names:
  --prefix=PREFIX         install architecture-independent
                           files in PREFIX
                           [/usr/local]
  --exec-prefix=PREFIX    install architecture-dependent files
                           in PREFIX
                           [same as prefix]
  --srcdir=DIR            find the sources in DIR [configure
                           dir or ..]
  --program-prefix=PREFIX prepend PREFIX to installed
      program names
  --program-suffix=SUFFIX append SUFFIX to installed
      program names
  --program-transform-name=PROGRAM run sed PROGRAM on installed
      program names
Host type:
  --build=BUILD           configure for building on BUILD
[BUILD=HOST]
  --host=HOST             configure for HOST [guessed]
  --target=TARGET         configure for TARGET [TARGET=HOST]
Features and packages:
  --disable-FEATURE       do not include FEATURE (same as
                            --enable-FEATURE=no)
  --enable-FEATURE[=ARG]  include FEATURE [ARG=yes]
  --with-PACKAGE[=ARG]    use PACKAGE [ARG=yes]
  --without-PACKAGE       do not use PACKAGE (same as
                            --with-PACKAGE=no)
  --x-includes=DIR        X include files are in DIR
  --x-libraries=DIR       X library files are in DIR
--enable and --with options recognized:
  --enable-gcc            allow use of gcc if available
  --disable-load          disallow dynamic loading and load
                           command
  --enable-shared         build libtcl as a shared library
```

The configuration options you are likely to want to set include:

--disable-load

> If the computer's operating system does not support run-time–linked shared libraries, you cannot use the load command, and you may as well disable it.

> BSD/OS 2.x, 3.x do not support run-time–linked shared libraries.

> Linux, Solaris, SunOS 4.1.3 and HP/UX do support run-time–linked shared libraries.

--enable-shared

> If your computer's operating system supports linked shared libraries you can create a libtcl that can be linked into your other applications.

--prefix=PREFIX

> By default Tcl installs itself in /usr/local/bin and /usr/local/lib. If you need to install Tcl elsewhere and you want the Tcl interpreter to find its initialization files in default locations, you can either define the prefix with this option, or edit the Makefile after the configure is complete.

7. Modify the Makefile, if required. For a normal installation, the Makefile that is created by configure can be used as is.

8. Make the distribution.

$> make

9. Test that the compile worked.

$> make test

On some systems the floating point tests will fail. This is usually not a real bug, but reflects slight differences in floating point emulation on different machines.

10. Install the Tcl interpreter, libraries and man pages

$> make install

To compile and install the Tk distribution, change to the unix directory under the Tk distribution, and repeat Steps 6–10.

B.3.2 Large Systems Installation

If you need to install Tcl/Tk on many machines you won't want to compile Tcl/Tk on each machine and perform the install.

The best solution is probably to NFS mount a common bin and library directory tree. If that's not possible you can distribute the software across your network using packages like `rdist` or `surd`.

If neither of these options are appropriate for your site, the Tcl `Makefile` can be used to install the Tcl package in a directory other than the one it was compiled for. For example, this lets you compile Tcl for `/usr/local`, and install it under `/tmp/usr/local`. You can then make an installation tar file from `/tmp` to use when installing the binaries on other systems.

The steps for doing this are:

1. Unpack and configure as above.
2. Edit the `Makefile`.

   Add a path for the temporary directory to the `INSTALL_ROOT` parameter. For example:

   ```
   INSTALL_ROOT = /tmp
   ```

3. Make the distribution.
4. Create the empty directory tree for the installation.

   ```
   mkdir /tmp/usr
   mkdir /tmp/usr/local
   ```

5. Make install.
6. Change to the parent of the temporary directory.

   ```
   cd /tmp/usr/local
   ```

7. Create a tar archive.

   ```
   tar -cvf tcl.install.tar
   ```

8. Copy the tar archive to the destination system and untar it.

   ```
   bar> rlogin foo
   foo> cd /usr/local
   foo> ftp bar
   ```

```
ftp> ...
ftp> get tcl.install.tar
ftp> quit
foo> tar -xvf tcl.install.tar
```

B.3.3 Installing Pre-Compiled Binaries for BSD/OS and Linux

The pre-compiled binaries and libraries files for BSD/OS and Linux are in the bsd_bin and lin_bin directories on the CD-ROM. These have been compiled with /usr/local as the root directory following the technique described in Section B.3.2.

The tar archive is generated from the root directory. These binaries can be unpacked into /usr/local with gunzip and tar or pax, and used with no further modifications.

If you need to install these under some other directory tree (for instance, /usr/contrib), you'll need to set the TCL_LIBRARY and TK_LIBRARY environment variables to point to the installation directories in order for the interpreters to find their initiation files.

The files in these directories are:

tcl76ful.tgz   Complete Tcl 7.6 installation.

tcl76min.tgz   Tcl 7.6 installation with no man pages.

tk42ful.tgz   Complete Tk 4.2 installation.

tk42min.tgz   Tk 4.2 installation with no man pages.

tcl80ful.tgz   Complete Tcl 8.0 installation.

tcl80min.tgz   Tcl 8.0 installation with no man pages.

tk80ful.tgz   Complete Tk 8.0 installation.

tk80min.tgz   Tk 8.0 installation with no man pages.

tcl81ful.tgz   Complete Tcl 8.1 installation.

tcl81min.tgz   Tcl 8.1 installation with no man pages.

`tk81ful.tgz`   Complete Tk 8.1 installation.

`tk81min.tgz`   Tk 8.1 installation with no man pages.

This procedure will install the Tcl and Tk binaries under /usr/local:

1. Mount the CD-ROM.

Linux: `mount -t iso9660 /dev/cdrom /cdrom`
BSD/OS: `mount -t 9660 /dev/sr0 /cdrom`

2. Change to the target directory.

`cd /usr/local`

3. Extract the archive for Tcl 8.0.

Linux: `gunzip -c /cdrom/lin_bin/tcl80ful.tgz | tar -xvof -`
BSD/OS: `gunzip -c /cdrom/bsd_bin/tcl80ful.tgz | tar -xvof -`

4. Extract the archive for Tk 8.0.

Linux: `gunzip -c /cdrom/lin_bin/tk80ful.tgz | tar -xvof -`
BSD/OS: `gunzip -c /cdrom/bsd_bin/tk80ful.tgz | tar -xvof -`

Installing Tcl/Tk Extensions

The CD-ROM contains several extensions to Tcl. Most of these are distributed as source code to be compiled with the Tcl library to create a new Tcl interpreter or loadable library.

The [incr Tcl], img, dash, plus, and TclX extensions are available as binaries for MS-Windows.

Only the [incr Tcl] extension is compiled for the Macintosh.

C.1 BLT

The BLT extension included on the CD-ROM is revision 2.4e, which can be used with Tk revisions 4.1, 4.2 and 8.0. This version is supported only for Unix, Linux, etc.

To use BLT, you'll first need to install Tcl/Tk on your system. See Appendix B for instructions on installing Tcl/Tk.

To install BLT, follow these steps (modified from the INSTALL file):

1. Uncompress and untar the distribution file.

   ```
   gunzip-c blt24e.tgz | tar -xvf -
   ```

   This will create a directory blt2.4e with the following subdirectories:

   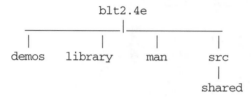

2. Run ./configure

   Go into the blt2.4e directory.

   ```
   cd blt2.4e
   ```

   and run the auto-configuration script (./configure). Tell configure where to find the Tcl and Tk header files and libraries with the --with-tcl switch.

   ```
   ./configure --with-tcl=/util/lang/tcl
   ```

   --with-tcl=dir

   > Top-level directory where the Tcl and/or Tk header files and libraries are installed. Will search both "$dir/include" and "$dir/lib".

   --with-tk=dir

   > Top-level directory where the Tk header files and libraries are installed.

   --with-cc=program

   > Lets you specify the C compiler, such as "acc" or "gcc".

   --prefix=path

   > By default, the bltwish demo program, the BLT header files, libraries, scripts, and manual pages are installed in "/usr/local/blt". This lets you pick another location.

   The configure script creates a header file src/bltConfig.h. It will also generate new Makefiles from their respective templates (Makefile.in).

3. Compile the libraries and build the demonstration program "bltwish".

   `make`

4. Test by running the demos.

   Go into the demos directory:

   `cd demos`

   and run the test scripts.

   `./graph`

   If your system doesn't support "#!" in shell scripts, then run

   `../bltwish ./graph`

5. Install BLT.

   `make install`

   The following directories will be created when BLT is installed. By default, the top directory is /usr/local/blt.

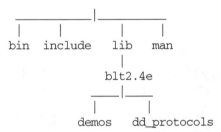

   You can change the top directory by supplying the `--prefix=dir` switch to: `./configure`.

6. (Optional) Compile BLT into your own custom "wish".

   (If your version of "wish" supports dynamic loading of packages you can simply add

   `package require BLT`

   to the start of your script.)

   Add the following lines to your program's Tcl_AppInit routine in `tkAppInit.c`

   ```
   if (Blt_Init(interp) != TCL_OK) {
           return TCL_ERROR;
       }
   ```

then link with `libBLT.a`. And that's all there's to it.

This revision of BLT places the new commands in the `blt::` namespace.

C.2 dash

The dash kit is a set of patches to the Tcl/Tk source code. This patch improves and extends the canvas widget. See the README file for more details.

C.2.1 Installing the **dash** Patch under MS-Windows

The dash, plus, and img patches are all applied to the MS-Windows executables contained in the self-extracting installation files `tk81plus.exe` under the plus directory. See Section C.7 for instructions on installing the plus extension.

C.2.2 Installing the **dash** Patch under Unix

You must have Larry Wall's patch program to install these patches (or be very patient and careful with a text editor!).

You must compile the appropriate version of Tcl before you can compile Tk. See Appendix B for details on compiling Tcl.

The steps for installing these patches are:

1. Mount the *Tcl/Tk for Real Programmers* CD-ROM.
2. Create a fresh, clean copy of the Tk distribution from the distribution, as described in Appendix B.
3. Change directory to the top of the Tk directory tree.
4. Apply the appropriate patch (tk42dash.ptc for Tk revision 4.2, or tk80dash.ptc for Tk revision 8.0p2) with the command:

   ```
   patch -p < /cdrom/extensns/dash/tk80dash.ptc
   ```
5. Compile wish as described in Appendix A.

C.3 Expect

Expect revision 5.26 is included on the CD-ROM in the file /extensns/
expect/expect.tgz. Expect is only supported on the Unix and Linux
operating systems.

Expect is distributed as source code, and you must compile and install Tcl
and Tk before you can make expect and expectk.

C.3.1 Building the **Expect** Extension under Unix

The steps for building expect under Unix or Linux are:

1. Build and install Tcl/Tk as described in Appendix B.
2. Mount the *Tcl/Tk for Real Programmers* CD-ROM.
3. Unpack the expect distribution.

   ```
   gunzip -c /cdrom/extensns/expect/expect.tgz | tar -xvf -
   ```
4. Change to the expect-5.26 directory.
5. Run the configure script to create a new Makefile.
6. Make the package.

C.4 Img

The CD-ROM contains the complete sources for the img wish extensions
(img11p3.tgz), and the binaries for MS-Windows platforms in a self-
extracting zip file (img11p3.exe).

The img gzipped tar (img11p3.tgz) distribution includes distributions for
the jpeg, tiff and png image libraries, and code and patches to link
these libraries into a new wish interpreter with support for jpeg, tiff
and png image types.

C.4.1 Installing the `img` Extension under MS-Windows

The image libraries and the `img` library files are included in the file `img11p3.exe`. This executable is created with `InstallShield` and can be installed by running the `img11p3.exe` file.

The image format libraries will be installed into a new directory named `img1.1` under your existing `Tcl/lib` directory. You may need to rebuild the `pkgIndex.tcl` file that is distributed in this .exe.

The new image formats can be accessed once you load the revision of the `img` library for the version of `wish` you are running: `img1176.dll` for `wish` revision 4.2, `img1180.dll` for `tclsh/wish` revision 8.0, or `img1181.dll` for `tclsh/wish` revision 8.1.

The `Img` extension can be loaded with a Tcl command resembling:

```
load C:/progra~1/tcl/lib/img1.1/img1180
```

The `dash`, `plus`, and `img` patches are all applied to the MS-Windows executables contained in the self-extracting installation files `tk81plus.exe` under the `plus` directory. See Section C.7 for instructions on installing the `plus` extension.

C.4.2 Building the `Img` Extension under Unix

To build the `Img` extensions under Unix, follow this procedure:

1. Mount the *Tcl/Tk for Real Programmers* CD-ROM.
2. Unpack the `Img` files with gunzip and tar.

   ```
   gunzip -c /cdrom/extensns/img/img11p3.tgz | tar -xvf -
   ```
3. Unpack the Tcl and Tk distributions at the same directory level (the same directory level is not required, but it makes life simpler).

   When this done, your build directory should resemble:

   ```
   $> ls
     img1.1  tcl8.0  tk8.0
   ```
4. Build Tcl following the instructions in Appendix B.
5. Configure Tk following the instructions in Appendix B.

6. Build the image handling libraries.

   The library directories libjpeg, libtiff, and libz have configure scripts which will generate a Makefile.

   In the libpng directory, copy the appropriate Makefile from the scripts directory and make.

7. Make the libimg library.

   Change to the img1.1 directory. Execute the configure script and run make.

   This creates a loadable library that can be inserted into your wish interpreter with the load command, or by creating a package index file (as described in Chapter 7) and including a package require Img command in your script.

   If your system does not support run-time linking, you'll need to create a non-shared library. To do this set the --disable-shared flag when you run the configure script.

   ```
   ./configure --disable-shared
   ```

   and then run make.

8. Copy the appropriate patch file for your version of wish from the img/patches directory to the top level of your Tk distribution and install the patches:

   ```
   $>   cd img1.1/patches
   $>   cp patch.tk8 ../../tk8.0
   $>   cd ../../tk8.0
   $>   patch < patch.tk8
   ```

9. Change to the unix directory, and make the distribution.

   ```
   $>   cd unix
   $>   make
   ```

   This creates a version of wish with several patches to extend the image commands. The new image formats are not loaded by default, however. If you want to access the new formats you must either load the libimg.1.so library or use the package require Img command.

10. To create a wish interpreter with the extended image types available by default (a requirement if your OS does not support run-time linking) you need to add a call to Img_Init to tkWindow.c and explicitly link with the image libraries.

Add the call to `Img_Init` to `tkWindow.c`

1. Change to the `generic` subdirectory of your Tk distribution.

2. Edit `tkWindow.c`

3. Modify the `Initialize` function by adding the line `Img_Init(interp);` just before the label `done:`. The code will now resemble:

```
code = TkpInit(interp);
          Img_Init(interp);
     done:
```

4. Change to the `unix` subdirectory.

5. Copy the image handling libraries to the `unix` directory.

```
cp ../../img1.1/*/*.a ../../img1.1/*.a .
```

6. Edit the `Makefile`, and add the image libraries to the `LIBS` definition. The `LIBS` definition line should resemble this when you are done:

```
LIBS = -limg1.1 -ljpeg -ltiff -lpng -lz \
     -L/usr/src/img/tcl8.0/unix...
```

7. Make the new `wish` interpreter.

C.5 incr_tcl

The [incr Tcl] extension is supported for Unix, Macintosh, and MS-Windows platforms. This version of [incr Tcl] supports Tcl revision 7.6 and Tk revision 4.2. The Macintosh and Windows versions of the distribution include executable versions of the [incr Tcl] interpreters.

C.5.1 Installing [incr Tcl] on a Macintosh

The [incr Tcl] distribution for the Macintosh is created as a self-extracting BinHex archive. The [incr Tcl] extension can be installed from this file using the Aladdin Systems StuffIt Expander package. The StuffIt Expander program is distributed with Netscape and can be obtained from http://www.aladdinsys.com.

To unpack the distribution using the StuffIt Expander follow these steps:

1. Place the *Tcl/Tk for Real Programmers* CD-ROM in the CD-ROM drive and confirm that it creates an icon on your screen when it loads.

2. Start the StuffIt Expander program.

3. Click the **File** menu in the upper-left corner of your screen.

4. Click the **Expand** menu option from that menu. Clicking the **Expand** option will bring up a file browsing window to select the installation file. Select the file to extract with the sequence:

   - Select the **desktop**
   - Double-click the name of the CD-ROM
   - Double-click **extensns**
   - Double-click **incr_tcl**

5. Double-click the 68000 or Power PC distribution of [incr Tcl] to install.

   - itcl_68K.hqx: For 680x0-based Macintoshes
   - itcl_ppc.hqx: For Power PC-based Macintoshes

6. Select the destination directory for the [incr Tcl] package.

7. Click the **Unstuff** button to unpack this distribution.

When StuffIt Expander is finished, you will have a new icon for [incr Tcl], and new interpreters to use.

C.5.2 Installing the [**incr Tcl**] Extension under MS-Windows

To install this distribution:

The [incr Tcl] extension is created with InstallShield. You can install [incr Tcl] by executing the img11p3.exe file.

When you execute the img11p3.exe program, you'll see the familiar blue screen. If you choose the defaults this program will install [incr Tcl] in C:\Program Files\Itcl2.2.

The new interpreters will be named `itclsh.exe` and `itkwish.exe`. These files will be placed in the `bin` subdirectory of the installation directory you specified during installation (by default, this will be `C:\Program Files\Itcl2.2\bin`).

C.5.3 Installing [`incr Tcl`] under Unix

The Unix distribution of [`incr Tcl`] is done as a gzipped tar file (`itcl2.2p2.tgz`). The distribution includes patched versions of the Tcl and Tk distributions.

This procedure will create the [`incr Tcl`] extension:

1. Mount the *Tcl/Tk for Real Programmers* CD-ROM.
2. Unpack the [`incr Tcl`] source files with gunzip and tar.

    `gunzip -c /cdrom/extensns/incr_tcl/itcl22p2.tgz | tar -xvf -`
3. Change to the `itcl2.2p2` directory.
4. Run the `configure` script to create the `Makefile`.
5. Run `make` to make the interpreters.

    On BSD/OS systems you may need to manually add `-ldl` to the `Makefile` after configure.

C.6 oratcl

The `oratcl` extension provided on the *Tcl/Tk for Real Programmers* CD-ROM supports Tcl revisions 7.6 and 8.0 , and Tk revisions 4.2 and 8.0. In order to use this extension you must also have access to an Oracle server (Version 6, 7.0, 7.1, 7.2, or 7.3).

C.6.1 Installing the oratcl Extension under MS-Windows

The `oratcl` .DLL files are stored in the self-extracting zip file `extensns\oratcl\oratcl25.exe`. In order to use `oratcl` you must also have the Oracle DLLs installed.

This installation requires that you unzip the files into a temporary directory, then run the `oratcl` installation script `install.tcl` to copy the appropriate files to your Tcl directories.

To install the `oratcl` .DLL's:

1. Place the *Tcl/Tk for Real Programmers* CD-ROM in the CD-ROM drive.
2. Open the Run dialog box.
3. Type or browse to select `D:\extensn\oratcl\oratcl25.exe` as the file to run.
4. Run the self-extracting zip file.

5. When the initial window appears, click the **OK** button.
6. The next window gives you the chance to select the installation directory.

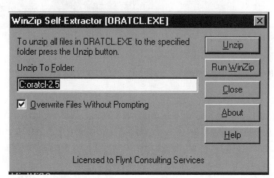

You may accept the default installation directory (`C:\ora_tmp`) or type in the directory path you prefer.

7. Click the **Unzip** button. You will see the usual progress bar as the extension is installed.

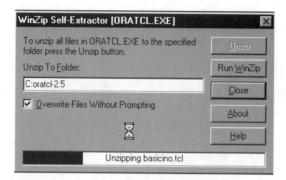

8. When the installation is complete click the **OK** button.

9. Exit the installation program by clicking the **Close** button.

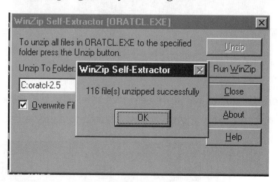

10. Change to the C:\oratcl2.5\win directory.

    cd C:\oratcl2.5\win

11. Run the install.tcl script, which will determine which version of Tcl you are running, and will copy the appropriate version of the oratcl DLL to a new directory named oratcl25 under your Tcl installation library directory.

You may need to add the new directory to the append_path variable in your scripts in order to load oratcl with a package require Oratcl command.

C.6.2 Installing the `oratcl` Extension under Unix

The `oratcl` source code is provided in a gzipped tar archive. In order to build this package you will need to have the Oracle C libraries installed on your system.

The steps for building `oratcl` under Unix or Linux are:

1. Build and install Tcl/Tk as described in Appendix B.
2. Mount the *Tcl/Tk for Real Programmers* CD-ROM.
3. Change to the parent directory of the Tcl and Tk distributions.
4. Unpack the `oratcl` distribution.

    ```
    gunzip -c /cdrom/extensns/oratcl/oratcl25.tgz | tar -xvf -
    ```

    At this point the directory tree should resemble:

    ```
    $> ls
    oratcl-2.5 tcl8.0 tk8.0
    ```

5. Change to the `oratcl-2.5` directory.
6. Run the `configure` script to create a new `Makefile`.
7. Make the package.

C.7 plus

The `plus` patch is supported for revisions 8.0 and 8.1 of Tcl and Tk.

C.7.1 Installing the `plus` Extension under MS-Windows

The `dash`, `plus`, and `img` patches are all applied to the MS-Windows executables contained in the self-extracting installation files `tk81plus.exe` under the `plus` directory.

The image libraries and the `img` library files are included in the file `tk81a2pl.exe`. This executable is created with `InstallShield` and can be installed by running the `tk81a2pl.exe` file.

Running this install program will create new copies of wish81.exe, and tclsh81.exe in the bin directory, and will place a copy of img11p3.dll in the lib\img1.1 directory.

In order to use the new formats supported by the img extension, you will need the command load C:\progra~1\tcl\lib\img1.1\img1181p3.DLL in your script.

C.7.2 Installing the plus Extension under Unix

The plus patches have already been applied to the Tcl and distributions in the gripped tar archives in the /cdrom/extensns/plus directory.

You can generate a new interpreter by following the instructions for compiling the Tcl and Tk interpreters in Appendix B, but extract the distributions from /cdrom/extensns/plus instead of the distributions under tcl_dist.

C.8 sybtcl

The sybtcl extension provided on the *Tcl/Tk for Real Programmers* CD-ROM supports Tcl revisions 7.6 and 8.0, and Tk revisions 4.2 and 8.0. In order to use this extension you must also have access to an Sybase SQL Server (version 4.x, System 10, or System 11), and have the Sybase Open Client available.

C.8.1 Installing the sybtcl Extension under MS-Windows

The sybtcl .DLL files are stored in the self-extracting zip file extensns\sybtcl\sybtcl25.exe. In order to use sybtcl you must also have the Sybase DLLs (libsybdb.dll) installed.

This installation requires that you unzip the files into a temporary directory, then run the sybtcl installation script install.tcl to copy the appropriate files to your Tcl directories.

To install the sybtcl .DLL's:

1. Place the *Tcl/Tk for Real Programmers* CD-ROM in the CD-ROM drive.
2. Open the **Run** dialog box.
3. Type or browse to select D:\extensn\sybtcl\sybtcl25.exe as the file to run.
4. Run the self-extracting zip file.
5. When the initial window appears, click the **OK** button.
6. The next window gives you the chance to select the installation directory.

    You may accept the default installation directory (C:\sybtcl2.5) or type in the directory path you prefer.
7. Click the **Unzip** button. You will see the usual progress bar as the extension is installed.
8. When the installation is complete click the **OK** button.
9. Exit the installation program by clicking the **Clear** button.
10. Change to the C:\sybtcl2.5\win directory.

    ```
    cd C:\sybtcl2.5\win
    ```
11. Run the install.tcl script, which will determine which version of Tcl you are running, and will copy the appropriate version of the sybtcl DLL to a new directory named sybtcl25 under your Tcl installation library directory.

You may need to add the new directory to the append_path variable in your scripts in order to load sybtcl with a package require sybtcl command.

C.8.2 Installing the **sybtcl** Extension under Unix

The sybtcl source code is provided in a gzipped tar archive. In order to build this package you will need to have the Sybase C libraries (libsybdb.a) installed on your system.

The steps for building sybtcl under Unix or Linux are:

1. Build and install Tcl/Tk as described in Appendix B.
2. Mount the *Tcl/Tk for Real Programmers* CD-ROM.

3. Change to the parent directory of the Tcl and Tk distributions.

4. Unpack the `sybtcl` distribution.

   `gunzip -c /cdrom/extensns/sybtcl/sybtcl25.tgz | tar -xvf -`

   At this point the directory tree should resemble:

   ```
   $>  ls
      sybtcl-2.5 tcl8.0 tk8.0
   ```

5. Change to the `sybtcl-2.5` directory.

6. Run the `configure` script to create a new `Makefile`.

7. Make the package.

C.9 TclX

The `TclX` extension is supported on Unix and Windows systems. The distributions for revisions 7.6 and 8.0 are included on the CD-ROM.

C.9.1 Installing the **TclX** Extension under MS-Windows

The Windows distributions for the `TclX` extension are supported in different formats for the different releases. Neosoft provides the Tcl 7.6 version of TclX compiled for Windows as a zip file, and the 8.0 version as a gzipped tar file.

I've repackaged these as self-extracting zip files, and put both the original distribution and my repackaged version on the CD-ROM.

To unpack the self-extracting zip files:

1. Place the *Tcl/Tk for Real Programmers* CD-ROM in the CD-ROM drive.

2. Open the **Run** dialog box.

3. Type or browse to select `D:\extensn\tclx\tclx800.exe` as the file to run.

4. Run the self-extracting zip file.

5. Click the **OK** button when you see this graphic.

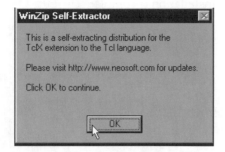

6. The next window gives you the chance to select the installation directory.

    You may accept the default installation directory (C:\tclx) or type in the directory path you prefer.

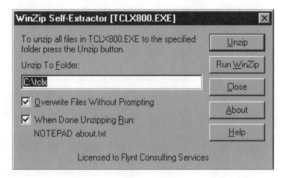

7. Click the **Unzip** button. You will see the usual progress bar as the extension is installed.

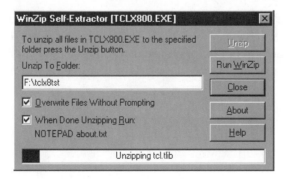

8. When the installation is complete click the **OK** button.

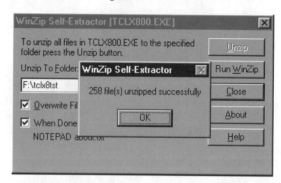

9. Exit the installation program by clicking the **Close** button.

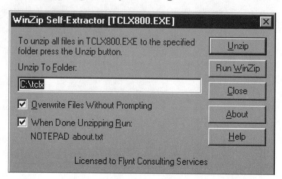

C.9.2 Installing the `Tclx` Extension under Unix

In order to configure and compile the `TclX` extension, you need to have the appropriate version of Tcl and Tk already compiled. The most straightforward method of building the extension is to have the `tclX8.0.2` directory at the same level as the Tcl and Tk source code directories.

```
$> ls
 tcl8.0          tclX8.0.2        tk8.0
```

Following this procedure will generate the TclX extension on your system:

1. Mount the *Tcl/Tk for Real Programmers* CD-ROM.
2. Extract the Tcl and Tk distributions.

   ```
   $> tar -xvf /cdrom/tcl_dist/full_src/8.0/tcl80p2.tar
   $> tar -xvf /cdrom/tcl_dist/full_src/8.0/tk80p2.tar
   ```

3. Extract the TclX distribution.

   ```
   gunzip -c /cdrom/extensns/tclx/tclX802.tgz | tar -xvf -
   ```

4. Build the Tcl and Tk interpreters as described in Appendix B.
5. Change to the tclX8.0.2/unix subdirectory.
6. Generate the Makefile by running the configure script.

   ```
   $> configure
   ```

7. Make the interpreters.

   ```
   $> make
   ```

8. Test the new Tcl interpreter.

   ```
   $> make test
   ```

9. Install the new Tcl interpreters.

   ```
   $> make install
   ```

APPENDIX D

Installing Tcl/Tk Packages

D.1 Installing the vs Package

The vs package distribution is under `packages/vs` on the CD-ROM. This package is distributed in gzipped tar archives for Unix systems, self-extracting zip files for MS-Windows and as BinHex archives for Macintosh.

Note that these packages were written before Tcl had been ported to Windows and Macintosh environments. The packages may not work correctly in those environments.

D.1.1 Installing the **vs** Packages under MS-Windows

To unpack the self-extracting zip files:

1. Place the *Tcl/Tk for Real Programmers* CD-ROM in the CD-ROM drive.
2. Open the **Run** dialog box.
3. Enter or browse to `D:\packages\vs\vsfrm10.exe`. Select this as the file to run.
4. Run the self-extracting zip file.
5. When the introduction window appears click the **OK** button.

6. The next window gives you the chance to select the installation directory.
   You may accept the default installation directory (C:\vsfrm) or type in the directory path you prefer.

7. Click the **Unzip** button. You will see the usual progress bar as the package is installed.

8. A window will appear when the installation is complete. Click the **OK** button in that window.

9. Exit the installation program by clicking the **Close** button.

D.1.2 Installing the **vs** Packages under Unix

1. Mount the *Tcl/Tk for Real Programmers* CD-ROM.

2. Change to the parent directory for this installation.

3. Unpack the vs package.

```
gunzip -c /cdrom/packages/vs/vsfrm10.tgz | tar -xvf -
```

D.1.3 Installing the **vs** Packages on a Macintosh

The VS package is packaged for the Macintosh as BinHex archives. The vs packages can be installed from these files using the Aladdin Systems StuffIt Expander package. The StuffIt Expander program is distributed with Netscape and can be obtained from http://www.aladdinsys.com.

To unpack these packages using the StuffIt Expander follow these steps:

1. Place the *Tcl/Tk for Real Programmers* CD-ROM in the CD-ROM drive and confirm that it creates an icon on your screen when it loads.

2. Start the StuffIt Expander program by double-clicking the Expander icon.

3. Click the **File** menu in the upper left corner of your screen.

4. Click the **Expand** menu option from that menu.

   Clicking the **Expand** option will bring up a file browsing window to select the installation file. Select the file to extract with the sequence:

   • Select the **desktop**

   • Double-click the name of the CD-ROM

- Double-click **packages**
- Double-click **vs**

5. Double-click the entry for the package you wish to install. For example, to install the VSForm package click **VSFRM10.HQX**.

6. Click the **Desktop** button. The contents of the desktop will now appear in the window, and the **Unstuff** button will no longer be grayed out.

7. Click the **Unstuff** button, or press the **Return** key.

8. `StuffIt Expander` will now unpack the files from the CD-ROM to a folder on your desktop.

D.2 TkCon

The `TkConsole` program can be run on the Macintosh, or under MS-Windows or Unix.

This package is distributed in gzipped tar archives for unix systems, as a self-extracting zip file for MS-Windows systems, and as a BinHex archive for the Macintosh.

D.2.1 Installing the **TkCon** Package under MS-Windows

To unpack the self-extracting zip files:

1. Place the *Tcl/Tk for Real Programmers* CD-ROM in the CD-ROM drive.

2. Open the **Run** dialog box.

3. Enter or browse to `D:\packages\tkcon\tkcon13.exe`. Select this as the file to run.

4. Run the self-extracting zip file.

5. When the introduction window appears click the **OK** button.

6. The next window gives you the chance to select the installation directory. You may accept the default installation directory (`C:\tkcon1.3`) or type in the directory path you prefer.

7. Click the **Unzip** button. You will see the usual progress bar as the package is installed.

8. A window will appear when the installation is complete. Click the **OK** button in that window.

9. Exit the installation program by clicking the **Close** button.

D.2.2 Installing the `TkCon` Package under Unix

1. Mount the *Tcl/Tk for Real Programmers* CD-ROM.

2. Change to the parent directory for this installation.

3. Unpack the `TkCon` package.

```
gunzip -c /cdrom/packages/tkcon/tkcon13.tgz | tar -xvf -
```

D.2.3 Installing the `TkCon` Package on a Macintosh

The `TkCon` package is packaged for the Macintosh as a BinHex archive. The `TkCon` package can be installed using the Aladdin Systems `StuffIt Expander` package. The `StuffIt Expander` program is distributed with `Netscape` and can be obtained from `http://www.aladdinsys.com`.

To unpack these packages using the `StuffIt Expander` follow these steps:

1. Place the *Tcl/Tk for Real Programmers* CD-ROM in the CD-ROM drive and confirm that it creates an icon on your screen when it loads.

2. Start the `StuffIt Expander` program by double-clicking the Expander icon.

3. Click the **File** menu in the upper-left corner of your screen.

4. Click the **Expand** menu option from that menu.

   Clicking the **Expand** option will bring up a file browsing window to select the installation file. Select the file to extract with the sequence:

   - Select the **desktop**
   - Double-click the name of the CD-ROM
   - Double-click **packages**
   - Double-click **tkcon**

5. Double-click the entry for the package you wish to install (**TKCON13.HQX**).

6. Click the **Desktop** button. The contents of the desktop will now appear in the window, and the **Unstuff** button will no longer be grayed out.

7. Click the **Unstuff** button, or press the **Return** key.

8. StuffIt Expander will now unpack the files from the CD-ROM to a folder on your desktop.

D.3 Frink

Frink is distributed as a gzipped tar archive (frink132.tgz) with a configure script for Unix systems. A compiled version of frink is in the D:\win_bin directory. The frink source code is also packaged as a self-extracting zip file.

D.3.1 Compiling **frink** under MS-Windows

To compile this package with VC++ 4.0 follow these steps:

1. Place the *Tcl/Tk for Real Programmers* CD-ROM in your CD-ROM drive.

2. Run the D:\devel\frink\frink132.exe self-extracting zip archive to extract the source code. By default this will be extracted into C:\frink1.32

3. Start up VC++.

4. Create a new project (**File - New - Project Workspace**).

5. Select Console Application from the listbox, and check **win32** under **Platform**.

6. Type in the path to the directory you created (but not the directory itself) in the **Location:** entry box (i.e., if you created a new directory C:\frink, type C: in the **Location:** entry box).

7. Type the name of the directory you created in the **Name:** entry box.

8. Click the **Create** button. The new project will now be created. Wait until the progress bars have been erased from your screen.

9. Open the **Insert Files into Project** window (**Insert - Files into Project**).

10. With the control key depressed, click each of the .c files with the left mouse button, then click the **Add** button.

11. Pull down the **Build** menu-button and select **Build All**.

D.3.2 Compiling `frink` under Unix

To compile `frink` on a Unix/Linux system:

1. Mount the *Tcl/Tk for Real Programmers* CD-ROM.
2. Change directory to the top of your source tree.
   ```
   cd /home/example/src
   ```
3. Unpack the `frink` source distribution.
   ```
   gunzip -c /cdrom/devel/frink/frink.tgz | tar -xvf -
   ```
4. Change to the `frink` directory.
   ```
   cd frink-1.2p32
   ```
5. Create the `Makefile` by running the `configure` script.
   ```
   configure
   ```
6. Make the `frink` executable.
   ```
   make
   ```

D.4 `Tcl_Cruncher`

The `tcl_cruncher` distribution is on the CD-ROM under the `devel/cruncher/cruncher.tgz` directory. This package does not compile with VC++.

To compile this package on a Unix system:

1. Mount the *Tcl/Tk for Real Programmers* CD-ROM.
2. Change directory to the top of your source tree.
   ```
   cd /home/example/src
   ```
3. Unpack the `tcl_cruncher` source distribution.
   ```
   gunzip -c /cdrom/devel/cruncher/cruncher.tgz | tar -xvf -
   ```
4. Change to the `tcl_crunch` directory.
   ```
   cd tcl_cruncher-1.11
   ```
5. Make the `tcl_cruncher` executable.
   ```
   make
   ```

D.5 tclcheck

Tclcheck is distributed as a gzipped tar archive (tclcheck.tgz) with a configure script for Unix systems. A compiled version of tclcheck is in the D:\win_bin directory. The tclcheck source code is also packaged as a self-extracting zip file.

D.5.1 Compiling tclcheck under MS-Windows

To compile this package with VC++ 4.0 follow these steps:

1. Place the *Tcl/Tk for Real Programmers* CD-ROM in your CD-ROM drive.
2. Run the D:\devel\tclcheck\tcl_check.exe self-extracting zip archive to extract the source code. By default this will be extracted into C:\check_1.112
3. Start up VC++.
4. Create a new project (**File - New - Project Workspace**).
5. Select Console Application from the listbox, and check **win32** under **Platform**.
6. Type in the path to the directory you created (but not the directory itself) in the **Location:** entry box (i.e., if you created a new directory C:\tclcheck, type C: in the **Location:** entry box).
7. Type the name of the directory you created in the **Name:** entry box.
8. Click the **Create** button. The new project will now be created. Wait until the progress bars have been erased from your screen.
9. Open the **Insert Files into Project** window (**Insert - Files into Project**).
10. With the control key depressed, click each of the .c files with the left mouse button, then click the **Add** button.
11. Pull down the **Build** menu-button and select **Build All**.

D.5.2 Compiling tclcheck under Unix

To compile tclcheck on a Unix/Linux system:

1. Mount the *Tcl/Tk for Real Programmers* CD-ROM.
2. Change directory to the top of your source tree.
   ```
   cd /home/example/src
   ```

3. Unpack the tclcheck source distribution.

   gunzip -c /cdrom/devel/tclcheck/tclcheck.tgz | tar -xvf -

4. Change to the tclcheck directory.

   cd tclcheck-1.1.12

5. Create the Makefile by running the configure script.

   configure

6. Make the tclcheck executable.

   make

D.6 tclparse

The tclparse distribution is on the CD-ROM in the file devel/tclparse/parse300.tgz. This package does not compile with VC++.

To compile this package on a Unix system:

1. Mount the *Tcl/Tk for Real Programmers* CD-ROM.

2. Change directory to the top of your source tree.

   cd /home/example/src

3. Unpack the tclparse source distribution.

   gunzip -c /cdrom/devel/tclparse/parse300.tgz | tar -xvf -

4. Change to the tclparse directory.

   cd tclparse-3.00

5. Make the tclparse executable.

   make

D.7 tcl-debug

The tcl-debug distribution is on the CD-ROM in the file devel/tcl-debug/tcldebug.tgz.

D.7.1 Compiling `tcl-debug` under Unix

The `tcl-debug` package is distributed as a gzipped tar archive with a `configure` file.

To compile `tcl-debug` on a Unix/Linux system:

1. Mount the *Tcl/Tk for Real Programmers* CD-ROM.
2. Change directory to the top of your source tree.
   ```
   cd /home/example/src
   ```
3. Unpack the `tcl-debug` source distribution.
   ```
   gunzip -c /cdrom/devel/tcl_debg/tcldebug.tgz | tar -xvf -
   ```
4. Change to the `tcl-debug` directory.
   ```
   cd tcl-debug-1.7
   ```
5. Create the `Makefile` by running the `configure` script.
   ```
   configure
   ```
6. Make the `tcl-debug` executable.
   ```
   make
   ```

D.8 Tuba

The Tuba debugger is a Tcl language package that is supported on Unix/ Linux and MS-Windows platforms. This revision does not work under Macintosh.

D.8.1 Installing the **Tuba** Debugger under MS-Windows

The MS-Windows distribution of the Tuba debugger is contained in the file `devel\tuba23.zip`. This can be extracted using the common `pkunzip`, `Gnu unzip` or `winzip` utilities.

D.8.2 Installing the Tuba Debugger under Unix

The Tuba debugger instruments the code that it will be debugging. For generic Unix systems, there are Tcl procedures to do the instrumenting. There are also high-speed C language subroutines to perform this task compiled for Sun/OS and Linux systems.

The Unix and Linux distributions of the Tuba debugger are in the following files:

tuba23Li.tgz   The Tuba distribution with Linux loadable libraries.

tuba23Su.tgz   The Tuba distribution with Sun/OS loadable libraries.

tuba23.tgz   The Tuba distribution with generic Tcl libraries.

To install the Tuba debugger:

1. Mount the *Tcl/Tk for Real Programmers* CD-ROM.
2. Select the appropriate gzipped tar archive, and extract it with a command resembling:

   ```
   gunzip -c /cdrom/devel/tuba/tuba23.tgz | tar -xvf -
   ```

D.8.3 Installing the Tuba Debugger on a Macintosh

The generic tuba distribution is packed in the file devel:tuba:tuba23.hqx. You can drag and drop this file to the StuffIt Expander icon to unpack the files.

If you make Tuba work, send your patches to John Stump (illiad@doitnow.com).

D.9 TDebug

The TDebug debugger is packaged as a gzipped tar archive for Unix systems, and as a self-extracting zip file for MS-Windows systems.

This package uses the send command, which is not implemented on the Macintosh, and is not implemented on the Windows platform in Tk revisions prior to 8.1.

D.9.1 Installing the **TDebug** Debugger under MS-Windows

The MS Windows distribution of the TDebug debugger is contained in the file `devel\tdebug\tdebug17.exe`.

1. Place the *Tcl/Tk for Real Programmers* CD-ROM in the CD-ROM drive.
2. Open the **Run** dialog box.
3. Enter or browse to `D:\devel\tdebug\tdebug17.exe`. Select this as the file to run.
4. Run the self-extracting zip file.
5. When the introduction window appears click the **OK** button.
6. The next window gives you the chance to select the installation directory. You may accept the default installation directory (`C:\tdebug1.7`) or type in the directory path you prefer.
7. Click the **Unzip** button. You will see the usual progress bar as the package is installed.
8. A window will appear when the installation is complete. Click the **OK** button in that window.
9. Exit the installation program by clicking the **Close** button.

D.9.2 Installing the **TDebug** Debugger under Unix

The Unix distribution of the TDebug debugger is in the file `devel/tdebug/Tdebug17.tgz`.

To install the TDebug debugger:

1. Mount the *Tcl/Tk for Real Programmers* CD-ROM.
2. Change to the destination directory for this package.
3. Unpack the TDebug debugger.

   ```
   gunzip -c /cdrom/devel/tdebug/tdebug17.tgz | tar -xvf -
   ```

D.10 SpecTcl

The `Spectcl` distribution is done as a gzipped tar archive for Unix systems, as a self-extracting zip file for MS-Windows systems, and as a self-extracting BinHex archive (to be unpacked with the StuffIt Expander for the Macintosh).

D.10.1 Installing SpecTcl under MS-Windows

The SpecTcl installation program (D:\devel\spec_tcl\spectcl.exe) is generated with InstallShield. When you invoke the program, you'll see the familiar blue screen.

To install SpecTcl from the D:\devel\spec_tcl\spectcl.exe file:

1. Place the *Tcl/Tk for Real Programmers* CD-ROM in your CD-ROM drive. The rest of these instructions assume that this is drive D.
2. Select **Start** and then **Run** from the Windows task button.
3. Enter or browse to D:\devel\spec_tcl\spectcl.exe and run that program.
4. The initial screen will inform you that this application will install Spec-Tcl onto your computer. Click the **OK** button.
5. The next screen contains the license agreement. Click the **Accept** button.
6. The next screen contains a browser to allow you to select the destination for the SpecTcl installation. Select the location for this installation and click the **OK** button.
7. After you click the **OK** button you will see the familiar progress bar as SpecTcl is installed.
8. When SpecTcl has been installed in the selected directory, a window will be displayed that asks if you would like to have a shortcut for Spec-Tcl created. Click the **Yes** button.
9. The final window will tell you how you can invoke SpecTcl.

D.10.2 Installing SpecTcl under Unix

To install SpecTcl under Unix:

1. Mount the *Tcl/Tk for Real Programmers* CD-ROM.
2. Change directory to the directory where you wish to install SpecTcl.
3. Unpack the SpecTcl distribution.
   ```
   gunzip -c /cdrom/devel/spec_tcl/spectcl.tgz | tar -xvf -
   ```

4. Change to the SpecTcl1.1/bin directory.

5. Edit specTcl and specJava.

   • Set the DIR variable to point to the current directory.

   • Optionally set the WISH variable to point to the version of wish that you want to use.

6. Add the $DIR/SpecTcl1.1/bin path to your $PATH environment variable, or copy the specTcl and specJava variables to a directory in your search path.

D.10.3 Installing SpecTcl on a PPC-Based Macintosh

The SpecTcl distribution for the Macintosh is a self-extracting BinHex archive. This file includes a stub for the Power PC version of the Macintosh. This will not work with a 680x0-based Macintosh. For a 680x0-based Mac, see Section D.10.4.

The first step is to convert the packed file into an installation file using the Aladdin Systems StuffIt Expander package. The StuffIt Expander program is distributed with Netscape and can be obtained from http://www.aladdinsys.com.

The second step is to run the installation program to install SpecTcl.

To unpack the distribution using the StuffIt Expander follow these steps:

1. Place the *Tcl/Tk for Real Programmers* CD-ROM in the CD-ROM drive and confirm that it creates an icon on your screen when it loads.

2. Start the StuffIt Expander program by double-clicking the Expander icon.

3. Click the **File** menu in the upper-left corner of your screen.

4. Click the **Expand** menu option from that menu.

   Clicking the **Expand** option will bring up a file browsing window to select the installation file. Select the file to extract with the sequence:

   • Select the **desktop**

   • Double-click the name of the CD-ROM

   • Double-click **devel**

   • Double-click **spec_tcl**

5. Double-click the entry **SPEC_SEA.HQX.**

6. Click the **Desktop** button. The contents of the desktop will now appear in the window, and the **Unstuff** button will no longer be grayed out.

7. Click the **Unstuff** button, or press the **Return** key.

8. `StuffIt Expander` will now convert the distribution file to an executable program on your desktop area.

9. When `StuffIt Expander` has completed the expansion of the distribution file, there will be a new icon on your desktop named `SpecTcl 1.1 Installer`.

10. Click the **SpecTcl 1.1 Installer** icon. This starts the `SpecTcl` installation.

11. The first window you'll see will have the Tcl/Tk license agreement. Click the **Continue** button.

12. The next screen informs you that this installation program will install the SpecTcl GUI Builder. Click the **Install** button.

13. The next window will allow you to select where you'd like to place the Tcl/Tk package.

    After you've selected the workspace for `SpecTcl` (perhaps the main desktop) click the **Install** button.

After your system has rebooted, there will be an icon for **SpecTcl Folder** in the workspace you selected for the installation.

You can now drag the **SpecTcl 1.1 Installation** icon to the trash bin. You won't need it again.

D.10.4 Installing `SpecTcl` on a 680x0-based Macintosh

A modified version of the `SpecTcl` GUI builder is in the file `devel:spec_tcl:spectcl.hqx`, which can be unpacked into a directory with the `StuffIt Expander`.

1. Place the *Tcl/Tk for Real Programmers* CD-ROM in the CD-ROM drive and confirm that it creates an icon on your screen when it loads.

2. Double-click the CD-ROM icon and step through the directories to `devel:spec_tcl`.

3. Drag the `spectcl.hqx` icon to the `StuffIt Expander` icon.

This will unpack the SpecTcl package into a directory on your desktop.

D.11 SWIG

The SWIG distribution is done as a gzipped tar archive for Unix systems, as a self-extracting zip file for MS-Windows systems, and as a self-extracting BinHex archive for the Macintosh.

D.11.1 Installing SWIG under MS-Windows

The SWIG distribution has been repackaged as a self-extracting zip file for this CD-ROM.

To install SWIG under MS-Windows:

1. Place the *Tcl/Tk for Real Programmers* CD-ROM in your CD-ROM drive. The rest of these instructions assume that this is drive D.
2. Select **Start** and then **Run** from the Windows task button.
3. Enter or browse to D:\devel\swig\swig11p5.exe and run that program.
4. The first window will inform you that this is the SWIG installation package. Click the **OK** button.
5. The next window will allow you to select the destination for this installation. If you do not want the default destinations (C:\swig) enter desired destination path. Click the **Unzip** button.
6. You'll see the familiar progress bar as SWIG is installed.
7. When the package is fully installed, a window will appear informing you that 1152 files were successfully installed. Click the **OK** button.
8. Close the installation window.

Instructions for compiling SWIG with VC++ or Borland C++ are in the file win\readme.txt under the directory you installed SWIG into.

D.11.2 Installing SWIG under Unix

To install SWIG under Unix:

1. Mount the *Tcl/Tk for Real Programmers* CD-ROM.
2. Change directory to the directory where you wish to install SWIG.

3. Unpack the `swig` source distribution.

   ```
   gunzip -c /cdrom/devel/swig/swig11p5.tgz | tar -xvf -
   ```

4. Change to the `SWIG1.1p5` directory. Check the `README` file for more options. To make a default installation, continue these instructions.

5. Create the `Makefile` by running `configure`.

   ```
   configure
   ```

6. Make the `swig` executable with `make`.

   ```
   make
   ```

7. Install the new executable with `make install`.

D.11.3 Installing `SWIG` on a Macintosh

The `SWIG` distribution for the Macintosh is a self-extracting BinHex archive. Note that this distribution is for a Power PC-based Macintosh. This executable will not work on a 680x0-based Macintosh.

The first step is to convert the packed file into an installation file using the Aladdin Systems `StuffIt Expander` package. The `StuffIt Expander` program is distributed with `Netscape` and can be obtained from `http://www.aladdinsys.com`.

The second step is to run the installation program to install `SWIG`.

To unpack the distribution using the `StuffIt Expander` follow these steps:

1. Place the *Tcl/Tk for Real Programmers* CD-ROM in the CD-ROM drive and confirm that it creates an icon on your screen when it loads.

2. Start the `StuffIt Expander` program by double-clicking the Expander icon.

3. Click the **File** menu in the upper-left corner of your screen.

4. Click the **Expand** menu option from that menu. Clicking the **Expand** option will bring up a file browsing window to select the installation file. Select the file to extract with the sequence:

   - Select the **desktop**
   - Double-click the name of the CD-ROM

- Double-click **devel**
- Double-click **swig**

5. Double-click the entry **SWIG_SEA.HQX**.

6. Click the **Desktop** button. The contents of the desktop will now appear in the window, and the **Unstuff** button will no longer be grayed out.

7. Click the **Unstuff** button, or press the **Return** key.

8. `StuffIt Expander` will now convert the distribution file to an executable program on your desktop area.

9. When `StuffIt Expander` has completed the expansion of the distribution file, there will be a new icon on your desktop named `MacSWIG1.1p2.sea`

10. Click the **MacSWIG1.1p2.sea** icon.

    This starts the `SWIG` installation.

11. The first window you will see has the information about the package used to create the archive.

    Click the **Continue** button.

12. The next window contains a file browser widget that will allow you to select where you wish to have SWIG installed.

    After you've selected the workspace for `SWIG` (perhaps the main desktop) click the **Save** button.

13. The `SWIG` will be unpacked into the directory you selected.

D.12 `megaWidget`

Jeff Hobbs's `megaWidget` *package* is included in the *packages/mega_wid* directory. This package is discussed in Chapter 11.

This package is being distributed as a gzipped tar archive for Unix-based systems, as a self-extracting zip file for MS-Windows-based systems, and as a BinHex archive for the Macintosh.

D.12.1 Unpacking the `megaWidget` Distribution under Windows

The `megaWidget` package has been repackaged as a self-extracting zip file for the Windows users.

To unpack the self-extracting zip files:

1. Place the *Tcl/Tk for Real Programmers* CD-ROM in the CD-ROM drive.
2. Open the **Run** dialog box.
3. Enter or browse to `D:\packages\mega_wid\widget09.exe`. Select this as the file to run.
4. Run the self-extracting zip file.
5. Click the **OK** button.
6. The next window gives you the chance to select the installation directory. You may accept the default installation directory (`C:\widget`) or type in the directory path you prefer.
7. Click the **Unzip** button. You will see the usual progress bar as the extension is installed.
8. When the installation is complete click the **OK** button.
9. Exit the installation program by clicking the **Clear** button.
10. Run the TOUR.tcl example with a command resembling:

    `C:\progra~1\tcl\bin\wish80 tour.tcl`

D.12.2 Unpacking the `megaWidget` Distribution under Unix

To unpack the `megaWidget` package on a Unix/Linux system:

1. Mount the *Tcl/Tk for Real Programmers* CD-ROM.
2. Change directory to the top of your source tree.

    `cd /home/example/src`
3. Unpack the `widget09` source distribution.

    `gunzip -c /cdrom/packages/mega_wid/widget09.tgz | tar -xvf -`
4. Change to the `widget` directory.

    `cd widget`
5. Run the TOUR.tcl example with a command resembling:

    `/usr/local/bin/wish TOUR.tcl`

D.12.3 Unpacking the **megaWidget** Distribution on a Macintosh

For the Macintosh, the files are packaged in the file `pack-ages:mega_wid:widget09.hqx`. You can drag and drop this file to the `StuffIt Expander` icon to unpack the files.

1. Place the *Tcl/Tk for Real Programmers* CD-ROM in the CD-ROM drive and confirm that it creates an icon on your screen when it loads.

2. Double-click the CD-ROM icon and step through the directories to `packages:mega_wid`.

3. Drag the `widget09.hqx` icon to the `StuffIt Expander` icon.

This will unpack the SpecTcl package into a directory on your desktop.

Bonus Book and Tutorials

Tcl/Tk for Real Programmers includes a bonus book! Several chapters that were originally written for a book about using Tcl/Tk in the Real World have been added to the CD-ROM.

The CD-ROM also includes several tutorials, and four reference guides.

E.1 Accessing the Real World Tcl Chapters

To access these chapters simply load the CD-ROM into your CD-ROM drive, point your browser at the file index.htm on that device and follow the references.

E.2 Accessing the Tutorials

The CD-ROM contains textual and HTML-based tutorials and the TclTutor package.

E.2.1 Accessing the Textual and HTML-Based Tutorials

The textual and HTML-based tutorials are referenced from the opening HTML page on the CD-ROM.

To access these tutorials, simply load the CD-ROM into your CD-ROM drive, and point your browser at the file index.htm on that device and follow the references.

E.3 TclTutor

TclTutor is a computer-aided instruction package for learning Tcl. It provides a brief description and an interactive example for all the Tcl commands. Experience has shown that people completely unfamiliar with Tcl can complete the Tutorial and be doing productive programming in just a few hours.

The TclTutor package is distributed as a self-extracting zip file and as a packaged runnable system (using the Scriptics Pro Wrapper) for Windows systems, as a gzipped tar file for Unix/Linux installations, and as a BinHex archive file for Macintosh systems.

The version of the TclTutor program created with the Scriptics Tcl Pro Wrapper program (tutor.exe) can be executed directly from the CD-ROM.

If you want to install TclTutor onto your hard drive, you must have wish installed on your system before starting the installation.

E.3.1 Installing TclTutor under MS-Windows

To install TclTutor under MS-Windows:

1. Place the *Tcl/Tk for Real Programmers* CD-ROM in your CD-ROM drive. The rest of these instructions assume that this is drive D.
2. Select **Start** and then **Run** from the Windows task bar.
3. Enter or browse to D:\devel\tcltutor\tutor097.exe and run that program.

4. The first window will inform you that this is the TclTutor installation package. Click the **OK** Button.

5. You'll see the familiar progress bar as TclTutor is installed into a temporary directory, following which the TclTutor installation menu should be displayed.

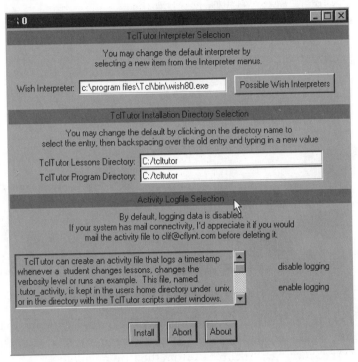

6. The installation window will allow you to select the destination for this installation, or the wish interpreter to use (if you have multiple wish interpreters installed on your system.)

If you do not want the default destinations (C:\TclTutor) enter the path to use in the entry widgets.

Click the **Install** button.

7. A new window will open showing you the installation progress.

8. When the installation is complete, the new window will display that information, and the **Abort** button will change to an **INSTALL COMPLETE - EXIT NOW** button.

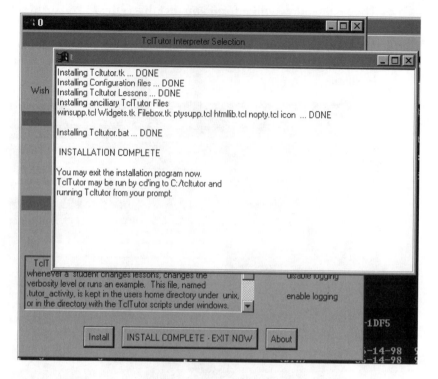

Click the INSTALL COMPLETE - EXIT NOW button.

You can run TclTutor by opening a DOS window, changing to the directory you chose for the installation and running `tcltutor`, or by selecting `C:\tcltutor\tcltutor.tcl` from the **Run** menu.

E.3.2 Installing TclTutor under Unix

To install `TclTutor` on a Unix/Linux system:

1. Mount the *Tcl/Tk for Real Programmers* CD-ROM.

2. Change directory to the top of your source tree.

   `cd /home/example/src`

3. Unpack the `TclTutor` distribution.

   `gunzip -c /cdrom/devel/tcltutor/tutor097.tgz | tar -xvf -`

4. Change to the TclTutor directory.

   cd TclTutor

5. Install the package by running the Configure script.

   Configure

6. When the Configure script starts up it will display a screen resembling this:

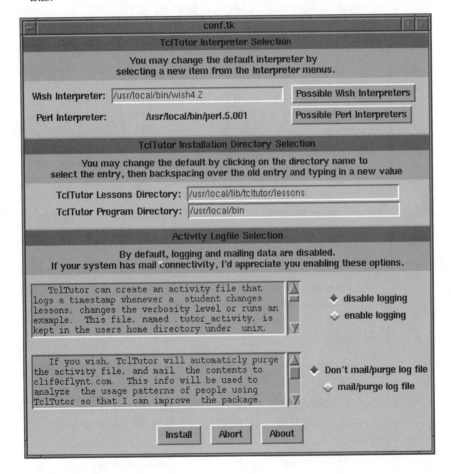

You can select the wish interpreter to use from the **Possible Wish Interpreters** pull-down menu.

The `Perl` interpreter is used for the demonstration `perl` lessons. The default `perl` interpreter can be selected from the **Possible Perl Interpreters** pull-down menu.

The installation directories for the lessons and binary objects can be selected by typing a new path into the **TclTutor Lessons Directory** or **TclTutor Program Directory** entry widget.

If you select the **enable logging** button, TclTutor will log when a user enters a lesson, runs examples, or changes verbosity levels.

This data file can be used by an instructor to monitor a student's progress.

If you select the **mail/purge log file** entry, the file will be cleared and mailed every five lessons. The default address in the mail field is the package author (me). In this case, the data is used to determine what lessons are being accessed most often, and which should be modified.

Modify these items until they match your requirements.

Click the **Install** button.

7. A new window will open showing you the installation progress.

8. When the installation is complete, the new window will display that information, and the **Abort** button will change to an **INSTALL COMPLETE - EXIT NOW** button.

   Click the **INSTALL COMPLETE - EXIT NOW** button.

9. If the Program directory you selected is in your default path, you will be able to execute `TclTutor.tcl` by typing `TclTutor.tcl`. If it is not in your path, you'll need to change to the installation directory in order to run TclTutor.

E.3.3 Installing TclTutor on a Macintosh

TclTutor is packaged in a BinHex archive (`tcltutor::tutor097.hqx`) for the Macintosh. You can drag and drop this file to the `StuffIt Expander` icon to unpack the files.

This version of TclTutor can be run by starting a wish session, using the Tcl `cd` command to change to the directory where TclTutor is installed, and then source `TclTutor`.

```
%   cd ..
%   ls
 Tcl/Tk Folder
 TclTutor
%   cd TclTutor
%   source TclTutor.tcl
```

E.4 Accessing the Extra Documentation

The docco directory contains additional documentation for using Tcl in Postscript format. These files include:

eng_man.ps   The Tcl Engineering Manual that describes conventions for creating Tcl Extensions.

style.ps   The Tcl Script style manual.

tkref40.tgz   Paul Raines Tcl/Tk pocket reference guide for Tcl revision 7.4 and Tk revision 4.0.

tkref80.tgz   Paul Raines Tcl/Tk pocket reference guide for Tcl and Tk revision 8.0.

Index
of Commands Used in Examples

Index of Commands Used in Examples

Index

This index consists of commands and topics discussed in the text. The meaning of the fonts is:

normal font	A topic, option name, variable name, program name, or term in general use.
`fixed font`	A command name.
`fixed italic font`	A widget command name.
bold font	The page number with the command definition.

Index

Index

(continued from back page)

- *Tcl Extensions*. The extensions discussed in Chapter 13 are included on the CD-ROM. See Appendix C for installation instructions.

- *Tcl Packages*. The development packages described in Chapter 14 and throughout the text of the book are included on the CD-ROM; for more information, point your browser to the index.htm file on the CD-ROM. See Appendix D for installation instructions.

- *Tcl Extension Skeletons*. The Tcl Extension templates in the `skeltns` directory will help you write Tcl extensions quickly and easily; for more information, point your browser to the index.htm file on the CD-ROM.

- *Documentation*. The Tcl Engineering Guide, Tcl Style guide, and Paul Raines' Tcl and Tk reference cards are included under the `docco` directory and are distributed in PostScript format. For more information, point your browser to the index.htm file on the CD-ROM.

- *Examples from the book*. The examples shown in the text of this book are included under the `examples` directory. The examples from each chapter are under the appropriate `chaptXX` directory. The example files are named the same as their example number in the book. For instance, Example 5.5.3-1 is in the directory `chapt5`, in file `e5_5_3_1.tcl`.

About the CD-ROM

The CD-RON
start progra

- *Binary*
  and BS
  1998
  one

  To install a Tc,
  of RAM. (Tcl7.6 will ru

  To install Tcl/Tk on an MS-Windo
  MB of RAM. Tcl/Tk will run on any 386-
  tem, but is sluggish if the clock speed is slower u

  To install Tcl/Tk on a Linux or BSD/OS system, you must i.
  8 MB of RAM. To run Tk you must have X windows installed. Tcl/
  will run on any 386-, 486-, or Pentium-based system, but is sluggish if
  the clock speed is slower than 100 MHz.

- *Source code distributions for Tcl and Tk.* Revisions 7.6p2, 8.0p2, 8.1a2 and
  8.0.3 (new in September 1998) are included. See Appendix B for installation instructions.

- *A bonus book of Real World Tcl application discussions.* Mount the CD-
  ROM and point your browser to the index.htm file on the CD-ROM to
  find these.

- *Extra Tcl Tutorials.* The TclTutor interactive CAI program and HTML-
  based tutorials that you can browse are included; for more information,
  point your browser to the index.htm file on the CD-ROM. See Appendix
  E for installation instructions.

(continued)